Python® for Data Science

for dummies®

A Wiley Brand

Python® for Data Science

2nd Edition

by John Paul Mueller
and Luca Massaron

A Wiley Brand

Python® for Data Science For Dummies®, 2nd Edition

Published by: **John Wiley & Sons, Inc.**, 111 River Street, Hoboken, NJ 07030-5774, www.wiley.com

Copyright © 2019 by John Wiley & Sons, Inc., Hoboken, New Jersey

Media and software compilation copyright © 2019 by John Wiley & Sons, Inc. All rights reserved.

Published simultaneously in Canada

For general information on our other products and services, please contact our Customer Care Department within the U.S. at 877-762-2974, outside the U.S. at 317-572-3993, or fax 317-572-4002. For technical support, please visit https://hub.wiley.com/community/support/dummies.

Wiley publishes in a variety of print and electronic formats and by print-on-demand. Some material included with standard print versions of this book may not be included in e-books or in print-on-demand. If this book refers to media such as a CD or DVD that is not included in the version you purchased, you may download this material at http://booksupport.wiley.com. For more information about Wiley products, visit www.wiley.com.

Library of Congress Control Number: 2018967877

ISBN: 978-1-119-54762-4; ISBN: 978-1-119-54766-2 (ebk); ISBN: 978-1-119-54764-8 (ebk)

Manufactured in the United States of America

C10007742_012319

Contents at a Glance

Table of Contents

Introduction

Data is increasingly used for every possible purpose, and many of those purposes elude attention, but every time you get on the Internet, you generate even more. It's not just you, either; the growth of the Internet has been phenomenal, according to Internet World Stats (`https://www.internet worldstats.com/emarketing.htm`). Data science turns this huge amount of data into something useful — something that you use absolutely every day to perform an amazing array of tasks or to obtain services from someone else.

In fact, you've probably used data science in ways that you never expected. For example, when you used your favorite search engine this morning to look for something, it made suggestions on alternative search terms. Those terms are supplied by data science. When you went to the doctor last week and discovered the lump you found wasn't cancer, the doctor likely made her prognosis with the help of data science. In fact, you might work with data science every day and not even know it. *Python for Data Science For Dummies,* 2nd Edition not only gets you started using data science to perform a wealth of practical tasks but also helps you realize just how many places data science is used. By knowing how to answer data science problems and where to employ data science, you gain a significant advantage over everyone else, increasing your chances at promotion or that new job you really want.

About This Book

The main purpose of *Python for Data Science For Dummies,* 2nd Edition is to take the scare factor out of data science by showing you that data science is not only really interesting but also quite doable using Python. You might assume that you need to be a computer science genius to perform the complex tasks normally associated with data science, but that's far from the truth. Python comes with a host of useful libraries that do all the heavy lifting for you in the background. You don't even realize how much is going on, and you don't need to care. All you really need to know is that you want to perform specific tasks, and Python makes these tasks quite accessible.

Part of the emphasis of this book is on using the right tools. You start with Anaconda, a product that includes IPython and Jupyter Notebook — two tools that take the sting out of working with Python. You experiment with IPython in a fully interactive environment. The code you place in Jupyter Notebook (also called just Notebook throughout the book) is presentation quality, and you can mix a number of presentation elements right there in your document. It's not really like using a development environment at all. To make this book easier to use on alternative platforms, you also discover an online Interactive Development Environment application (IDE) named Google Colab that allows you to interact with most, but not quite all, of the book examples using your favorite tablet or (assuming that you can squint well enough) your smart phone.

You also discover some interesting techniques in this book. For example, you can create plots of all your data science experiments using MatPlotLib, and this book gives you all the details for doing that. This book also spends considerable time showing you available resources (such as packages) and how you can use Scikit-learn to perform some really interesting calculations. Many people would like to know how to perform handwriting recognition, and if you're one of them, you can use this book to get a leg up on the process.

Of course, you might still be worried about the whole programming environment issue, and this book doesn't leave you in the dark there, either. At the beginning, you find complete installation instructions for Anaconda, which are followed by the methods you need to get started with data science using Jupyter Notebook or Google Colab. The emphasis is on getting you up and running as quickly as possible, and to make examples straightforward and simple so that the code doesn't become a stumbling block to learning.

This second edition of the book provides you with updated examples using Python 3.x so that you're using the most modern version of Python while reading. In addition, you find a stronger emphasis on making examples simpler, but also making the environment more inclusive by adding material on deep learning. Consequently, you get a lot more out of this edition of the book as a result of the input provided by hundreds of readers before you.

To make absorbing the concepts even easier, this book uses the following conventions:

>> Text that you're meant to type just as it appears in the book is in **bold**. The exception is when you're working through a step list: Because each step is bold, the text to type is not bold.

>> When you see words in *italics* as part of a typing sequence, you need to replace that value with something that works for you. For example, if you

see "Type **Your Name** and press Enter," you need to replace *Your Name* with your actual name.

» Web addresses and programming code appear in monofont. If you're reading a digital version of this book on a device connected to the Internet, note that you can click the web address to visit that website, like this: http://www.dummies.com.

» When you need to type command sequences, you see them separated by a special arrow, like this: File ➪ New File. In this example, you go to the File menu first and then select the New File entry on that menu.

Foolish Assumptions

You might find it difficult to believe that we've assumed anything about you — after all, we haven't even met you yet! Although most assumptions are indeed foolish, we made these assumptions to provide a starting point for the book.

You need to e familiar with the platform you want to use because the book doesn't offer any guidance in this regard. (Chapter 3 does, however, provide Anaconda installation instructions, and Chapter 4 gets you started with Google Colab.) To provide you with maximum information about Python concerning how it applies to data science, this book doesn't discuss any platform-specific issues. You really do need to know how to install applications, use applications, and generally work with your chosen platform before you begin working with this book.

You must know how to work with Python. This edition of the book no longer contains a Python primer because you can find such as wealth of tutorials online (see https://www.w3schools.com/python/ and https://www.tutorialspoint.com/python/ as examples).

This book isn't a math primer. Yes, you see lots of examples of complex math, but the emphasis is on helping you use Python and data science to perform analysis tasks rather than teaching math theory. Chapters 1 and 2 give you a better understanding of precisely what you need to know to use this book successfully.

This book also assumes that you can access items on the Internet. Sprinkled throughout are numerous references to online material that will enhance your learning experience. However, these added sources are useful only if you actually find and use them.

Icons Used in This Book

As you read this book, you see icons in the margins that indicate material of interest (or not, as the case may be). This section briefly describes each icon in this book.

TIP

Tips are nice because they help you save time or perform some task without a lot of extra work. The tips in this book are time-saving techniques or pointers to resources that you should try in order to get the maximum benefit from Python or in performing data science–related tasks.

WARNING

We don't want to sound like angry parents or some kind of maniacs, but you should avoid doing anything that's marked with a Warning icon. Otherwise, you might find that your application fails to work as expected, you get incorrect answers from seemingly bulletproof equations, or (in the worst-case scenario) you lose data.

TECHNICAL STUFF

Whenever you see this icon, think advanced tip or technique. You might find these tidbits of useful information just too boring for words, or they could contain the solution you need to get a program running. Skip these bits of information when-ever you like.

REMEMBER

If you don't get anything else out of a particular chapter or section, remember the material marked by this icon. This text usually contains an essential process or a bit of information that you must know to work with Python or to perform data science–related tasks successfully.

Beyond the Book

This book isn't the end of your Python or data science experience — it's really just the beginning. We provide online content to make this book more flexible and better able to meet your needs. That way, as we receive e-mail from you, we can address questions and tell you how updates to either Python or its associated add-ons affect book content. In fact, you gain access to all these cool additions:

>> **Cheat sheet:** You remember using crib notes in school to make a better mark on a test, don't you? You do? Well, a cheat sheet is sort of like that. It provides you with some special notes about tasks that you can do with Python, IPython, IPython Notebook, and data science that not every other person knows. You can find the cheat sheet by going to www.dummies.com, searching this book's title, and scrolling down the page that appears. The cheat sheet contains really

neat information such as the most common programming mistakes that cause people woe when using Python.

>> **Updates:** Sometimes changes happen. For example, we might not have seen an upcoming change when we looked into our crystal ball during the writing of this book. In the past, this possibility simply meant that the book became outdated and less useful, but you can now find updates to the book by searching this book's title at `www.dummies.com`.

In addition to these updates, check out the blog posts with answers to reader questions and demonstrations of useful book-related techniques at `http://blog.johnmuellerbooks.com/`.

>> **Companion files:** Hey! Who really wants to type all the code in the book and reconstruct all those plots manually? Most readers would prefer to spend their time actually working with Python, performing data science tasks, and seeing the interesting things they can do, rather than typing. Fortunately for you, the examples used in the book are available for download, so all you need to do is read the book to learn Python for data science usage techniques. You can find these files at `www.dummies.com`. Search this book's title, and on the page that appears, scroll down to the image of the book cover and click it. Then click the More about This Book button and on the page that opens, go to the Downloads tab.

Where to Go from Here

It's time to start your Python for data science adventure! If you're completely new to Python and its use for data science tasks, you should start with Chapter 1 and progress through the book at a pace that allows you to absorb as much of the material as possible.

If you're a novice who's in an absolute rush to get going with Python for data science as quickly as possible, you can skip to Chapter 3 with the understanding that you may find some topics a bit confusing later. Skipping to Chapter 5 is okay if you already have Anaconda (the programming product used in the book) installed, but be sure to at least skim Chapter 3 so that you know what assumptions we made when writing this book. If you plan to use your tablet to work with this book, be certain to review Chapter 4 so that you understand the limitations presented by Google Colab in running the example code; not all of the examples work in this IDE. Make sure to install Anaconda with Python version 3.6.5 installed to obtain the best results from the book's source code.

Readers who have some exposure to Python and have Anaconda installed can save reading time by moving directly to Chapter 5. You can always go back to earlier chapters as necessary when you have questions. However, you should understand how each technique works before moving to the next one. Every technique, coding example, and procedure has important lessons for you, and you could miss vital content if you start skipping too much information.

1

Getting Started with Data Science and Python

IN THIS PART . . .

Understanding how Python can make data science easier.

Defining the Python features commonly used for data science.

Creating a Python setup of your own.

Working with Google Colab on alternative devices.

Chapter **1**

Discovering the Match between Data Science and Python

Data science may seem like one of those technologies that you'd never use, but you'd be wrong. Yes, data science involves the use of advanced math techniques, statistics, and big data. However, data science also involves helping you make smart decisions, creating suggestions for options based on previous choices, and making robots see objects. In fact, people use data science in so many different ways that you literally can't look anywhere or do anything without feeling the effects of data science on your life. In short, data science is the person behind the partition in the experience of the wonderment of technology. Without data science, much of what you accept as typical and expected today wouldn't even be possible. This is the reason that being a data scientist is the sexiest job of the twenty-first century.

REMEMBER

To make data science doable by someone who's less than a math genius, you need tools. You could use any of a number of tools to perform data science tasks, but Python is uniquely suited to making it easier to work with data science. For one thing, Python provides an incredible number of math-related libraries that help you perform tasks with a less-than-perfect understanding of precisely what is going on. However, Python goes further by supporting multiple coding styles (programming paradigms) and doing other things to make your job easier. Therefore, yes, you could use other languages to write data science applications, but Python reduces your workload, so it's a natural choice for those who really don't want to work hard, but rather to work smart.

This chapter gets you started with Python. Even though this book isn't designed to provide you with a complete Python tutorial, exploring some basic Python issues will reduce the time needed for you to get up to speed. (If you do need a good starting tutorial, please get *Beginning Programming with Python For Dummies*, 2nd Edition, by John Mueller (Wiley). You'll find that the book provides pointers to tutorials and other aids as needed to fill in any gaps that you may have in your Python education.

CHOOSING A DATA SCIENCE LANGUAGE

There are many different programming languages in the world — and most were designed to perform tasks in a certain way or even make it easier for a particular profession's work to be done with greater ease. Choosing the correct tool makes your life easier. It's akin to using a hammer to drive a screw rather than a screwdriver. Yes, the hammer works, but the screwdriver is much easier to use and definitely does a better job. Data scientists usually use only a few languages because they make working with data easier. With this in mind, here are the top languages for data science work in order of preference:

- **Python (general purpose):** Many data scientists prefer to use Python because it provides a wealth of libraries, such as NumPy, SciPy, MatPlotLib, pandas, and Scikit-learn, to make data science tasks significantly easier. Python is also a precise language that makes it easy to use multi-processing on large datasets — reducing the time required to analyze them. The data science community has also stepped up with specialized IDEs, such as Anaconda, that implement the Jupyter Notebook concept, which makes working with data science calculations significantly easier (Chapter 3 demonstrates how to use Jupyter Notebook, so don't worry about it in this chapter). Besides all of these things in Python's favor, it's also an excellent language for creating glue code with languages such as C/C++ and Fortran. The Python documentation actually shows how to create the required extensions. Most Python users rely on the language to see patterns, such as allowing a robot to see a group of pixels as an object. It also sees use for all sorts of scientific tasks.

- **R (special purpose statistical):** In many respects, Python and R share the same sorts of functionality but implement it in different ways. Depending on which source you view, Python and R have about the same number of proponents, and some people use Python and R interchangeably (or sometimes in tandem). Unlike

Python, R provides its own environment, so you don't need a third-party product such as Anaconda. However, R doesn't appear to mix with other languages with the ease that Python provides.

- **SQL (database management):** The most important thing to remember about Structured Query Language (SQL) is that it focuses on data rather than tasks. Businesses can't operate without good data management — the data is the business. Large organizations use some sort of relational database, which is normally accessible with SQL, to store their data. Most Database Management System (DBMS) products rely on SQL as their main language, and DBMS usually has a large number of data analysis and other data science features built in. Because you're accessing the data natively, there is often a significant speed gain in performing data science tasks this way. Database Administrators (DBAs) generally use SQL to manage or manipulate the data rather than necessarily perform detailed analysis of it. However, the data scientist can also use SQL for various data science tasks and make the resulting scripts available to the DBAs for their needs.

- **Java (general purpose):** Some data scientists perform other kinds of programming that require a general purpose, widely adapted and popular, language. In addition to providing access to a large number of libraries (most of which aren't actually all that useful for data science, but do work for other needs), Java supports object orientation better than any of the other languages in this list. In addition, it's strongly typed and tends to run quite quickly. Consequently, some people prefer it for finalized code. Java isn't a good choice for experimentation or ad hoc queries.

- **Scala (general purpose):** Because Scala uses the Java Virtual Machine (JVM) it does have some of the advantages and disadvantages of Java. However, like Python, Scala provides strong support for the functional programming paradigm, which uses lambda calculus as its basis (see *Functional Programmming For Dummies*, by John Mueller [Wiley] for details). In addition, Apache Spark is written in Scala, which means that you have good support for cluster computing when using this language; — think huge dataset support. Some of the pitfalls of using Scala are that it's hard to set up correctly, it has a steep learning curve, and it lacks a comprehensive set of data science specific libraries.

Defining the Sexiest Job of the 21st Century

At one point, the world viewed anyone working with statistics as a sort of accountant or perhaps a mad scientist. Many people consider statistics and analysis of data boring. However, data science is one of those occupations in which the more you learn, the more you want to learn. Answering one question often spawns more questions that are even more interesting than the one you just answered.

However, the thing that makes data science so sexy is that you see it everywhere and used in an almost infinite number of ways. The following sections provide you with more details on why data science is such an amazing field of study.

Considering the emergence of data science

Data science is a relatively new term. William S. Cleveland coined the term in 2001 as part of a paper entitled "Data Science: An Action Plan for Expanding the Technical Areas of the Field of Statistics." It wasn't until a year later that the International Council for Science actually recognized data science and created a committee for it. Columbia University got into the act in 2003 by beginning publication of the *Journal of Data Science.*

REMEMBER

However, the mathematical basis behind data science is centuries old because data science is essentially a method of viewing and analyzing statistics and probability. The first essential use of statistics as a term comes in 1749, but statistics are certainly much older than that. People have used statistics to recognize patterns for thousands of years. For example, the historian Thucydides (in his History of the Peloponnesian War) describes how the Athenians calculated the height of the wall of Platea in fifth century BC by counting bricks in an unplastered section of the wall. Because the count needed to be accurate, the Athenians took the average of the count by several solders.

The process of quantifying and understanding statistics is relatively new, but the science itself is quite old. An early attempt to begin documenting the importance of statistics appears in the ninth century when Al-Kindi wrote *Manuscript on Deciphering Cryptographic Messages.* In this paper, Al-Kindi describes how to use a combination of statistics and frequency analysis to decipher encrypted messages. Even in the beginning, statistics saw use in practical application of science to tasks that seemed virtually impossible to complete. Data science continues this process, and to some people it might actually seem like magic.

Outlining the core competencies of a data scientist

As is true of anyone performing most complex trades today, the data scientist requires knowledge of a broad range of skills to perform the required tasks. In fact, so many different skills are required that data scientists often work in teams. Someone who is good at gathering data might team up with an analyst and someone gifted in presenting information. It would be hard to find a single person with all the required skills. With this in mind, the following list describes areas in which a data scientist could excel (with more competencies being better):

>> **Data capture:** It doesn't matter what sort of math skills you have if you can't obtain data to analyze in the first place. The act of capturing data begins by managing a data source using database management skills. However, raw data isn't particularly useful in many situations — you must also understand the data domain so that you can look at the data and begin formulating the sorts of questions to ask. Finally, you must have data-modeling skills so that you understand how the data is connected and whether the data is structured.

>> **Analysis:** After you have data to work with and understand the complexities of that data, you can begin to perform an analysis on it. You perform some analysis using basic statistical tool skills, much like those that just about everyone learns in college. However, the use of specialized math tricks and algorithms can make patterns in the data more obvious or help you draw conclusions that you can't draw by reviewing the data alone.

>> **Presentation:** Most people don't understand numbers well. They can't see the patterns that the data scientist sees. It's important to provide a graphical presentation of these patterns to help others visualize what the numbers mean and how to apply them in a meaningful way. More important, the presentation must tell a specific story so that the impact of the data isn't lost.

Linking data science, big data, and AI

Interestingly enough, the act of moving data around so that someone can perform analysis on it is a specialty called Extract, Transformation, and Loading (ETL). The ETL specialist uses programming languages such as Python to extract the data from a number of sources. Corporations tend not to keep data in one easily accessed location, so finding the data required to perform analysis takes time. After the ETL specialist finds the data, a programming language or other tool transforms it into a common format for analysis purposes. The loading process takes many forms, but this book relies on Python to perform the task. In a large, real-world operation, you might find yourself using tools such as Informatica, MS SSIS, or Teradata to perform the task.

REMEMBER

Data science isn't necessarily a means to an end; it may instead be a step along the way. As a data scientist works through various datasets and finds interesting facts, these facts may act as input for other sorts of analysis and AI applications. For example, consider that your shopping habits often suggest what books you might like or where you might like to go for a vacation. Shopping or other habits can also help others understand other, sometimes less benign, activities as well. *Machine Learning For Dummies* and *AI For Dummies*, both by John Mueller and Luca Massaron (Wiley) help you understand these other uses of data science. For now, consider the fact that what you learn in this book can have a definite effect on a career path that will go many other places.

Understanding the role of programming

A data scientist may need to know several programming languages in order to achieve specific goals. For example, you may need SQL knowledge to extract data from relational databases. Python can help you perform data loading, transformation, and analysis tasks. However, you might choose a product such as MATLAB (which has its own programming language) or PowerPoint (which relies on VBA) to present the information to others. (If you're interested to see how MATLAB compares to the use of Python, you can get my book, *MATLAB For Dummies*, published by John Wiley & Sons, Inc.) The immense datasets that data scientists rely on often require multiple levels of redundant processing to transform into useful processed data. Manually performing these tasks is time consuming and error prone, so programming presents the best method for achieving the goal of a coherent, usable data source.

Given the number of products that most data scientists use, it may not be possible to use just one programming language. Yes, Python can load data, transform it, analyze it, and even present it to the end user, but it works only when the language provides the required functionality. You may have to choose other languages to fill out your toolkit. The languages you choose depend on a number of criteria. Here are the things you should consider:

>> How you intend to use data science in your code (you have a number of tasks to consider, such as data analysis, classification, and regression)

>> Your familiarity with the language

>> The need to interact with other languages

>> The availability of tools to enhance the development environment

>> The availability of APIs and libraries to make performing tasks easier

Creating the Data Science Pipeline

Data science is partly art and partly engineering. Recognizing patterns in data, considering what questions to ask, and determining which algorithms work best are all part of the art side of data science. However, to make the art part of data science realizable, the engineering part relies on a specific process to achieve specific goals. This process is the data science pipeline, which requires the data scientist to follow particular steps in the preparation, analysis, and presentation of the data. The following sections help you understand the data science pipeline better so that you can understand how the book employs it during the presentation of examples.

Preparing the data

The data that you access from various sources doesn't come in an easily packaged form, ready for analysis — quite the contrary. The raw data not only may vary substantially in format, but you may also need to transform it to make all the data sources cohesive and amenable to analysis. Transformation may require changing data types, the order in which data appears, and even the creation of data entries based on the information provided by existing entries.

Performing exploratory data analysis

The math behind data analysis relies on engineering principles in that the results are provable and consistent. However, data science provides access to a wealth of statistical methods and algorithms that help you discover patterns in the data. A single approach doesn't ordinarily do the trick. You typically use an iterative process to rework the data from a number of perspectives. The use of trial and error is part of the data science art.

Learning from data

As you iterate through various statistical analysis methods and apply algorithms to detect patterns, you begin learning from the data. The data might not tell the story that you originally thought it would, or it might have many stories to tell. Discovery is part of being a data scientist. In fact, it's the fun part of data science because you can't ever know in advance precisely what the data will reveal to you.

REMEMBER

Of course, the imprecise nature of data and the finding of seemingly random patterns in it means keeping an open mind. If you have preconceived ideas of what the data contains, you won't find the information it actually does contain. You miss the discovery phase of the process, which translates into lost opportunities for both you and the people who depend on you.

Visualizing

Visualization means seeing the patterns in the data and then being able to react to those patterns. It also means being able to see when data is not part of the pattern. Think of yourself as a data sculptor — removing the data that lies outside the patterns (the outliers) so that others can see the masterpiece of information beneath. Yes, you can see the masterpiece, but until others can see it, too, it remains in your vision alone.

Obtaining insights and data products

The data scientist may seem to simply be looking for unique methods of viewing data. However, the process doesn't end until you have a clear understanding of what the data means. The insights you obtain from manipulating and analyzing the data help you to perform real-world tasks. For example, you can use the results of an analysis to make a business decision.

In some cases, the result of an analysis creates an automated response. For example, when a robot views a series of pixels obtained from a camera, the pixels that form an object have special meaning and the robot's programming may dictate some sort of interaction with that object. However, until the data scientist builds an application that can load, analyze, and visualize the pixels from the camera, the robot doesn't see anything at all.

Understanding Python's Role in Data Science

Given the right data sources, analysis requirements, and presentation needs, you can use Python for every part of the data science pipeline. In fact, that's precisely what you do in this book. Every example uses Python to help you understand another part of the data science equation. Of all the languages you could choose for performing data science tasks, Python is the most flexible and capable because it supports so many third-party libraries devoted to the task. The following sections help you better understand why Python is such a good choice for many (if not most) data science needs.

Considering the shifting profile of data scientists

Some people view the data scientist as an unapproachable nerd who performs miracles on data with math. The data scientist is the person behind the curtain in an Oz-like experience. However, this perspective is changing. In many respects, the world now views the data scientist as either an adjunct to a developer or as a new type of developer. The ascendance of applications of all sorts that can learn is the essence of this change. For an application to learn, it has to be able to manipulate large databases and discover new patterns in them. In addition, the application must be able to create new data based on the old data — making an informed prediction of sorts. The new kinds of applications affect people in ways that would have seemed like science fiction just a few years ago. Of course, the most noticeable of these applications define the behaviors of robots that will interact far more closely with people tomorrow than they do today.

From a business perspective, the necessity of fusing data science and application development is obvious: Businesses must perform various sorts of analysis on the huge databases it has collected — to make sense of the information and use it to predict the future. In truth, however, the far greater impact of the melding of these two branches of science — data science and application development — will be felt in terms of creating altogether new kinds of applications, some of which aren't even possibly to imagine with clarity today. For example, new applications could help students learn with greater precision by analyzing their learning trends and creating new instructional methods that work for that particular student. This combination of sciences might also solve a host of medical problems that seem impossible to solve today — not only in keeping disease at bay, but also by solving problems, such as how to create truly usable prosthetic devices that look and act like the real thing.

Working with a multipurpose, simple, and efficient language

Many different ways are available for accomplishing data science tasks. This book covers only one of the myriad methods at your disposal. However, Python represents one of the few single-stop solutions that you can use to solve complex data science problems. Instead of having to use a number of tools to perform a task, you can simply use a single language, Python, to get the job done. The Python difference is the large number scientific and math libraries created for it by third parties. Plugging in these libraries greatly extends Python and allows it to easily perform tasks that other languages could perform, but with great difficulty.

TIP

Python's libraries are its main selling point; however, Python offers more than reusable code. The most important thing to consider with Python is that it supports four different coding styles:

>> **Functional:** Treats every statement as a mathematical equation and avoids any form of state or mutable data. The main advantage of this approach is having no side effects to consider. In addition, this coding style lends itself better than the others to parallel processing because there is no state to consider. Many developers prefer this coding style for recursion and for lambda calculus.

>> **Imperative:** Performs computations as a direct change to program state. This style is especially useful when manipulating data structures and produces elegant, but simple, code.

>> **Object-oriented:** Relies on data fields that are treated as objects and manipulated only through prescribed methods. Python doesn't fully support this coding form because it can't implement features such as data hiding. However, this is a useful coding style for complex applications because it supports encapsulation and polymorphism. This coding style also favors code reuse.

>> **Procedural:** Treats tasks as step-by-step iterations where common tasks are placed in functions that are called as needed. This coding style favors iteration, sequencing, selection, and modularization.

Learning to Use Python Fast

It's time to try using Python to see the data science pipeline in action. The following sections provide a brief overview of the process you explore in detail in the rest of the book. You won't actually perform the tasks in the following sections. In fact, you don't install Python until Chapter 3, so for now, just follow along in the text. This book uses a specific version of Python and an IDE called Jupyter Notebook, so please wait until Chapter 3 to install these features (or skip ahead, if you insist, and install them now). Don't worry about understanding every aspect of the process at this point. The purpose of these sections is to help you gain an understanding of the flow of using Python to perform data science tasks. Many of the details may seem difficult to understand at this point, but the rest of the book will help you understand them.

REMEMBER

The examples in this book rely on a web-based application named Jupyter Notebook. The screenshots you see in this and other chapters reflect how Jupyter Notebook looks in Firefox on a Windows 7 system. The view you see will contain the same data, but the actual interface may differ a little depending on platform (such as using a notebook instead of a desktop system), operating system, and browser. Don't worry if you see some slight differences between your display and the screenshots in the book.

TIP

You don't have to type the source code for this chapter in by hand. In fact, it's a lot easier if you use the downloadable source (see the Introduction for details on downloading the source code). The source code for this chapter appears in the P4DS4D2_01_Quick_Overview.ipynb source code file.

Loading data

Before you can do anything, you need to load some data. The book shows you all sorts of methods for performing this task. In this case, Figure 1-1 shows how to load a dataset called Boston that contains housing prices and other facts about houses in the Boston area. The code places the entire dataset in the boston variable and then places parts of that data in variables named X and y. Think of variables as you would storage boxes. The variables are important because they make it possible to work with the data.

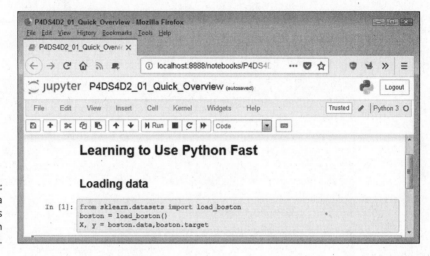

FIGURE 1-1: Loading data into variables so that you can manipulate it.

```
In [1]: from sklearn.datasets import load_boston
        boston = load_boston()
        X, y = boston.data, boston.target
```

Training a model

Now that you have some data to work with, you can do something with it. All sorts of algorithms are built into Python. Figure 1-2 shows a linear regression model. Again, don't worry precisely how this works; later chapters discuss linear regression in detail. The important thing to note in Figure 1-2 is that Python lets you perform the linear regression using just two statements and to place the result in a variable named hypothesis.

Viewing a result

Performing any sort of analysis doesn't pay unless you obtain some benefit from it in the form of a result. This book shows all sorts of ways to view output, but Figure 1-3 starts with something simple. In this case, you see the coefficient output from the linear regression analysis.

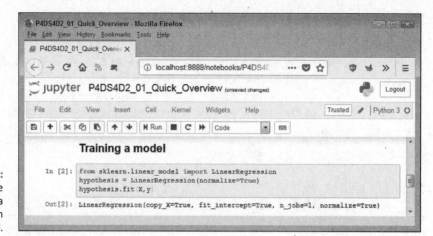

FIGURE 1-2:
Using the variable content to train a linear regression model.

FIGURE 1-3:
Outputting a result as a response to the model.

TIP

One of the reasons that this book uses Jupyter Notebook is that the product helps you to create nicely formatted output as part of creating the application. Look again at Figure 1-3 and you see a report that you could simply print and offer to a colleague. The output isn't suitable for many people, but those experienced with Python and data science will find it quite usable and informative.

Chapter **2**

Introducing Python's Capabilities and Wonders

ll computers run on just one language — machine code. However, unless you want to learn how to talk like a computer in 0s and 1s, machine code isn't particularly useful. You'd never want to try to define data science problems using machine code. It would take an entire lifetime (if not longer) just to define one problem. Higher-level languages make it possible to write a lot of code that humans can understand quite quickly. The tools used with these languages make it possible to translate the human-readable code into machine code that the machine understands. Therefore, the choice of languages depends on the human need, not the machine need. With this in mind, this chapter introduces you to the capabilities that Python provides that make it a practical choice for the data scientist. After all, you want to know why this book uses Python and not another language, such as Java or C++. These other languages are perfectly good choices for some tasks, but they're not as suited to meet data science needs.

The chapter begins with a short history of Python so that you know a little about why developers created Python in the first place. You also see some simple Python examples to get a taste for the language. As part of exploring Python in this chapter, you discover all sorts of interesting features that Python provides. Python gives you access to a host of libraries that are especially suited to meet the needs of the data scientist. In fact, you use a number of these libraries throughout the book as you work through the coding examples. Knowing about these libraries in advance will help you understand the programming examples and why the book shows how to perform tasks in a certain way.

REMEMBER

Even though this chapter does show examples of working with Python, you don't really begin using Python in earnest until Chapter 6. This chapter provides you with an overview so that you can better understand what Python can do. Chapter 3 shows how to install the particular version of Python used for this book. Chapters 4 and 5 are about tools you can use, with Chapter 4 emphasizing Google's Colab, an alternative environment for coding. In short, if you don't quite understand an example in this chapter, don't worry: You get plenty of additional information in later chapters.

Why Python?

Python is the vision of a single person, Guido van Rossum. You might be surprised to learn that Python has been around a long time — Guido started the language in December 1989 as a replacement for the ABC language. Not much information is available as to the precise goals for Python, but it does retain ABC's ability to create applications using less code. However, it far exceeds the ability of ABC to create applications of all types, and in contrast to ABC, boasts four programming styles. In short, Guido took ABC as a starting point, found it limited, and created a new language without those limitations. It's an example of creating a new language that really is better than its predecessor.

Python has gone through a number of iterations and currently has two development paths. The 2.x path is backward compatible with previous versions of Python, while the 3.x path isn't. The compatibility issue is one that figures into how data science uses Python because a few of the libraries won't work with 3.x. However, this issue is slowly being resolved, and you should use 3.x for all new development because the end of the line is coming for the 2.x versions (see https://pythonclock.org/ for details). As a result, this edition of the book uses 3.x code. In addition, some versions use different licensing because Guido was working at various companies during Python's development. You can see a listing of the versions and their respective licenses at https://docs.python.org/3/license.html. The Python Software Foundation (PSF) owns all current versions of Python, so unless you use an older version, you really don't need to worry about the licensing issue.

Grasping Python's Core Philosophy

Guido actually started Python as a skunkworks project. The core concept was to create Python as quickly as possible, yet create a language that is flexible, runs on any platform, and provides significant potential for extension. Python provides all these features and many more. Of course, there are always bumps in the road, such as figuring out just how much of the underlying system to expose. You can read more about the Python design philosophy at `http://python-history.blogspot.com/2009/01/pythons-design-philosophy.html`. The history of Python at `http://python-history.blogspot.com/2009/01/introduction-and-overview.html` also provides some useful information.

Contributing to data science

Because this is a book about data science, you're probably wondering how Python contributes toward better data science and what the word *better* actually means in this case. Knowing that a lot of organizations use Python doesn't help you because it doesn't really say much about how they use Python, and if you want to match your choice of language to your particular need, answering how they use Python becomes important.

One such example appears at `https://www.datasciencegraduateprograms.com/python/`. In this case, the article talks about Forecastwatch.com (`https://forecastwatch.com/`), which actually does watch the weather and try to make predictions better. Every day, Forecastwatch.com compares 36,000 forecasts with the actual weather that people experience and then uses the results to create better forecasts. Trying to aggregate and make sense of the weather data for 800 U.S. cities is daunting, so Forecastwatch.com needed a language that could do what it needed with the least amount of fuss. Here are the reasons Forecast.com chose Python:

>> **Library support:** Python provides support for a large number of libraries, more than any one organization will ever need. According to `https://www.python.org/about/success/forecastwatch/`, Forecastwatch.com found the regular expression, thread, object serialization, and gzip data compression libraries especially useful.

>> **Parallel processing:** Each of the forecasts is processed as a separate thread so that the system can work through them quickly. The thread data includes the web page URL that contains the required forecast, along with category information, such as city name.

>> **Data access:** This huge amount of data can't all exist in memory, so Forecast.com relies on a MySQL database accessed through the MySQLdb (`https://sourceforge.net/projects/mysql-python/`) library, which is one of those few libraries that hasn't moved on to Python 3.x yet. However, the associated website promises the required support soon.

>> **Data display:** Originally, PHP produced the Forecastwatch.com output. However, by using Quixote (`https://www.mems-exchange.org/software/quixote/`), which is a display framework, Forecastwatch.com was able to move everything to Python.

Discovering present and future development goals

The original development (or design) goals for Python don't quite match what has happened to the language since Guido initially thought about it. Guido originally intended Python as a second language for developers who needed to create one-off code but who couldn't quite achieve their goals using a scripting language. The original target audience for Python was the C developer. You can read about these original goals in the interview at `http://www.artima.com/intv/pyscale.html`.

You can find a number of applications written in Python today, so the idea of using it solely for scripting didn't come to fruition. In fact, you can find listings of Python applications at `https://www.python.org/about/apps/` and `https://www.python.org/about/success/`. As of this writing, Python is the fourth-ranked language in the world (see `https://www.tiobe.com/tiobe-index/`). It continues to move up the scale because developers see it as one of the best ways to create modern applications, many of which rely on data science.

Naturally, with all these success stories to go on, people are enthusiastic about adding to Python. You can find lists of Python Enhancement Proposals (PEPs) at http://legacy.python.org/dev/peps/. These PEPs may or may not see the light of day, but they prove that Python is a living, growing language that will continue to provide features that developers truly need to create great applications of all types, not just those for data science.

Working with Python

This book doesn't provide you with a full Python tutorial. (However, you can get a great start with *Beginning Programming with Python For Dummies*, 2nd Edition, by John Paul Mueller (Wiley). For now, it's helpful to get a brief overview of what Python looks like and how you interact with it, as in the following sections.

TIP

You don't have to type the source code for this chapter manually. You'll find using the downloadable source a lot easier (see the Introduction for details on downloading the source code). The source code for this chapter appears in the P4DS4D2_02_Using_Python.ipynb source code file.

Getting a taste of the language

Python is designed to provide clear language statements but to do so in an incredibly small space. A single line of Python code may perform tasks that another language usually takes several lines to perform. For example, if you want to display something on-screen, you simply tell Python to print it, like this:

```
print("Hello There!")
```

TIP

This is an example of a 3.*x* print() function. (The 2.*x* version of Python includes both a function form of print, which requires parentheses, and a statement form of print, which omits the parentheses.) The "Why Python?" section of this chapter mentions some differences between the 2.*x* path and the 3.*x* path. If you use the print() function without parentheses in 3.*x*, you get an error message:

```
File "<Jupyter-input-1-fe18535d9681>", line 1
    print "Hello There!"
                       ^
SyntaxError: Missing parentheses in call to 'print'. Did you
    mean print("Hello There!")?
```

The point is that you can simply tell Python to output text, an object, or anything else using a simple statement. You don't really need too much in the way of advanced programming skills. When you want to end your session using a command line environment such as IDLE, you simply type quit() and press Enter. This book relies on a much better environment, Jupyter Notebook, which really does make your code look as though it came from someone's notebook.

Understanding the need for indentation

Python relies on indentation to create various language features, such as conditional statements. One of the most common errors that developers encounter is not providing the proper indentation for code. You see this principle in action later in the book, but for now, always be sure to pay attention to indentation as you work through the book examples. For example, here is an if statement (a conditional that says that if something meets the condition, perform the code that follows) with proper indentation.

```
if 1 < 2:
    print("1 is less than 2")
```

The print statement must appear indented below the conditional statement. Otherwise, the condition won't work as expected, and you might see an error message, too.

UNDERSTANDING THE ANACONDA PACKAGE

The book approaches Anaconda as a product. In fact, you do install and interact with Anaconda as you would any other single product. However, Anaconda is actually a compilation of several open source applications. You can use these applications individually or in cooperation with each other to achieve specific coding goals. In most of the book, you use a single application, Jupyter Notebook, to accomplish tasks. However, you want to know about the other applications bundled in Anaconda to get the best use out of the product as a whole.

A large number of data scientists rely on the Anaconda product bundling, which is why this book uses it. However, you might find that some of the open source products come in a newer form when downloaded separately. For example, Jupyter Notebook actually comes in a newer form than found in the Anaconda bundle (http://jupyter.org/). Because of the differences in Jupyter Notebook versions you need to install the version of Jupyter Notebook specified for this book, which means using the Anaconda package, rather than a separate download.

Working at the command line or in the IDE

Anaconda is a product that makes using Python even easier. It comes with a number of utilities that help you work with Python in a variety of ways. The vast majority of this book relies on Jupyter Notebook, which is part of the Anaconda installation you create in Chapter 3. You saw this editor used in Chapter 1 and you see it again later in the book. In fact, this book doesn't use any of the other Anaconda utilities much at all. However, they do exist, and sometimes they're helpful in playing with Python. The following sections provide a brief overview of the other Anaconda utilities for creating Python code. You may want to experiment with them as you work through various coding techniques in the book.

Creating new sessions with Anaconda Command Prompt

Only one of the Anaconda utilities provides direct access to the command line, Anaconda Prompt. When you start this utility, you see a command prompt at which you can type commands. The main advantage of this utility is that you can start an Anaconda utility with any of the switches it provides to modify that utility's standard environment. Of course, you start many of the utilities using the Python interpreter that you access using the python.exe command. (If you have both Python 3.6 and Python 2.7 installed on your system and open a regular command prompt or terminal window, you may see the Python 2.7 version start instead of the Python 3.6 version, so it's always best to open an Anaconda Command Prompt to ensure that you get the right version of Python.) So you could simply type **python** and press Enter to start a copy of the Python interpreter should you wish to do so. Figure 2-1 shows how the plain Python interpreter looks.

FIGURE 2-1:
A view of the plain Python interpreter.

```
python
(base) C:\Users\John>python
Python 3.6.4 |Anaconda, Inc.| (default, Jan 16 2018, 10:22:32) [MSC v.1900 64 bi
t (AMD64)] on win32
Type "help", "copyright", "credits" or "license" for more information.
>>> _
```

You quit the interpreter by typing **quit()** and pressing Enter. Once back at the command line, you can discover the list of python.exe command-line switches by typing **python -?** and pressing Enter. Figure 2-2 shows just some of the ways in which you can change the Python interpreter environment.

If you want, you can create a modified form of any of the utilities provided by Anaconda by starting the interpreter with the correct script. The scripts appear in the `scripts` subdirectory. For example, type **python Anaconda3/scripts/Jupyter-script.py** and press Enter to start the Jupyter environment without using the graphical command for your platform. You can also add command-line arguments to further modify the script's behavior. When working with this script, you can get information about Jupyter by using the following command-line arguments:

>> `--version`: Obtains the version of Jupyter Notebook in use.

>> `--config-dir`: Displays the configuration directory for Jupyter Notebook (where the configuration information is stored).

>> `--data-dir`: Displays the storage location of Jupyter application data, rather than projects. Your projects generally appear in your user folder.

>> `--runtime-dir`: Shows the location of the Jupyter runtime files, which is normally a subdirectory of the data directory.

>> `--paths`: Creates a list of paths that Jupyter is configured to use.

Consequently, if you want to obtain a list of Jupyter paths, you type **python Anaconda3/scripts/Jupyter-script.py --paths** and press Enter. The `scripts` sub-directory also contains a wealth of executable files. Often, these files are compiled versions of scripts and may execute more quickly as a result. If you want to start the Jupyter Notebook browser environment, you can either type **python Anaconda3/scripts/Jupyter-notebook-script.py** and press Enter to use the script version or execute `Jupyter-notebook.exe`. The result is the same in either case.

Entering the IPython environment

The Interactive Python (IPython) environment provides enhancements to the standard Python interpreter. To start this environment, you use the `IPython` command, rather than the standard `Python` command, at the Anaconda Prompt. The main purpose of the environment shown in Figure 2-3 is to help you use Python with less work. Note that the Python version is the same as when using the `Python` command, but that the IPython version is different and that you see a different prompt. To see these enhancements (as shown in the figure), type **%quickref** and press Enter.

FIGURE 2-3: The Jupyter environment is easier to use than the standard Python interpreter.

One of the more interesting additions to IPython is a fully functional clear screen (`cls`) command. You can't clear the screen easily when working in the Python interpreter, which means that things tend to get a bit messy after a while. It's also possible to perform tasks such as searching for variables using wildcard matches. Later in the book, you see how to use the magic functions to perform tasks such as capturing the amount of time it takes to perform a task for the purpose of optimization.

Entering Jupyter QTConsole environment

Trying to remember Python commands and functions is hard — and trying to remember the enhanced Jupyter additions is even harder. In fact, some people would say that the task is impossible (and perhaps they're right). This is where the Jupyter QTConsole comes into play. It adds a graphical user interface (GUI) on top of Jupyter that makes using the enhancements that Jupyter provides a lot easier.

You may think that QTConsole is missing if you used previous versions of Anaconda, but it's still present. Only the direct access method is gone. To start QTConsole, open an Anaconda Prompt, type **Jupyter QTConsole**, and press Enter. You see QTConsole start, as shown in Figure 2-4. Of course, you give up a little screen real estate to get this feature, and some hardcore programmers don't like the idea of using a GUI, so you have to choose what sort of environment to work with when programming.

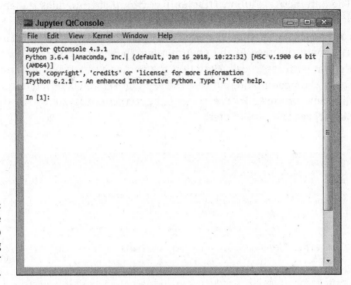

FIGURE 2-4:
Use the QTConsole to make working with Jupyter easier.

Some of the enhanced commands appear in menus across the top of the window. All you need to do is choose the command you want to use. For example, to restart the kernel, you choose Kernel ➪ Restart Current Kernel. You also have the same access to IPython commands. For example, type **%magic** and press Enter to see a list of magic commands.

Editing scripts using Spyder

Spyder is a fully functional Integrated Development Environment (IDE). You use it to load scripts, edit them, run them, and perform debugging tasks. Figure 2-5 shows the default windowed environment.

The Spyder IDE is much like any other IDE that you might have used in the past. The left side contains an editor in which you type code. Any code you create is placed in a script file, and you must save the script before running it. The upper-right window contains various tabs for inspecting objects, exploring variables, and interacting with files. The lower-right window contains the Python console, a history log, and the Jupyter console. Across the top, you see menu options for performing all the tasks that you normally associate with working with an IDE.

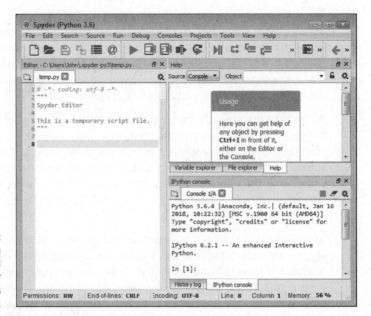

FIGURE 2-5:
Spyder is a traditional style IDE for developers who need one.

Performing Rapid Prototyping and Experimentation

Python is all about creating applications quickly and then experimenting with them to see how things work. The act of creating an application design in code without necessarily filling in all the details is *prototyping*. Python uses less code than other languages to perform tasks, so prototyping goes faster. The fact that many of the actions you need to perform are already defined as part of libraries that you load into memory makes things go faster still.

Data science doesn't rely on static solutions. You may have to try multiple solutions to find the particular solution that works best. This is where experimentation comes into play. After you create a prototype, you use it to experiment with various algorithms to determine which algorithm works best in a particular situation. The algorithm you use varies depending on the answers you see and the data you use, so there are too many variables to consider for any sort of canned solution.

TECHNICAL STUFF

The prototyping and experimentation process occurs in several phases. As you go through the book, you discover that these phases have distinct uses and appear in a particular order. The following list shows the phases in the order in which you normally perform them.

1. **Building a data pipeline.** To work with the data, you must create a pipeline to it. It's possible to load some data into memory. However, after the dataset gets to a certain size, you need to start working with it on disk or by using other means to interact with it. The technique you use for gaining access to the data is important because it impacts how fast you get a result.

2. **Performing the required shaping.** The shape of the data — the way in which it appears and its characteristics (such as data type), is important in performing analysis. To perform an apples-to-apples comparison, like data has to be shaped the same. However, just shaping the data the same isn't enough. The shape has to be correct for the algorithms you employ to analyze it. Later chapters (starting with Chapter 7) help you understand the need to shape data in various ways.

3. **Analyzing the data.** When analyzing data, you seldom employ a single algorithm and call it good enough. You can't know which algorithm will produce the same results at the outset. To find the best result from your dataset, you experiment on it using several algorithms. This practice is emphasized in the later chapters of the book when you start performing serious data analysis.

4. **Presenting a result.** A picture is worth a thousand words, or so they say. However, you need the picture to say the correct words or your message gets lost. Using the MATLAB-like plotting functionality provided by the `matplotlib` library, you can create multiple presentations of the same data, each of which describes the data graphically in different ways. To ensure that your meaning really isn't lost, you must experiment with various presentation methods and determine which one works best.

Considering Speed of Execution

Computers are known for their prowess in crunching numbers. Even so, analysis takes considerable processing power. The datasets are so large that you can bog down even an incredibly powerful system. In general, the following factors control the speed of execution for your data science application:

>> **Dataset size:** Data science relies on huge datasets in many cases. Yes, you can make a robot see objects using a modest dataset size, but when it comes to making business decisions, larger is better in most situations. The application type determines the size of your dataset in part, but dataset size also relies on the size of the source data. Underestimating the effect of dataset size is deadly in data science applications, especially those that need to operate in real time (such as self-driving cars).

>> **Loading technique:** The method you use to load data for analysis is critical, and you should always use the fastest means at your disposal, even if it means upgrading your hardware to do so. Working with data in memory is always faster than working with data stored on disk. Accessing local data is always faster than accessing it across a network. Performing data science tasks that rely on Internet access through web services is probably the slowest method of all. Chapter 6 helps you understand loading techniques in more detail. You also see the effects of loading technique later in the book.

>> **Coding style:** Some people will likely try to tell you that Python's programming paradigms make writing a slow application nearly impossible. They're wrong. Anyone can create a slow application using any language by employing coding techniques that don't make the best use of programming language functionality. To create fast data science applications, you must use best-of-method coding techniques. The techniques demonstrated in this book are a great starting point.

>> **Machine capability:** Running data science applications on a memory-constrained system with a slower processor is impossible. The system you use needs to have the best hardware you can afford. Given that data science applications are both processor and disk bound, you can't really cut corners in any area and expect great results.

>> **Analysis algorithm:** The algorithm you use determines the kind of result you obtain and controls execution speed. Many of the chapters in the latter parts of this book demonstrate multiple methods to achieve a goal using different algorithms. However, you must still experiment to find the best algorithm for your particular dataset.

REMEMBER

A number of the chapters in this book emphasize performance, most notably speed and reliability, because both factors are critical to data science applications. Even though database applications tend to emphasize the need for speed and reliability to some extent, the combination of huge dataset access (disk-bound issues) and data analysis (processor-bound issues) in data science applications makes the need to make good choices even more critical.

Visualizing Power

Python makes it possible to explore the data science environment without resorting to using a debugger or debugging code, as would be needed in many other languages. The print statement (or function, depending on the version of Python you use) and dir() function let you examine any object interactively. In short, you can load something up and play with it for a while to see just how the developer put it together. Playing with the data, visualizing what it means to you personally, can often help you gain new insights and create new ideas. Judging by many online conversations, playing with the data is the part of data science that its practitioners find the most fun.

You can play with data using any of the tools found in Anaconda, but one of the best tools for the job is IPython (see the "Entering the IPython environment" section, earlier in of this chapter, for details) because you don't really have to worry too much about the environment, and nothing you create is permanent. After all, you're playing with the data. Therefore, you can load a dataset to see just what it has to offer, as shown in Figure 2-6. Don't worry if this code looks foreign and hard to understand right now. Beginning with Chapter 4, you start to play with code more, and the various sections give you more details. You can also obtain the book *Beginning Programming with Python For Dummies,* 2nd Edition, by John Paul Mueller (Wiley) if you want a more detailed tutorial. Just follow along with the concept of playing with data for now.

```
(base) C:\Users\John>iPython
Python 3.6.4 |Anaconda, Inc.| (default, Jan 16 2018, 10:22:32) [MSC v.1900 64 bi
t (AMD64)]
Type 'copyright', 'credits' or 'license' for more information
IPython 6.2.1 -- An enhanced Interactive Python. Type '?' for help.

In [1]: import sklearn as sk

In [2]: items = dir(sk.utils.Bunch)

In [3]: for item in items:
   ...:     if 'key' in item:
   ...:         print(item)
   ...:
fromkeys
keys

In [4]:
```

FIGURE 2-6:
Load a dataset and play with it a little.

Scikit-learn datasets appear within *bunches* (a bunch is a kind of data structure). When you import a dataset, that dataset will have certain functions that you can use with it that are determined by the code used to define the datastructure — a bunch. This code shows which functions deal with *keys* — the data identifiers for the *values* (one or more columns of information) in the dataset. Each row in the dataset has a unique key, even if the values in that row repeat another row in the dataset. You can use these functions to perform useful work with the dataset as part of building your application.

Before you can work with a dataset, you must provide access to it in the local environment. Figure 2-7 shows the import process and demonstrates how you can use the keys() function to display a list of keys that you can use to access data within the dataset.

FIGURE 2-7:
Use a function
to learn more
information.

When you have a list of keys you can use, you can access individual data items. For example, Figure 2-8 shows a list of all the feature names contained in the Boston dataset. Python really does make it possible to know quite a lot about a dataset before you have to work with it in depth.

FIGURE 2-8:
Access specific
data using a key.

Using the Python Ecosystem for Data Science

You have already seen the need to load libraries in order to perform data science tasks in Python. The following sections provide an overview of the libraries you use for the data science examples in this book. Various book examples show the libraries at work.

Accessing scientific tools using SciPy

The SciPy stack (http://www.scipy.org/) contains a host of other libraries that you can also download separately. These libraries provide support for mathematics, science, and engineering. When you obtain SciPy, you get a set of libraries designed to work together to create applications of various sorts. These libraries are

>> NumPy

>> SciPy

>> matplotlib

>> Jupyter

>> Sympy

>> pandas

The SciPy library itself focuses on numerical routines, such as routines for numerical integration and optimization. SciPy is a general-purpose library that provides functionality for multiple problem domains. It also provides support for domain-specific libraries, such as Scikit-learn, Scikit-image, and statsmodels.

Performing fundamental scientific computing using NumPy

The NumPy library (`http://www.numpy.org/`) provides the means for performing n-dimensional array manipulation, which is critical for data science work. The Boston dataset used in the examples in Chapters 1 and 2 is an example of an n-dimensional array, and you couldn't easily access it without NumPy functions that include support for linear algebra, Fourier transform, and random-number generation (see the listing of functions at `http://docs.scipy.org/doc/numpy/reference/routines.html`).

Performing data analysis using pandas

The pandas library (`http://pandas.pydata.org/`) provides support for data structures and data analysis tools. The library is optimized to perform data science tasks especially fast and efficiently. The basic principle behind pandas is to provide data analysis and modeling support for Python that is similar to other languages, such as R.

Implementing machine learning using Scikit-learn

The Scikit-learn library (`http://scikit-learn.org/stable/`) is one of a number of Scikit libraries that build on the capabilities provided by NumPy and SciPy to allow Python developers to perform domain-specific tasks. In this case, the library focuses on data mining and data analysis. It provides access to the following sorts of functionality:

>> Classification

>> Regression

- » Clustering
- » Dimensionality reduction
- » Model selection
- » Preprocessing

A number of these functions appear as chapter headings in the book. As a result, you can assume that Scikit-learn is the most important library for the book (even though it relies on other libraries to perform its work).

Going for deep learning with Keras and TensorFlow

Keras (`https://keras.io/`) is an application programming interface (API) that is used to train deep learning models. An *API* often specifies a model for doing something, but it doesn't provide an implementation. Consequently, you need an implementation of Keras to perform useful work, which is where TensorFlow (`https://www.tensorflow.org/`) comes into play. You can also use Microsoft's Cognitive Toolkit, CNTK (`https://www.microsoft.com/en-us/cognitive-toolkit/`), or Theano (`https://github.com/Theano`), to implement Keras, but this book focuses on TensorFlow.

When working with an API, you're looking for ways to simplify things. Keras makes things easy in the following ways:

- » **Consistent interface:** The Keras interface is optimized for common use cases with an emphasis on actionable feedback for fixing user errors.

- » **Lego approach:** Using a black-box approach makes it easy to create models by connecting configurable building blocks together with only a few restrictions on how you can connect them.

- » **Extendable:** You can easily add custom building blocks to express new ideas for research that include new layers, loss functions, and models.

- » **Parallel processing:** To run applications fast today, you need good parallel processing support. Keras runs on both CPUs and GPUs.

- » **Direct Python support:** You don't have to do anything special to make the TensorFlow implementation of Keras work with Python, which can be a major stumbling block when working with other sorts of APIs.

Plotting the data using matplotlib

The matplotlib library (http://matplotlib.org/) gives you a MATLAB-like interface for creating data presentations of the analysis you perform. The library is currently limited to 2-D output, but it still provides you with the means to express graphically the data patterns you see in the data you analyze. Without this library, you couldn't create output that people outside the data science community could easily understand.

Creating graphs with NetworkX

To properly study the relationships between complex data in a networked system (such as that used by your GPS setup to discover routes through city streets), you need a library to create, manipulate, and study the structure of network data in various ways. In addition, the library must provide the means to output the resulting analysis in a form that humans understand, such as graphical data. NetworkX (https://networkx.github.io/) enables you to perform this sort of analysis. The advantage of NetworkX is that nodes can be anything (including images) and edges can hold arbitrary data. These features allow you to perform a much broader range of analysis with NetworkX than using custom code would (and such code would be time consuming to create).

Parsing HTML documents using Beautiful Soup

The Beautiful Soup library (http://www.crummy.com/software/Beautiful Soup/) download is actually found at https://pypi.python.org/pypi/beautiful soup4/4.3.2. This library provides the means for parsing HTML or XML data in a manner that Python understands. It allows you to work with tree-based data.

TECHNICAL STUFF

Besides providing a means for working with tree-based data, Beautiful Soup takes a lot of the work out of working with HTML documents. For example, it automatically converts the *encoding* (the manner in which characters are stored in a document) of HTML documents from UTF-8 to Unicode. A Python developer would normally need to worry about things like encoding, but with Beautiful Soup, you can focus on your code instead.

Chapter **3**

Setting Up Python for Data Science

Before you can do too much with Python or use it to solve data science problems, you need a workable installation. In addition, you need access to the datasets and code used for this book. Downloading the sample code and installing it on your system is the best way to get a good learning experience from the book. This chapter helps you get your system set up so that you can easily follow the examples in the remainder of the book.

This book relies on Jupyter Notebook version 5.5.0 supplied with the Anaconda 3 environment (version 5.2.0) that supports the Python version 3.6.5 to create the coding examples. For the examples to work, you must use Python 3.6.5 and the packages' version as present in the Anaconda 3 version 5.2.0. Older versions of both Python and its packages tend to lack needed features, and newer versions tend to produce breaking changes. If you use some other version of Python, the examples are likely not going to work as intended. However, you can find other development tools that you may prefer to Jupyter Notebook. As part of looking at tools that you can use to write Python code, this chapter also reviews a few other offerings. If you choose one of these other offerings, your screenshots won't match those provided in the book and you won't be able to following the procedures, but if the package you choose supports Python 3.6.5, the code should still run as described in the book.

REMEMBER

Using the downloadable source doesn't prevent you from typing the examples on your own, following them using a debugger, expanding them, or working with the code in all sorts of ways. The downloadable source is there to help you get a good start with your data science and Python learning experience. After you see how the code works when it's correctly typed and configured, you can try to create the examples on your own. If you make a mistake, you can compare what you've typed with the downloadable source and discover precisely where the error exists. You can find the downloadable source for this chapter in the P4DS4D2_03_Sample.ipynb and P4DS4D2_03_Dataset_Load.ipynb files. (The Introduction tells you where to download the source code for this book.)

Considering the Off-the-Shelf Cross-Platform Scientific Distributions

It's entirely possible to obtain a generic copy of Python and add all of the required data science libraries to it. The process can be difficult because you need to ensure that you have all the required libraries in the correct versions to ensure success. In addition, you need to perform the configuration required to ensure that the libraries are accessible when you need them. Fortunately, going through the required work is not necessary because a number of Python data science products are available for you to use. These products provide everything needed to get started with data science projects.

REMEMBER

You can use any of the packages mentioned in the following sections to work with the examples in this book. However, the book's source code and downloadable source rely on Continuum Analytics Anaconda because this particular package works on every platform this book is designed to support: Linux, Mac OS X, and Windows. The book doesn't mention a specific package in the chapters that follow, but any screenshots reflect how things look when using Anaconda on Windows. You may need to tweak the code to use another package, and the screens will look different if you use Anaconda on some other platform.

Getting Continuum Analytics Anaconda

The basic Anaconda package is a free download that you obtain at https://www. anaconda.com/download/ (you may need to go to https://repo.anaconda.com/ archive/ to obtain the 5.2.0 version used in this book if a newer version of the product is available when you visit the main site). Simply click one of the Python 3.6 Version links to obtain access to the free product. The filename you want begins with Anaconda3-5.2.0- followed by the platform and 32-bit or 64-bit version, such as `Anaconda3-5.2.0-Windows-x86_64.exe` for the Windows 64-bit version. Anaconda supports the following platforms:

>> Windows 32-bit and 64-bit (the installer may offer you only the 64-bit or 32-bit version, depending on which version of Windows it detects)

>> Linux 32-bit and 64-bit

>> Mac OS X 64-bit

The default download version installed Python 3.6, which is the version used in this book. You can also choose to install Python 2.7 by clicking one of the Python 2.7 Version links. Both Windows and Mac OS X provide graphical installers. When using Linux, you rely on the `bash` utility.

TIP

Obtaining Anaconda with older versions of Python is possible. If you want to use an older version of Python, click the installer archive link about halfway down the page. You should use only an older version of Python when you have a pressing need to do so.

The free product is all you need for this book. However, when you look on the site, you see that many other add-on products are available. These products can help you create robust applications. For example, when you add Accelerate to the mix, you obtain the ability to perform multicore and GPU-enabled operations. The use of these add-on products is outside the scope of this book, but the Anaconda site provides details on using them.

Getting Enthought Canopy Express

Enthought Canopy Express is a free product for producing both technical and sci-entific applications using Python. You can obtain it at `https://www.enthought.com/canopy-express/`. Click Download on the main page to see a listing of the versions that you can download. Only Canopy Express is free, the full Canopy product comes at a cost. Canopy Express supports the following platforms:

>> Windows 32-bit and 64-bit

>> Linux 32-bit and 64-bit

>> Mac OS X 32-bit and 64-bit

WARNING

As of this writing, Canopy supports Python 3.5. You need Python 3.6 to ensure that the examples will run as anticipated. Make sure to download a version of Canopy that provides Python 3.6 support or be aware that some examples in the book may not work. The page at `https://www.enthought.com/product/canopy/#/package-index` lists packages that work with Python 3.6.

Choose the platform and version you want to download. When you click Download Canopy Express, you see an optional form for providing information about yourself. The download starts automatically, even if you don't provide personal information to the company.

One of the advantages of Canopy Express is that Enthought is heavily involved in providing support for both students and teachers. People also can take classes, including online classes, that teach the use of Canopy Express in various ways (see https://training.enthought.com/courses). Also offered is live classroom training specifically designed for the data scientist; read about this training at https://www.enthought.com/services/training/data-science.

Getting WinPython

The name tells you that WinPython is a Windows-only product, which you can find at http://winpython.github.io/. That site provides Python 3.5, 3.6 and 3.7 support. This product is actually a takeoff of Python(x,y) (an IDE that went dormant in 2015 and stopped being developed; see http://python-xy.github.io/) and isn't simply meant to replace it. Quite the contrary: WinPython gives you a more flexible way to work with Python(x,y). You can read about the initial motivation for creating WinPython at http://sourceforge.net/p/winpython/wiki/ Roadmap/ and about its most recent development roadmap at https://github.com/winpython/winpython/wiki/Roadmap.

The bottom line for this product is that you gain flexibility at the cost of friendliness and a little platform integration. However, for developers who need to maintain multiple versions of an IDE, WinPython may make a significant difference. When using WinPython with this book, make sure to pay particular attention to configuration issues or you'll find that even the downloadable code has little chance of working.

Installing Anaconda on Windows

Anaconda comes with a graphical installation application for Windows, so getting a good install means using a wizard, much as you would for any other installation. Of course, you need a copy of the installation file before you begin, and you can find the required download information in the "Getting Continuum Analytics Anaconda" section of this chapter. The following procedure should work fine on any Windows system, whether you use the 32-bit or the 64-bit version of Anaconda.

1. **Locate the downloaded copy of Anaconda on your system.**

   The name of this file varies, but normally it appears as Anaconda3-5.2.0-Windows-x86.exe for 32-bit systems and Anaconda3-5.2.0-Windows-x86_64.exe for 64-bit systems. The version number is embedded as part of the filename. In this case, the filename refers to version 5.2.0, which is the version used for this book. If you use some other version, you may experience problems with the source code and need to make adjustments when working with it.

2. **Double-click the installation file.**

   (You may see an Open File – Security Warning dialog box that asks whether you want to run this file. Click Run if you see this dialog box pop up.) You see an Anaconda 5.2.0 Setup dialog box similar to the one shown in Figure 3-1. The exact dialog box you see depends on which version of the Anaconda installation program you download. If you have a 64-bit operating system, it's always best to use the 64-bit version of Anaconda so that you obtain the best possible performance. This first dialog box tells you when you have the 64-bit version of the product.

FIGURE 3-1:
The setup process begins by telling you whether you have the 64-bit version.

3. **Click Next.**

   The wizard displays a licensing agreement. Be sure to read through the licensing agreement so that you know the terms of usage.

4. **Click I Agree if you agree to the licensing agreement.**

   You're asked what sort of installation type to perform, as shown in Figure 3-2. In most cases, you want to install the product just for yourself. The exception is if you have multiple people using your system and they all need access to Anaconda.

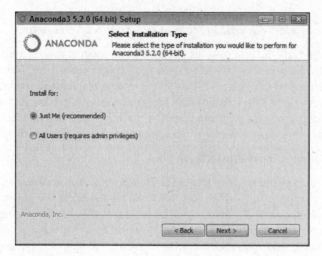

FIGURE 3-2:
Tell the wizard
how to install
Anaconda on
your system.

5. **Choose one of the installation types and then click Next.**

   The wizard asks where to install Anaconda on disk, as shown in Figure 3-3. The book assumes that you use the default location. If you choose some other location, you may have to modify some procedures later in the book to work with your setup.

FIGURE 3-3:
Specify an
installation
location.

6. **Choose an installation location (if necessary) and then click Next.**

   You see the Advanced Installation Options, shown in Figure 3-4. These options are selected by default and there isn't a good reason to change them in most cases. You might need to change them if Anaconda won't provide your default Python 3.6 setup. However, the book assumes that you've set up Anaconda using the default options.

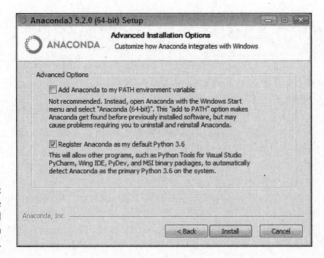

FIGURE 3-4:
Configure the
advanced
installation
options.

TIP

The Add Anaconda to My PATH Environment Variable option is cleared by default, and you should leave it cleared. Adding it to the PATH environment variable does offer the ability to locate the Anaconda files when using a standard command prompt, but if you have multiple versions of Anaconda installed, only the first version you installed is accessible. Opening an Anaconda Prompt instead is far better so that you gain access to the version you expect.

7. Change the advanced installation options (if necessary) and then click Install.

You see an Installing dialog box with a progress bar. The installation process can take a few minutes, so get yourself a cup of coffee and read the comics for a while. When the installation process is over, you see a Next button enabled.

8. Click Next.

The wizard tells you that the installation is complete.

9. Click Next.

Anaconda offers you the chance to integrate Visual Studio code support. You don't need this support for this book, and adding it could potentially change the way that the Anaconda tools work. Unless you absolutely need Visual Studio support, you want to keep the Anaconda environment pure.

10. Click Skip.

You see a completion screen. This screen contains options to discover more about Anaconda Cloud and obtain information about starting your first Anaconda project. Selecting these options (or clearing them) depends on what you want to do next; the options don't affect your Anaconda setup.

11. Select any required options. Click Finish.

You're ready to begin using Anaconda.

A WORD ABOUT THE SCREENSHOTS

As you work your way through the book, you'll use an IDE of your choice to open the Python and Jupyter Notebook files containing the book's source code. Every screenshot that contains IDE-specific information relies on Anaconda because Anaconda runs on all three platforms supported by the book. The use of Anaconda doesn't imply that it's the best IDE or that the authors are making any sort of recommendation for it — Anaconda simply works well as a demonstration product.

When you work with Anaconda, the name of the graphical (GUI) environment, Jupyter Notebook, is precisely the same across all three platforms, and you won't even see any significant difference in the presentation. The differences you do see are minor, and you should ignore them as you work through the book. With this in mind, the book does rely heavily on Windows 7 screenshots. When working on a Linux, Mac OS X, or other Windows version platform, you should expect to see some differences in presentation, but these differences shouldn't reduce your ability to work with the examples.

Installing Anaconda on Linux

You use the command line to install Anaconda on Linux — there is no graphical installation option. Before you can perform the install, you must download a copy of the Linux software from the Continuum Analytics site. You can find the required download information in the "Getting Continuum Analytics Anaconda" section of this chapter. The following procedure should work fine on any Linux system, whether you use the 32-bit or the 64-bit version of Anaconda.

1. **Open a copy of Terminal.**

    You see the Terminal window appear.

2. **Change directories to the downloaded copy of Anaconda on your system.**

    The name of this file varies, but normally it appears as Anaconda3-5.2.0-Linux-x86.sh for 32-bit systems and Anaconda3-5.2.0-Linux-x86_64.sh for 64-bit systems. The version number is embedded as part of the filename. In this case, the filename refers to version 5.2.0, which is the version used for this book. If you use some other version, you may experience problems with the source code and need to make adjustments when working with it.

3. **Type** bash Anaconda3-5.2.0-Linux-x86 **(for the 32-bit version) or** Anaconda3-5.2.0-Linux-x86_64.sh **(for the 64-bit version) and press Enter.**

    An installation wizard starts that asks you to accept the licensing terms for using Anaconda.

4. **Read the licensing agreement and accept the terms using the method required for your version of Linux.**

   The wizard asks you to provide an installation location for Anaconda. The book assumes that you use the default location of ~/anaconda. If you choose some other location, you may have to modify some procedures later in the book to work with your setup.

5. **Provide an installation location (if necessary) and press Enter (or click Next).**

   You see the application extraction process begin. After the extraction is complete, you see a completion message.

6. **Add the installation path to your PATH statement using the method required for your version of Linux.**

   You're ready to begin using Anaconda.

Installing Anaconda on Mac OS X

The Mac OS X installation comes only in one form: 64-bit. Before you can perform the install, you must download a copy of the Mac software from the Continuum Analytics site. You can find the required download information in the "Getting Continuum Analytics Anaconda" section of this chapter. The following steps help you install Anaconda 64-bit on a Mac system.

1. **Locate the downloaded copy of Anaconda on your system.**

   The name of this file varies, but normally it appears as Anaconda3-5.2.0-MacOSX-x86_64.pkg. The version number is embedded as part of the filename. In this case, the filename refers to version 5.2.0, which is the version used for this book. If you use some other version, you may experience problems with the source code and need to make adjustments when working with it.

2. **Double-click the installation file.**

   You see an introduction dialog box.

3. **Click Continue.**

   The wizard asks whether you want to review the Read Me materials. You can read these materials later. For now, you can safely skip the information.

4. **Click Continue.**

   The wizard displays a licensing agreement. Be sure to read through the licensing agreement so that you know the terms of usage.

5. **Click I Agree if you agree to the licensing agreement.**

   The wizard asks you to provide a destination for the installation. The destination controls whether the installation is for an individual user or a group.

WARNING

   You may see an error message stating that you can't install Anaconda on the system. The error message occurs because of a bug in the installer and has nothing to do with your system. To get rid of the error message, choose the Install Only for Me option. You can't install Anaconda for a group of users on a Mac system.

6. **Click Continue.**

   The installer displays a dialog box containing options for changing the installation type. Click Change Install Location if you want to modify where Anaconda is installed on your system (the book assumes that you use the default path of ~/anaconda). Click Customize if you want to modify how the installer works. For example, you can choose not to add Anaconda to your PATH statement. However, the book assumes that you have chosen the default install options and there isn't a good reason to change them unless you have another copy of Python 2.7 installed somewhere else.

7. **Click Install.**

   You see the installation begin. A progress bar tells you how the installation process is progressing. When the installation is complete, you see a completion dialog box.

8. **Click Continue.**

   You're ready to begin using Anaconda.

Downloading the Datasets and Example Code

This book is about using Python to perform data science tasks. Of course, you could spend all your time creating the example code from scratch, debugging it, and only then discovering how it relates to data science, or you can take the easy way and download the prewritten code so that you can get right to work. Likewise, creating datasets large enough for data science purposes would take quite a while. Fortunately, you can access standardized, precreated datasets quite easily using features provided in some of the data science libraries. The following sections help you download and use the example code and datasets so that you can save time and get right to work with data science–specific tasks.

Using Jupyter Notebook

To make working with the relatively complex code in this book easier, you use Jupyter Notebook. This interface makes it easy to create Python notebook files that can contain any number of examples, each of which can run individually. The program runs in your browser, so which platform you use for development doesn't matter; as long as it has a browser, you should be OK.

Starting Jupyter Notebook

Most platforms provide an icon to access Jupyter Notebook. All you need to do is open this icon to access Jupyter Notebook. For example, on a Windows system, you choose Start⇨All Programs⇨Anaconda3⇨Jupyter Notebook. Figure 3-5 shows how the interface looks when viewed in a Firefox browser. The precise appearance on your system depends on the browser you use and the kind of platform you have installed.

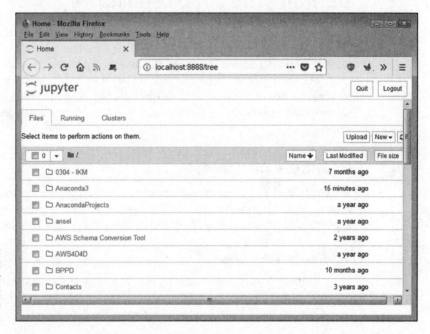

FIGURE 3-5: Jupyter Notebook provides an easy method to create data science examples.

If you have a platform that doesn't offer easy access through an icon, you can use these steps to access Jupyter Notebook:

1. **Open an Anaconda Prompt, Command Prompt, or Terminal Window on your system.**

    You see the window open so that you can type commands.

2. **Change directories to the** `\Anaconda3\Scripts` **directory on your machine.**

   Most systems let you use the CD command for this task.

3. **Type** ..\python Jupyter-script.py notebook **and press Enter.**

   The Jupyter Notebook page opens in your browser.

Stopping the Jupyter Notebook server

No matter how you start Jupyter Notebook (or just Notebook, as it appears in the remainder of the book), the system generally opens a command prompt or terminal window to host Notebook. This window contains a server that makes the application work. After you close the browser window when a session is complete, select the server window and press Ctrl+C or Ctrl+Break to stop the server.

Defining the code repository

The code you create and use in this book will reside in a repository on your hard drive. Think of a *repository* as a kind of filing cabinet where you put your code. Notebook opens a drawer, takes out the folder, and shows the code to you. You can modify it, run individual examples within the folder, add new examples, and simply interact with your code in a natural manner. The following sections get you started with Notebook so that you can see how this whole repository concept works.

Defining a new folder

You use folders to hold your code files for a particular project. The project for this book is P4DS4D2 (which stands for *Python for Data Science For Dummies*, 2nd Edition). The following steps help you create a new folder for this book.

1. **Choose New ⇨ Folder.**

   Notebook creates a new folder for you. The name of the folder can vary, but for Windows users, it's simply listed as Untitled Folder. You may have to scroll down the list of available folders to find the folder in question.

2. **Place a check in the box next to Untitled Folder.**

3. **Click Rename at the top of the page.**

   You see the Rename Directory dialog box, shown in Figure 3-6.

4. **Type** P4DS4D2 **and press Enter.**

   Notebook renames the folder for you.

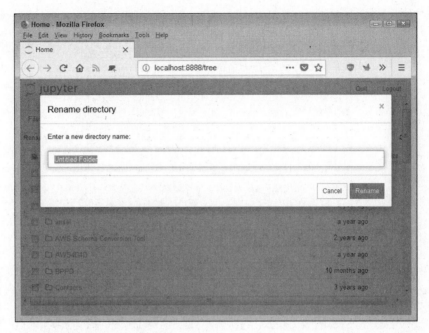

FIGURE 3-6:
Create a folder to
use to hold the
book's code.

Creating a new notebook

Every new notebook is like a file folder. You can place individual examples within the file folder, just as you would sheets of paper into a physical file folder. Each example appears in a cell. You can put other sorts of things in the file folder, too, but you see how these things work as the book progresses. Use these steps to create a new notebook.

1. **Click the P4DS4D2 entry on the Home page.**

You see the contents of the project folder for this book, which will be blank if you're performing this exercise from scratch.

2. **Choose New ⇨ Python 3.**

You see a new tab open in the browser with the new notebook, as shown in Figure 3-7. Notice that the notebook contains a cell and that Notebook has highlighted the cell so that you can begin typing code in it. The title of the notebook is Untitled right now. That's not a particularly helpful title, so you need to change it.

3. **Click Untitled on the page.**

Notebook asks whether you want to use a new name, as shown in Figure 3-8.

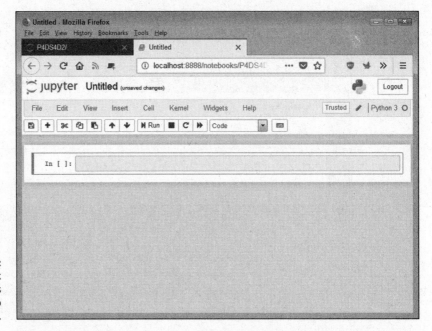

FIGURE 3-7:
A notebook contains cells that you use to hold code.

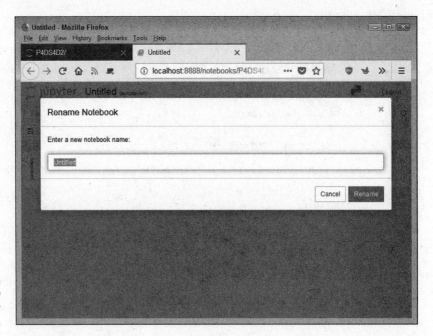

FIGURE 3-8:
Provide a new name for your notebook.

4. **Type** P4DS4D2_03_Sample **and press Enter.**

The new name tells you that this is a file for *Python for Data Science For Dummies,* 2nd Edition, Chapter 3, Sample.ipynb. Using this naming convention will let you easily differentiate these files from other files in your repository.

Adding notebook content

Of course, the Sample notebook doesn't contain anything just yet. This book follows a convention of putting the source code files together that makes them easy to use. The following steps tell you about this convention:

1. **Choose Markdown from the drop-down list that currently contains the word** *Code.*

A Markdown cell contains documentation text. You can put anything in a Markdown cell because Notebook won't interpret it. By using Markdown cells, you can easily document precisely what you mean when writing code.

2. **Type** # Downloading the Datasets and Example Code **and click Run (the button with the right-pointing arrow on the toolbar).**

The hash mark (#) creates a heading. A single # creates a first-level heading. The text that follows contains that actual heading information. Clicking Run turns the formatted text into a heading, as shown in Figure 3-9. Notice that Notebook automatically creates a new cell for you to use.

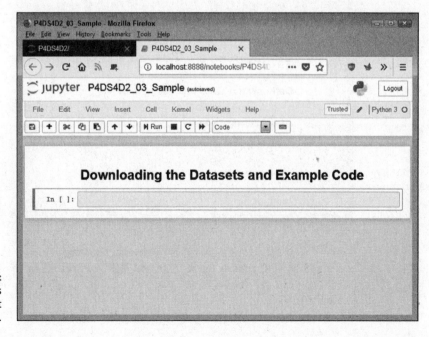

FIGURE 3-9:
Create headings
to document
your code.

3. **Choose Markdown, type** ## Defining the code repository**, and click Run.**

   Notebook creates a second-level heading, which looks smaller than a first-level heading.

4. **Choose Markdown, type** ### Adding notebook content**, and click Run.**

   Notebook creates a third-level heading. Your headings now match the hierarchy that starts with the first-level heading for this section. Using this approach helps you to easily locate a particular piece of code in the downloadable source. As always, Notebook creates a new cell for you, and the cell type automatically changes to Code, so you're ready to type some code for this example.

5. **Type** print('Python is really cool!') **and click Run.**

   Notice that the code is color coded so that you can tell the different between a function (`print`) and its associated data (`'Python is really cool!'`). You see the output shown in Figure 3-10. The output is part of the same cell as the code. However, Notebook visually separates the output from the code so that you can tell them apart. Notebook automatically creates a new cell for you.

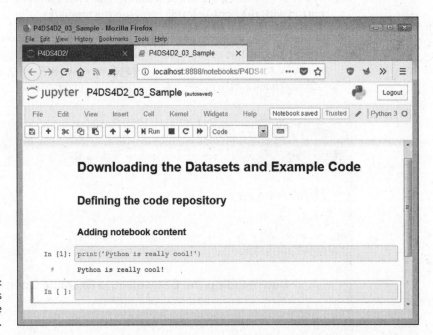

FIGURE 3-10: Notebook uses cells to store your code.

When you finish working with a notebook, shutting it down is important. To close a notebook, choose File ⇨ Close and Halt. You return to the P4DS4D2 page, where you can see the notebook you just created added to the list, as shown in Figure 3-11.

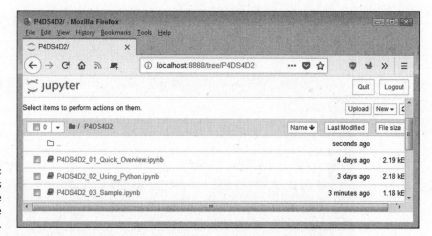

FIGURE 3-11:
Any notebooks you create appear in the repository list.

Exporting a notebook

It isn't much fun to create notebooks and keep them all to yourself. At some point, you want to share them with other people. To perform this task, you must export your notebook from the repository to a file. You can then send the file to someone else who will import it into his or her repository.

The previous section shows how to create a notebook named P4DS4D2_03_ Sample. You can open this notebook by clicking its entry in the repository list. The file reopens so that you can see your code again. To export this code, choose File ➪ Download As ➪ Notebook (.ipynb). What you see next depends on your browser, but you generally see some sort of dialog box for saving the notebook as a file. Use the same method for saving the Notebook file as you use for any other file you save using your browser.

Removing a notebook

Sometimes notebooks get outdated or you simply don't need to work with them any longer. Rather than allow your repository to get clogged with files you don't need, you can remove these unwanted notebooks from the list. Notice the check box next to the P4DS4D2_03_Sample.ipynb entry in Figure 3-11. Use these steps to remove the file:

1. **Select the check box next to the** P4DS4D2_03_Sample.ipynb **entry.**

2. **Click the Delete (trashcan) icon.**

   You see a Delete notebook warning message like the one shown in Figure 3-12.

3. **Click Delete.**

   Notebook removes the notebook file from the list.

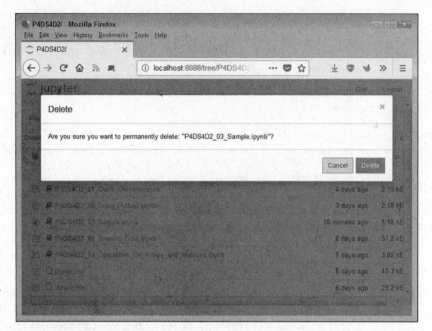

FIGURE 3-12:
Notebook warns
you before
removing any
files from the
repository.

Importing a notebook

To use the source code from this book, you must import the downloaded files into your repository. The source code comes in an archive file that you extract to a location on your hard drive. The archive contains a list of .ipynb (IPython Notebook) files containing the source code for this book (see the Introduction for details on downloading the source code). The following steps tell how to import these files into your repository:

1. **Click Upload on the Notebook P4DS4D2 page.**

What you see depends on your browser. In most cases, you see some type of File Upload dialog box that provides access to the files on your hard drive.

2. **Navigate to the directory containing the files you want to import into Notebook.**

3. **Highlight one or more files to import and click the Open (or other, similar) button to begin the upload process.**

You see the file added to an upload list, as shown in Figure 3-13. The file isn't part of the repository yet — you've simply selected it for upload.

4. **Click Upload.**

Notebook places the file in the repository so that you can begin using it.

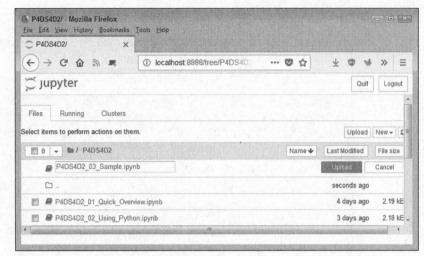

Understanding the datasets used in this book

This book uses a number of datasets, all of which appear in the Scikit-learn library. These datasets demonstrate various ways in which you can interact with data, and you use them in the examples to perform a variety of tasks. The following list provides a quick overview of the function used to import each of the datasets into your Python code:

» `load_boston()`: Regression analysis with the Boston house-prices dataset

» `load_iris()`: Classification with the Iris dataset

» `load_diabetes()`: Regression with the diabetes dataset

» `load_digits([n_class])`: Classification with the digits dataset

» `fetch_20newsgroups(subset='train')`: Data from 20 newsgroups

» `fetch_olivetti_faces()`: Olivetti faces dataset from AT&T

The technique for loading each of these datasets is the same across examples. The following example shows how to load the Boston house-prices dataset. You can find the code in the `P4DS4D2_03_Dataset_Load.ipynb` notebook.

```
from sklearn.datasets import load_boston
Boston = load_boston()
print(Boston.data.shape)
```

To see how the code works, click Run Cell. The output from the `print` call is (506L, 13L). You can see the output shown in Figure 3-14. (Be patient; the dataset load can require a few seconds to complete.)

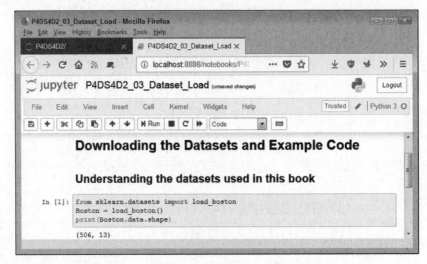

FIGURE 3-14:
The Boston object contains the loaded dataset.

Chapter **4**

Working with Google Colab

olaboratory (`https://colab.research.google.com/notebooks/welcome.ipynb`), or Colab for short, is a Google cloud-based service that replicates Jupyter Notebook in the cloud. You don't have to install anything on your system to use it. In most respects, you use Colab as you would a desktop installation of Jupyter Notebook (also called Notebook throughout the book). This book includes this chapter mainly for those readers who use something other than a standard desktop setup to work through the examples.

REMEMBER

Because you may not be using the same versions of products that appear in this book, the book's example source code may or may not work precisely as described in the text when you use Colab. Also when using Colab, you may not see the results as presented in this book because of the differences in hardware between platforms. The introductory sections of this chapter go into more detail about Colab and help you understand what you can expect from it. However, the most important thing to remember is that Colab isn't a replacement for Jupyter Notebook and the examples aren't tested to specifically work with it, but you can try it with your alternative device if desired to follow the examples.

To use Colab, you must have a Google account and then access Colab using your account. Otherwise, most of the Colab features won't work. The next section of the chapter gets you started with Google and helps you access Colab.

As with Notebook, you can use Colab to perform specific tasks in a cell-oriented paradigm. The next sections of the chapter go through a range of task-related topics that start with the use of notebooks. If you've used Notebook in previous chapters, you notice a strong resemblance between Notebook and Colab. Of course, you also want to perform other sorts of tasks, such as creating various cell types and using them to create notebooks that look like those you create with Notebook.

Finally, this chapter can't address every aspect of Colab, so the final section of the chapter serves as a handy resource for locating the most reliable information about Colab.

Defining Google Colab

Google Colab is the cloud version of Notebook. In fact, the Welcome page makes this fact apparent. It even uses IPython (the previous name for Jupyter) Notebook (.ipynb) files for the site. That's right, you're viewing a Notebook right there in your browser. Even though the two applications are similar and they both use .ipynb files, they do have some differences that you need to know about. The following sections help you understand the Colab differences.

Understanding what Google Colab does

You can use Colab to perform many tasks, but for the purpose of this book, you use it to write and run code, create its associated documentation, and display graphics, just as you do with Notebook. The techniques you use are similar, in fact, to using Notebook, but later in the chapter, you find out the small differences between the two. Even so, the downloadable source for this book should run without much effort on your part.

Notebook is a localized application in that you use local resources with it. You could potentially use other sources, but doing so could prove inconvenient or impossible in some cases. For example, according to https://help.github.com/articles/working-with-jupyter-notebook-files-on-github/, your Notebook files will appear as static HTML pages when you use a GitHub repository. In fact, some features won't work at all. Colab enables you to fully interact with your Notebook files using GitHub as a repository. In fact, Colab supports a number of online storage options, so you can regard Colab as your online partner in creating Python code.

SOME FIREFOX ODDITIES

Even with online help, you may still find that your copy of Firefox displays a `SecurityError: The operation is insecure.` error message. The initial error dialog box will point to some unrelated issue, such as cookies, but you see this error message when you click Details. Simply dismissing the dialog box by clicking OK will make Colab appear to be working because it displays your code, but you won't see results from running the code.

As a first step to fixing this problem, make sure that your copy of Firefox is current; older versions won't provide the required support. After you've updated your copy, setting the `network.websocket.allowInsecureFromHTTPS` preference using `About:Config` to `True` should resolve the problem, but sometimes it doesn't. In this case, verify that Firefox actually does allow third-party cookies by selecting Always for the Accept Third Party Cookies and Site Data option and selecting Remember History in the History section on the Privacy & Security tab of the Options dialog box. Restart Firefox after each change and then try Colab again. If none of these fixes works, you must use Chrome to work with Colab on your system.

The other reason that you really need to know about Colab is that you can use it with your alternative device. During the writing process, some of the example code was tested on an Android-based tablet (an ASUS ZenPad 3S 10). The target tablet has Chrome installed and executes the code well enough to follow the examples. All this said, you likely won't want to try to write code using a tablet of that size — the text was incredibly small, for one thing, and the lack of a keyboard could be a problem, too. The point is that you don't absolutely have to have a Windows, Linux, or OS X system to try the code, but the alternatives might not provide quite the performance you expect.

REMEMBER

Google Colab generally doesn't work with browsers other than Chrome or Firefox. In most cases, you see an error message and no other display if you try to start Colab in a browser that it doesn't support. Your copy of Firefox may also need some configuration to work properly (see the "Using local runtime support" section, later in this chapter, for details). The amount of configuration that you perform depends on which Colab features you choose to use. Many examples work fine in Firefox without any modification.

Considering the online coding difference

For the most part, you use Colab just as you would Notebook. However, some features work differently. For example, to execute the code within a cell, you select that cell and click the run button (right-facing arrow) for that cell. The current cell remains selected, which means that you must actually initiate the selection of the next cell as a separate action. A block next to the output lets you clear just that output without affecting any other cell. Hovering the mouse over the block tells you when someone executed the content. On the right side of the cell, you see a vertical ellipsis that you can click to see a menu of options for that cell. The result is the same as when using Notebook, but the process for achieving the result is different.

REMEMBER

The actual process for working with the code also differs from Notebook. Yes, you still type the code as you always have and the resulting code executes without problem in Notebook. The difference is in the way you can manage the code. You can upload code from your local drive as desired and then save it to a Google Drive or GitHub. The code becomes accessible from any device at this point by accessing those same sources. All you need to do is load Colab to access it.

If you use Chrome when working with Colab and choose to sync your copy of Chrome among various devices, all your code becomes available on any device you choose to work with. Syncing transfers your choices to all your devices as long as those devices are also set to synchronize their settings. Consequently, you can write code on your desktop, test it on your tablet, and then review it on your smart phone. It's all the same code, all the same repository, and the same Chrome setup, just a different device.

What you may find, however, is that all this flexibility comes at the price of speed and ergonomics. In reviewing the various options, a local copy of Notebook executes the code in this book faster than a copy of Colab using any of the available configurations (even when working with a local copy of the .ipynb file). So, you trade speed for flexibility when working with Colab. In addition, viewing the source code on a tablet is hard; viewing it on a smart phone is nearly impossible. If you make the text large enough to see, you can't see enough of the code to make any sort of reasonable editing possible. At best, you could review the code one line at a time to determine how it works.

TIP

Using Notebook has other benefits, too. For example, when working with Colab, you have options to download your source files only as .ipynb or .py files. Colab doesn't include all the other download options, including (but not limited to) HTML, LaTeX, and PDF. Consequently, your options for creating presentations from the online content are also limited to some extent. In short, using Colab and Notebook provides different coding experiences to some degree. They're not mutually exclusive, however, because they share file formats. Theoretically, switching between the two as needed is possible.

One thing to consider when using Notebook and Colab is that the two products use most of the same terminology and many of the same features, but they're not completely the same. The methods used to perform tasks differ, and some of the terminology does as well. For example, a Markdown cell in Notebook is a Text cell in Colab. The "Performing Common Tasks" section of this chapter tells you about other differences you need to consider.

Using local runtime support

The only time you really need local runtime support is when you want to work within a team environment and you need the speed or resource access advantage offered by a local runtime. Using a local runtime normally produces better speed than you obtain when relying on the cloud. In addition, a local runtime enables you to access files on your machine. A local runtime also gives you control over the version of Notebook used to execute code. You can read more about local runtime support at `https://research.google.com/colaboratory/local-runtimes.html`.

WARNING

You need to consider several issues when determining the need for local runtime support. The most obvious is that you need a local runtime, which means that this option won't work with your laptop or tablet unless your laptop has Windows, Linux, or OS X and the appropriate version of Notebook installed. Your laptop or tablet will also need an appropriate browser; Internet Explorer is almost guaranteed to cause problems, assuming that it works at all.

The most important consideration when using a local runtime, however, is that your machine is now open to possible infection from Notebook code. You need to trust the party supplying the code. The local runtime option doesn't open your machine to others that you share code with, however; they must either use their own local runtimes or rely on the cloud to execute code.

TIP

When working with Colab on using local runtime support and Firefox, you must perform some special setups. Make sure to read the Browser Specific Setups section on the Local Runtimes page to ensure that you have Firefox configured correctly. Always verify your setup. Firefox may appear to work correctly with Colab. However, a configuration issue arises when you perform tasks with it, and Colab shows error messages that say the code didn't execute (or something else that isn't particularly helpful).

Getting a Google Account

Before you can perform any significant tasks using Colab, you must have a Google account. You can use the same account for all sorts of purposes, not just development. For example, a Google account gives you access to Google Docs (`https://www.google.com/docs/about/`), an online document management system similar to Office 365.

Creating the account

To create a Google account, simply navigate to `https://account.google.com/` and click the Create Your Google Account link. This page also contains a wealth of information about what a Google account can provide. When you click Create Your Google Account, you see the page shown in Figure 4-1. The account creation process consumes several pages. You just provide the required information in each page and click Next.

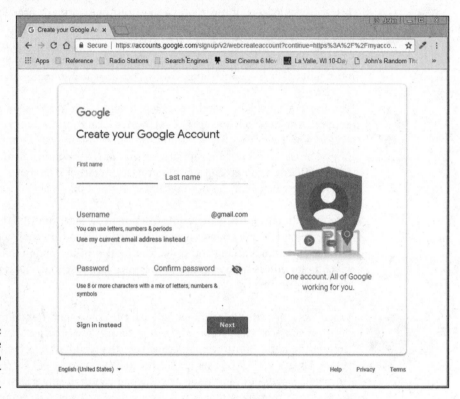

FIGURE 4-1:
Follow the prompts to create your Google account.

Signing in

After you create and verify your account, you can sign into it. Before you can use Colab effectively, you must sign into your account. That's because Colab relies on your Google Drive for certain tasks. You can also store notebooks in other places, such as GitHub, but having your Google account ensures that everything works as planned. To sign into your account, navigate to `https://accounts.google.com/`, provide your e-mail address and password, and then click Next. You see the sign-in page shown in Figure 4-2.

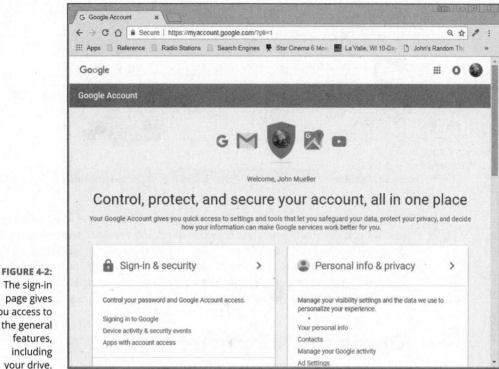

FIGURE 4-2:
The sign-in
page gives
you access to
all the general
features,
including
your drive.

Working with Notebooks

As with Jupyter Notebook, the notebook forms the basis of interactions with Colab. In fact, Colab is built on notebooks, as previously mentioned. When you place the mouse on certain parts of the Welcome page at `https://colab.research.google.com/notebooks/welcome.ipynb`, you see opportunities for interacting with the page by adding either code or text entries (which you can use for notes as needed). These entries are active, so you can interact with them. You can also move cells around and copy the resulting material to your Google Drive. Of course, while interacting with the Welcome page is both unexpected and fun, the real purpose of this chapter is to demonstrate how to interact with Colab notebooks. The following sections describe how to perform basic notebook-related tasks with Colab.

Creating a new notebook

To create a new notebook, choose File ➪ New Python 3 Notebook. You see a new Python 3 notebook like the one shown in Figure 4-3. The new notebook looks similar to, but not precisely the same as, those found in Notebook. However, all the same functionality exists. You can also create a new Python 2 notebook if desired, but this book doesn't rely on Python 2.

FIGURE 4-3:
Create a new
Python 3
Notebook
using the same
techniques
as normal.

The notebook shown in Figure 4-3 lets you change the filename by clicking on it, just as you do when working in Notebook. Some features work differently but provide the same results. For example, to run the code in a particular cell, you click the right-pointing arrow on the left side of that cell. In contrast to Notebook, the cell focus doesn't change to the next cell, so you must choose the next cell directly or by clicking the Next Cell or Previous Cell buttons on the toolbar.

Opening existing notebooks

You can open existing notebooks found in local storage, on Google Drive, or on GitHub. You can also open any of the Colab examples or upload files from sources that you can access, such as a network drive on your system. In all cases, you begin by choosing File⇨Open Notebook. You see the dialog box shown in Figure 4-4.

The default view shows all the files you opened recently, regardless of location. The files appear in alphabetical order. You can filter the number of items displayed by typing a string into the Filter Notebooks field. Across the top are other options for opening notebooks.

TIP

Even if you're not logged in, you can still access the Colab example projects. These projects help you understand Colab but won't allow you to do anything with your own projects. Even so, you can still experiment with Colab without logging into Google first. The following sections discuss these options in more detail.

Using Google Drive for existing notebooks

Google Drive is the default location for many operations in Colab, and you can always choose it as a destination. When working with Drive, you see a list of files similar to those shown in Figure 4-4. To open a particular file, you click its link in the dialog box. The file opens in the current tab of your browser.

FIGURE 4-4:
Use this dialog box to open existing notebooks.

Using GitHub for existing notebooks

When working with GitHub, you initially need to provide the location of the source code online, as shown in Figure 4-5. The location must point to a public project; you can't use Colab to access private projects.

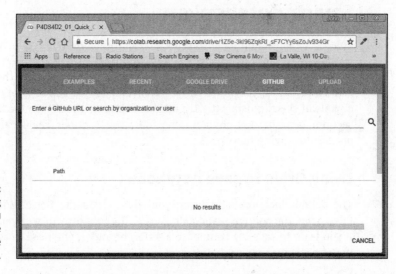

FIGURE 4-5:
When using GitHub, you must provide the location of the source code.

After you make the connection to GitHub, you see two lists: repositories, which are containers for code related to a particular project; and branches, a particular implementation of the code. Selecting a repository and branch displays a list of notebook files that you can load into Colab. Simply click the required link and it loads as if you were using a Google Drive.

Using local storage for existing notebooks

If you want to use the downloadable source for this book, or any local source for that matter, you select the Upload tab of the dialog box. In the center is a single button, Choose File. Clicking this button opens the File Open dialog box for your browser. You locate the file you want to upload, just as you normally would for opening any file.

REMEMBER

Selecting a file and clicking Open uploads the file to Google Drive. If you make changes to the file, those changes appear on Google Drive, not on your local drive. Depending on your browser, you usually see a new window open with the code loaded. However, you could also simply see a success message, in which case you must now open the file using the same technique as you would when using Google Drive. In some case, your browser asks whether you want to leave the current page. You should tell the browser to do so.

TIP

The File⇨Upload Notebook command also uploads a file to Google Drive. In fact, uploading a notebook works like uploading any other kind of file, and you see the same dialog box. If you want to upload other kinds of files, using the File⇨Upload Notebook command is likely faster.

Saving notebooks

Colab provides a significant number of options for saving your notebook. However, none of these options works with your local drive. After you upload content from your local drive to Google Drive or GitHub, Colab manages the content in the cloud and not on your local drive. To save updates to your local drive, you must download the file using the techniques found in the "Downloading notebooks" section, later in this chapter. The following sections review the cloud-based options for saving notebooks.

Using Drive to save notebooks

The default location for storing your data is Google Drive. When you choose File⇨Save, the content you create goes to the root directory of your Google Drive. If you want to save the content to a different folder, you need to select that folder in Google Drive (https://drive.google.com/).

REMEMBER

Colab tracks the versions of your project as you perform saves. However, as these revisions age, Colab removes them. To save a version that won't age, you use the File⇨Save and Pin Revision command. To see the revisions for your project, choose File⇨Revision History. You see the output shown in Figure 4-6. Notice that the first entry is pinned. You can also pin entries by checking the entry in the History list. The revision history also shows you the modification date, who made the revision, and the size of the resulting file. You can use this list to restore a previous revision or download the revision to your local drive.

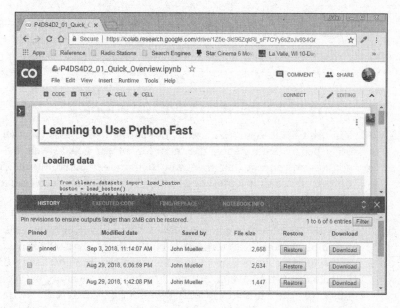

FIGURE 4-6:
Colab maintains a history of the revisions for your project.

You can also save a copy of your project by choosing File ⇨ Save a Copy In Drive. The copy receives the word *Copy* as part of its name. Of course, you can rename it later. Colab stores the copy in the current Google Drive folder.

Using GitHub to save notebooks

GitHub provides an alternative to Google Drive for saving content. It offers an organized method of sharing code for the purpose of discussion, review, and distribution. You can find GitHub at `https://github.com/`.

REMEMBER

You may use only public repositories when working with GitHub from Colab, even though GitHub also supports private repositories. To save a file to GitHub, choose File ⇨ Save a Copy in GitHub. If you aren't already signed into GitHub, Colab displays a window that requests your sign-in information. After you sign in, you see a dialog box similar to the one shown in Figure 4-7.

Notice that this account doesn't currently have a repository. You must either create a new repository or choose an existing repository in which to store your data. After you save the file, it will appear in your GitHub repository of your choice. The repository will include a link to open the data in Colab by default, unless you choose not to include this feature.

FIGURE 4-7:
Using GitHub
means storing
your data in a
repository.

Using GitHubGist to save notebooks

You use GitHub Gists as a means of sharing single files or other resources with other people. Some people use them for full projects as well, but the idea is that you have a concept that you want to share — something that isn't quite fully formed and doesn't represent a usable application. You can read more about Gists at https://help.github.com/articles/about-gists/.

As with GitHub, Gists come in both public and secret form. You can access both public and secret Gists from Colab, but Colab automatically keeps your files secret. To save your current project as a Gist, you choose File⇨ Save a Copy as a GitHub Gist. Unlike GitHub, you don't need to create a repository or do anything fancy in this case. The file saves as a Gist without any extra effort. The resulting entry always contains a View in Colaboratory link, as shown in Figure 4-8.

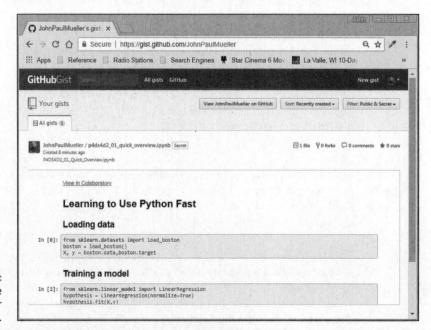

FIGURE 4-8:
Use Gists to store
individual files or
other resources.

Downloading notebooks

Colab supports two methods for downloading notebooks to your local drive: .ipynb files (using File➪Download .ipynb) and .py files (using File➪Download .py). In both cases, the file appears in the default download directory for your browser; Colab doesn't offer a method for downloading the file to a specific directory.

Performing Common Tasks

Most tasks in Colab work similar to their Notebook counterparts. For example, you can create code cells just as you do in Notebook. Markdown cells come in three forms: text, heading, and table of contents. They work somewhat differently from the Markdown cells found in Notebook, but the idea is the same. You can also edit and move cells, just as you do with Notebook. One important difference is that you can't change a cell type. A cell that you create as a header can't suddenly transform into a code cell. The following sections provide a brief overview of the various features.

Creating code cells

The first cell that Colab creates for you is a code cell. The code you create in Colab uses all the same features that you find in Notebook. However, off to the side of the cell, you see a menu of extras that you can use with Colab that aren't present in Notebook, as shown in Figure 4-9.

FIGURE 4-9: Colab code cells contain a few extras not found in Notebook.

You use the options shown in Figure 4-9 to augment your Colab code experience. The following list provides a short description of these features:

>> **Link to Cell:** Displays a dialog box containing a link you can use to access a specific cell within the notebook. You can embed this link anywhere on a web page or within a notebook to allow someone to access that specific cell. The person still sees the entire notebook but doesn't have to search for the cell you want to discuss.

>> **Delete Cell:** Removes the cell from the notebook.

>> **Clear Output:** Removes the output from the cell. You must run the code again to regenerate the output.

>> **View Output Fullscreen:** Displays the output (not the entire cell or any other part of the notebook) in full-screen mode on the host device. This option is useful when displaying a significant amount of content or when a detailed view of graphics helps explain a topic. Press Esc to exit full-screen mode.

>> **Add a Comment:** Creates a comment balloon to the right of the cell. This is not the same as a code comment, which exists in line with the code but affects the entire cell. You can edit, delete, or resolve comments. A resolved comment is one that receives attention and is no longer applicable.

>> **Add a Form:** Inserts a form into the cell to the right of the code. You use forms to provide a graphical input for parameters. Forms don't appear in Notebook, but because of how you create them, they won't prevent you from running the code in Notebook. You can read more about forms at `https://colab.research.google.com/notebooks/forms.ipynb`.

Code cells also tell you about the code and its execution. The little icon next to the output displays information about the execution when you hover your mouse over it, as shown in Figure 4-10. Clicking the icon clears the output. You must run the code again to regenerate the output.

Creating text cells

Text cells work much like Markup cells in Notebook. However, Figure 4-11 shows that you receive additional help in formatting the text using a graphical interface. The markup is the same, but you have the option of allowing the GUI to help you create the markup. For example, in this case, to create the # sign for a heading, you click the double T icon that appears first in the list. Clicking the double T icon again would increase the header level. To the right, you see how the text will appear in the notebook.

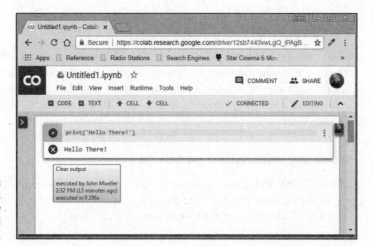

FIGURE 4-10:
Colab code cells contain a few extras not found in Notebook.

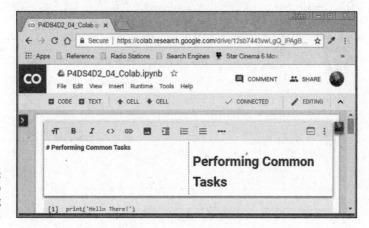

FIGURE 4-11:
Use the GUI to make formatting your text easier.

Notice the menu to the right of the text cell. This menu contains many of the same options that a code cell does. For example, you can create a list of links to help people access specific parts of your notebook through an index. Unlike Notebook, you can't execute text cells to resolve the markup they contain.

Creating special cells

The special cells that Colab provides are variations of the text cell. These special cells, which you access using the Insert menu option, make creating the required cells faster. The following sections describe each of these special cell types.

Working with headings

When you choose Insert⇨Section Header Cell, you see a new cell created below the currently selected cell that has the appropriate header level 1 entry in it. You can increase the heading level by clicking the double T icon. The GUI looks the same as the one in Figure 4-11, so you have all the standard formatting features for your text.

Working with table of contents

An interesting addition to Colab is the automatic generation of a table of contents for your notebook. To use this feature, choose Insert⇨Table of Contents Cell. Figure 4-12 shows the output for this particular example.

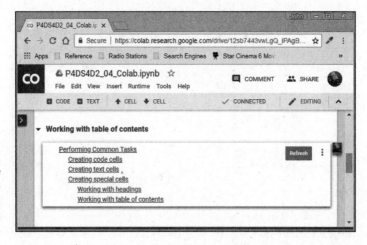

FIGURE 4-12: Adding a table of contents to your notebook makes the information more accessible.

The Table of Contents cell contains a heading in the actual cell that you can modify in the same way as any other heading in your notebook. The table of contents appears in the cell output. To update the table of contents, click Refresh to the right of the cell output. You also have access to all the usual text cell features when working with a Table of Contents cell.

WARNING

The table of contents feature does appear in Notebook, but it's not usable. If you plan to share the notebook with people who use Notebook, you should remove the table of contents to avoid potential confusion.

Editing cells

Both Colab and Notebook have Edit menus that contain the options you except, such as the ability to cut, copy, and paste cells. The two products have some interesting differences. For example, Notebook allows you to split and merge cells. Colab contains an option to show or hide the code as a toggle. These differences give each product a slightly different flavor but don't really change your ability to use it to create and modify Python code.

Moving cells

The same technique you use for moving cells in Notebook also works with Colab. The only difference is that Colab relies exclusively on toolbar buttons, while Notebook also has cell movement options on the Edit menu.

Using Hardware Acceleration

Your Colab code executes on a Google server. All your computing device does is host a browser that displays the code and its results. Consequently, any special hardware on your computing device is ignored unless you choose to execute code locally.

TIP

Fortunately, you do have another option when working with Colab. Choose Edit ⇨ Notebook Settings to display the Notebook Settings dialog box shown in Figure 4-13. This dialog box lets you choose the Python runtime and gives you a way to add GPU execution for your code. The article at `https://medium.com/deep-learning-turkey/google-colab-free-gpu-tutorial-e113627b9f5d` provides additional details on how this feature works. The availability of a GPU isn't an invitation to run large computations using Colab. The content at `https://research.google.com/colaboratory/faq.html#gpu-availability` tells you about the limitations of the Colab hardware acceleration (including that it may not be available when you need it).

Notebook settings

Runtime type
Python 3 ▾

Hardware accelerator
None ▾ ⑦

☐ Omit code cell output when saving this notebook

CANCEL   SAVE

FIGURE 4-13: Hardware acceleration speeds code execution.

The Notebook Settings dialog box also lets you choose whether to include cell output when saving the notebook. Given that you store your notebook in the cloud in most cases and that loading large files into your browser can be time consuming, this feature enables you to restart a session more quickly. Of course, the trade-off is that you must now regenerate all the outputs you need.

Executing the Code

For your to be useful, you need to run it at some point. Previous sections have mentioned the right-pointing arrow that appears in the current cell. Clicking it runs just the current cell. Of course, you have other options than clicking the right-pointing arrow, and all these options appear on the Runtime menu. The following list summarizes these options:

>> **Running the current cell:** Besides clicking the right-pointing arrow, you can also choose Runtime ➪ Run the Focused Cell to execute the code in the current cell.

>> **Running other cells:** Colab provides options on the Runtime menu for executing the code in the next cell, the previous cell, or a selection of cells. Simply choose the option that matches the cell or set of cells you want to execute.

>> **Running all the cells:** In some cases, you want to execute all the code in a notebook. In this case, choose Runtime ➪ Run All. Execution starts at the top of the notebook, in the first cell containing code, and continues to the last cell that contains code in the notebook. You can stop execution at any time by choosing Runtime ➪ Interrupt Execution.

TIP

Choosing Runtime ➪ Manage Sessions displays a dialog box containing a list of all the sessions that are currently executing for your account on Colab. You can use this dialog box to determine when the code in that notebook last executed and how much memory the notebook consumes. Click Terminate to end execution for a particular notebook. Click Close to close the dialog box and return to your current notebook.

Viewing Your Notebook

A notebook has a right-pointing arrow in its left margin. Clicking this icon displays a pane containing tabs that show various kinds of information about your notebook. You can also choose specific pieces of information to see from the View menu. To close this pane, click the *X* in the upper-right corner of the pane. The following sections describe each of these pieces of information.

Displaying the table of contents

Choose View⇨Table of Contents to see a table of contents for your notebook, as shown in Figure 4-14. Clicking any of the entries takes you to that section of the notebook.

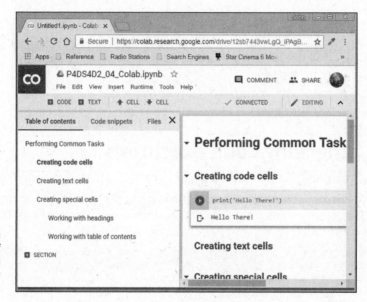

FIGURE 4-14:
Use the table of contents to navigate your notebook.

At the bottom of the pane is a + Section button. Click this button to create a new header cell below the currently selected cell.

Getting notebook information

When you choose View⇨Notebook Information, you see a pane open at the bottom of the browser, as shown in Figure 4-15. This pane contains the notebook size, settings, and owner. Notice that the display also tells you the maximum notebook size.

The Notebook Info tab also includes a Modify link (two of them). Both links display the Notebook Settings dialog box, in which you can choose the runtime type and whether the notebook relies on hardware acceleration, as described in the "Using Hardware Acceleration" section, earlier in this chapter.

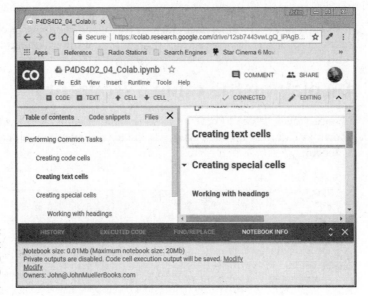

FIGURE 4-15:
The notebook
information
includes both
size and settings.

Checking code execution

Colab keeps track of your code as you execute it. Choose View⇨Executed Code
History to display the Executed Code tab in the pane at the bottom of the window,
as shown in Figure 4-16. Note that the number associated with the entries in the

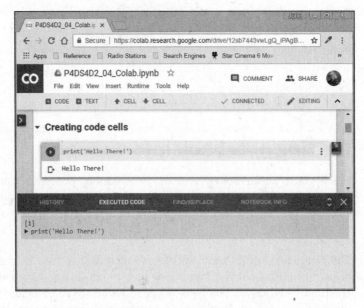

FIGURE 4-16:
Colab tracks
which code you
execute and in
what order.

Executed Code tab may not match the numbers associated with the associated cells. In addition, each unique execution of code receives a separate number.

Sharing Your Notebook

You can share your Colab notebooks in a number of ways. For example, you can save it to GitHub or GitHub Gists. However, the two most direct methods are the following:

» Create a share message and send it to the recipient.

» Obtain a link to the code and send the link to the recipient.

In both cases, you click the Share button in the upper right of the Colab window. The Share with Others dialog box opens (see Figure 4-17).

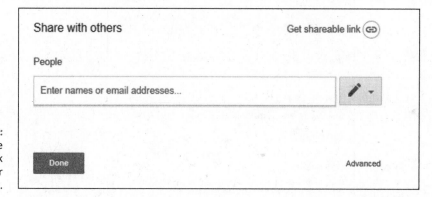

FIGURE 4-17: Send a message or obtain a link to share your notebook.

When you enter one or more names in the People field, an additional field opens in which to add a sharing message. You can type a message and click Send to send the link immediately. If you click Advanced instead, you see another dialog box, where you can define how to share the notebook.

In the upper-right corner of the Share with Others dialog box, you see the Get Shareable Link button. Click this button to display a dialog box containing the link for your notebook. Clicking Copy Link places the URL on the Clipboard for your device, and you can paste it into messages or other forms of communication with others.

Getting Help

The most obvious place to obtain help with Colab is from the Colab Help menu. This menu contains all the usual entries for accessing frequently asked questions (FAQs) pages. The menu doesn't have a link to general help, but you can find general help at `https://colab.research.google.com/notebooks/welcome.ipynb` (which requires you to log into the Colab site). The menu also provides options for submitting a bug and sending feedback.

One of the more intriguing Help menu entries is Search Code Snippets. This option opens the pane shown in Figure 4-18, in which you can search for example code that could meet your needs with a little modification. Clicking the Insert button inserts the code at the current cursor location in the cell that has focus. Each of the entries also shows an example of the code.

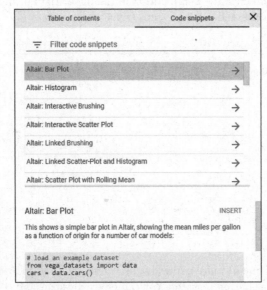

FIGURE 4-18: Use code snippets to write your applications more quickly.

Colab enjoys strong community support. Choosing Help ⇨ Ask a Question on Stack Overflow displays a new browser tab, where you can ask questions from other users. You see a login screen if you haven't already logged into Stack Overflow.

2

Getting Your Hands Dirty with Data

Chapter **5**

Understanding the Tools

U p to this point, the book spends a lot of time working with Python to perform data science tasks without actually engaging the tools provided by
Anaconda much. Yes, a good deal of what you do involves typing in code
and seeing what happens. However, if you don't actually know how to use your
tools well, you miss opportunities to perform tasks easier and faster. Automation
is an essential part of performing data science tasks in Python.

This chapter is about working with the two main Anaconda tools, Jupyter console
and Jupyter Notebook. Earlier chapters give you some experience with both tools,
but those chapters don't explore either tool in any detail, and you need to know
these tools a lot better for upcoming chapters. The skills you develop in this
chapter will help you perform tasks in later chapters with greater speed and far
less effort.

The chapter also looks at tasks you can perform with your newfound skills. You
develop even more skills as the book progresses, but these tasks help put your new
skills into perspective and appreciate how you can use them to make working with
Python even easier.

REMEMBER

You don't have to manually type the source code for this chapter. In fact, it's a lot
easier if you use the downloadable source. The source code for this chapter appears
in the P4DS4D2_05_Understanding the Tools.ipynb source code file. (See the
Introduction for details on where to locate this file.)

Using the Jupyter Console

The Python console (accessible through the Anaconda Prompt) is where you can experiment with data science interactively. You can try things and see the results immediately. If you make a mistake, you can simply close the console and create a new one. The console is for playing around and considering what might be possible. The following sections help you understand what you can do to make your Jupyter console experience better.

REMEMBER

The standard Python console that comes with a downloaded copy of Python and the Anaconda version of the Python console (accessed with the IPython command) look similar, and you can perform many of the same tasks using them. (From this point on, the Anaconda version of the Python console appears simply as the IPython console in the text for the sake of simplicity.) If you already know how to use the standard Python console, you have an advantage when it comes to working with the IPython console. However, they also have differences. The IPython console provides enhancements that don't come with the standard Python console. In addition, performing certain tasks, such as pasting large amounts of text, differs between the two consoles, so even if you know how to use the standard Python console, reading the sections that follow will help you.

Interacting with screen text

When you first start the IPython console by typing **ipython** at the Anaconda Prompt and pressing Enter, you see a screen similar to the one shown in Figure 5-1. The screen seems loaded with text, but all of it provides useful information. The top line tells you about your version of Python and Anaconda. Below that are three help terms (copyright, credits, and license) that you type to obtain more information about your version of these two products. For example, when you type **credits** and press Enter, you see a listing of the contributors to this version of the product.

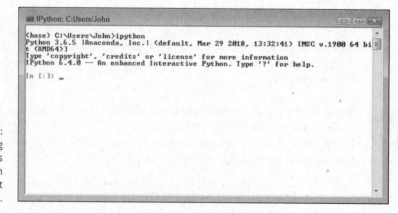

FIGURE 5-1:
The opening screen provides information on where to get additional help.

Note that you see a line telling you about enhanced help. If you type **?** and press Enter, you see five commands, which you use for the following tasks:

>> ?: Using Jupyter to perform useful work

>> object?: Discovering facts about the packages, objects, and methods that you use in Python to interact with data

>> object??: Obtaining verbose information about the packages, objects, and methods (often pages worth that can become cumbersome to read)

>> %quickref: Obtaining information about the magic functions that Jupyter provides

>> help: Learning about the Python programming language (help and ? aren't the same — the first is for Python and the second is for IPython features)

Depending on your operating system, you should be able to right-click the Anaconda Prompt window and see a context menu containing options for working with the text in the window. Figure 5-2 shows the context menu for Windows. This menu is important because it lets you interact with the text and copy the results of your experimentation in a more permanent form.

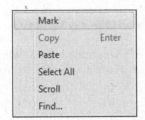

FIGURE 5-2:
You can cut, copy, and paste text using this context menu.

You can obtain access to the same menu of options by choosing the System menu (click the icon in the upper-left corner of the window) and selecting the Edit menu. The options you commonly see are the following:

>> **Mark:** Selects the specific text you want to copy.

>> **Copy:** Places the text you have marked onto the Clipboard (you can also press Enter after marking the text to perform a copy).

REMEMBER

>> **Paste:** Moves text from the Clipboard to the window. Unfortunately, this command doesn't work right with the IPython console for copying multiple lines of text. Use the %paste magic function to copy multiple lines of text instead.

>> **Select All:** Performs a mark on all the text visible in the window.

» **Scroll:** Makes it possible to scroll the window when using the arrow keys. Press Enter to stop scrolling.

» **Find:** Displays a Find dialog box that you can use to locate text anywhere in the screen buffer. This is actually an exceptionally useful command because you can quickly locate text that you previously entered and want to reuse in some way.

TIP

One feature that the IPython console provides, and that you don't find when working with the standard Python console, is cls, or clear screen. To clear the screen and make typing new commands easier, simply type **cls** and press Enter. You can also use the following code to reset the shell, similar to restarting the kernel in Notebook:

```
import IPython
app = IPython.Application.instance()
app.shell.reset()
```

In this case, the numbering starts over, letting you see the sequence of execution better. If your only goal is to clear variables from memory, use the %reset magic function instead.

Changing the window appearance

The Windows console lets you change the Anaconda Prompt window appearance with ease. Depending on the console and platform you use, you may find that you have other options as well. If your platform doesn't provide any flexibility in changing the Anaconda Prompt window appearance, you can still do so using a magic function as described in the "Using magic functions" section later in the chapter to change the window appearance. To change the Windows console, click the system menu and choose Properties. You see a dialog box like the one shown in Figure 5-3.

Each tab controls a different aspect of the window appearance. Even though you're working with IPython, the underlying console still affects what you see. Here are the purposes for each of the tabs shown in Figure 5-3:

» **Options:** Determines the size of the cursor (a large cursor works better in bright settings), how many commands the window remembers, and how editing works (such as whether you're in Insert mode).

» **Font:** Defines the font used to display text in the window. The Raster Fonts option appears to work best for most people, but trying other font options may help you see the text better under certain conditions.

FIGURE 5-3:
The Properties
dialog box makes
it possible to
control the
appearance of
your window.

>> **Layout:** Specifies the window size, position onscreen, and size of the buffer used to hold information that scrolls out of view. If you find that old commands scroll off too quickly, increasing the size of the window can help. Likewise, if you find that you can't locate older commands, increasing the size of the buffer can help.

>> **Colors:** Determines the basic color settings for the window. The default setting of a black background with gray text is hard for many people to use. Using a white background with black text is much easier. However, you need to choose the color settings that work best for you. These colors are augmented by the colors used by the %colors magic function.

Getting Python help

No one can remember absolutely everything about a programming language. Even the best coders have memory lapses. This is why having language-specific help is so important. Without this help, programmers would spend a great deal of time researching packages, classes, methods, and properties online. Yes, they've used them in the past, but they can't quite bring the required information to mind today.

REMEMBER

The Python portion of the IPython console provides two methods of getting help: help mode and interactive help. You use help mode when you want to explore the language and plan to spend some while doing it. Interactive help is better when you know specifically what you need help with and don't want to spend a lot of time looking at other sorts of information. The following sections tell you how to get help on the Python language whenever you need it.

Entering help mode

To enter help mode, type **help( )** and press Enter. The console enters a new mode, in which you can type help-related commands as needed to discover more about Python. You can't type Python commands in this mode. The prompt changes to a help> prompt, as shown in Figure 5-4, to remind you that you're in help mode.

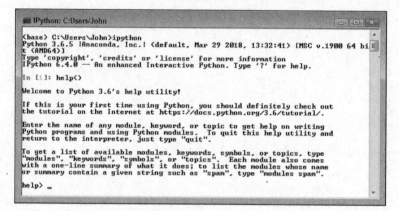

FIGURE 5-4:
Help mode relies on a special help> prompt.

To obtain help about any object or command, simply type the object or command name and press Enter. You can also type any of the following commands to obtain a listing of other topics of discussion.

» modules: Compiles a list of the currently loaded modules. This list varies by how your copy of Python (the underlying language) is configured at any given time, so the list won't be the same every time you use this command. The command can take a while to execute, and the output list is usually quite large.

» keywords: Presents a list of Python keywords that you can ask about. For example, you can type **assert** and learn more about the assert keyword.

» symbols: Shows the list of symbols that have special meaning in Python, such as * for multiplication and << for a left shift.

» topics: Displays a list of general Python topics, such as CONVERSIONS. The topics appear in uppercase rather than lowercase.

Requesting help in help mode

To obtain help in help mode, you simply type the name of the module, keyword, symbol, or topic that you want to learn more about and press Enter. Help mode is Python specific, which means that you can ask about a list, but not an object based on a list named `mylist`. You also can't ask about IPython-specific features, such as the `cls` command.

When working with features that are part of a module, you need to include the module name. For example, if you want to find out about the `version()` method within the `sys` module, you type **sys.version** and press Enter at the help prompt, rather than just type **version**.

If a help topic is too large to present as a single screen of information, you see `-- More --` at the bottom of the display. Press Enter to advance the help information one line at a time or the spacebar to advance the help information a full screen a time. You can't go backward in the help listing. Pressing Q (or q) ends the help information immediately.

Exiting help mode

After you finish exploring help, you need to get back to the Python prompt to type more commands. Simply press Enter without entering anything at the help prompt or type **quit** (without parentheses) and press Enter at the help prompt.

Getting interactive help

Sometimes you don't want to leave the Python prompt to get help. In this case, you can type `help('<topic>')` and press Enter to obtain help information. For example, to receive help on the print command, you type **help('print')** and press Enter. Notice that the help topic is in single quotation marks. If you try to request help without enclosing the topic in single quotation marks, you see an error message.

TIP

Interactive help works with any module, keyword, or topic that Python supports. For example, you can type **help('CONVERSIONS')** and press Enter to receive help about the `CONVERSIONS` topic. It's important to note that case is still important when working with interactive help. Typing **help('conversions')** and pressing Enter displays a message telling you that help isn't available.

Getting IPython help

Getting help with IPython is different from getting help with Python. When you obtain IPython help, you work with the development environment rather than the programming language. To obtain IPython help, type **?** and press Enter. You see a long listing of the various ways in which you can use IPython help.

Some of the more essential forms of help rely on typing a keyword with a question mark. For example, if you want to learn more about the `cls` command, you type cls? or ?cls and press Enter. It doesn't matter whether the question mark appears before or after the command.

TIP

Interestingly enough, you can kick IPython help up a notch. If you want to obtain more details about a command or other IPython feature, use two question marks. For example, ??cls displays the source code for the cls command. The double question mark (??) may not always return additional information if there isn't any more information to find.

If you want to stop displaying IPython information early, press Q to quit. Otherwise, you can press Space or Enter to display each screen of information until the help system has displayed everything available.

Using magic functions

Amazingly, you really can get magic on your computer! Jupyter provides a special feature called magic functions. The functions let you perform all sorts of amazing tasks with your Jupyter console. The following sections provide an overview of the magic functions. You do see some of them used later in the book as well. However, it pays to spend some time checking out these functions for yourself.

Obtaining the magic functions list

The best way to start working with magic functions is to obtain a list of them by typing **%quickref** and pressing Enter. What you see is a help screen similar to the one shown in Figure 5-5. The listing can be a little confusing to read, so make sure you take your time with it.

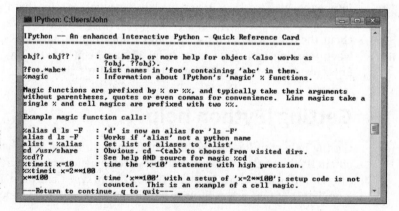

FIGURE 5-5:
Take your time going through the magic function help; it has a lot of information.

Working with magic functions

Most magic functions start with either a single percent sign (%) or two percent signs (%%). Those with a single percent sign work at the command-line level, while those that have two percent signs work at the cell level. The Jupyter Notebook discussion later in the chapter talks more about cells. For now, all you really need to know is that you generally use magic functions with a single percent sign within the IPython console.

REMEMBER

Most of the magic functions display status information when you use them by themselves. For example, when you type **%cd** and press Enter, you see the current directory. To change directories, you type %cd plus the new directory location on your system. There are some exceptions to this rule, however. For example, %cls clears the screen when used alone because it doesn't take any parameters.

One of the more interesting magic functions is %colors. You can use this function to change the colors used to display information onscreen, which is helpful when you use various devices. The available options are NoColor (everything is in black and white), Linux (the default setting), and LightBG (which uses a blue-and-green color scheme). This particular function is another exception to the rule. Typing %colors alone doesn't display the current color scheme but displays an error message instead.

Discovering objects

Python is all about objects. In fact, you can't do anything in Python without working with some sort of object. With this in mind, it's a good idea to know how to discover precisely what object you're working with and what features it provides. The following sections help you discover the Python objects you use as you code.

Getting object help

With IPython, you can request information about specific objects using the object name and a question mark (?). For example, if you want to know more about a list object named mylist, simply type **mylist?** and press Enter. You see output showing the mylist type, content in string form, length, and a document string providing a quick overview of mylist.

When you need detailed help about mylist, you type **help(mylist)** and press Enter instead. You see the same help that you should when requesting information about the Python list. However, you receive the information that's appropriate to the particular object you need help with, rather than having to first discover the object type and then request information for that object.

Obtaining object specifics

The dir() function is often overlooked, but it's an essential way to learn about object specifics. To see a list of properties and methods associated with any object, use dir(<object name>). For example, if you create a list called mylist and want to know what sorts of things you can do with it, type **dir(mylist)** and press Enter. The IPython console displays a list of methods and properties that are specific to mylist.

Using IPython object help

Python provides one level of help about your objects — and IPython provides another. When you want to know more about your object than Python tells you, try using the question mark with it. For example, when working with a list named mylist, you can type **mylist?** and press Enter to discover the object type, content, length, and associated docstring. The docstring provides you with a quick overview of usage information for the type — enough that you can find more details with what you now know about the object.

Using a single question mark does cause IPython to clip long content. If you want to obtain the full content for an object, you need to use the double question mark (??). For example, type **mylist??** and press Enter to see any clipped details (although there may not be any additional details). Whenever possible, IPython provides you with the full source code for the object (assuming that the source code is available).

You can use magic functions with objects as well. These functions simplify the help output and provide only the information you need, as shown here:

>> %pdoc: Displays the docstring for the object

>> %pdef: Shows how to call the object (assuming that the object is callable)

>> %source: Displays the source code for the object (assuming that the source is available)

>> %file: Outputs the name of the file that contains the source code for the object

>> %pinfo: Displays detailed information about the object (often more than provided by help alone)

>> %pinfo2: Displays extra detailed information about the object (when available)

Using Jupyter Notebook

You generally use the IPython console described in previous sections to play with code, and that's about it. Of course, it works fine for that purpose. However, the Jupyter Notebook Integrated Development Environment (IDE), which is another part of the Anaconda suite of tools, can do more for you. The following sections help you understand some of the interesting things that Jupyter Notebook (simply called Notebook) can help you do.

Working with styles

Here's one of the ways in which Notebook excels over just about any other IDE that you'll ever use: It helps you to create nice-looking output. Rather than have a screen full of a whole bunch of plain-old code, you can use Notebook to create sections and add styles so that the output is nicely formatted. What you can end up with is a good-looking report that just happens to contain executable code. The reason for this improved output is the use of styles.

When you type code into Notebook, you place the code in a cell. Each section of code that you create goes into a separate cell. When you need to create a new cell, you click Insert Cell Below (the button with a plus sign) on the toolbar. Likewise, when you decide that you no longer need a cell, you select it and then click Cut Cell (the button with a scissors) to place the deleted cell on the Clipboard, or choose Edit⇨Delete Cell to remove it completely.

The default style for a cell is Code. However, when you click the down arrow next to the Code entry, you see a listing of styles, as shown in Figure 5-6.

FIGURE 5-6: Notebook makes adding styles to your work easy.

The various styles shown help you format content in various ways. The Markdown style is most definitely used to separate varies entries. To try it for yourself, choose Markdown from the drop-down list, type the heading for this main chapter section, **# Using Jupyter Notebook**, in the first cell; next, click Run. The content changes to a heading. The single hash (#) tells Notebook that this is a first-level heading. Notice that clicking Run automatically adds a new cell and places the cursor in it. To add a second-level heading, choose Markdown from the drop-down list, type **## Working with styles**, and click Run. Figure 5-7 shows that the two entries are indeed headings and that the second entry is smaller than the first.

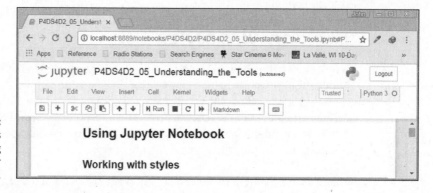

FIGURE 5-7:
Adding headings makes separating content in your notebooks easy.

The Markdown style also lets you add HTML content, which can contain anything a web page contains with regard to standard HTML tags. Another way to create a first-level heading is to define the cell type as Markdown, type **<h1>Using Jupyter Notebook</h1>**, and then click Run. In general, you use HTML to provide documentation and links to outside material. Relying on HTML tags makes it possible to include things like lists or even pictures. In short, you can actually include an HTML document fragment as part of your notebook, which makes Notebook much more than a simple means of writing down code.

The use of the Raw NBConvert formatting option is outside the scope of this book. However, it provides you with the means for included information that shouldn't be modified by the notebook converter (NBConvert). You can output notebooks in a variety of formats, and NBConvert performs this task for you. You can read about this feature at https://nbconvert.readthedocs.io/en/latest/. The goal of the Raw NBConvert style is to allow you to include special content, such as Lamport TeX (LaTeX) content. The LaTeX document system isn't tied to a particular editor — it's simply a means of encoding scientific documents.

Restarting the kernel

Every time you perform a task in your notebook, you create variables, import modules, and perform a wealth of other tasks that corrupt the environment. At some point, you can't really be sure that something is working as it should.

To overcome this problem, you click Restart Kernel (the button with an open circle with an arrow at one end) after saving your document by clicking Save and Checkpoint (the button containing a floppy disk symbol). You can then run your code again to ensure that it does work as you thought it would.

Sometimes an error also causes the kernel to crash. Your document starts acting oddly, updates slowly, or shows other signs of corruption. Again, the answer is to restart the kernel to ensure that you have a clean environment and that the kernel is running as it should.

WARNING

Whenever you click Restart Kernel, you see the warning message shown in Figure 5-8. Make certain that you pay attention to the warning because you could lose temporary changes during a kernel restart. Always save your document before you restart the kernel.

FIGURE 5-8:
Save your document before restarting the kernel.

Restart kernel?   ✕

Do you want to restart the current kernel? All variables will be lost.

                                        Continue Running   Restart

Restoring a checkpoint

At some point, you may find that you made a mistake. Notebook is notably missing an Undo button: You won't find one anywhere. Instead, you create checkpoints each time you finish a task. Creating checkpoints when your document is stable and working properly helps you recover faster from mistakes.

WARNING

To restore your setup to the condition contained in a checkpoint, choose File ➪ Revert to Checkpoint. You see a listing of available checkpoints. Simply select the one you want to use. When you select the checkpoint, you see a warning message like the one shown in Figure 5-9. When you click Revert, any old information is gone and the information found in the checkpoint becomes the current information.

FIGURE 5-9:
Revert to a previous notebook setup to undo a mistake.

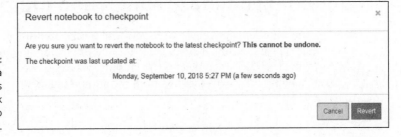

Revert notebook to checkpoint   ✕

Are you sure you want to revert the notebook to the latest checkpoint? **This cannot be undone.**

The checkpoint was last updated at:
                    Monday, September 10, 2018 5:27 PM (a few seconds ago)

                                              Cancel   Revert

Performing Multimedia and Graphic Integration

Pictures say a lot of things that words can't say (or at least they do it with far less effort). Notebook is both a coding platform and a presentation platform. You may be surprised at just what you can do with it. The following sections provide a brief overview of some of the more interesting features.

Embedding plots and other images

At some point, you might have spotted a notebook with multimedia or graphics embedded into it and wondered why you didn't see the same effects in your own files. In fact, all the graphics examples in the book appear as part of the code. Fortunately, you can perform some more magic by using the `%matplotlib` magic function. The possible values for this function are: `'gtk'`, `'gtk3'`, `'inline'`, `'nbagg'`, `'osx'`, `'qt'`, `'qt4'`, `'qt5'`, `'tk'`, and `'wx'`, each of which defines a different plotting backend (the code used to actually render the plot) used to present information onscreen.

When you run `%matplotlib inline`, any plots you create appear as part of the document. That's how Figure 8-1 (see the section about using NetworkX basics in Chapter 8) shows the plot that it creates immediately below the affected code.

Loading examples from online sites

Because some examples you see online can be hard to understand unless you have them loaded on your own system, you should also keep the `%load` magic function in mind. All you need is the URL of an example you want to see on your system. For example, try `%load https://matplotlib.org/_downloads/pyplot_text.py`. When you click Run Cell, Notebook loads the example directly in the cell and comments the `%load` call out. You can then run the example and see the output from it on your own system.

Obtaining online graphics and multimedia

A lot of the functionality required to perform special multimedia and graphics processing appears within `Jupyter.display`. By importing a required class, you can perform tasks such as embedding images into your notebook. Here's an example of embedding one of the pictures from the author's blog into the notebook for this chapter:

```
from IPython.display import Image
Embed = Image(
'http://blog.johnmuellerbooks.com/' +
'wp-content/uploads/2015/04/Layer-Hens.jpg')
Embed
```

The code begins by importing the required class, Image, and then using features from it to first define what to embed and then actually embed the image. The output you see from this example appears in Figure 5-10.

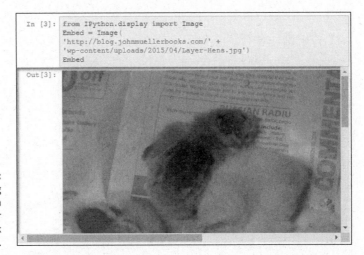

FIGURE 5-10:
Embedding images can dress up your notebook presentation.

TIP

If you expect an image to change over time, you might want to create a link to it instead of embedding it. You must refresh a link because the content in the notebook is only a reference rather than the actual image. However, as the image changes, you see the change in your notebook as well. To accomplish this task, you use SoftLinked = Image(url='http://blog.johnmuellerbooks.com/wp-content/uploads/2015/04/Layer-Hens.jpg') instead of Embed.

When working with embedded images on a regular basis, you might want to set the form in which the images are embedded. For example, you may prefer to embed them as PDFs. To perform this task, you use code similar to this:

```
from IPython.display import set_matplotlib_formats
set_matplotlib_formats('pdf', 'svg')
```

You have access to a wide number of formats when working with a notebook. The commonly supported formats are `'png'`, `'retina'`, `'jpeg'`, `'svg'`, and `'pdf'`.

The IPython display system is nothing short of amazing, and this section hasn't even begun to tap the surface for you. For example, you can import a YouTube video and place it directly into your notebook as part of your presentation if you want. You can see quite a few more of the display features demonstrated at `http://nbviewer.jupyter.org/github/ipython/ipython/blob/1.x/examples/notebooks/Part%205%20-%20Rich%20Display%20System.ipynb`.

IN THIS CHAPTER

» **Manipulating data streams**

» **Working with flat and unstructured files**

» **Interacting with relational databases**

» **Using NoSQL as a data source**

» **Interacting with web-based data**

Chapter **6**

Working with Real Data

ata science applications require data by definition. It would be nice if you could simply go to a data store somewhere, purchase the data you need in an easy-open package, and then write an application to access that data. However, data is messy. It appears in all sorts of places, in many different forms, and you can interpret it in many different ways. Every organization has a different method of viewing data and stores it in a different manner as well. Even when the data management system used by one company is the same as the data management system used by another company, the chances are slim that the data will appear in the same format or even use the same data types. In short, before you can do any data science work, you must discover how to access the data in all its myriad forms. Real data requires a lot of work to use and fortunately, Python is up to the task of manipulating it as needed.

This chapter helps you understand the techniques required to access data in a number of forms and locations. For example, memory streams represent a form of data storage that your computer supports natively; flat files exist on your hard drive; relational databases commonly appear on networks (although smaller relational databases, such as those found in Access, could appear on your hard drive as well); and web-based data usually appears on the Internet. You won't visit every form of data storage available (such as that stored on a point-of-sale, or POS, system). Quite possibly, an entire book on the topic wouldn't suffice to cover the topic of data formats in any detail. However, the techniques in this chapter do demonstrate how to access data in the formats you most commonly encounter when working with real-world data.

TIP

The Scikit-learn library includes a number of *toy* datasets (small datasets meant for you to play with). These datasets are complex enough to perform a number of tasks, such as experimenting with Python to perform data science tasks. Because this data is readily available, and making the examples too complicated to understand is a bad idea, this book relies on these toy datasets as input for many of the examples. Even though the book does use these toy datasets for the sake of reducing complexity and making the examples clearer, the techniques that the book demonstrates work equally well on real-world data that you access using the techniques shown in this chapter.

You don't have to type the source code for this chapter in by hand. In fact, it's a lot easier if you use the downloadable source (see the Introduction for download instructions). The source code for this chapter appears in the `P4DS4D2_06_Dataset_Load.ipynb` source code file.

WARNING

It's essential that the `Colors.txt`, `Titanic.csv`, `Values.xls`, `Colorblk.jpg`, and `XMLData.xml` files that come with the downloadable source code appear in the same folder (directory) as your Notebook files. Otherwise, the examples in the following sections fail with an input/output (IO) error. The file location varies according to the platform you're using. For example, on a Windows system, you find the notebooks stored in the `C:\Users\`*Username*`\P4DS4D2` folder, where *Username* is your login name. (The book assumes that you've used the prescribed folder location of P4DS4D2, as described in the "Defining the code repository" section of Chapter 3.) To make the examples work, simply copy the four files from the downloadable source folder into your Notebook folder.

Uploading, Streaming, and Sampling Data

Storing data in local computer memory represents the fastest and most reliable means to access it. The data could reside anywhere. However, you don't actually interact with the data in its storage location. You load the data into memory from the storage location and then interact with it in memory. This is the technique the book uses to access all the toy datasets found in the Scikit-learn library, so you see this technique used relatively often in the book.

REMEMBER

Data scientists call the columns in a database *features* or *variables*. The rows are *cases*. Each row represents a collection of variables that you can analyze.

Uploading small amounts of data into memory

The most convenient method that you can use to work with data is to load it directly into memory. This technique shows up a couple of times earlier in the book but uses the toy dataset from the Scikit-learn library. This section uses the `Colors.txt` file, shown in Figure 6-1, for input.

FIGURE 6-1:
Format of the `Colors.txt` file.

The example also relies on native Python functionality to get the task done. When you load a file (of any type), the entire dataset is available at all times and the loading process is quite short. Here is an example of how this technique works.

```
with open("Colors.txt", 'r') as open_file:
    print('Colors.txt content:\n' + open_file.read())
```

The example begins by using the `open()` method to obtain a `file` object. The `open()` function accepts the filename and an access mode. In this case, the access mode is read (`r`). It then uses the `read()` method of the file object to read all the data in the file. If you were to specify a size argument as part of `read()`, such as `read(15)`, Python would read only the number of characters that you specify or stop when it reaches the End Of File (EOF). When you run this example, you see the following output:

```
Colors.txt content:
Color    Value
Red      1
Orange   2
Yellow   3
Green    4
Blue     5
```

```
Purple    6
Black     7
White     8
```

WARNING

The entire dataset is loaded from the library into free memory. Of course, the loading process will fail if your system lacks sufficient memory to hold the dataset. When this problem occurs, you need to consider other techniques for working with the dataset, such as streaming it or sampling it. In short, before you use this technique, you must ensure that the dataset will actually fit in memory. You won't normally experience any problems when working with the toy datasets in the Scikit-learn library.

Streaming large amounts of data into memory

Some datasets will be so large that you won't be able to fit them entirely in memory at one time. In addition, you may find that some datasets load slowly because they reside on a remote site. Streaming answers both needs by making it possible to work with the data a little at a time. You download individual pieces, making it possible to work with just part of the data and to work with it as you receive it, rather than waiting for the entire dataset to download. Here's an example of how you can stream data using Python:

```
with open("Colors.txt", 'r') as open_file:
    for observation in open_file:
        print('Reading Data: ' + observation)
```

This example relies on the Colors.txt file, which contains a header, and then a number of records that associate a color name with a value. The open_file file object contains a pointer to the open file.

As the code performs data reads in the for loop, the file pointer moves to the next record. Each record appears one at a time in observation. The code outputs the value in observation using a print statement. You should receive this output:

```
Reading Data: Color    Value

Reading Data: Red       1

Reading Data: Orange    2

Reading Data: Yellow    3
```

```
Reading Data: Green     4

Reading Data: Blue      5

Reading Data: Purple    6

Reading Data: Black     7

Reading Data: White     8
```

Python streams each record from the source. This means that you must perform a read for each record you want.

Generating variations on image data

At times, you need to import and analyze image data. The source and type of the image does make a difference. You see a number of examples of working with images throughout the book. However, a good starting point is to simply read a local image in, obtain statistics about that image, and display the image onscreen, as shown in the following code:

```
import matplotlib.image as img
import matplotlib.pyplot as plt
%matplotlib inline

image = img.imread("Colorblk.jpg")
print(image.shape)
print(image.size)
plt.imshow(image)
plt.show()
```

The example begins by importing two matplotlib libraries, image and pyplot. The image library reads the image into memory, while the pyplot library displays it onscreen.

After the code reads the file, it begins by displaying the image shape property — the number of horizontal pixels, vertical pixels, and pixel depth. Figure 6-2 shows that the image is 100 x 100 x 3 pixels. The image size property is the combination of these three elements, or 30,000 bytes.

The next step is to load the image for plotting using imshow(). The final call, plt.show(), displays the image onscreen, as shown in Figure 6-2. This technique represents just one of a number of methods for interacting with images using Python so that you can analyze them in some manner.

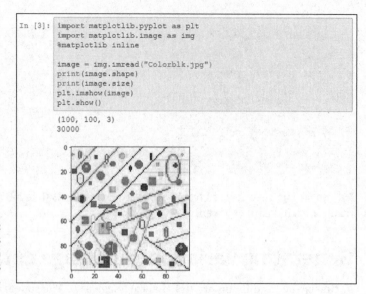

```
In [3]: import matplotlib.pyplot as plt
        import matplotlib.image as img
        %matplotlib inline

        image = img.imread("Colorblk.jpg")
        print(image.shape)
        print(image.size)
        plt.imshow(image)
        plt.show()

        (100, 100, 3)
        30000
```

FIGURE 6-2:
The test image is 100 pixels high and 100 pixels long.

Sampling data in different ways

Data streaming obtains all the records from a data source. You may find that you don't need all the records. You can save time and resources by simply sampling the data. This means retrieving records a set number of records apart, such as every fifth record, or by making random samples. The following code shows how to retrieve every other record in the Colors.txt file:

```
n = 2
with open("Colors.txt", 'r') as open_file:
    for j, observation in enumerate(open_file):
        if j % n==0:
            print('Reading Line: ' + str(j) +
            ' Content: ' + observation)
```

The basic idea of sampling is the same as streaming. However, in this case, the application uses enumerate() to retrieve a row number. When j % n == 0, the row is one that you want to keep and the application outputs the information. In this case, you see the following output:

```
Reading Line: 0 Content: Color Value

Reading Line: 2 Content: Orange 2

Reading Line: 4 Content: Green 4
```

```
Reading Line: 6 Content: Purple 6

Reading Line: 8 Content: White 8
```

The value of n is important in determining which records appear as part of the dataset. Try changing n to 3. The output will change to sample just the header and rows 3 and 6.

You can perform random sampling as well. All you need to do is randomize the selector, like this:

```
from random import random
sample_size = 0.25
with open("Colors.txt", 'r') as open_file:
    for j, observation in enumerate(open_file):
        if random()<=sample_size:
            print('Reading Line: ' + str(j) +
            ' Content: ' + observation)
```

To make this form of selection work, you must import the random class. The random() method outputs a value between 0 and 1. However, Python randomizes the output so that you don't know what value you receive. The sample_size variable contains a number between 0 and 1 to determine the sample size. For example, 0.25 selects 25 percent of the items in the file.

The output will still appear in numeric order. For example, you won't see Green come before Orange. However, the items selected are random, and you won't always get precisely the same number of return values. The spaces between return values will differ as well. Here is an example of what you might see as output (although your output will likely vary):

```
Reading Line: 1 Content: Red 1

Reading Line: 4 Content: Green 4

Reading Line: 8 Content: White 8
```

Accessing Data in Structured Flat-File Form

In many cases, the data you need to work with won't appear within a library, such as the toy datasets in the Scikit-learn library. Real-world data usually appears in a file of some type. A flat file presents the easiest kind of file to work with.

The data appears as a simple list of entries that you can read one at a time, if desired, into memory. Depending on the requirements for your project, you can read all or part of the file.

A problem with using native Python techniques is that the input isn't intelligent. For example, when a file contains a header, Python simply reads it as yet more data to process, rather than as a header. You can't easily select a particular column of data. The pandas library used in the sections that follow makes it much easier to read and understand flat-file data. Classes and methods in the pandas library interpret (parse) the flat-file data to make it easier to manipulate.

REMEMBER

The least formatted and therefore easiest-to-read flat-file format is the text file. However, a text file also treats all data as strings, so you often have to convert numeric data into other forms. A comma-separated value (CSV) file provides more formatting and more information, but it requires a little more effort to read. At the high end of flat-file formatting are custom data formats, such as an Excel file, which contains extensive formatting and could include multiple datasets in a single file.

The following sections describe these three levels of flat-file dataset and show how to use them. These sections assume that the file structures the data in some way. For example, the CSV file uses commas to separate data fields. A text file might rely on tabs to separate data fields. An Excel file uses a complex method to separate data fields and to provide a wealth of information about each field. You can work with unstructured data as well, but working with structured data is much easier because you know where each field begins and ends.

Reading from a text file

Text files can use a variety of storage formats. However, a common format is to have a header line that documents the purpose of each field, followed by another line for each record in the file. The file separates the fields using tabs. Refer to Figure 6-1 for an example of the Colors.txt file used for the example in this section.

Native Python provides a wide variety of methods you can use to read such a file. However, it's far easier to let someone else do the work. In this case, you can use the pandas library to perform the task. Within the pandas library, you find a set of *parsers,* code used to read individual bits of data and determine the purpose of each bit according to the format of the entire file. Using the correct parser is essential if you want to make sense of file content. In this case, you use the read_table() method to accomplish the task, as shown in the following code:

```
import pandas as pd
color_table = pd.io.parsers.read_table("Colors.txt")
print(color_table)
```

The code imports the pandas library, uses the `read_table()` method to read `Colors.txt` into a variable named `color_table`, and then displays the resulting memory data onscreen using the `print` function. Here's the output you can expect to see from this example.

```
    Color Value
0      Red    1
1   Orange    2
2   Yellow    3
3    Green    4
4     Blue    5
5   Purple    6
6    Black    7
7    White    8
```

Notice that the parser correctly interprets the first row as consisting of field names. It numbers the records from 0 through 7. Using `read_table()` method arguments, you can adjust how the parser interprets the input file, but the default settings usually work best. You can read more about the `read_table()` arguments at `http://pandas.pydata.org/pandas-docs/version/0.23.0/generated/pandas.read_table.html`.

Reading CSV delimited format

A CSV file provides more formatting than a simple text file. In fact, CSV files can become quite complicated. There is a standard that defines the format of CSV files, and you can see it at `https://tools.ietf.org/html/rfc4180`. The CSV file used for this example is quite simple:

» A header defines each of the fields

» Fields are separated by commas

» Records are separated by linefeeds

» Strings are enclosed in double quotes

» Integers and real numbers appear without double quotes

Figure 6-3 shows the raw format for the `Titanic.csv` file used for this example. You can see the raw format using any text editor.

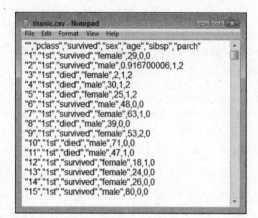

FIGURE 6-3:
The raw format of a CSV file is still text and quite readable.

Applications such as Excel can import and format CSV files so that they become easier to read. Figure 6-4 shows the same file in Excel.

FIGURE 6-4:
Use an application such as Excel to create a formatted CSV presentation.

Excel actually recognizes the header as a header. If you were to use features such as data sorting, you could select header columns to obtain the desired result. Fortunately, pandas also makes it possible to work with the CSV file as formatted data, as shown in the following example:

```
import pandas as pd
titanic = pd.io.parsers.read_csv("Titanic.csv")
X = titanic[['age']]
print(X)
```

Notice that the parser of choice this time is `read_csv()`, which understands CSV files and provides you with new options for working with it. (You can read more about this parser at `http://pandas.pydata.org/pandas-docs/version/0.23.0/`

generated/pandas.read_csv.html.) Selecting a specific field is quite easy — you just supply the field name as shown. The output from this example looks like this (some values omitted for the sake of space):

```
           age
0      29.0000
1       0.9167
2       2.0000
3      30.0000
4      25.0000
5      48.0000
...
1304   14.5000
1305 9999.0000
1306   26.5000
1307   27.0000
1308   29.0000
[1309 rows x 1 columns]
```

TIP

Of course, a human readable output like this one is nice when working through an example, but you might also need the output as a list. To create the output as a list, you simply change the third line of code to read X = titanic[['age']].values. Notice the addition of the values property. The output changes to something like this (some values omitted for the sake of space):

```
[[ 29. ]
 [  0.91670001]
 [  2. ]
 ...,
 [ 26.5 ]
 [ 27. ]
 [ 29. ]]
```

Reading Excel and other Microsoft Office files

Excel and other Microsoft Office applications provide highly formatted content. You can specify every aspect of the information these files contain. The Values. xls file used for this example provides a listing of sine, cosine, and tangent values for a random list of angles. You can see this file in Figure 6-5.

FIGURE 6-5:
An Excel file is highly formatted and might contain information of various types.

	A	B	C	D	E
1	Angle (Degrees)	Sine	Cosine	Tangent	
2	40.29472	0.646719	0.762728	0.847903	
3	216.71810	-0.597878	-0.801587	0.745868	
4	105.17861	0.965114	-0.261829	-3.686049	
5	97.38824	0.991698	-0.128592	-7.711971	
6	120.87683	0.858272	-0.513194	-1.672413	
7	316.08650	-0.693572	0.720388	-0.962775	
8	317.88761	-0.670587	0.741831	-0.903962	
9	60.82377	0.873124	0.487497	1.791034	
10	34.41988	0.565253	0.824917	0.685224	
11	92.81788	0.998791	-0.049161	-20.316545	

When you work with Excel or other Microsoft Office products, you begin to experience some complexity. For example, an Excel file can contain more than one worksheet, so you need to tell pandas which worksheet to process. In fact, you can choose to process multiple worksheets, if desired. When working with other Office products, you have to be specific about what to process. Just telling pandas to process something isn't good enough. Here's an example of working with the Values.xls file.

```
import pandas as pd
xls = pd.ExcelFile("Values.xls")
trig_values = xls.parse('Sheet1', index_col=None,
                        na_values=['NA'])
print(trig_values)
```

The code begins by importing the pandas library as normal. It then creates a pointer to the Excel file using the ExcelFile() constructor. This pointer, xls, lets you access a worksheet, define an index column, and specify how to present empty values. The index column is the one that the worksheet uses to index the records. Using a value of None means that pandas should generate an index for you. The parse() method obtains the values you request. You can read more about the Excel parser options at https://pandas.pydata.org/pandas-docs/stable/generated/pandas.ExcelFile.parse.html.

You don't absolutely have to use the two-step process of obtaining a file pointer and then parsing the content. You can also perform the task using a single step like this: trig_values = pd.read_excel("Values.xls", 'Sheet1', index_col=None, na_values=['NA']). Because Excel files are more complex, using the two-step process is often more convenient and efficient because you don't have to reopen the file for each read of the data.

Sending Data in Unstructured File Form

Unstructured data files consist of a series of bits. The file doesn't separate the bits from each other in any way. You can't simply look into the file and see any structure because there isn't any to see. Unstructured file formats rely on the file user to know how to interpret the data. For example, each pixel of a picture file could consist of three 32-bit fields. Knowing that each field is 32-bits is up to you. A header at the beginning of the file may provide clues about interpreting the file, but even so, it's up to you to know how to interact with the file.

The example in this section shows how to work with a picture as an unstructured file. The example image is a public domain offering from `http://commons.wikimedia.org/wiki/Main_Page`. To work with images, you need to access the Scikit-image library (`http://scikit-image.org/`), which is a free-of-charge collection of algorithms used for image processing. You can find a tutorial for this library at `http://scipy-lectures.github.io/packages/scikit-image/`. The first task is to be able to display the image onscreen using the following code. (This code can require a little time to run. The image is ready when the busy indicator disappears from the Notebook tab.)

```
from skimage.io import imread
from skimage.transform import resize
from matplotlib import pyplot as plt
import matplotlib.cm as cm

example_file = ("http://upload.wikimedia.org/" +
    "wikipedia/commons/7/7d/Dog_face.png")
image = imread(example_file, as_grey=True)
plt.imshow(image, cmap=cm.gray)
plt.show()
```

The code begins by importing a number of libraries. It then creates a string that points to the example file online and places it in `example_file`. This string is part of the `imread()` method call, along with `as_grey`, which is set to `True`. The `as_grey` argument tells Python to turn any color images into gray scale. Any images that are already in gray scale remain that way.

Now that you have an image loaded, it's time to render it (make it ready to display onscreen. The `imshow()` function performs the rendering and uses a grayscale color map. The `show()` function actually displays `image` for you, as shown in Figure 6-6.

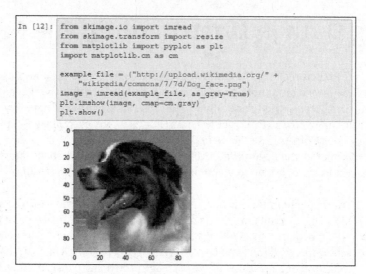

```
In [12]:  from skimage.io import imread
          from skimage.transform import resize
          from matplotlib import pyplot as plt
          import matplotlib.cm as cm

          example_file = ("http://upload.wikimedia.org/" +
              "wikipedia/commons/7/7d/Dog_face.png")
          image = imread(example_file, as_grey=True)
          plt.imshow(image, cmap=cm.gray)
          plt.show()
```

FIGURE 6-6:
The image
appears onscreen
after you render
and show it.

You now have an image in memory and you may want to find out more about it. When you run the following code, you discover the image type and size:

```
print("data type: %s, shape: %s" %
      (type(image), image.shape))
```

The output from this call tells you that the image type is a numpy.ndarray and that the image size is 90 pixels by 90 pixels. The image is actually an array of pixels that you can manipulate in various ways. For example, if you want to crop the image, you can use the following code to manipulate the image array:

```
image2 = image[5:70,0:70]
plt.imshow(image2, cmap=cm.gray)
plt.show()
```

The numpy.ndarray in image2 is smaller than the one in image, so the output is smaller as well. Figure 6-7 shows typical results. The purpose of cropping the image is to make it a specific size. Both images must be the same size for you to analyze them. Cropping is one way to ensure that the images are the correct size for analysis.

Another method that you can use to change the image size is to resize it. The following code resizes the image to a specific size for analysis:

```
image3 = resize(image2, (30, 30), mode='symmetric')
plt.imshow(image3, cmap=cm.gray)
print("data type: %s, shape: %s" %
      (type(image3), image3.shape))
```

```
In [14]: image2 = image[5:70,0:70]
         plt.imshow(image2, cmap=cm.gray)
         plt.show()
```

FIGURE 6-7:
Cropping the image makes it smaller.

The output from the print() function tells you that the image is now 30 pixels by 30 pixels in size. You can compare it to any image with the same dimensions.

After you have all the images the right size, you need to flatten them. A dataset row is always a single dimension, not two dimensions. The image is currently an array of 30 pixels by 30 pixels, so you can't make it part of a dataset. The following code flattens image3 so that it becomes an array of 900 elements that is stored in image_row.

```
image_row = image3.flatten()
print("data type: %s, shape: %s" %
      (type(image_row), image_row.shape))
```

Notice that the type is still a numpy.ndarray. You can add this array to a dataset and then use the dataset for analysis purposes. The size is 900 elements, as anticipated.

Managing Data from Relational Databases

Databases come in all sorts of forms. For example, AskSam (http://asksam.en.softonic.com/) is a kind of free-form textual database. However, the vast majority of data used by organizations rely on relational databases because these databases provide the means for organizing massive amounts of complex data in an organized manner that makes the data easy to manipulate. The goal of a database manager is to make data easy to manipulate. The focus of most data storage is to make data easy to retrieve.

Relational databases accomplish both the manipulation and data retrieval objectives with relative ease. However, because data storage needs come in all shapes and sizes for a wide range of computing platforms, there are many different relational database products. In fact, for the data scientist, the proliferation of different Database Management Systems (DBMSs) using various data layouts is one of the main problems you encounter with creating a comprehensive dataset for analysis.

The one common denominator between many relational databases is that they all rely on a form of the same language to perform data manipulation, which does make the data scientist's job easier. The Structured Query Language (SQL) lets you perform all sorts of management tasks in a relational database, retrieve data as needed, and even shape it in a particular way so that the need to perform additional shaping is unnecessary.

Creating a connection to a database can be a complex undertaking. For one thing, you need to know how to connect to that particular database. However, you can divide the process into smaller pieces. The first step is to gain access to the database engine. You use two lines of code similar to the following code (but the code presented here is not meant to execute and perform a task):

```
from sqlalchemy import create_engine
engine = create_engine('sqlite:///:memory:')
```

After you have access to an engine, you can use the engine to perform tasks specific to that DBMS. The output of a read method is always a DataFrame object that contains the requested data. To write data, you must create a DataFrame object or use an existing DataFrame object. You normally use these methods to perform most tasks:

» read_sql_table(): Reads data from a SQL table to a DataFrame object

» read_sql_query(): Reads data from a database using a SQL query to a DataFrame object

» read_sql(): Reads data from either a SQL table or query to a DataFrame object

» DataFrame.to_sql(): Writes the content of a DataFrame object to the specified tables in the database

The sqlalchemy library provides support for a broad range of SQL databases. The following list contains just a few of them:

- » SQLite

- » MySQL

- » PostgreSQL

- » SQL Server

- » Other relational databases, such as those you can connect to using Open Database Connectivity (ODBC)

You can discover more about working with databases at `https://docs.sqlalchemy.org/en/latest/core/engines.html`. The techniques that you discover in this book using the toy databases also work with relational databases.

Interacting with Data from NoSQL Databases

In addition to standard relational databases that rely on SQL, you find a wealth of databases of all sorts that don't have to rely on SQL. These Not only SQL (NoSQL) databases are used in large data storage scenarios in which the relational model can become overly complex or can break down in other ways. The databases generally don't use the relational model. Of course, you find fewer of these DBMSes used in the corporate environment because they require special handling and training. Still, some common DBMSes are used because they provide special functionality or meet unique requirements. The process is essentially the same for using NoSQL databases as it is for relational databases:

1. Import required database engine functionality.

2. Create a database engine.

3. Make any required queries using the database engine and the functionality supported by the DBMS.

The details vary quite a bit, and you need to know which library to use with your particular database product. For example, when working with MongoDB (`https://www.mongodb.org/`), you must obtain a copy of the PyMongo library (`https://api.mongodb.org/python/current/`) and use the `MongoClient` class to create the required engine. The MongoDB engine relies heavily on the `find()` function to locate data. Following is a pseudo-code example of a MongoDB session. (You won't be able to execute this code in Notebook; it's shown only as an example.)

```
import pymongo
import pandas as pd
from pymongo import Connection
connection = Connection()
db = connection.database_name
input_data = db.collection_name
data = pd.DataFrame(list(input_data.find()))
```

Accessing Data from the Web

It would be incredibly difficult (perhaps impossible) to find an organization today that doesn't rely on some sort of web-based data. Most organizations use web services of some type. A *web service* is a kind of web application that provides a means to ask questions and receive answers. Web services usually host a number of input types. In fact, a particular web service may host entire groups of query inputs.

APIs AND OTHER WEB ENTITIES

A data scientist may have a reason to rely on various web Application Programming Interfaces (APIs) to access and manipulate data. In fact, the focus of an analysis might be the API itself. This book doesn't discuss APIs in any detail because each API is unique, and APIs operate outside the normal scope of what a data scientist might do. For example, you might use a product such as jQuery (http://jquery.com/) to access data and manipulate it in various ways when working with a web application. However, the techniques for doing so are more along the lines of writing an application than employing a data science technique.

It's important to realize that APIs can be data sources and that you might need to use one to achieve some data input or data-shaping goals. In fact, you find many data entities that resemble APIs but don't appear in this book. Windows developers can create Component Object Model (COM) applications that output data onto the web that you could possibly use for analysis purposes. In fact, the number of potential sources is nearly endless. This book focuses on the sources that you use most often and in the most conventional manner. Keeping your eyes open for other possibilities, though, is always a good idea.

Another type of query system is the microservice. Unlike the web service, *microservices* have a specific focus and provide only one specific query input and output. Using microservices has specific benefits that are outside the scope of this book to address, but essentially they work like tiny web services, so that's how this book addresses them.

One of the most beneficial data access techniques to know when working with web data is accessing XML. All sorts of content types rely on XML, even some web pages. Working with web services and microservices means working with XML (in most cases). With this in mind, the example in this section works with XML data found in the `XMLData.xml` file, shown in Figure 6-8. In this case, the file is simple and uses only a couple of levels. XML is hierarchical and can become quite a few levels deep.

FIGURE 6-8: XML is a hierarchical format that can become quite complex.

The technique for working with XML, even simple XML, can be a bit harder than anything else you've worked with so far. Here's the code for this example:

```python
from lxml import objectify
import pandas as pd

xml = objectify.parse(open('XMLData.xml'))
root = xml.getroot()

df = pd.DataFrame(columns=('Number', 'String', 'Boolean'))
```

```
for i in range(0,4):
    obj = root.getchildren()[i].getchildren()
    row = dict(zip(['Number', 'String', 'Boolean'],
                   [obj[0].text, obj[1].text,
                    obj[2].text]))
    row_s = pd.Series(row)
    row_s.name = i
    df = df.append(row_s)

print(df)
```

The example begins by importing libraries and parsing the data file using the objectify.parse() method. Every XML document must contain a root node, which is <MyDataset> in this case. The root node encapsulates the rest of the content, and every node under it is a child. To do anything practical with the document, you must obtain access to the root node using the getroot() method.

The next step is to create an empty DataFrame object that contains the correct column names for each record entry: Number, String, and Boolean. As with all other pandas data handling, XML data handling relies on a DataFrame. The for loop fills the DataFrame with the four records from the XML file (each in a <Record> node).

The process looks complex but follows a logical order. The obj variable contains all the children for one <Record> node. These children are loaded into a dictionary object in which the keys are Number, String, and Boolean to match the DataFrame columns.

There is now a dictionary object that contains the row data. The code creates an actual row for the DataFrame next. It gives the row the value of the current for loop iteration. It then appends the row to the DataFrame. To see that everything worked as expected, the code prints the result, which looks like this:

```
  Number String Boolean
0      1  First    True
1      2 Second   False
2      3  Third    True
3      4 Fourth   False
```

USING THE JSON ALTERNATIVE

You shouldn't get the idea that all data you work with on the web is in XML format. You may need to consider other popular alternatives as part of your development plans. One of the most popular today is JavaScript Object Notation (JSON) (http://www.json.org/). JSON proponents state that JSON takes less space, is faster to use, and is easier to work with than XML (see https://www.w3schools.com/js/js_json_xml.asp and https://blog.cloud-elements.com/json-better-xml for details). Consequently, you may find that your next project relies on JSON output, rather than XML, when dealing with certain web services and microservices.

If your data formatting choices consisted of just XML and JSON, you might feel that interacting with data is quite manageable. However, a lot of other people have ideas of how to format data so that you can parse it quickly and easily. In addition, developers now have a stronger emphasis on understanding the data stream, so some formatting techniques emphasize human readability. You can read about some of these other alternative at https://insights.dice.com/2018/01/05/5-xml-alternatives-to-consider-in-2018/. One of the more important of these alternatives is Yet Another Markup Language or YAML Ain't Markup Language (YAML), depending on whom you talk to and which resources you use (http://yaml.org/spec/1.2/spec.html), but be prepared to do your homework when working through the particulars of any new projects.

Chapter 7

Conditioning Your Data

T he characteristics, content, type, and other elements that define your data in its entirety is the data *shape*. The shape of your data determines the kinds of tasks you can perform with it. In order to make your data amenable to certain types of analysis, you must shape it into a different form. Think of the data as clay and you as the potter, because that's the sort of relationship that exists. However, instead of using your hands to shape the data, you rely on functions and algorithms to perform the task. This chapter helps you understand the tools you have available to shape data and the ramifications of shaping it.

Also in this chapter, you consider the problems associated with shaping. For example, you need to know what to do when data is missing from a dataset. It's important to shape the data correctly or you end up with an analysis that simply doesn't make sense. Likewise, some data types, such as dates, can present problems. Again, you need to tread carefully to ensure that you get the desired result so that the dataset becomes more useful and amenable to analysis of various sorts.

REMEMBER

The goal of some types of data shaping is to create a larger dataset. In many cases, the data you need to perform an analysis doesn't appear in a single database or in a particular form. You need to shape the data and then combine it so that you have a single dataset in a known format before you can begin the analysis. Combining data successfully can be an art form because data often defies simple analysis or quick fixes.

TIP

You don't have to type the source code for this chapter in by hand. In fact, it's a lot easier if you use the downloadable source. The source code for this chapter appears in the P4DS4D2_07_Getting_Your_Data_in_Shape.ipynb source code file; see the Introduction for the location of this file.

WARNING

Make sure that the XMLData2.xml file that comes with the downloadable source code appears in the same folder (directory) as your Notebook files. Otherwise, the examples in the following sections fail with an input/output (I/O) error. The file location varies according to the platform you're using. For example, on a Windows system, you find the notebooks stored in the C:\Users\Username\P4DS4D2 folder, where *Username* is your login name. (The book assumes that you've used the prescribed folder location of P4DS4D2, as described in the "Defining the code repository" section of Chapter 3.) To make the examples work, simply copy the file from the downloadable source folder into your Notebook folder. See the Introduction for instructions on downloading the source code.

Juggling between NumPy and pandas

There is no question that you need NumPy at all times. The pandas library is actually built on top of NumPy. However, you do need to make a choice between NumPy and pandas when performing tasks. You need the low-level functionality of NumPy to perform some tasks, but pandas makes things so much easier that you want to use it as often as possible. The following sections describe when to use each library in more detail.

Knowing when to use NumPy

Developers built pandas on top of NumPy. As a result, every task you perform using pandas also goes through NumPy. To obtain the benefits of pandas, you pay a performance penalty that some testers say is 100 times slower than NumPy for a similar task (see http://penandpants.com/2014/09/05/performance-of-pandas-series-vs-numpy-arrays/). Given that computer hardware can make up for a lot of performance differences today, the speed issue may not be a concern at times, but when speed is essential, NumPy is always the better choice.

Knowing when to use pandas

You use pandas to make writing code easier and faster. Because pandas does a lot of the work for you, you could make a case for saying that using pandas also reduces the potential for coding errors. The essential consideration, though, is that the pandas library provides rich time-series functionality, data alignment, NA-friendly statistics, groupby, merge, and join methods. Normally, you need to code these features when using NumPy, which means you keep reinventing the wheel.

As the book progresses, you discover just how useful pandas can be performing such tasks as *binning* (a data preprocessing technique designed to reduce the effect of observational errors) and working with a *dataframe* (a two-dimensional labeled data structure with columns that can potentially contain different data types) so that you can calculate statistics on it. For example, in Chapter 9, you discover how to perform both discretization and binning. Chapter 13 shows actual binning examples, such as obtaining a frequency for each categorical variable of a dataset. In fact, many of the examples in Chapter 13 don't work without binning. In other words, don't worry too much right now about knowing precisely what binning is or why you need to use it — examples later in the book discuss the topic in detail. All you really need to know is that pandas does make your work considerably easier.

IT'S ALL IN THE PREPARATION

This book may seem to spend a lot of time massaging data and little time in actually analyzing it. However, the majority of a data scientist's time is actually spent preparing data because the data is seldom in any order to actually perform analysis. To prepare data for use, a data scientist must:

- Get the data

- Aggregate the data

- Create data subsets

- Clean the data

- Develop a single dataset by merging various datasets together

Fortunately, you don't need to die of boredom while wading your way through these various tasks. Using Python and the various libraries it provides makes the task a lot simpler, faster, and more efficient, which is the point of spending all of the time on seemingly mundane topics in these early chapters. The better you know how to use Python to speed your way through these repetitive tasks, the sooner you begin having fun performing various sorts of analysis on the data.

Validating Your Data

When it comes to data, no one really knows what a large database contains. Yes, everyone has seen bits and pieces of it, but when you consider the size of some databases, viewing it all would be physically impossible. Because you don't know what's in there, you can't be sure that your analysis will actually work as desired and provide valid results. In short, you must validate your data before you use it to ensure that the data is at least close to what you expect it to be. This means performing tasks such as removing duplicate records before you use the data for any sort of analysis (duplicates would unfairly weight the results).

REMEMBER

However, you do need to consider what validation actually does for you. It doesn't tell you that the data is correct or that there won't be values outside the expected range. In fact, later chapters help you understand the techniques for handling these sorts of issues. What validation does is ensure that you can perform an analysis of the data and reasonably expect that analysis to succeed. Later, you need to perform additional massaging of the data to obtain the sort of results that you need in order to perform the task you set out to perform in the first place.

Figuring out what's in your data

Figuring out what your data contains is important because checking data by hand is sometimes simply impossible due to the number of observations and variables. In addition, hand verifying the content is time consuming, error prone, and, most important, really boring. Finding duplicates is important because you end up

» Spending more computational time to process duplicates, which slows your algorithms down.

» Obtaining false results because duplicates implicitly overweight the results. Because some entries appear more than once, the algorithm considers these entries more important.

As a data scientist, you want your data to enthrall you, so it's time to get it to talk to you — not figuratively, of course, but through the wonders of pandas, as shown in the following example:

```
from lxml import objectify
import pandas as pd

xml = objectify.parse(open('XMLData2.xml'))
root = xml.getroot()
df = pd.DataFrame(columns=('Number', 'String', 'Boolean'))
```

```
for i in range(0,4):
    obj = root.getchildren()[i].getchildren()
    row = dict(zip(['Number', 'String', 'Boolean'],
                   [obj[0].text, obj[1].text,
                    obj[2].text]))
    row_s = pd.Series(row)
    row_s.name = i
    df = df.append(row_s)

search = pd.DataFrame.duplicated(df)
print(df)
print()
print(search[search == True])
```

This example shows how to find duplicate rows. It relies on a modified version of the XMLData.xml file, XMLData2.xml, which contains a simple repeated row in it. A real data file contains thousands (or more) of records and possibly hundreds of repeats, but this simple example does the job. The example begins by reading the data file into memory using the same technique you explored in Chapter 6. It then places the data into a DataFrame.

At this point, your data is corrupted because it contains a duplicate row. However, you can get rid of the duplicated row by searching for it. The first task is to create a search object containing a list of duplicated rows by calling pd.DataFrame.duplicated(). The duplicated rows contain a True next to their row number.

Of course, now you have an unordered list of rows that are and aren't duplicated. The easiest way to determine which rows are duplicated is to create an index in which you use search == True as the expression. Following is the output you see from this example. Notice that row 3 is duplicated in the DataFrame output and that row 3 is also called out in the search results:

```
   Number  String  Boolean
0       1   First     True
1       2  Second    False
2       3   Third     True
3       3   Third     True

3    True
dtype: bool
```

Removing duplicates

To get a clean dataset, you want to remove the duplicates from it. Fortunately, you don't have to write any weird code to get the job done — pandas does it for you, as shown in the following example:

```
from lxml import objectify
import pandas as pd

xml = objectify.parse(open('XMLData2.xml'))
root = xml.getroot()
df = pd.DataFrame(columns=('Number', 'String', 'Boolean'))
for i in range(0,4):
    obj = root.getchildren()[i].getchildren()
    row = dict(zip(['Number', 'String', 'Boolean'],
                   [obj[0].text, obj[1].text,
                    obj[2].text]))
    row_s = pd.Series(row)
    row_s.name = i
    df = df.append(row_s)

print(df.drop_duplicates())
```

As with the previous example, you begin by creating a DataFrame that contains the duplicate record. To remove the errant record, all you need to do is call drop_duplicates(). Here's the result you get.

	Number	String	Boolean
0	1	First	True
1	2	Second	False
2	3	Third	True

Creating a data map and data plan

You need to know about your dataset — that is, how it looks statically. A *data map* is an overview of the dataset. You use it to spot potential problems in your data, such as

>> Redundant variables

>> Possible errors

>> Missing values

>> Variable transformations

Checking for these problems goes into a *data plan*, which is a list of tasks you have to perform to ensure the integrity of your data. The following example shows a data map, A, with two datasets, B and C:

```
import pandas as pd
pd.set_option('display.width', 55)

df = pd.DataFrame({'A': [0,0,0,0,0,1,1],
                   'B': [1,2,3,5,4,2,5],
                   'C': [5,3,4,1,1,2,3]})

a_group_desc = df.groupby('A').describe()
print(a_group_desc)
```

In this case, the data map uses 0s for the first series and 1s for the second series. The groupby() function places the datasets, B and C, into groups. To determine whether the data map is viable, you obtain statistics using describe(). What you end up with is a dataset B, series 0 and 1, and dataset C, series 0 and 1, as shown in the following output.

	B							\
	count	mean	std	min	25%	50%	75%	max
A								
0	5.0	3.0	1.581139	1.0	2.00	3.0	4.00	5.0
1	2.0	3.5	2.121320	2.0	2.75	3.5	4.25	5.0

	C							
	count	mean	std	min	25%	50%	75%	max
A								
0	5.0	2.8	1.788854	1.0	1.00	3.0	4.00	5.0
1	2.0	2.5	0.707107	2.0	2.25	2.5	2.75	3.0

These statistics tell you about the two dataset series. The breakup of the two datasets using specific cases is the *data plan*. As you can see, the statistics tell you that this data plan may not be viable because some statistics are relatively far apart.

TIP

The default output from describe() shows the data unstacked. Unfortunately, the unstacked data can print out with an unfortunate break, making it very hard to read. To keep this from happening, you set the width you want to use for the data by calling pd.set_option('display.width', 55). You can set a number of pandas options this way by using the information found at https://pandas.pydata.org/pandas-docs/stable/generated/pandas.set_option.html.

Although the unstacked data is relatively easy to read and compare, you may prefer a more compact presentation. In this case, you can stack the data using the following code:

```
stacked = a_group_desc.stack()
print(stacked)
```

Using stack() creates a new presentation. Here's the output shown in a compact form:

```
              B          C
A
0  count  5.000000   5.000000
   mean   3.000000   2.800000
   std    1.581139   1.788854
   min    1.000000   1.000000
   25%    2.000000   1.000000
   50%    3.000000   3.000000
   75%    4.000000   4.000000
   max    5.000000   5.000000
1  count  2.000000   2.000000
   mean   3.500000   2.500000
   std    2.121320   0.707107
   min    2.000000   2.000000
   25%    2.750000   2.250000
   50%    3.500000   2.500000
   75%    4.250000   2.750000
   max    5.000000   3.000000
```

Of course, you may not want all the data that describe() provides. Perhaps you really just want to see the number of items in each series and their mean. Here's how you reduce the size of the information output:

```
print(a_group_desc.loc[:,(slice(None),['count','mean']),])
```

Using loc lets you obtain specific columns. Here's the final output from the example showing just the information you absolutely need to make a decision:

```
        B          C
   count mean count mean
A
0   5.0  3.0   5.0  2.8
1   2.0  3.5   2.0  2.5
```

Manipulating Categorical Variables

In data science, a *categorical variable* is one that has a specific value from a limited selection of values. The number of values is usually fixed. Many developers will know categorical variables by the moniker *enumerations*. Each of the potential values that a categorical variable can assume is a *level*.

To understand how categorical variables work, say that you have a variable expressing the color of an object, such as a car, and that the user can select blue, red, or green. To express the car's color in a way that computers can represent and effectively compute, an application assigns each color a numeric value, so blue is 1, red is 2, and green is 3. Normally when you print each color, you see the value rather than the color.

If you use `pandas.DataFrame` (`http://pandas.pydata.org/pandas-docs/dev/generated/pandas.DataFrame.html`), you can still see the symbolic value (blue, red, and green), even though the computer stores it as a numeric value. Sometimes you need to rename and combine these named values to create new symbols. Symbolic variables are just a convenient way of representing and storing qualitative data.

CHECKING YOUR VERSION OF PANDAS

The categorical variable examples in this section depend on your having a minimum version of pandas 0.23.0 installed on your system. However, your version of Anaconda may have a previous pandas version installed instead. Use the following code to check your version of pandas:

```
import pandas as pd
print(pd.__version__)
```

You see the version number of pandas you have installed. Another way to check the version is to open the Anaconda Prompt, type **pip show pandas**, and press Enter. If you have an older version, open the Anaconda Prompt, type **pip install pandas --upgrade**, and press Enter. The update process will occur automatically, along with a check of associated packages. When working with Windows, you may need to open the Anaconda Prompt using the Administrator option (right click the Anaconda Prompt entry in the Start menu and choose Run as Administrator from the context menu).

When using categorical variables for machine learning, it's important to consider the algorithm used to manipulate the variables. Some algorithms, such as trees and ensembles of three, can work directly with the numeric variables behind the symbols. Other algorithms, such as linear and logistic regression and SVM, require that you encode the categorical values into binary variables. For example, if you have three levels for a color variable (blue, red, and green), you have to create three binary variables:

» One for blue (1 when the value is blue, 0 when it is not)

» One for red (1 when the value is red, 0 when it is not)

» One for green (1 when the value is green, 0 when it is not)

Creating categorical variables

Categorical variables have a specific number of values, which makes them incredibly valuable in performing a number of data science tasks. For example, imagine trying to find values that are out of range in a huge dataset. In this example, you see one method for creating a categorical variable and then using it to check whether some data falls within the specified limits:

```
import pandas as pd

car_colors = pd.Series(['Blue', 'Red', 'Green'],
                    dtype='category')

car_data = pd.Series(
    pd.Categorical(
        ['Yellow', 'Green', 'Red', 'Blue', 'Purple'],
                categories=car_colors, ordered=False))

find_entries = pd.isnull(car_data)

print(car_colors)
print()
print(car_data)
print()
print(find_entries[find_entries == True])
```

The example begins by creating a categorical variable, car_colors. The variable contains the values Blue, Red, and Green as colors that are acceptable for a car. Notice that you must specify a dtype property value of category.

The next step is to create another series. This one uses a list of actual car colors, named car_data, as input. Not all the car colors match the predefined acceptable values. When this problem occurs, pandas outputs Not a Number (NaN) instead of the car color.

Of course, you could search the list manually for the nonconforming cars, but the easiest method is to have pandas do the work for you. In this case, you ask pandas which entries are null using isnull() and place them in find_entries. You can then output just those entries that are actually null. Here's the output you see from the example:

```
0       Blue
1        Red
2      Green
dtype: category
Categories (3, object): [Blue, Green, Red]

0        NaN
1      Green
2        Red
3       Blue
4        NaN
dtype: category
Categories (3, object): [Blue, Green, Red]

0       True
4       True
dtype: bool
```

Looking at the list of car_data outputs, you can see that entries 0 and 4 equal NaN. The output from find_entries verifies this fact for you. If this were a large dataset, you could quickly locate and correct errant entries in the dataset before performing an analysis on it.

Renaming levels

There are times when the naming of the categories you use is inconvenient or otherwise wrong for a particular need. Fortunately, you can rename the categories as needed using the technique shown in the following example.

```
import pandas as pd

car_colors = pd.Series(['Blue', 'Red', 'Green'],
                       dtype='category')
```

```
car_data = pd.Series(
    pd.Categorical(
        ['Blue', 'Green', 'Red', 'Blue', 'Red'],
        categories=car_colors, ordered=False))

car_colors.cat.categories = ["Purple", "Yellow", "Mauve"]
car_data.cat.categories = car_colors

print(car_data)
```

All you really need to do is set the cat.categories property to a new value, as shown. Here is the output from this example:

```
0    Purple
1    Yellow
2     Mauve
3    Purple
4     Mauve
dtype: category
Categories (3, object): [Purple, Yellow, Mauve]
```

Combining levels

A particular categorical level might be too small to offer significant data for analysis. Perhaps there are only a few of the values, which may not be enough to create a statistical difference. In this case, combining several small categories might offer better analysis results. The following example shows how to combine categories:

```
import pandas as pd

car_colors = pd.Series(['Blue', 'Red', 'Green'],
    dtype='category')
car_data = pd.Series(
    pd.Categorical(
        ['Blue', 'Green', 'Red', 'Green', 'Red', 'Green'],
        categories=car_colors, ordered=False))

car_data = car_data.cat.set_categories(
    ["Blue", "Red", "Green", "Blue_Red"])
print(car_data.loc[car_data.isin(['Red'])])
car_data.loc[car_data.isin(['Red'])] = 'Blue_Red'
car_data.loc[car_data.isin(['Blue'])] = 'Blue_Red'
```

```
car_data = car_data.cat.set_categories(
    ["Green", "Blue_Red"])

print()
print(car_data)
```

What this example shows you is that there is only one Blue item and only two Red items, but there are three Green items, which places Green in the majority. Combining Blue and Red together is a two-step process. First, you add the Blue_Red category to car_data. Then you change the Red and Blue entries to Blue_Red, which creates the combined category. As a final step, you can remove the unneeded categories.

However, before you can change the Red entries to Blue_Red entries, you must find them. This is where a combination of calls to isin(), which locates the Red entries, and loc[], which obtains their index, provides precisely what you need. The first print statement shows the result of using this combination. Here's the output from this example.

```
2      Red
4      Red
dtype: category
Categories (4, object): [Blue, Red, Green, Blue_Red]

0      Blue_Red
1         Green
2      Blue_Red
3         Green
4      Blue_Red
5         Green
dtype: category
Categories (2, object): [Green, Blue_Red]
```

Notice that there are now three Blue_Red entries and three Green entries. The Blue and Red categories are no longer in use. The result is that the levels are now combined as expected.

Dealing with Dates in Your Data

Dates can present problems in data. For one thing, dates are stored as numeric values. However, the precise value of the number depends on the representation for the particular platform and could even depend on the users' preferences. For example, Excel users can choose to start dates in 1900 or 1904 (https://support.microsoft.com/en-us/help/214330/differences-between-the-1900-and-the-1904-date-system-in-excel). The numeric encoding for each is different, so the same date can have two numeric values depending on the starting date.

In addition to problems of representation, you also need to consider how to work with time values. Creating a time value format that represents a value the user can understand is hard. For example, you might need to use Greenwich Mean Time (GMT) in some situations but a local time zone in others. Transforming between various times is also problematic. With this in mind, the following sections provide you with details on dealing with time issues.

Formatting date and time values

Obtaining the correct date and time representation can make performing analysis a lot easier. For example, you often have to change the representation to obtain a correct sorting of values. Python provides two common methods of formatting date and time. The first technique is to call str(), which simply turns a datetime value into a string without any formatting. The strftime() function requires more work because you must define how you want the datetime value to appear after conversion. When using strftime(), you must provide a string containing special directives that define the formatting. You can find a listing of these directives at http://strftime.org/.

Now that you have some idea of how time and date conversions work, it's time to see an example. The following example creates a datetime object and then converts it into a string using two different approaches:

```
import datetime as dt

now = dt.datetime.now()

print(str(now))
print(now.strftime('%a, %d %B %Y'))
```

In this case, you can see that using str() is the easiest approach. However, as shown by the following output, it may not provide the output you need. Using strftime() is infinitely more flexible.

```
2018-09-21 11:39:49.698891
Fri, 21 September 2018
```

Using the right time transformation

Time zones and differences in local time can cause all sorts of problems when performing analysis. For that matter, some types of calculations simply require a time shift in order to get the right results. No matter what the reason, you may need to transform one time into another time at some point. The following examples show some techniques you can employ to perform the task:

```
import datetime as dt

now = dt.datetime.now()
timevalue = now + dt.timedelta(hours=2)

print(now.strftime('%H:%M:%S'))
print(timevalue.strftime('%H:%M:%S'))
print(timevalue - now)
```

The `timedelta()` function makes the time transformation straightforward. You can use any of these parameter names with `timedelta()` to change a time and date value:

>> days

>> seconds

>> microseconds

>> milliseconds

>> minutes

>> hours

>> weeks

You can also manipulate time by performing addition or subtraction on time values. You can even subtract two time values to determine the difference between them. Here's the output from this example:

```
11:42:22
13:42:22
2:00:00
```

Note that `now` is the local time, `timevalue` is two time zones different from this one, and there is a two-hour difference between the two times. You can perform all sorts of transformations using these techniques to ensure that your analysis always shows precisely the time-oriented values you need.

Dealing with Missing Data

Sometimes the data you receive is missing information in specific fields. For example, a customer record might be missing an age. If enough records are missing entries, any analysis you perform will be skewed and the results of the analysis weighted in an unpredictable manner. Having a strategy for dealing with missing data is important. The following sections give you some ideas on how to work through these issues and produce better results.

Finding the missing data

Finding missing data in your dataset is essential to avoid getting incorrect results from your analysis. The following code shows how you can obtain a listing of missing values without too much effort:

```
import pandas as pd
import numpy as np

s = pd.Series([1, 2, 3, np.NaN, 5, 6, None])

print(s.isnull())

print()
print(s[s.isnull()])
```

A dataset can represent missing data in several ways. In this example, you see missing data represented as np.NaN (NumPy Not a Number) and the Python None value.

Use the isnull() method to detect the missing values. The output shows True when the value is missing. By adding an index into the dataset, you obtain just the entries that are missing. The example shows the following output:

```
0    False
1    False
2    False
3     True
4    False
5    False
6     True
dtype: bool
```

```
3    NaN
6    NaN
dtype: float64
```

Encoding missingness

After you figure out that your dataset is missing information, you need to consider what to do about it. The three possibilities are to ignore the issue, fill in the missing items, or remove (drop) the missing entries from the dataset. Ignoring the problem could lead to all sorts of problems for your analysis, so it's the option you use least often. The following example shows one technique for filling in missing data or dropping the errant entries from the dataset:

```
import pandas as pd
import numpy as np

s = pd.Series([1, 2, 3, np.NaN, 5, 6, None])

print(s.fillna(int(s.mean())))
print()
print(s.dropna())
```

The two methods of interest are `fillna()`, which fills in the missing entries, and `dropna()`, which drops the missing entries. When using `fillna()`, you must provide a value to use for the missing data. This example uses the mean of all the values, but you could choose a number of other approaches. Here's the output from this example:

```
0    1.0
1    2.0
2    3.0
3    3.0
4    5.0
5    6.0
6    3.0
dtype: float64

0    1.0
1    2.0
2    3.0
4    5.0
5    6.0
dtype: float64
```

Working with a series is straightforward because the dataset is so simple. When working with a `DataFrame`, however, the problem becomes significantly more complicated. You still have the option of dropping the entire row. When a column is sparsely populated, you might drop the column instead. Filling in the data also becomes more complex because you must consider the dataset as a whole, in addition to the needs of the individual feature.

Imputing missing data

The previous section hints at the process of imputing missing data (ascribing characteristics based on how the data is used). The technique you use depends on the sort of data you're working with. For example, when working with a tree ensemble (you can find discussions of trees in the "Performing Hierarchical Clustering" section of Chapter 15 and the "Starting with a Plain Decision Tree" section of Chapter 20), you may simply replace missing values with a −1 and rely on the imputer (a transformer algorithm used to complete missing values) to define the best possible value for the missing data. The following example shows a technique you can use to impute missing data values:

```
import pandas as pd
import numpy as np
from sklearn.preprocessing import Imputer

s = [[1, 2, 3, np.NaN, 5, 6, None]]

imp = Imputer(missing_values='NaN',
              strategy='mean', axis=0)

imp.fit([[1, 2, 3, 4, 5, 6, 7]])

x = pd.Series(imp.transform(s).tolist()[0])

print(x)
```

In this example, s is missing some values. The code creates an `Imputer` to replace these missing values. The `missing_values` parameter defines what to look for, which is NaN. You set the `axis` parameter to 0 to impute along columns and 1 to impute along rows. The `strategy` parameter defines how to replace the missing values. (You can discover more about the Imputer parameters at https://scikit-learn.org/stable/modules/generated/sklearn.preprocessing.Imputer.html).

>> **mean**: Replaces the values by using the mean along the axis

>> **median**: Replaces the values by using the medium along the axis

>> **most_frequent**: Replaces the values by using the most frequent value along the axis

Before you can impute anything, you must provide statistics for the Imputer to use by calling fit(). The code then calls transform() on s to fill in the missing values. In this case, the example needs to display the result as a series. To create a series, you must convert the Imputer output to a list and use the resulting list as input to Series(). Here's the result of the process with the missing values filled in:

```
0  1
1  2
2  3
3  4
4  5
5  6
6  7
dtype: float64
```

Slicing and Dicing: Filtering and Selecting Data

You may not need to work with all the data in a dataset. In fact, looking at just one particular column might be beneficial, such as age, or a set of rows with a significant amount of information. You perform two steps to obtain just the data you need to perform a particular task:

1. Filter rows to create a subject of the data that meets the criterion you select (such as all the people between the ages of 5 and 10).

2. Select data columns that contain the data you need to analyze. For example, you probably don't need the individuals' names unless you want to perform some analysis based on name.

The act of slicing and dicing data, gives you a subset of the data suitable for analysis. The following sections describe various ways to obtain specific pieces of data to meet particular needs.

Slicing rows

Slicing can occur in multiple ways when working with data, but the technique of interest in this section is to slice data from a row of 2-D or 3-D data. A 2-D array may contain temperatures (x axis) over a specific time frame (y axis). Slicing a row would mean seeing the temperatures at a specific time. In some cases, you might associate rows with cases in a dataset.

A 3-D array might include an axis for place (x axis), product (y axis), and time (z axis) so that you can see sales for items over time. Perhaps you want to track whether sales of an item are increasing, and specifically where they are increasing. Slicing a row would mean seeing all the sales for one specific product for all locations at any time. The following example demonstrates how to perform this task:

```
x = np.array([[[1, 2, 3], [4, 5, 6], [7, 8, 9],],
              [[11,12,13], [14,15,16], [17,18,19],],
              [[21,22,23], [24,25,26], [27,28,29]]])
x[1]
```

In this case, the example builds a 3-D array. It then slices row 1 of that array to produce the following output:

```
array([[11, 12, 13],
       [14, 15, 16],
       [17, 18, 19]])
```

Slicing columns

Using the examples from the previous section, slicing columns would obtain data at a 90-degree angle from rows. In other words, when working with the 2-D array, you would want to see the times at which specific temperatures occurred. Likewise, you might want to see the sales of all products for a specific location at any time when working with the 3-D array. In some cases, you might associate columns with features in a dataset. The following example demonstrates how to perform this task using the same array as in the previous section:

```
x = np.array([[[1, 2, 3], [4, 5, 6], [7, 8, 9],],
              [[11,12,13], [14,15,16], [17,18,19],],
              [[21,22,23], [24,25,26], [27,28,29]]])
x[:,1]
```

Note that the indexing now occurs at two levels. The first index refers to the row. Using the colon (:) for the row means to use all the rows. The second index refers to a column. In this case, the output will contain column 1. Here's the output you see:

```
array([[ 4,  5,  6],
       [14, 15, 16],
       [24, 25, 26]])
```

REMEMBER

This is a 3-D array. Therefore, each of the columns contains all the z axis elements. What you see is every row — 0 through 2 for column 1 with every z axis element 0 through 2 for that column.

Dicing

The act of dicing a dataset means to perform both row and column slicing such that you end up with a data wedge. For example, when working with the 3-D array, you might want to see the sales of a specific product in a specific location at any time. The following example demonstrates how to perform this task using the same array as in the previous two sections:

```
x = np.array([[[1, 2, 3], [4, 5, 6], [7, 8, 9],],
              [[11,12,13], [14,15,16], [17,18,19],],
              [[21,22,23], [24,25,26], [27,28,29]]])
print(x[1,1])
print(x[:,1,1])
print(x[1,:,1])
print()
print(x[1:2, 1:2])
```

This example dices the array in four different ways. First, you get row 1, column 1. Of course, what you may actually want is column 1, z axis 1. If that's not quite right, you could always request row 1, z axis 1 instead. Then again, you may want rows 1 and 2 of columns 1 and 2. Here's the output of all four requests:

```
[14 15 16]
[ 5 15 25]
[12 15 18]

[[[14 15 16]]]
```

Concatenating and Transforming

Data used for data science purposes seldom comes in a neat package. You may need to work with multiple databases in various locations — each of which has its own data format. It's impossible to perform analysis on such disparate sources of information with any accuracy. To make the data useful, you must create a single dataset (by *concatenating*, or combining, the data from various sources).

Part of the process is to ensure that each field you create for the combined dataset has the same characteristics. For example, an age field in one database might appear as a string, but another database could use an integer for the same field. For the fields to work together, they must appear as the same type of information.

The following sections help you understand the process involved in concatenating and transforming data from various sources to create a single dataset. After you have a single dataset from these sources, you can begin to perform tasks such as analysis on the data. Of course, the trick is to create a single dataset that truly represents the data in all those disparate datasets — modifying the data would result in skewed results.

Adding new cases and variables

You often find a need to combine datasets in various ways or even to add new information for the sake of analysis purposes. The result is a combined dataset that includes either new cases or variables. The following example shows techniques for performing both tasks:

```python
import pandas as pd

df = pd.DataFrame({'A': [2,3,1],
                   'B': [1,2,3],
                   'C': [5,3,4]})

df1 = pd.DataFrame({'A': [4],
                    'B': [4],
                    'C': [4]})

df = df.append(df1)
df = df.reset_index(drop=True)
print(df)
```

```
df.loc[df.last_valid_index() + 1] = [5, 5, 5]
print()
print(df)

df2 = pd.DataFrame({'D': [1, 2, 3, 4, 5]})

df = pd.DataFrame.join(df, df2)
print()
print(df)
```

The easiest way to add more data to an existing DataFrame is to rely on the append() method. You can also use the concat() method (a technique shown in Chapter 13). In this case, the three cases found in df are added to the single case found in df1. To ensure that the data is appended as anticipated, the columns in df and df1 must match. When you append two DataFrame objects in this manner, the new DataFrame contains the old index values. Use the reset_index() method to create a new index to make accessing cases easier.

You can also add another case to an existing DataFrame by creating the new case directly. Any time you add a new entry at a position that is one greater than the last_valid_index(), you get a new case as a result.

Sometimes you need to add a new variable (column) to the DataFrame. In this case, you rely on join() to perform the task. The resulting DataFrame will match cases with the same index value, so indexing is important. In addition, unless you want blank values, the number of cases in both DataFrame objects must match. Here's the output from this example:

```
   A  B  C
0  2  1  5
1  3  2  3
2  1  3  4
3  4  4  4

   A  B  C
0  2  1  5
1  3  2  3
2  1  3  4
3  4  4  4
4  5  5  5
```

```
   A  B  C  D
0  2  1  5  1
1  3  2  3  2
2  1  3  4  3
3  4  4  4  4
4  5  5  5  5
```

Removing data

At some point, you may need to remove cases or variables from a dataset because they aren't required for your analysis. In both cases, you rely on the drop() method to perform the task. The difference in removing cases or variables is in how you describe what to remove, as shown in the following example:

```
import pandas as pd

df = pd.DataFrame({'A': [2,3,1],
                   'B': [1,2,3],
                   'C': [5,3,4]})

df = df.drop(df.index[[1]])
print(df)

df = df.drop('B', 1)
print()
print(df)
```

The example begins by removing a case from df. Notice how the code relies on an index to describe what to remove. You can remove just one case (as shown), ranges of cases, or individual cases separated by commas. The main concern is to ensure that you have the correct index numbers for the cases you want to remove.

Removing a column is different. This example shows how to remove a column using a column name. You can also remove a column by using an index. In both cases, you must specify an axis as part of the removal process (normally 1). Here's the output from this example:

```
   A  B  C
0  2  1  5
2  1  3  4

   A  C
0  2  5
2  1  4
```

Sorting and shuffling

Sorting and shuffling are two ends of the same goal — to manage data order. In the first case, you put the data into order, while in the second, you remove any systematic patterning from the order. In general, you don't sort datasets for the purpose of analysis because doing so can cause you to get incorrect results. However, you might want to sort data for presentation purposes. The following example shows both sorting and shuffling:

```python
import pandas as pd
import numpy as np

df = pd.DataFrame({'A': [2,1,2,3,3,5,4],
                   'B': [1,2,3,5,4,2,5],
                   'C': [5,3,4,1,1,2,3]})

df = df.sort_values(by=['A', 'B'], ascending=[True, True])
df = df.reset_index(drop=True)
print(df)

index = df.index.tolist()
np.random.shuffle(index)
df = df.loc[df.index[index]]
df = df.reset_index(drop=True)
print()
print(df)
```

It turns out that sorting the data is a bit easier than shuffling it. To sort the data, you use the sort_values() method and define which columns to use for indexing purposes. You can also determine whether the index is in ascending or descending order. Make sure to always call reset_index() when you're done so that the index appears in order for analysis or other purposes.

To shuffle the data, you first acquire the current index using df.index.tolist() and place it in index. A call to random.shuffle() creates a new order for the index. You then apply the new order to df using loc[]. As always, you call reset_index() to finalize the new order. Here's the output from this example (but note that the second output may not match your output because it has been shuffled):

```
   A  B  C
0  1  2  3
1  2  1  5
2  2  3  4
3  3  4  1
```

```
4  3  5  1
5  4  5  3
6  5  2  2

   A  B  C
0  2  1  5
1  2  3  4
2  3  4  1
3  1  2  3
4  3  5  1
5  4  5  3
6  5  2  2
```

Aggregating Data at Any Level

Aggregation is the process of combining or grouping data together into a set, bag, or list. The data may or may not be alike. However, in most cases, an aggregation function combines several rows together statistically using algorithms such as average, count, maximum, median, minimum, mode, or sum. There are several reasons to aggregate data:

>> Make it easier to analyze

>> Reduce the ability of anyone to deduce the data of an individual from the dataset for privacy or other reasons

>> Create a combined data element from one data source that matches a combined data element in another source

The most important use of data aggregation is to promote anonymity in order to meet legal or other concerns. Sometimes even data that should be anonymous turns out to provide identification of an individual using the proper analysis techniques. For example, researchers have found that it's possible to identify individuals based on just three credit card purchases (see https://www.computerworld.com/article/2877935/how-three-small-credit-card-transactions-could-reveal-your-identity.html for details). Here's an example that shows how to perform aggregation tasks:

```
import pandas as pd

df = pd.DataFrame({'Map': [0,0,0,1,1,2,2],
                   'Values': [1,2,3,5,4,2,5]})

df['S'] = df.groupby('Map')['Values'].transform(np.sum)
df['M'] = df.groupby('Map')['Values'].transform(np.mean)
df['V'] = df.groupby('Map')['Values'].transform(np.var)

print(df)
```

In this case, you have two initial features for this DataFrame. The values in Map define which elements in Values belong together. For example, when calculating a sum for Map index 0, you use the Values 1, 2, and 3.

To perform the aggregation, you must first call groupby() to group the Map values. You then index into Values and rely on transform() to create the aggregated data using one of several algorithms found in NumPy, such as np.sum. Here are the results of this calculation:

```
   Map  Values  S    M    V
0    0       1  6  2.0  1.0
1    0       2  6  2.0  1.0
2    0       3  6  2.0  1.0
3    1       5  9  4.5  0.5
4    1       4  9  4.5  0.5
5    2       2  7  3.5  4.5
6    2       5  7  3.5  4.5
```

Chapter **8**

Shaping Data

C hapter 7 demonstrates techniques for working with data as an entity — as something you work with in Python. However, data doesn't exist in a vacuum. It doesn't just suddenly appear within Python for absolutely no reason at all. As demonstrated in Chapter 6, you load the data. However, loading may not be enough — you may have to shape the data as part of loading it. That's the purpose of this chapter. You discover how to work with a variety of container types in a way that makes it possible to load data from a number of complex container types, such as HTML pages. In fact, you even work with graphics, images, and sounds.

REMEMBER

As you progress through the book, you discover that data takes all kinds of forms and shapes. As far as the computer is concerned, data consists of 0s and 1s. Humans give the data meaning by formatting, storing, and interpreting it in a certain way. The same group of 0s and 1s could be a number, date, or text, depending on the interpretation. The data container provides clues as to how to interpret the data, so that's why this chapter is so important to you as a data scientist using Python to discover data patterns. You find that you can discover patterns in places where you might have thought patterns couldn't exist.

You don't have to type the source code for this chapter manually. In fact, it's a lot easier if you use the downloadable source (see the Introduction for download instructions). The source code for this chapter appears in the P4DS4D2_08_ Shaping_Data.ipynb source code file.

Working with HTML Pages

HTML pages contain data in a hierarchical format. You often find HTML content in a strict HTML form or as XML. The HTML form can present problems because it doesn't always necessarily follow strict formatting rules. XML does follow strict formatting rules because of the standards used to define it, which makes it easier to parse. However, in both cases, you use similar techniques to parse a page. The first section that follows describes how to parse HTML pages in general.

Sometimes you don't need all the data on a page. Instead you need specific data, which is where XPath comes into play. You can use XPath to locate specific data on the HTML page and extract it for your particular needs.

Parsing XML and HTML

Simply extracting data from an XML file as you do in Chapter 6 may not be enough. The data may not be in the correct format. Using the approach in Chapter 6, you end up with a DataFrame containing three columns of type str. Obviously, you can't perform much data manipulation with strings. The following example shapes the XML data from Chapter 6 to create a new DataFrame containing just the <Number> and <Boolean> elements in the correct format.

```
from lxml import objectify
import pandas as pd
from distutils import util

xml = objectify.parse(open('XMLData.xml'))
root = xml.getroot()
df = pd.DataFrame(columns=('Number', 'Boolean'))

for i in range(0, 4):
    obj = root.getchildren()[i].getchildren()
    row = dict(zip(['Number', 'Boolean'],
                    [obj[0].pyval,
                     bool(util.strtobool(obj[2].text))]))
    row_s = pd.Series(row)
    row_s.name = obj[1].text
    df = df.append(row_s)

print(type(df.loc['First']['Number']))
print(type(df.loc['First']['Boolean']))
```

The DataFrame df is initially instantiated as empty, but as the code loops through the root node's children, it extracts a list containing the following

>> A ‹Number› element (expressed as an int)

>> An ordinal element (a string)

>> A ‹Boolean› element (expressed as a string)

that the code uses to increment df. In fact, the code relies on the ordinal number element as the index label and constructs a new individual row to append to the existing DataFrame. This operation programmatically converts the information contained in the XML tree into the right data type to place into the existing variables in df. The number elements are already available as int type; the conversion of the ‹Boolean› element is a little harder. You must convert the string to a numeric value using the strtobool() function in distutils.util. The output is a 0 for False values and a 1 for True values. However, that's still not a Boolean value. To create a Boolean value, you must convert the 0 or 1 using bool().

TIP

This example also shows how to access individual values in the DataFrame. Notice that the name property now uses the ‹String› element value for easy access. You provide an index value using loc and then access the individual feature using a second index. The output from this example is

```
<class 'int'>
<class 'bool'>
```

Using XPath for data extraction

Using XPath to extract data from your dataset can greatly reduce the complexity of your code and potentially make it faster as well. The following example shows an XPath version of the example in the previous section. Notice that this version is shorter and doesn't require the use of a for loop.

```
from lxml import objectify
import pandas as pd
from distutils import util

xml = objectify.parse(open('XMLData.xml'))
root = xml.getroot()

map_number = map(int, root.xpath('Record/Number'))
map_bool = map(str, root.xpath('Record/Boolean'))
map_bool = map(util.strtobool, map_bool)
```

```
map_bool = map(bool, map_bool)
map_string = map(str, root.xpath('Record/String'))

data = list(zip(map_number, map_bool))

df = pd.DataFrame(data,
                  columns=('Number', 'Boolean'),
                  index = list(map_string))

print(df)
print(type(df.loc['First']['Number']))
print(type(df.loc['First']['Boolean']))
```

The example begins just like the previous example, with the importing of data and obtaining of the root node. At this point, the example creates a data object that contains record number and Boolean value pairs. Because the XML file entries are all strings, you must use the map() function to convert the strings to the appropriate values. Working with the record number is straightforward — all you do is map it to an int. The xpath() function accepts a path from the root node to the data you need, which is 'Record/Number' in this case.

Mapping the Boolean value is a little more difficult. As in the previous section, you must use the util.strtobool() function to convert the string Boolean values to a number that bool() can convert to a Boolean equivalent. However, if you try to perform just a double mapping, you'll encounter an error message saying that lists don't include a required function, tolower().To overcome this obstacle, you perform a triple mapping and convert the data to a string using the str() function first.

Creating the DataFrame is different, too. Instead of adding individual rows, you add all the rows at one time by using data. Setting up the column names is the same as before. However, now you need some way of adding the row names, as in the previous example. This task is accomplished by setting the index parameter to a mapped version of the xpath() output for the 'Record/String' path. Here's the output you can expect:

```
        Number Boolean
First       1    True
Second      2   False
Third       3    True
Fourth      4   False
<type 'numpy.int64'>
<type 'numpy.bool_'>
```

Working with Raw Text

Even though it might seem as if raw text wouldn't present a problem in parsing because it doesn't contain any special formatting, you do have to consider how the text is stored and whether it contains special words within it. The multiple forms of Unicode can present interpretation problems that you need to consider as you work through the text. Using regular expressions can help you locate specific information within a raw-text file. You can use regular expressions for both data cleaning and pattern matching. The following sections help you understand the techniques used to shape raw-text files.

Dealing with Unicode

Text files are pure text — this much is certain. The way the text is encoded can differ. For example, a character can use seven, eight, or more bits for encoding purposes. The use of special characters can differ as well. In short, the interpretation of bits used to create characters differs from encoding to encoding. You can see a host of encodings at `http://www.i18nguy.com/unicode/codepages.html`.

REMEMBER

Sometimes you need to work with encodings other than the default encoding set within the Python environment. When working with Python 3.*x*, you must rely on Universal Transformation Format 8-bit (UTF-8) as the encoding used to read and write files. This environment is always set for UTF-8, and trying to change it causes an error message. The article at `https://docs.python.org/3/howto/unicode.html` provides insights on how to get around the Unicode problems in Python.

WARNING

Dealing with encoding in the incorrect way can prevent you from performing tasks such as importing modules or processing text. Make sure to test your code carefully and completely to ensure that any problem with encoding won't affect your ability to run the application. Good additional articles to read on this topic appear at `http://blog.notdot.net/2010/07/Getting-unicode-right-in-Python` and `http://web.archive.org/web/20120722170929/http://boodebr.org/main/python/all-about-python-and-unicode`.

Stemming and removing stop words

Stemming is the process of reducing words to their stem (or root) word. This task isn't the same as understanding that some words come from Latin or other roots, but instead makes like words equal to each other for the purpose of comparison or sharing. For example, the words *cats*, *catty*, and *catlike* all have the stem *cat*. The act of stemming helps you analyze sentences by tokenizing them in a more efficient way because the machine learning algorithm has to learn about the stem *cat* and not about all its variants.

Removing suffixes to create stem words and generally tokenizing sentences are only two parts of the process, however, of creating something like a natural language interface. Languages include a great number of glue words that don't mean much to a computer but have significant meaning to humans, such as *a, as, the, that,* and so on in English. These short, less useful words are *stop* words. Sentences don't make sense without them to humans, but for your computer, they can act as a means of stopping sentence analysis.

The act of stemming and removing stop words simplifies the text and reduces the number of textual elements so that just the essential elements remain. In addition, you keep just the terms that are nearest to the true sense of the phrase. By reducing phrases in such a fashion, a computational algorithm can work faster and process the text more effectively.

WARNING

This example requires the use of the Natural Language Toolkit (NLTK), which Anaconda (see Chapter 3 for details on Anaconda) doesn't install by default. To use this example, you must download and install NLTK using the instructions found at http://www.nltk.org/install.html for your platform. Make certain that you install the NLTK for whatever version of Python you're using for this book when you have multiple versions of Python installed on your system. After you install NLTK, you must also install the packages associated with it. The instructions at http://www.nltk.org/data.html tell you how to perform this task (install all the packages to ensure you have everything).

The following example demonstrates how to perform stemming and remove stop words from a sentence. It begins by training an algorithm to perform the required analysis using a test sentence. Afterward, the example checks a second sentence for words that appear in the first.

```
from sklearn.feature_extraction.text import *
from nltk import word_tokenize
from nltk.stem.porter import PorterStemmer

stemmer = PorterStemmer()

def stem_tokens(tokens, stemmer):
    stemmed = []
    for item in tokens:
        stemmed.append(stemmer.stem(item))
    return stemmed
```

```
def tokenize(text):
    tokens = word_tokenize(text)
    stems = stem_tokens(tokens, stemmer)
    return stems

vocab = ['Sam loves swimming so he swims all the time']
vect = CountVectorizer(tokenizer=tokenize,
                       stop_words='english')
vec = vect.fit(vocab)

sentence1 = vec.transform(['George loves swimming too!'])

print(vec.get_feature_names())
print(sentence1.toarray())
```

At the outset, the example creates a vocabulary using a test sentence and places it in vocab. It then creates a CountVectorizer, vect, to hold a list of stemmed words, but excludes the stop words. The tokenizer parameter defines the function used to stem the words. The stop_words parameter refers to a pickle file that contains stop words for a specific language, which is English in this case. There are also files for other languages, such as French and German. (You can see other parameters for the CountVectorizer() at https://scikit-learn.org/stable/modules/generated/sklearn.feature_extraction.text.CountVectorizer.html.) The vocabulary is fitted into another CountVectorizer, vec, which is used to perform the actual transformation on a test sentence using the transform() function. Here's the output from this example.

```
['love', 'sam', 'swim', 'time']
[[1 0 1 0]]
```

The first output shows the stemmed words. Notice that the list contains only *swim*, not *swimming* and *swims*. All the stop words are missing as well. For example, you don't see the words *so, he, all,* or *the*.

The second output shows how many times each stemmed word appears in the test sentence. In this case, a *love* variant appears once and a *swim* variant appears once as well. The words *sam* and *time* don't appear in the second sentence, so those values are set to 0.

Introducing regular expressions

Regular expressions present the data scientist with an interesting array of tools for parsing raw text. At first, it may seem daunting to figure out precisely how regular expressions work. However, sites such as https://regexr.com/ let you play with regular expressions so that you can see how the use of various expressions performs specific types of pattern matching. Of course, the first requirement is to discover *pattern matching*, which is the use of special characters to tell a parsing engine what to find in the raw text file. Table 8-1 provides a list of pattern-matching characters and tells you how to use them.

TABLE 8-1   **Pattern-Matching Characters Used in Python**

Character	Interpretation
(re)	Groups regular expressions and remembers the matched text
(?: re)	Groups regular expressions without remembering matched text
(?#...)	Indicates a comment, which isn't processed
re?	Matches 0 or 1 occurrence of preceding expression (but no more than 0 or 1 occurrence)
re*	Matches 0 or more occurrences of the preceding expression
re+	Matches 1 or more occurrences of the preceding expression
(?> re)	Matches an independent pattern without backtracking
.	Matches any single character except the newline (\n) character (adding the m option allows it to match the newline character as well)
[^...]	Matches any single character or range of characters not found within the brackets
[...]	Matches any single character or range of characters that appears within the brackets
re{ n, m}	Matches at least n and at most m occurrences of the preceding expression
\n, \t, etc.	Matches control characters such as newlines (\n), carriage returns (\r), and tabs (\t)
\d	Matches digits (which is equivalent to using [0–9])
a|b	Matches either a or b
re{ n}	Matches exactly the number of occurrences of preceding expression specified by n
re{ n,}	Matches n or more occurrences of the preceding expression
\D	Matches nondigits
\S	Matches nonwhitespace
\B	Matches nonword boundaries
\W	Matches nonword characters

Character	Interpretation
\1...\9	Matches nth grouped subexpression
\10	Matches nth grouped subexpression if it matched already (otherwise, the pattern refers to the octal representation of a character code)
\A	Matches the beginning of a string
^	Matches the beginning of the line
\z	Matches the end of a string
\Z	Matches the end of string (when a newline exists, it matches just before newline)
$	Matches the end of the line
\G	Matches the point where the last match finished
\s	Matches whitespace (which is equivalent to using [\t\n\r\f])
\b	Matches word boundaries when outside the brackets; matches the backspace (0x08) when inside the brackets
\w	Matches word characters
(?= re)	Specifies a position using a pattern (This pattern doesn't have a range.)
(?! re)	Specifies a position using pattern negation (This pattern doesn't have a range.)
(?-imx)	Toggles the i, m, or x options temporarily off within a regular expression (when this pattern appears in parentheses, only the area within the parentheses is affected)
(?imx)	Toggles the i, m, or x options temporarily on within a regular expression (when this pattern appears in parentheses, only the area within the parentheses is affected)
(?-imx: re)	Toggles the i, m, or x options within parentheses temporarily off
(?imx: re)	Toggles the i, m, or x options within parentheses temporarily on

Using regular expressions helps you manipulate complex text before using other techniques described in this chapter. In the following example, you see how to extract a telephone number from a sentence no matter where the telephone number appears. This sort of manipulation is helpful when you have to work with text of various origins and in irregular format. You can see some additional telephone number manipulation routines at http://www.diveintopython.net/ regular_expressions/phone_numbers.html. The big thing is that this example helps you understand how to extract any text you need from text you don't.

```
import re

data1 = 'My phone number is: 800-555-1212.'
data2 = '800-555-1234 is my phone number.'

pattern = re.compile(r'(\d{3})-(\d{3})-(\d{4})')

dmatch1 = pattern.search(data1).groups()
dmatch2 = pattern.search(data2).groups()

print(dmatch1)
print(dmatch2)
```

The example begins with two telephone numbers placed in sentences in various locations. Before you can do much, you need to create a pattern. Always read a pattern from left to right. In this case, the pattern is looking for three digits, followed by a dash, three more digits, followed by another dash, and finally four digits.

To make the process faster and easier, the code calls the `compile()` function to create a compiled version of the pattern so that Python doesn't have to recreate the pattern every time you need it. The compiled pattern appears in `pattern`.

The `search()` function looks for the pattern in each of the test sentences. It then places any matched text that it finds into groups and outputs a tuple into one of two variables. Here's the output from this example.

```
('800', '555', '1212')
('800', '555', '1234')
```

Using the Bag of Words Model and Beyond

The goal of most data imports is to perform some type of analysis. Before you can perform analysis on textual data, you must tokenize every word within the dataset. The act of tokenizing the words creates a *bag of words*. You can then use the bag of words to train *classifiers*, a special kind of algorithm used to break words down into categories. The following section provides additional insights into the bag of words model and shows how to work with it.

Understanding the bag of words model

As mentioned in the introduction, in order to perform textual analysis of various sorts, you need to first tokenize the words and create a bag of words from them. The bag of words uses numbers to represent words, word frequencies, and word locations that you can manipulate mathematically to see patterns in the way that the words are structured and used. The bag of words model ignores grammar and even word order — the focus is on simplifying the text so that you can easily analyze it.

The creation of a bag of words revolves around Natural Language Processing (NLP) and Information Retrieval (IR). Before you perform this sort of processing, you normally remove any special characters (such as HTML formatting from a web source), remove the stop words, and possibly perform stemming as well (as described in the "Stemming and removing stop words" section, earlier this chapter). For the purpose of this example, you use the 20 Newsgroups dataset directly. Here's an example of how you can obtain textual input and create a bag of words from it:

```
from sklearn.datasets import fetch_20newsgroups
from sklearn.feature_extraction.text import *

categories = ['comp.graphics', 'misc.forsale',
              'rec.autos', 'sci.space']
```

```
twenty_train = fetch_20newsgroups(subset='train',
                                  categories=categories,
                                  shuffle=True,
                                  random_state=42)


count_vect = CountVectorizer()
X_train_counts = count_vect.fit_transform(
    twenty_train.data)


print("BOW shape:", X_train_counts.shape)
caltech_idx = count_vect.vocabulary_['caltech']
print('"Caltech": %i' % X_train_counts[0, caltech_idx])
```

REMEMBER

A number of the examples you see online are unclear as to where the list of categories they use come from. The host site at http://qwone.com/~jason/20Newsgroups/ provides you with a listing of the categories you can use. The category list doesn't come from a magic hat somewhere, but many examples online simply don't bother to document some information sources. Always refer to the host site when you have questions about issues such as dataset categories.

The call to fetch_20newsgroups() loads the dataset into memory. You see the resulting training object, twenty_train, described as a *bunch*. At this point, you have an object that contains a listing of categories and associated data, but the application hasn't tokenized the data, and the algorithm used to work with the data isn't trained.

Now that you have a bunch of data to use, you can begin creating a bag of words with it. The bag of words process begins by assigning an integer value (an index of a sort) to each unique word in the training set. In addition, each document receives an integer value. The next step is to count every occurrence of these words in each document and create a list of document and count pairs so that you know which words appear how often in each document.

Naturally, some words from the master list aren't used in some documents, thereby creating a *high-dimensional sparse dataset.* The scipy.sparse matrix is a data structure that lets you store only the nonzero elements of the list in order to save memory. When the code makes the call to count_vect.fit_transform(), it places the resulting bag of words into X_train_counts. You can see the resulting number of entries by accessing the shape property and the counts for the word "Caltech" in the first document:

```
BOW shape: (2356, 34750)
"Caltech": 3
```

Working with n-grams

An *n-gram* is a continuous sequence of items in the text you want to analyze. The items are phonemes, syllables, letters, words, or base pairs. The *n* in n-gram refers to a size. An n-gram that has a size of one, for example, is a unigram. The example in this section uses a size of three, making a trigram. You use n-grams in a probabilistic manner to perform tasks such as predicting the next sequence in a series, which wouldn't seem very useful until you start thinking about applications such as search engines that try to predict the word you want to type based on the previous letters you've supplied. However, the technique has all sorts of applications, such as in DNA sequencing and data compression. The following example shows how to create n-grams from the 20 Newsgroups dataset.

```python
from sklearn.datasets import fetch_20newsgroups
from sklearn.feature_extraction.text import *

categories = ['sci.space']

twenty_train = fetch_20newsgroups(subset='train',
                                  categories=categories,
                                  remove=('headers',
                                          'footers',
                                          'quotes'),
                                  shuffle=True,
                                  random_state=42)

count_chars = CountVectorizer(analyzer='char_wb',
                              ngram_range=(3,3),
                              max_features=10)

count_chars.fit(twenty_train['data'])

count_words = CountVectorizer(analyzer='word',
                              ngram_range=(2,2),
                              max_features=10,
                              stop_words='english')

count_words.fit(twenty_train['data'])

X = count_chars.transform(twenty_train.data)

print(count_chars.get_feature_names())
print(X[1].todense())
print(count_words.get_feature_names())
```

The beginning code is the same as in the previous section. You still begin by fetching the dataset and placing it into a bunch. However, in this case, the vectorization process takes on new meaning. The arguments process the data in a special way.

In this case, the `analyzer` parameter determines how the application creates the n-grams. You can choose words (`word`), characters (`char`), or characters within word boundaries (`char_wb`). The `ngram_range` parameter requires two inputs in the form of a tuple: The first determines the minimum n-gram size and the second determines the maximum n-gram size. The third argument, `max_features`, determines how many features the vectorizer returns. In the second vectorizer call, the `stop_words` argument removes the terms contained in the English pickle (see the "Stemming and removing stop words" section, earlier in the chapter, for details). At this point, the application fits the data to the transformation algorithm.

The example provides three outputs. The first shows the top ten trigrams for characters from the document. The second is the n-gram for the first document. It shows the frequency of the top ten trigrams. The third is the top ten trigrams for words. Here's the output from this example:

```
[' an', ' in', ' of', ' th', ' to', 'he ', 'ing', 'ion',
 'nd ', 'the']
[[0 0 2 5 1 4 2 2 0 5]]
['anonymous ftp', 'commercial space', 'gamma ray',
'nasa gov', 'national space', 'remote sensing',
'sci space', 'space shuttle', 'space station',
'washington dc']
```

Implementing TF-IDF transformations

The *Term Frequency times Inverse Document Frequency (TF-IDF)* transformation is a technique used to help compensate for words found relatively often in different documents, which makes it hard to distinguish between the documents because they are too common (stop words are a good example). What this transformation is really telling you is the importance of a particular word to the uniqueness of a document. The greater the frequency of a word in a document, the more important it is to that document. However, the measurement is offset by the document size — the total number of words the document contains — and by how often the word appears in other documents.

Even if a word appears many times inside a document, that doesn't imply that the word is important for understanding the document itself; in many documents, you find stop words with the same frequency as the words that relate to the document's general topics. For example, if you analyze documents with scifi-related discussions (such as in the 20 Newsgroups dataset), you may find that many of them deal with UFOs; therefore, the acronym *UFO* can't represent a distinction between different documents. Moreover, longer documents contain more words than shorter ones, and repeated words are easily found when the text is abundant.

REMEMBER

In fact, a word found a few times in a single document (or possibly a few others) could prove quite distinctive and helpful in determining the document type. If you are working with documents discussing scifi and automobile sales, the acronym *UFO* can be distinctive because it easily separates the two topic types in your documents.

Search engines often need to weight words in a document in a way that helps determine when the word is important in the text. You use words with the higher weight to index the document so that when you search for those words, the search engine will retrieve that document. This is the reason that the TD-IDF transformation is used quite often in search engine applications.

Getting into more details, the TF part of the TF-IDF equation determines how frequently the term appears in the document, while the IDF part of the equation determines the term's importance because it represents the inverse of the frequency of that word among all the documents. A large IDF implies a seldom-found word and that the TF-IDF weight will also be larger. A small IDF means that the word is common, and that will result in a small TF-IDF weight. You can see some actual calculations of this particular measure at http://www.tfidf.com/. Here's an example of how to calculate TF-IDF using Python:

```python
from sklearn.datasets import fetch_20newsgroups
from sklearn.feature_extraction.text import *

categories = ['comp.graphics', 'misc.forsale',
              'rec.autos', 'sci.space']
twenty_train = fetch_20newsgroups(subset='train',
                                  categories=categories,
                                  shuffle=True,
                                  random_state=42)

count_vect = CountVectorizer()
X_train_counts = count_vect.fit_transform(
    twenty_train.data)
```

```
tfidf = TfidfTransformer().fit(X_train_counts)
X_train_tfidf = tfidf.transform(X_train_counts)

caltech_idx = count_vect.vocabulary_['caltech']
print('"Caltech" scored in a BOW:')
print('count: %0.3f' % X_train_counts[0, caltech_idx])
print('TF-IDF: %0.3f' % X_train_tfidf[0, caltech_idx])
```

This example begins much like the other examples in this section have, by fetching the 20 Newsgroups dataset. It then creates a word bag, much like the example in the "Understanding the bag of words model" section, earlier in this chapter. However, now you see something you can do with the word bag.

In this case, the code calls upon `TfidfTransformer()` to convert the raw newsgroup documents into a matrix of TF-IDF features. The `use_idf` controls the use of inverse-document-frequency reweighting, which it turned on in this case. The vectorized data is fitted to the transformation algorithm. The next step, calling `tfidf.transform()`, performs the actual transformation process. Here's the result you get from this example:

```
"Caltech" scored in a BOW:
count: 3.000
TF-IDF: 0.123
```

Notice how the word *Caltech* now has a lower value in the first document compared to the example in the previous paragraph, where the counting of occurrences for the same word in the same document scored a value of 3. To understand how counting occurrences relates to TF-IDF, compute the average word count and average TF-IDF:

```
import numpy as np
count = np.mean(X_train_counts[X_train_counts>0])
tfif = np.mean(X_train_tfidf[X_train_tfidf>0])
print('mean count: %0.3f' % np.mean(count))
print('mean TF-IDF: %0.3f' % np.mean(tfif))
```

The results demonstrate that no matter how you count occurrences of *Caltech* in the first document or use its TF-IDF, the value is always double the average word, revealing that it is a keyword for modeling the text:

```
mean count: 1.698
mean TF-IDF: 0.064
```

TF–IDF helps you to locate the most important word or n–grams and exclude the least important ones. It is also very helpful as an input for linear models, because they work better with TF–IDF scores than word counts. At this point, you normally train a classifier and perform various sorts of analysis. Don't worry about this next part of the process just yet. Starting with Chapters 12 and 15, you get introduced to classifiers. In Chapter 17, you begin working with classifiers in earnest.

Working with Graph Data

Imagine data points that are connected to other data points, such as how one web page is connected to another web page through hyperlinks. Each of these data points is a *node.* The nodes connect to each other using *links.* Not every node links to every other node, so the node connections become important. By analyzing the nodes and their links, you can perform all sorts of interesting tasks in data science, such as defining the best way to get from work to your home using streets and highways. The following sections describe how graphs work and how to perform basic tasks with them.

Understanding the adjacency matrix

An *adjacency matrix* represents the connections between nodes of a graph. When a connection exists between one node and another, the matrix indicates it as a value greater than 0. The precise representation of connections in the matrix depends on whether the graph is directed (where the direction of the connection matters) or undirected.

A problem with many online examples is that the authors keep them simple for explanation purposes. However, real–world graphs are often immense and defy easy analysis simply through visualization. Just think about the number of nodes that even a small city would have when considering street intersections (with the links being the streets themselves). Many other graphs are far larger, and simply looking at them will never reveal any interesting patterns. Data scientists call the problem in presenting any complex graph using an adjacency matrix a *hairball.*

One key to analyzing adjacency matrices is to sort them in specific ways. For example, you might choose to sort the data according to properties other than the actual connections. A graph of street connections might include the date the street was last paved with the data, enabling you to look for patterns that direct someone based on the streets that are in the best repair. In short, making the graph data useful becomes a matter of manipulating the organization of that data in specific ways.

Using NetworkX basics

Working with graphs could become difficult if you had to write all the code from scratch. Fortunately, the NetworkX package for Python makes it easy to create, manipulate, and study the structure, dynamics, and functions of complex networks (or graphs). Even though this book covers only graphs, you can use the package to work with digraphs and multigraphs as well.

The main emphasis of NetworkX is to avoid the whole issue of hairballs. The use of simple calls hides much of the complexity of working with graphs and adjacency matrices from view. The following example shows how to create a basic adjacency matrix from one of the NetworkX-supplied graphs:

```
import networkx as nx

G = nx.cycle_graph(10)
A = nx.adjacency_matrix(G)

print(A.todense())
```

The example begins by importing the required package. It then creates a graph using the `cycle_graph()` template. The graph contains ten nodes. Calling `adjacency_matrix()` creates the adjacency matrix from the graph. The final step is to print the output as a matrix, as shown here:

```
[[0 1 0 0 0 0 0 0 0 1]
 [1 0 1 0 0 0 0 0 0 0]
 [0 1 0 1 0 0 0 0 0 0]
 [0 0 1 0 1 0 0 0 0 0]
 [0 0 0 1 0 1 0 0 0 0]
 [0 0 0 0 1 0 1 0 0 0]
 [0 0 0 0 0 1 0 1 0 0]
 [0 0 0 0 0 0 1 0 1 0]
 [0 0 0 0 0 0 0 1 0 1]
 [1 0 0 0 0 0 0 0 1 0]]
```

TIP

You don't have to build your own graph from scratch for testing purposes. The NetworkX site documents a number of standard graph types that you can use, all of which are available within IPython. The list appears at https://networkx.github.io/documentation/latest/reference/generators.html.

It's interesting to see how the graph looks after you generate it. The following code displays the graph for you. Figure 8-1 shows the result of the plot.

```
import matplotlib.pyplot as plt
%matplotlib inline
nx.draw_networkx(G)
plt.show()
```

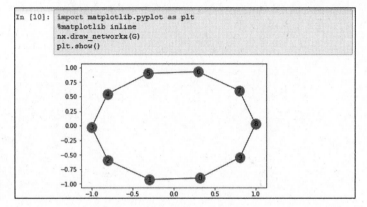

FIGURE 8-1:
Plotting the
original graph.

The plot shows that you can add an edge between nodes 1 and 5. Here's the code needed to perform this task using the add_edge() function. Figure 8-2 shows the result.

```
G.add_edge(1,5)
nx.draw_networkx(G)
plt.show()
```

FIGURE 8-2:
Plotting the
graph addition.

Chapter **9**

Putting What You Know in Action

Previous chapters have all been preparatory in nature. You have discovered how to perform essential data science tasks using Python. In addition, you spent time working with the various tools that Python provides to make data science tasks easier. All this information is essential, but it doesn't help you see the big picture — where all the pieces go. This chapter shows you how to employ the techniques you discovered in previous chapters to solve real data science problems.

REMEMBER

This chapter isn't the end of the journey — it's the beginning. Think of previous chapters in the same way as you think about packing your bags, making reservations, and creating an itinerary before you go on a trip. This chapter is the trip to the airport, during which you start to see everything come together.

The chapter begins by looking at the aspects you normally have to consider when trying to solve a data science problem. You can't just jump in and start performing an analysis; you must understand the problem first, as well as consider the resources (in the form of data, algorithms, computational resources) to solve it. Putting the problem into a context, a setting of a sort, helps you understand the problem and define how the data relates to that problem. The context is essential because, like language, context alters the meaning of both the problem and its associated data. For example, when you say, "I have a red rose" to your significant other, the meaning behind the sentence has one connotation. If you say the same sentence to a fellow gardener, the connotation is different. The red rose is a sort of data and the person you're speaking to is the context. There is no meaning to saying, "I have a red rose." unless you know the context in which the statement is made. Likewise, data has no meaning; it doesn't answer any question until you know the context in which the data is used. Saying "I have data" expresses a question, "What does the data mean?"

In the end, you'll need one or more datasets. Two-dimensional datatables (datasets) consist of *cases* (the rows) and *features* (the columns). You can also refer to features as *variables* when using a statistical terminology. The features you decide to use for any given dataset determine the kinds of analysis you can perform, the ways in which you can manipulate the data, and ultimately the sorts of results you obtain. Determining what sorts of features you can create from source data and how you must transform the data to ensure that it works for the analysis you want to perform is an essential part of developing a data science solution.

After you get a picture of what your problem is, the resources you have to solve it, and the inputs you need to work with to solve it, you're ready to perform some actual work. The last section of this chapter shows you how to perform simple tasks efficiently. You can usually perform tasks using more than one methodology, but when working with big data, the fastest routes are better. By working with arrays and matrices to perform specific tasks, you'll notice that certain operations can take a long time unless you leverage some computational tricks. Using computational tricks is one of the most basic forms of manipulation you perform, but knowing about them from the beginning is essential. Applying these techniques paves the road to later chapters when you start to look at the magic that data science can truly accomplish in helping you see more in the data you have than is nominally apparent.

REMEMBER

You don't have to type the source code for this chapter manually. In fact, it's a lot easier if you use the downloadable source (see the Introduction for download instructions). The source code for this chapter appears in the P4DS4D2_09_ Operations_On_Arrays_and_Matrices.ipynb source code file.

Contextualizing Problems and Data

Putting your problem in the correct context is an essential part of developing a data science solution for any given problem and associated data. Data science is definitively applied science, and abstract manual approaches may not work all that well on your specific situation. Running a Hadoop cluster or building a deep neural network may sound cool in front of fellow colleagues and make you feel you are doing great data science projects, but they may not provide what you need to solve your problem. Putting the problem in the correct context isn't just a matter of deliberating whether to use a certain algorithm or that you must transform the data in a certain way — it's the art of critically examining the problem and the available resources and creating an environment in which to solve the problem and obtain a desired solution.

REMEMBER

The key point here is the *desired* solution, in that you could come up with solutions that aren't desirable because they don't tell you what you need to know — or, even when they do tell you what you need to know, they waste too much time and resources. The following sections provide an overview of the process you follow to contextualize both problems and data.

Evaluating a data science problem

When working through a data science problem, you need to start by considering your goal and the resources you have available for achieving that goal. The resources are data, computational resources such as available memory, CPUs, and disk space. In the real world, no one will hand you ready-made data and tell you to perform a particular analysis on it. Most of the time, you have to face completely new problems, and you have to build your solution from scratch. During your first evaluation of a data science problem, you need to consider the following:

>> **The data available in terms of accessibility, quantity, and quality.** You must also consider the data in terms of possible biases that could influence or even distort its characteristics and content. Data never contains absolute truths, only relative truths that offer you a more or less useful view of a problem (see the "Considering the five mistruths in data" sidebar for details). Always be aware of the truthfulness of data and apply critical reasoning as part of your analysis of it.

>> **The methods you can feasibly use to analyze the dataset.** Consider whether the methods are simple or complex. You must also decide how well you know a particular methodology. Start by using simple approaches, and never fall in love with any particular technique. There are neither free lunches nor Holy Grails in data science.

>> **The questions you want to answer by performing your analysis and how you can quantitatively measure whether you achieved a satisfactory answer to them.** "If you can not measure it, you can not improve it," as Lord Kelvin stated (see https://zapatopi.net/kelvin/quotes/). If you can measure performance, you can determine the impact of your work and even make a monetary estimation. Stakeholders will be delighted to know that you've figured out what to do and what benefits your data science project will bring about.

CONSIDERING THE FIVE MISTRUTHS IN DATA

Humans are used to seeing data for what it is in many cases: an opinion. In fact, in some cases, people skew data to the point where it becomes useless, a *mistruth*. A computer can't tell the difference between truthful and untruthful data; all it sees is data. Consequently, as you perform analysis with data, you must consider the truth value of that data as part of your analysis. The best you can hope to achieve is to see the errant data as outliers and then filter it out, but that technique doesn't necessarily solve the problem because a human would still use the data and attempt to determine a truth based on the mistruths it contains. Here are the five mistruths you commonly find in data (using a car accident reporting process as an illustration):

- **Commission:** Mistruths of commission are those that reflect an outright attempt to substitute truthful information for untruthful information. For example, when filling out an accident report, someone could state that the sun momentarily blinded them, making it impossible to see someone they hit. In reality, perhaps the person was distracted by something else or wasn't actually thinking about driving (possibly considering a nice dinner). If no one can disprove this theory, the person might get by with a lesser charge. However, the point is that the data would also be contaminated.

- **Omission:** Mistruths of omission occur when a person tells the truth in every stated fact but leaves out an important fact that would change the perception of an incident as a whole. Thinking again about the accident report, say that someone strikes a deer, causing significant damage to his car. He truthfully says that the road was wet; it was near twilight so the light wasn't as good as it could be; he was a little late in pressing on the brake; and the deer simply ran out from a thicket at the side of the road. The conclusion would be that the incident is simply an accident. However, the person has left out an important fact. He was texting at the time. If law enforcement knew about the texting, it would change the reason for the accident to inattentive driving. The driver might be fined and the insurance adjuster would use a different reason when entering the incident into the database.

- **Perspective:** Mistruths of perspective occur when multiple parties view an incident from multiple vantage points. For example, in considering an accident involving a struck pedestrian, the person driving the car, the person getting hit by the car, and a bystander who witnessed the event would all have different perspectives. An officer taking reports from each person would understandably get different facts from each one, even assuming that each person tells the truth as each knows it. In fact, experience shows that this is almost always the case, and what the officer submits as a report is the middle ground of what each of those involved state, augmented by personal experience. In other words, the report will be close to the truth, but not completely true. When dealing with perspective, it's important to consider vantage point. The driver of the car can see the dashboard and knows the car's condition at the time of the accident. This is information that the other two parties lack. Likewise, the person getting hit by the car has the best vantage point for seeing the driver's facial expression (intent). The bystander might be in the best position to see whether the driver made an attempt to stop, and assess issues such as whether the driver tried to swerve. Each party will have to make a report based on seen data without the benefit of hidden data.

- **Bias:** Mistruths of bias occur when someone is able to see the truth, but personal concerns or beliefs distort or obscure that vision. For example, when thinking about an accident, a driver might focus attention so completely on the middle of the road that the deer at the edge of the road becomes virtually invisible. Consequently, the driver has no time to react when the deer suddenly decides to bolt out into the middle of the road in an effort to cross. A problem with bias is that it can be incredibly hard to categorize. For example, a driver who fails to see the deer can have a genuine accident, meaning that the deer was hidden from view by shrubbery. However, the driver might also be guilty of inattentive driving because of incorrect focus. The driver might also experience a momentary distraction. In short, the fact that the driver didn't see the deer isn't the question; instead, it's a matter of why the driver didn't see the deer. In many cases, confirming the source of bias becomes important when creating an algorithm designed to avoid a bias source.

- **Frame of reference:** Of the five mistruths, frame of reference need not actually be the result of any sort of error, but one of understanding. A frame-of-reference mistruth occurs when one party describes something, such as an event like an accident, and the second party's lack of experience with the event makes the details muddled or completely misunderstood. Comedy routines abound that rely on frame-of-reference errors. One famous example is from Abbott and Costello, *Who's On First?*, as shown at https://www.youtube.com/watch?v=kTcRRaXV-fg. Getting one person to understand what a second person is saying can be impossible when the first person lacks experiential knowledge — the frame of reference.

Researching solutions

Data science is a complex system of knowledge at the intersection of computer science, math, statistics, and business. Very few people can know everything about it, and, if someone has already faced the same problem or dilemmas as you face, reinventing the wheel makes little sense. Now that you have contextualized your project, you know what you're looking for and you can search for it in different ways.

» **Check the Python documentation.** You might be able to find examples that suggest a possible solution. NumPy (https://docs.scipy.org/doc/numpy/user/), SciPy (https://docs.scipy.org/doc/), pandas (https://pandas.pydata.org/pandas-docs/version/0.23.2/), and especially Scikit-learn (https://scikit-learn.org/stable/user_guide.html) have detailed in-line and online documentation with plenty of data science–related examples.

» **Seek out online articles and blogs that hint at how other practitioners solved similar problems.** Q&A websites such as Quora (https://www.quora.com/), Stack Overflow (https://stackoverflow.com/), and Cross Validated (https://stats.stackexchange.com/) can provide you with plenty of answers to similar problems.

» **Consult academic papers.** For example, you can query your problem on Google Scholar at https://scholar.google.it/ or Microsoft Academic Search at https://academic.microsoft.com/. You can find a series of scientific papers that can tell you about preparing the data or detail the kind of algorithms that work better for a particular problem.

REMEMBER

It may seem trivial, but the solutions you create have to reflect the problem you're trying to solve. As you research solutions, you may find that some of them seem promising at first, but then you can't successfully apply them to your case because something in their context is different. For instance, your dataset may be incomplete or may not provide enough input to solve the problem. In addition, the analysis model you select may not actually provide the answer you need or the answer might prove inaccurate. As you work through the problem, don't be afraid to perform your research multiple times as you discover, test, and evaluate possible solutions that you could apply given the resources available and your actual constraints.

Formulating a hypothesis

At some point, you have everything you think you need to solve the problem. Of course, it's a mistake to assume now that the solutions you create can actually solve the problem. You have a hypothesis, rather than a solution, because you have to demonstrate the efficacy of the potential solution in a scientific way. In order to form and test a hypothesis, you must train a model using a training dataset and then test it using an entirely different dataset. Later chapters in the book spend a great deal of time helping you through the process of training and testing the algorithms used to perform analysis, so don't worry too much if you don't understand this aspect of the process right now.

Preparing your data

After you have some idea of the problem and its solution, you know the inputs required to make the algorithm work. Unfortunately, your data probably appears in multiple forms, you get it from multiple sources, and some data is missing entirely. Moreover, the developers of the features that existing data sources provide may have devised them for different purposes (such as accounting or marketing) than yours and you have to transform them so that you can use your algorithm at its fullest power. To make the algorithm work, you must prepare the data. This means checking for missing data, creating new features as needed, and possibly manipulating the dataset to get it into a form that your algorithm can actually use to make a prediction.

Considering the Art of Feature Creation

Features have to do with the columns in your dataset. Of course, you need to determine what those columns should contain. They might not end up looking precisely like the data in the original data source. The original data source may present the data in a form that leads to inaccurate analysis or even prevent you from getting a desired outcome because it's not completely suited to your algorithm or your objectives. For example, the data may contain too much information redundancy inside multiple variables, which is a problem called *multivariate correlation*. The task of making the columns work in the best manner for data analysis purposes is *feature creation* (also called feature engineering). The following sections help you understand feature creation and why it's important. (Future chapters provide all sorts of examples of how you actually employ feature creation to perform analysis.)

Defining feature creation

Feature creation may seem a bit like magic or weird science to some people, but it really does have a firm basis in math. The task is to take existing data and transform it into something that you can work with to perform an analysis. For example, numeric data could appear as strings in the original data source. To perform an analysis, you must convert the string data to numeric values in many cases. The immediate goal of feature creation is to achieve better performance from the algorithms used to accomplish the analysis than you can when using the original data.

In many cases, the transformation is less than straightforward. You may have to combine values in some way or perform math operations on them. The information you can access may appear in all sorts of forms, and the transformation process lets you work with the data in new ways so that you can see patterns in it. For example, consider this popular Kaggle competition: `https://www.kaggle.com/c/march-machine-learning-mania-2015`. The goal is to use all sorts of statistics to determine who will win the NCAA Basketball Tournament. Imagine trying to derive disparate measures from public information on a match, such as the geographic location the team will travel to or the unavailability of key players, and you can begin to grasp the need to create features in a dataset.

REMEMBER

As you might imagine, feature creation truly is an art form, and everyone has an opinion on precisely how to perform it. This book provides you with some good basic information on feature creation as well as a number of examples, but it leaves advanced techniques to experimentation and trial. As Pedro Domingos, professor at Washington University, stated in his Data Science paper, "A Few Useful Things to Know about Machine Learning" (see `https://homes.cs.washington.edu/~pedrod/papers/cacm12.pdf`), feature engineering is "easily the most important factor" in determining the success or failure of a machine-learning project, and nothing can really replace the "smarts you put into feature engineering."

Combining variables

Data often comes in a form that doesn't work at all for an algorithm. Consider a simple real-life situation in which you need to determine whether one person can lift a board at a lumber yard. You receive two datatables. The first contains the height, width, thickness, and wood types of boards. The second contains a list of wood types and the amount they weigh per board foot (a piece of wood 12" x 12" x 1"). Not every wood type comes in every size, and some shipments come unmarked, so you don't actually know what type of wood you're working with. The goal is to create a prediction so that the company knows how many people to send to work with the shipments.

In this case, you create a two-dimensional dataset by combining variables. The resulting dataset contains only two features. The first feature contains just the length of the boards. It's reasonable to expect a single person to carry a board that is up to ten feet long, but you want two people carrying a board ten feet or longer. The second feature is the weight of the board. A board that is 10 feet long, 12 inches wide, and 2 inches thick contains 20 board feet. If the board is made of ponderosa pine (with a board foot rating, BFR, of 2.67), the overall weight of the board is 53.4 pounds — one person could probably lift it. However, when the board is made of hickory (with a BFR of 4.25), the overall weight is now 85 pounds. Unless you have the Hulk working for you, you really do need two people lifting that board, even though the board is short enough for one person to lift.

Getting the first feature for your dataset is easy. All you need is the lengths of each of the boards that you stock. However, the second feature requires that you combine variables from both tables:

```
Length (feet) * Width (feet) * Thickness (inches) * BFR
```

The resulting dataset will contain the weight for each length of each kind of wood you stock. Having this information means that you can create a model that predicts whether a particular task will require one, two, or even three people to perform.

Understanding binning and discretization

In order to perform some types of analysis, you need to break numeric values into classes. For example, you might have a dataset that includes entries for people from ages 0 to 80. To derive statistics that work in this case (such as running the Naïve Bayes algorithm), you might want to view the variable as a series of levels in ten-year increments. The process of breaking the dataset up into these ten-year increments is *binning*. Each bin is a numeric category that you can use.

Binning may improve the accuracy of predictive models by reducing noise or by helping model nonlinearity. In addition, it allows easy identification of *outliers* (values outside the expected range) and invalid or missing values of numerical variables.

Binning works exclusively with single numeric features. *Discretization* is a more complex process, in which you place combinations of values from different features in a bucket — limiting the number of states in any given bucket. In contrast to binning, discretization works with both numeric and string values. It's a more generalized method of creating categories. For example, you can obtain a discretization as a byproduct of cluster analysis.

Using indicator variables

Indicator variables are features that can take on a value of 0 or 1. Another name for indicator variables is dummy variables. No matter what you call them, these variables serve an important purpose in making data easier to work with. For example, if you want to create a dataset in which individuals under 25 are treated one way and individuals 25 and over are treated another, you could replace the age feature with an indicator variable that contains a 0 when the individual is under 25 or a 1 when the individual is 25 and older.

TIP

Using an indicator variable lets you perform analysis faster and categorize cases with greater accuracy than you can without this variable. The indicator variable removes shades of gray from the dataset. Someone is either under 25 or 25 and older — there is no middle ground. Because the data is simplified, the algorithm can perform its task faster, and you have less ambiguity to contend with.

Transforming distributions

A *distribution* is an arrangement of the values of a variable that shows the frequency at which various values occur. After you know how the values are distributed, you can begin to understand the data better. All sorts of distributions exist (see a gallery of distributions at `https://www.itl.nist.gov/div898/handbook/eda/section3/eda366.htm`), and most algorithms can easily deal with them. However, you must match the algorithm to the distribution.

WARNING

Pay particular attention to uniform and skewed distributions. They are quite difficult to deal with for different reasons. The bell-shaped curve, the normal distribution, is always your friend. When you see a distribution shaped differently from a bell distribution, you should think about performing a transformation.

When working with distributions, you might find that the distribution of values is skewed in some way and that, because of the skewed values, any algorithm applied to the set of values produces output that simply won't match your expectations. Transforming a distribution means to apply some sort of function to the values in order to achieve specific objectives, such as fixing the data skew, so that the output of your algorithm is closer to what you expected. In addition, transformation helps make the distribution friendlier, such as when you transform a dataset to appear as a normal distribution. Transformations that you should always try on your numeric features are

>> Logarithm np.log(x) and exponential np.exp(x)

>> Inverse 1/x, square root np.sqrt(x), and cube root x**(1.0/3.0)

>> Polynomial transformations such as, x**2, x**3, and so on

Performing Operations on Arrays

A basic form of data manipulation is to place the data in an array or matrix and then use standard math-based techniques to modify its form. Using this approach puts the data in a convenient form to perform other operations done at the level of every single observation, such as in iterations, because they can leverage your computer architecture and some highly optimized numerical linear algebra routines present in CPUs. These routines are callable from every operating system. The larger the data and the computations, the more time you can save. In addition, using these techniques also spare you writing long and complex Python code. The following sections describe how to work with arrays for data science purposes.

Using vectorization

Your computer provides you with powerful routine calculations, and you can use them when your data is in the right format. NumPy's ndarray is a multidimensional data storage structure that you can use as a dimensional datatable. In fact, you can use it as a cube or even a hypercube when there are more than three dimensions.

Using ndarray makes computations easy and fast. The following example creates a dataset of three observations with seven features for each observation. In this case, the example obtains the maximum value for each observation and subtracts it from the minimum value to obtain the range of values for each observation.

```
import numpy as np
dataset = np.array([[2, 4, 6, 8, 3, 2, 5],
                    [7, 5, 3, 1, 6, 8, 0],
                    [1, 3, 2, 1, 0, 0, 8]])
print(np.max(dataset, axis=1) - np.min(dataset, axis=1))
```

The print statement obtains the maximum value from each observation using np.max() and then subtracts it from the minimum value using np.min(). The maximum value in each observation is [8 8 8]. The minimum value for each observation is [2 0 0]. As a result, you get the following output:

```
[6 8 8]
```

Performing simple arithmetic on vectors and matrices

Most operations and functions from NumPy that you apply to arrays leverage vectorization, so they're fast and efficient — much more efficient than any other solution or handmade code. Even the simplest operations such as additions or divisions can take advantage of vectorization.

For instance, many times, the form of the data in your dataset won't quite match the form you need. A list of numbers could represent percentages as whole numbers when you really need them as fractional values. In this case, you can usually perform some type of simple math to solve the problem, as shown here:

```
import numpy as np
a = np.array([15.0, 20.0, 22.0, 75.0, 40.0, 35.0])
a = a*.01
print(a)
```

The example creates an array, fills it with whole number percentages, and then uses 0.01 as a multiplier to create fractional percentages. You can then multiply these fractional values against other numbers to determine how the percentage affects that number. The output from this example is

```
[0.15 0.2 0.22 0.75 0.4 0.35]
```

Performing matrix vector multiplication

The most efficient vectorization operations are matrix manipulations in which you add and multiply multiple values against other multiple values. NumPy makes performing multiplication of a vector by a matrix easy, which is handy if you have to estimate a value for each observation as a weighted summation of the features. Here's an example of this technique:

```
import numpy as np
a = np.array([2, 4, 6, 8])
b = np.array([[1, 2, 3, 4],
              [2, 3, 4, 5],
              [3, 4, 5, 6],
              [4, 5, 6, 7]])
c = np.dot(a, b)
print(c)
```

Notice that the array formatted as a vector must appear before the array formatted as a matrix in the multiplication or you get an error. The example outputs these values:

```
[60 80 100 120]
```

To obtain the values shown, you multiply every value in the array against the matching column in the matrix; that is, you multiply the first value in the array against the first column, first row of the matrix. For example, the first value in the output is 2 * 1 + 4 * 2 + 6 * 3 + 8 * 4, which equals 60.

Performing matrix multiplication

You can also multiply one matrix against another. In this case, the output is the result of multiplying rows in the first matrix against columns in the second matrix. Here is an example of how you multiply one NumPy matrix against another:

```
import numpy as np

a = np.array([[2, 4, 6, 8],
              [1, 3, 5, 7]])
b = np.array ([[1, 2],
               [2, 3],
               [3, 4],
               [4, 5]])
c = np.dot(a, b)
print(c)
```

In this case, you end up with a 2 x 2 matrix as output. Here are the values you should see when you run the application:

```
[[60 80]
 [50 66]]
```

Each row in the first matrix is multiplied by each column of the second matrix. For example, to get the value 50 shown in row 2, column 1 of the output, you match up the values in row two of matrix a with column 1 of matrix b, like this: $1 * 1 + 3 * 2 + 5 * 3 + 7 * 4$.

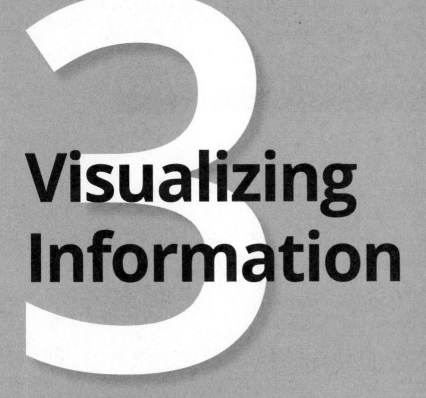

3

Visualizing Information

Chapter **10**

Getting a Crash Course in MatPlotLib

Most people visualize information better when they see it in graphic, versus textual, format. Graphics help people see relationships and make comparisons with greater ease. Even if you can deal with the abstraction of textual data with ease, performing data analysis is all about communication. Unless you can communicate your ideas to other people, the act of obtaining, shaping, and analyzing the data has little value beyond your own personal needs. Fortunately, Python makes the task of converting your textual data into graphics relatively easy using MatPlotLib, which is actually a simulation of the MATLAB application. You can see a comparison of the two at https://pyzo.org/python_vs_matlab.html.

TIP

If you already know how to use MATLAB (see *MATLAB For Dummies*, by John Paul Mueller [Wiley]), if you'd like to learn), moving over to MatPlotLib is relatively easy because they both use the same sort of state machine to perform tasks and they have a similar method of defining graphic elements. A number of people feel that MatPlotLib is superior to MATLAB because you can do things like perform tasks using less code when working with MatPlotLib than when using MATLAB (see https://phillipmfeldman.org/Python/Advantages_of_Python_Over_Matlab.html). Others have noted that the transition from MATLAB to

MatPlotLib is relatively straightforward (see `https://vnoel.wordpress.com/2008/05/03/bye-matlab-hello-python-thanks-sage/`). However, what matters most is what you think. You may find that you like to experiment with data using MATLAB and then create applications based on your findings using Python with MatPlotLib. It's a matter of personal taste rather than one of a strict correct answer.

This chapter focuses on getting you up to speed quickly with MatPlotLib. You do use MatPlotLib quite a few times later in the book, so this short overview of how it works is important, even if you already know how to work with MATLAB. That said, the MATLAB experience will be incredibly helpful as you progress through the chapter, and you may find that you can simply skim through some sections. Make sure to keep this chapter in mind as you start working with MatPlotLib in more detail later in the book.

REMEMBER

You don't have to type the source code for this chapter manually. In fact, it's a lot easier if you use the downloadable source code. The source code for this chapter appears in the `P4DS4D2_10_Getting_a_Crash_Course_in_MatPlotLib.ipynb` source code file (see the Introduction for where to find this code).

Starting with a Graph

A graph or chart is simply a visual representation of numeric data. MatPlotLib makes a large number of graph and chart types available to you. Of course, you can choose any of the common graph and graph types such as bar charts, line graphs, or pie charts. As with MATLAB, you also have access to a huge number of statistical plot types, such as boxplots, error bar charts, and histograms. You can see a gallery of the various graph types that MatPlotLib supports at `https://matplotlib.org/gallery.html`. However, it's important to remember that you can combine graphic elements in an almost infinite number of ways to create your own presentation of data no matter how complex that data might be. The following sections describe how to create a basic graph, but remember that you have access to a lot more functionality than these sections tell you about.

Defining the plot

Plots show graphically what you've defined numerically. To define a plot, you need some values, the `matplotlib.pyplot` module, and an idea of what you want to display, as shown in the following code.

```
import matplotlib.pyplot as plt
%matplotlib inline

values = [1, 5, 8, 9, 2, 0, 3, 10, 4, 7]
plt.plot(range(1,11), values)
plt.show()
```

In this case, the code tells the plt.plot() function to create a plot using x-axis values between 1 and 11 and y-axis values as they appear in values. Calling plot. show() displays the plot in a separate dialog box, as shown in Figure 10-1. Notice that the output is a line graph. Chapter 11 shows you how to create other chart and graph types.

FIGURE 10-1:
Creating a basic plot that shows just one line.

Drawing multiple lines and plots

You encounter many situations in which you must use multiple plot lines, such as when comparing two sets of values. To create such plots using MatPlotLib, you simply call plt.plot() multiple times — once for each plot line, as shown in the following example.

```
import matplotlib.pyplot as plt
%matplotlib inline

values = [1, 5, 8, 9, 2, 0, 3, 10, 4, 7]
values2 = [3, 8, 9, 2, 1, 2, 4, 7, 6, 6]
plt.plot(range(1,11), values)
plt.plot(range(1,11), values2)
plt.show()
```

When you run this example, you see two plot lines, as shown in Figure 10-2. Even though you can't see it in the printed book, the line graphs are different colors so that you can tell them apart.

```
In [2]:  import matplotlib.pyplot as plt
         %matplotlib inline

         values = [1, 5, 8, 9, 2, 0, 3, 10, 4, 7]
         values2 = [3, 8, 9, 2, 1, 2, 4, 7, 6, 6]
         plt.plot(range(1,11), values)
         plt.plot(range(1,11), values2)
         plt.show()
```

FIGURE 10-2:
Defining a plot that contains multiple lines.

Saving your work to disk

Jupyter Notebook makes it easy to include your graphs within the notebooks you create, so that you can define reports that everyone can easily understand. When you do need to save a copy of your work to disk for later reference or to use it as part of a larger report, you save the graphic programmatically using the plt.savefig() function, as shown in the following code:

```
import matplotlib.pyplot as plt
%matplotlib auto


values = [1, 5, 8, 9, 2, 0, 3, 10, 4, 7]
plt.plot(range(1,11), values)
plt.ioff()
plt.savefig('MySamplePlot.png', format='png')
```

In this case, you must provide a minimum of two inputs. The first input is the filename. You may optionally include a path for saving the file. The second input is the file format. In this case, the example saves the file in Portable Network Graphic (PNG) format, but you have other options: Portable Document Format (PDF), Postscript (PS), Encapsulated Postscript (EPS), and Scalable Vector Graphics (SVG).

Note the presence of the `%matplotlib auto` magic in this case. Using this call removes the inline display of the graph. You do have options for other MatPlotLib backends, depending on which version of Python and MatPlotLib you use. For example, some developers prefer the `notebook` backend to the `inline` backend because it provides additional functionality. However, to use the `notebook` backend, you must also restart the kernel, and you may not always see what you expect. To see the backend list, use the `%matplotlib -l` magic. In addition, calling `plt.ioff()` turns plot interaction off.

Setting the Axis, Ticks, Grids

It's hard to know what the data actually means unless you provide a unit of measure or at least some means of performing comparisons. The use of axes, ticks, and grids make it possible to illustrate graphically the relative size of data elements so that the viewer gains an appreciation of comparative measure. You won't use these features with every graphic, and you may employ the features differently based on viewer needs, but it's important to know that these features exist and how you can use them to help document your data within the graphic environment.

The following examples use the `%matplotlib notebook` magic so that you can see the difference between it and the `%matplotlib inline` magic. The two inline displays rely on a different graphic engine. Consequently, you must choose Kernel⇨Restart to restart the kernel before you run any of the examples in the sections that follow.

Getting the axes

The axes define the x and y plane of the graphic. The x axis runs horizontally, and the y axis runs vertically. In many cases, you can allow MatPlotLib to perform any required formatting for you. However, sometimes you need to obtain access to the axes and format them manually. The following code shows how to obtain access to the axes for a plot:

```
import matplotlib.pyplot as plt
%matplotlib notebook

values = [0, 5, 8, 9, 2, 0, 3, 10, 4, 7]
ax = plt.axes()
plt.plot(range(1,11), values)
plt.show()
```

The reason you place the axes in a variable, ax, instead of manipulating them directly is to make writing the code simpler and more efficient. In this case, you simply turn on the default axes by calling plt.axes(); then you place a handle to the axes in ax. A *handle* is a sort of pointer to the axes. Think of it as you would a frying pan. You wouldn't lift the frying pan directly but would instead use its handle when picking it up.

Formatting the axes

Simply displaying the axes won't be enough in many cases. You want to change the way MatPlotLib displays them. For example, you may not want the highest value t to reach to the top of the graph. The following example shows just a small number of tasks you can perform after you have access to the axes:

```
import matplotlib.pyplot as plt
%matplotlib notebook

values = [0, 5, 8, 9, 2, 0, 3, 10, 4, 7]
ax = plt.axes()
ax.set_xlim([0, 11])
ax.set_ylim([-1, 11])
ax.set_xticks([1, 2, 3, 4, 5, 6, 7, 8, 9, 10])
ax.set_yticks([0, 1, 2, 3, 4, 5, 6, 7, 8, 9, 10])
plt.plot(range(1,11), values)
plt.show()
```

In this case, the set_xlim() and set_ylim() calls change the axes limits — the length of each axis. The set_xticks() and set_yticks() calls change the ticks used to display data. The ways in which you can change a graph using these calls can become quite detailed. For example, you can choose to change individual tick labels if you want. Figure 10-3 shows the output from this example. Notice how the changes affect how the line graph displays.

TECHNICAL
STUFF

As you can see by viewing the differences between Figures 10-1, 10-2, and 10-3, the %matplotlib notebook magic produces a significantly different display. The controls at the bottom of the display let you pan and zoom the display, move between views you've created, and download the figure to disk. The button to the right of the Figure 1 heading in Figure 10-3 lets you stop interacting with the graph after you've finished working with it. Any changes you've made to the presentation of the graph remain afterward so that anyone looking at your notebook will see the graph in the manner you intended for them to see it. The ability to interact with the graph ends when you display another graph.

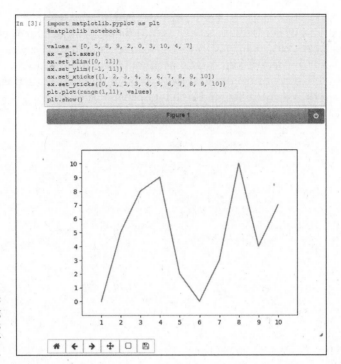

FIGURE 10-3:
Specifying how the axes should appear to the viewer.

Adding grids

Grid lines enable you to see the precise value of each element of a graph. You can more quickly determine both the x and y coordinates, which allow you to perform comparisons of individual points with greater ease. Of course, grids also add noise and make seeing the actual flow of data harder. The point is that you can use grids to good effect to create particular effects. The following code shows how to add a grid to the graph in the previous section:

```python
import matplotlib.pyplot as plt
%matplotlib notebook

values = [0, 5, 8, 9, 2, 0, 3, 10, 4, 7]
ax = plt.axes()
ax.set_xlim([0, 11])
ax.set_ylim([-1, 11])
ax.set_xticks([1, 2, 3, 4, 5, 6, 7, 8, 9, 10])
ax.set_yticks([0, 1, 2, 3, 4, 5, 6, 7, 8, 9, 10])
ax.grid()
plt.plot(range(1,11), values)
plt.show()
```

All you really need to do is call the grid() function. As with many other MatPlotLib functions, you can add parameters to create the grid precisely as you want to see it. For example, you can choose whether to add the x grid lines, y grid lines, or both. The output from this example appears in Figure 10-4. In this case, the figure shows the notebook backend with interaction turned off.

```
In [4]:  import matplotlib.pyplot as plt
         %matplotlib notebook

         values = [0, 5, 8, 9, 2, 0, 3, 10, 4, 7]
         ax = plt.axes()
         ax.set_xlim([0, 11])
         ax.set_ylim([-1, 11])
         ax.set_xticks([1, 2, 3, 4, 5, 6, 7, 8, 9, 10])
         ax.set_yticks([0, 1, 2, 3, 4, 5, 6, 7, 8, 9, 10])
         ax.grid()
         plt.plot(range(1,11), values)
         plt.show()
```

FIGURE 10-4:
Adding grids makes the values easier to read.

Defining the Line Appearance

Just drawing lines on a page won't do much for you if you need to help the viewer understand the importance of your data. In most cases, you need to use different line styles to ensure that the viewer can tell one data grouping from another. However, to emphasize the importance or value of a particular data grouping, you need to employ color. The use of color communicates all sorts of ideas to the viewer. For example, green often denotes that something is safe, while red communicates danger. The following sections help you understand how to work with line style and color to communicate ideas and concepts to the viewer without using any text.

MAKING GRAPHICS ACCESSIBLE

Avoiding assumptions about someone's ability to see your graphic presentation is essential. For example, someone who is color blind may not be able to tell that one line is green and the other red. Likewise, someone with low-vision problems may not be able to distinguish between a line that is dashed and one that has a combination of dashes and dots. Using multiple methods to distinguish each line helps ensure that everyone can see your data in a manner that is comfortable to each person.

Working with line styles

Line styles help differentiate graphs by drawing the lines in various ways. Using a unique presentation for each line helps you distinguish each line so that you can call it out (even when the printout is in shades of gray). You could also call out a particular line graph by using a different line style for it (and using the same style for the other lines). Table 10-1 shows the various MatPlotLib line styles.

TABLE 10-1 ### MatPlotLib Line Styles

Character	Line Style
'-'	Solid line
'--'	Dashed line
'-.'	Dash-dot line
':'	Dotted line

The line style appears as a third argument to the plot() function call. You simply provide the desired string for the line type, as shown in the following example.

```
import matplotlib.pyplot as plt
%matplotlib inline

values = [1, 5, 8, 9, 2, 0, 3, 10, 4, 7]
values2 = [3, 8, 9, 2, 1, 2, 4, 7, 6, 6]
plt.plot(range(1,11), values, '--')
plt.plot(range(1,11), values2, ':')
plt.show()
```

In this case, the first line graph uses a dashed line style, while the second line graph uses a dotted line style. You can see the results of the changes in Figure 10-5.

```
In [1]: import matplotlib.pyplot as plt
        %matplotlib inline

        values = [1, 5, 8, 9, 2, 0, 3, 10, 4, 7]
        values2 = [3, 8, 9, 2, 1, 2, 4, 7, 6, 6]
        plt.plot(range(1,11), values, '--')
        plt.plot(range(1,11), values2, ':')
        plt.show()
```

FIGURE 10-5:
Line styles help
differentiate
between plots.

Using colors

Color is another way in which to differentiate line graphs. Of course, this method has certain problems. The most significant problem occurs when someone makes a black-and-white copy of your colored graph — hiding the color differences as shades of gray. Another problem is that someone with color blindness may not be able to tell one line from the other. All this said, color does make for a brighter, eye-grabbing presentation. Table 10-2 shows the colors that MatPlotLib supports.

TABLE 10-2

MatPlotLib Colors

Character	Color
'b'	Blue
'g'	Green
'r'	Red
'c'	Cyan
'm'	Magenta
'y'	Yellow
'k'	Black
'w'	White

As with line styles, the color appears in a string as the third argument to the `plot()` function call. In this case, the viewer sees two lines — one in red and the other in magenta. The actual presentation looks like Figure 10-2, shown previously, but with specific colors, rather than the default colors used in that screenshot. If you're reading the printed version of the book, Figure 10-2 actually uses shades of gray.

```
import matplotlib.pyplot as plt
%matplotlib inline

values = [1, 5, 8, 9, 2, 0, 3, 10, 4, 7]
values2 = [3, 8, 9, 2, 1, 2, 4, 7, 6, 6]
plt.plot(range(1,11), values, 'r')
plt.plot(range(1,11), values2, 'm')
plt.show()
```

Adding markers

Markers add a special symbol to each data point in a line graph. Unlike line style and color, markers tend to be a little less susceptible to accessibility and printing issues. Even when the specific marker isn't clear, people can usually differentiate one marker from the other. Table 10-3 shows the list of markers that MatPlotLib provides.

TABLE 10-3   **MatPlotLib Markers**

Character	Marker Type
'.'	Point
','	Pixel
'o'	Circle
'v'	Triangle 1 down
'^'	Triangle 1 up
'<'	Triangle 1 left
'>'	Triangle 1 right
'1'	Triangle 2 down

(continued)

TABLE 10-3 *(continued)*

Character	Marker Type
'2'	Triangle 2 up
'3'	Triangle 2 left
'4'	Triangle 2 right
's'	Square
'p'	Pentagon
'*'	Star
'h'	Hexagon style 1
'H'	Hexagon style 2
'+'	Plus
'x'	X
'D'	Diamond
'd'	Thin diamond
'|'	Vertical line
'_'	Horizontal line

As with line style and color, you add markers as the third argument to a `plot()` call. In the following example, you see the effects of combining line style with a marker to provide a unique line graph presentation.

```
import matplotlib.pyplot as plt
%matplotlib inline

values = [1, 5, 8, 9, 2, 0, 3, 10, 4, 7]
values2 = [3, 8, 9, 2, 1, 2, 4, 7, 6, 6]
plt.plot(range(1,11), values, 'o--')
plt.plot(range(1,11), values2, 'v:')
plt.show()
```

Notice how the combination of line style and marker makes each line stand out in Figure 10-6. Even when printed in black and white, you can easily differentiate one line from the other, which is why you usually want to combine presentation techniques.

```
In [3]: import matplotlib.pyplot as plt
        %matplotlib inline

        values = [1, 5, 8, 9, 2, 0, 3, 10, 4, 7]
        values2 = [3, 8, 9, 2, 1, 2, 4, 7, 6, 6]
        plt.plot(range(1,11), values, 'o--')
        plt.plot(range(1,11), values2, 'v:')
        plt.show()
```

FIGURE 10-6:
Markers help
to emphasize
individual values.

Using Labels, Annotations, and Legends

To fully document your graph, you usually have to resort to labels, annotations, and legends. Each of these elements has a different purpose, as follows:

>> **Label:** Provides positive identification of a particular data element or grouping. The purpose is to make it easy for the viewer to know the name or kind of data illustrated.

>> **Annotation:** Augments the information the viewer can immediately see about the data with notes, sources, or other useful information. In contrast to a label, the purpose of annotation is to help extend the viewer's knowledge of the data rather than simply identify it.

>> **Legend:** Presents a listing of the data groups within the graph and often provides cues (such as line type or color) to make identification of the data group easier. For example, all the red points may belong to group A, while all the blue points may belong to group B.

The following sections help you understand the purpose and usage of various documentation aids provided with MatPlotLib. These documentation aids help you create an environment in which the viewer is certain as to the source, purpose, and usage of data elements. Some graphs work just fine without any documentation aids, but in other cases, you might find that you need to use all three in order to communicate with your viewer fully.

Adding labels

Labels help people understand the significance of each axis of any graph you create. Without labels, the values portrayed don't have any significance. In addition to a moniker, such as rainfall, you can also add units of measure, such as inches or centimeters, so that your audience knows how to interpret the data shown. The following example shows how to add labels to your graph:

```
import matplotlib.pyplot as plt
%matplotlib inline

values = [1, 5, 8, 9, 2, 0, 3, 10, 4, 7]
plt.xlabel('Entries')
plt.ylabel('Values')
plt.plot(range(1,11), values)
plt.show()
```

The call to xlabel() documents the x axis of your graph, while the call the ylabel() documents the y axis of your graph. Figure 10-7 shows the output of this example.

FIGURE 10-7:
Use labels to
identify the axes.

Annotating the chart

You use annotation to draw special attention to points of interest on a graph. For example, you may want to point out that a specific data point is outside the usual range expected for a particular dataset. The following example shows how to add annotation to a graph.

```
import matplotlib.pyplot as plt
%matplotlib inline

values = [1, 5, 8, 9, 2, 0, 3, 10, 4, 7]
plt.annotate(xy=[1,1], s='First Entry')
plt.plot(range(1,11), values)
plt.show()
```

The call to annotate() provides the labeling you need. You must provide a location for the annotation by using the xy parameter, as well as provide text to place at the location by using the s parameter. The annotate() function also provides other parameters that you can use to create special formatting or placement onscreen. Figure 10-8 shows the output from this example.

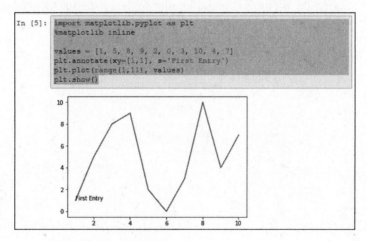

FIGURE 10-8: Annotation can identify points of interest.

Creating a legend

A legend documents the individual elements of a plot. Each line is presented in a table that contains a label for it so that people can differentiate between each line. For example, one line may represent sales in 2017 and another line may represent sales in 2018, so you include an entry in the legend for each line that is labeled 2017 and 2018. The following example shows how to add a legend to your plot.

```
import matplotlib.pyplot as plt
%matplotlib inline

values = [1, 5, 8, 9, 2, 0, 3, 10, 4, 7]
values2 = [3, 8, 9, 2, 1, 2, 4, 7, 6, 6]
```

```
line1 = plt.plot(range(1,11), values)
line2 = plt.plot(range(1,11), values2)
plt.legend(['First', 'Second'], loc=4)
plt.show()
```

The call to legend() occurs after you create the plots, not before, as with some of the other functions described in this chapter. You must provide a handle to each of the plots. Notice how line1 is set equal to the first plot() call and line2 is set equal to the second plot() call.

TIP

The default location for the legend is the upper-right corner of the plot, which proved inconvenient for this particular example. Adding the loc parameter lets you place the legend in a different location. See the legend() function documentation at https://matplotlib.org/api/pyplot_api.html#matplotlib.pyplot.legend for additional legend locations. Figure 10-9 shows the output from this example.

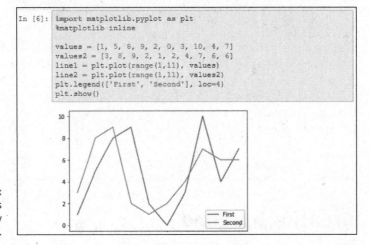

FIGURE 10-9:
Use legends to identify individual lines.

Chapter **11**

Visualizing the Data

Chapter 10 helped you understand the mechanics of working with MatPlotLib, which is an important first step toward using it. This chapter takes the next step in helping you use MatPlotLib to perform useful work. The main goal of this chapter is to help you visualize your data in various ways. Creating a graphic presentation of your data is essential if you want to help other people understand what you're trying to say. Even though you can see what the numbers mean in your mind, other people will likely need graphics to see what point you're trying to make by manipulating data in various ways.

The chapter starts by looking at some basic graph types that MatPlotLib supports. You don't find the full list of graphs and plots listed in this chapter — it could take an entire book to explore them all in detail. However, you do find the most common types.

In the remainder of the chapter, you begin exploring specific sorts of plotting as it relates to data science. Of course, no book on data science would be complete without exploring scatterplots, which are used to help people see patterns in seemingly unrelated data points. Because much of the data that you work with today is time related or geographic in nature, the chapter devotes two special sections to these topics. You also get to work with both directed and undirected graphs, which is fine for social media analysis.

REMEMBER

You don't have to type the source code for this chapter manually. In fact, it's a lot easier if you use the downloadable source. The source code for this chapter appears in the P4DS4D2_11_Visualizing_the_Data.ipynb source code file (see the Introduction for details on how to find that source file).

Choosing the Right Graph

The kind of graph you choose determines how people view the associated data, so choosing the right graph from the outset is important. For example, if you want to show how various data elements contribute toward a whole, you really need to use a pie chart. On the other hand, when you want people to form opinions on how data elements compare, you use a bar chart. The idea is to choose a graph that naturally leads people to draw the conclusion that you need them to draw about the data that you've carefully massaged from various data sources. (You also have the option of using line graphs — a technique demonstrated in Chapter 10.) The following sections describe the various graph types and provide you with basic examples of how to use them.

Showing parts of a whole with pie charts

Pie charts focus on showing parts of a whole. The entire pie would be 100 percent. The question is how much of that percentage each value occupies. The following example shows how to create a pie chart with many of the special features in place:

```
import matplotlib.pyplot as plt
%matplotlib inline

values = [5, 8, 9, 10, 4, 7]
colors = ['b', 'g', 'r', 'c', 'm', 'y']
labels = ['A', 'B', 'C', 'D', 'E', 'F']
explode = (0, 0.2, 0, 0, 0, 0)

plt.pie(values, colors=colors, labels=labels,
        explode=explode, autopct='%1.1f%%',
        counterclock=False, shadow=True)
plt.title('Values')

plt.show()
```

The essential part of a pie chart is the values. You could create a basic pie chart using just the values as input.

The `colors` parameter lets you choose custom colors for each pie wedge. You use the `labels` parameter to identify each wedge. In many cases, you need to make one wedge stand out from the others, so you add the `explode` parameter with list of explode values. A value of 0 keeps the wedge in place — any other value moves the wedge out from the center of the pie.

Each pie wedge can show various kinds of information. This example shows the percentage occupied by each wedge with the `autopct` parameter. You must provide a format string to format the percentages.

TIP

Some parameters affect how the pie chart is drawn. Use the `counterclock` parameter to determine the direction of the wedges. The `shadow` parameter determines whether the pie appears with a shadow beneath it (for a 3-D effect). You can find other parameters at `https://matplotlib.org/api/pyplot_api.html`.

In most cases, you also want to give your pie chart a title so that others know what it represents. You do this using the `title()` function. Figure 11-1 shows the output from this example.

```
In [1]: import matplotlib.pyplot as plt
        %matplotlib inline

        values = [5, 8, 9, 10, 4, 7]
        colors = ['b', 'g', 'r', 'c', 'm', 'y']
        labels = ['A', 'B', 'C', 'D', 'E', 'F']
        explode = (0, 0.2, 0, 0, 0, 0)

        plt.pie(values, colors=colors, labels=labels,
                explode=explode, autopct='%1.1f%%',
                counterclock=False, shadow=True)
        plt.title('Values')

        plt.show()
```

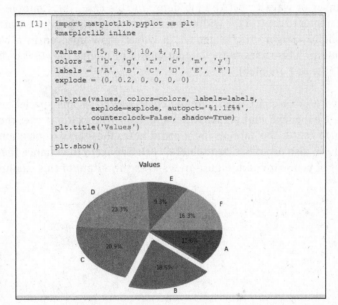

FIGURE 11-1:
Pie charts show a percentage of the whole.

Creating comparisons with bar charts

Bar charts make comparing values easy. The wide bars and segregated measurements emphasize the differences between values, rather than the flow of one value to another as a line graph would do. Fortunately, you have all sorts of methods at your disposal for emphasizing specific values and performing other tricks. The following example shows just some of the things you can do with a vertical bar chart.

```
import matplotlib.pyplot as plt
%matplotlib inline
```

```
values = [5, 8, 9, 10, 4, 7]
widths = [0.7, 0.8, 0.7, 0.7, 0.7, 0.7]
colors = ['b', 'r', 'b', 'b', 'b', 'b']
plt.bar(range(0, 6), values, width=widths,
        color=colors, align='center')

plt.show()
```

To create even a basic bar chart, you must provide a series of x coordinates and the heights of the bars. The example uses the `range()` function to create the x coordinates, and `values` contains the heights.

Of course, you may want more than a basic bar chart, and MatPlotLib provides a number of ways to get the job done. In this case, the example uses the `width` parameter to control the width of each bar, emphasizing the second bar by making it slightly larger. The larger width would show up even in a black-and-white printout. It also uses the `color` parameter to change the color of the target bar to red (the rest are blue).

As with other chart types, the bar chart provides some special features that you can use to make your presentation stand out. The example uses the `align` parameter to center the data on the x coordinate (the standard position is to the left). You can also use other parameters, such as `hatch`, to enhance the visual appearance of your bar chart. Figure 11-2 shows the output of this example.

FIGURE 11-2:
Bar charts make it easier to perform comparisons.

TIP

This chapter helps you get started using MatPlotLib to create a variety of chart and graph types. Of course, more examples are better, so you can also find some more advanced examples on the MatPlotLib site at `https://matplotlib.org/1.2.1/ examples/index.html`. Some of the examples, such as those that demonstrate animation techniques, become quite advanced, but with practice you can use any of them to improve your own charts and graphs.

Showing distributions using histograms

Histograms categorize data by breaking it into *bins*, where each bin contains a subset of the data range. A histogram then displays the number of items in each bin so that you can see the distribution of data and the progression of data from bin to bin. In most cases, you see a curve of some type, such as a bell curve. The following example shows how to create a histogram with randomized data:

```
import numpy as np
import matplotlib.pyplot as plt
%matplotlib inline

x = 20 * np.random.randn(10000)

plt.hist(x, 25, range=(-50, 50), histtype='stepfilled',
         align='mid', color='g', label='Test Data')
plt.legend()
plt.title('Step Filled Histogram')
plt.show()
```

In this case, the input values are a series of random numbers. The distribution of these numbers should show a type of bell curve. As a minimum, you must provide a series of values, x in this case, to plot. The second argument contains the number of bins to use when creating the data intervals. The default value is 10. Using the `range` parameter helps you focus the histogram on the relevant data and exclude any outliers.

You can create multiple histogram types. The default setting creates a bar chart. You can also create a stacked bar chart, stepped graph, or filled stepped graph (the type shown in the example). In addition, it's possible to control the orientation of the output, with vertical as the default.

As with most other charts and graphs in this chapter, you can add special features to the output. For example, the `align` parameter determines the alignment of each bar along the baseline. Use the `color` parameter to control the colors of the bars. The `label` parameter doesn't actually appear unless you also create a legend (as shown in this example). Figure 11-3 shows typical output from this example.

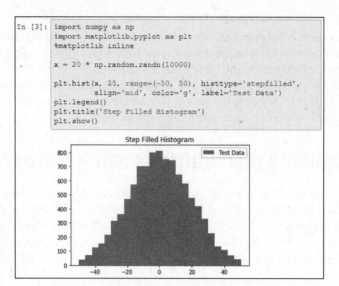

```
In [3]: import numpy as np
        import matplotlib.pyplot as plt
        %matplotlib inline

        x = 20 * np.random.randn(10000)

        plt.hist(x, 25, range=(-50, 50), histtype='stepfilled',
                align='mid', color='g', label='Test Data')
        plt.legend()
        plt.title('Step Filled Histogram')
        plt.show()
```

FIGURE 11-3:
Histograms let you see distributions of numbers.

REMEMBER

Random data varies call by call. Every time you run the example, you see slightly different results because the random-generation process differs.

Depicting groups using boxplots

Boxplots provide a means of depicting groups of numbers through their *quartiles* (three points dividing a group into four equal parts). A boxplot may also have lines, called *whiskers*, indicating data outside the upper and lower quartiles. The spacing shown within a boxplot helps indicate the skew and dispersion of the data. The following example shows how to create a boxplot with randomized data.

```
import numpy as np
import matplotlib.pyplot as plt
%matplotlib inline


spread = 100 * np.random.rand(100)
center = np.ones(50) * 50
flier_high = 100 * np.random.rand(10) + 100
flier_low = -100 * np.random.rand(10)
data = np.concatenate((spread, center,
                       flier_high, flier_low))

plt.boxplot(data, sym='gx', widths=.75, notch=True)
plt.show()
```

To create a usable dataset, you need to combine several different number-generation techniques, as shown at the beginning of the example. Here are how these techniques work:

» `spread`: Contains a set of random numbers between 0 and 100

» `center`: Provides 50 values directly in the center of the range of 50

» `flier_high`: Simulates outliers between 100 and 200

» `flier_low`: Simulates outliers between 0 and –100

The code combines all these values into a single dataset using `concatenate()`. Being randomly generated with specific characteristics (such as a large number of points in the middle), the output will show specific characteristics but will work fine for the example.

The call to `boxplot()` requires only `data` as input. All other parameters have default settings. In this case, the code sets the presentation of outliers to green Xs by setting the `sym` parameter. You use `widths` to modify the size of the box (made extra large in this case to make the box easier to see). Finally, you can create a square box or a box with a notch using the `notch` parameter (which normally defaults to False). Figure 11-4 shows typical output from this example.

```
In [4]: import numpy as np
        import matplotlib.pyplot as plt
        %matplotlib inline

        spread = 100 * np.random.rand(100)
        center = np.ones(50) * 50
        flier_high = 100 * np.random.rand(10) + 100
        flier_low = -100 * np.random.rand(10)
        data = np.concatenate((spread, center,
                               flier_high, flier_low))

        plt.boxplot(data, sym='gx', widths=.75, notch=True)
        plt.show()
```

FIGURE 11-4:
Use boxplots to present groups of numbers.

The box shows the three data points as the box, with the red line in the middle being the median. The two black horizontal lines connected to the box by whiskers show the upper and lower limits (for four quartiles). The outliers appear above and below the upper and lower limit lines as green Xs.

Seeing data patterns using scatterplots

Scatterplots show clusters of data rather than trends (as with line graphs) or discrete values (as with bar charts). The purpose of a scatterplot is to help you see data patterns. The following example shows how to create a scatterplot using randomized data:

```
import numpy as np
import matplotlib.pyplot as plt
%matplotlib inline

x1 = 5 * np.random.rand(40)
x2 = 5 * np.random.rand(40) + 25
x3 = 25 * np.random.rand(20)
x = np.concatenate((x1, x2, x3))

y1 = 5 * np.random.rand(40)
y2 = 5 * np.random.rand(40) + 25
y3 = 25 * np.random.rand(20)
y = np.concatenate((y1, y2, y3))

plt.scatter(x, y, s=[100], marker='^', c='m')
plt.show()
```

The example begins by generating random x and y coordinates. For each x coordinate, you must have a corresponding y coordinate. It's possible to create a scatterplot using just the x and y coordinates.

It's possible to dress up a scatterplot in a number of ways. In this case, the s parameter determines the size of each data point. The marker parameter determines the data point shape. You use the c parameter to define the colors for all the data points, or you can define a separate color for individual data points. Figure 11-5 shows the output from this example.

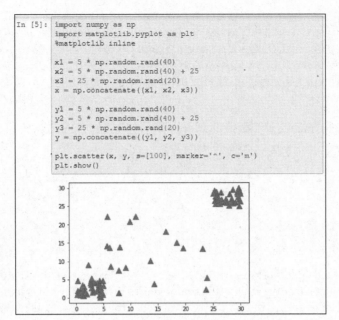

FIGURE 11-5:
Use scatterplots
to show groups
of data points
and their
associated
patterns.

Creating Advanced Scatterplots

Scatterplots are especially important for data science because they can show data patterns that aren't obvious when viewed in other ways. You can see data groupings with relative ease and help the viewer understand when data belongs to a particular group. You can also show overlaps between groups and even demonstrate when certain data is outside the expected range. Showing these various kinds of relationships in the data is an advanced technique that you need to know in order to make the best use of MatPlotLib. The following sections demonstrate how to perform these advanced techniques on the scatterplot you created earlier in the chapter.

Depicting groups

Color is the third axis when working with a scatterplot. Using color lets you highlight groups so that others can see them with greater ease. The following example shows how you can use color to show groups within a scatterplot:

```
import numpy as np
import matplotlib.pyplot as plt
%matplotlib inline
```

```
x1 = 5 * np.random.rand(50)
x2 = 5 * np.random.rand(50) + 25
x3 = 30 * np.random.rand(25)
x = np.concatenate((x1, x2, x3))

y1 = 5 * np.random.rand(50)
y2 = 5 * np.random.rand(50) + 25
y3 = 30 * np.random.rand(25)
y = np.concatenate((y1, y2, y3))

color_array = ['b'] * 50 + ['g'] * 50 + ['r'] * 25

plt.scatter(x, y, s=[50], marker='D', c=color_array)
plt.show()
```

The example works essentially the same as the scatterplot example in the previous section, except that this example uses an array for the colors. Unfortunately, if you're seeing this in the printed book, the differences between the shades of gray in Figure 11-6 will be hard to see. However, the first group is blue, followed by green for the second group. Any outliers appear in red.

FIGURE 11-6: Color arrays can make the scatterplot groups stand out better.

Showing correlations

In some cases, you need to know the general direction that your data is taking when looking at a scatterplot. Even if you create a clear depiction of the groups, the actual direction that the data is taking as a whole may not be clear. In this case, you add a trendline to the output. Here's an example of adding a trendline to a scatterplot that includes groups but isn't quite as clear as the scatterplot shown previously in Figure 11-6.

```
import numpy as np
import matplotlib.pyplot as plt
import matplotlib.pylab as plb
%matplotlib inline

x1 = 15 * np.random.rand(50)
x2 = 15 * np.random.rand(50) + 15
x3 = 30 * np.random.rand(25)
x = np.concatenate((x1, x2, x3))

y1 = 15 * np.random.rand(50)
y2 = 15 * np.random.rand(50) + 15
y3 = 30 * np.random.rand(25)
y = np.concatenate((y1, y2, y3))

color_array = ['b'] * 50 + ['g'] * 50 + ['r'] * 25
plt.scatter(x, y, s=[90], marker='*', c=color_array)
z = np.polyfit(x, y, 1)
p = np.poly1d(z)
plb.plot(x, p(x), 'm-')

plt.show()
```

The code for creating the scatterplot is essentially the same as in the example in the "Depicting groups" section, earlier in the chapter, but the plot doesn't define the groups as clearly. Adding a trendline means calling the NumPy polyfit() function with the data, which returns a vector of coefficients, p, that minimizes the least-squares error. (Least-square regression is a method for finding a line that summarizes the relationship between two variables, x and y in this case, at least within the domain of the explanatory variable x. The third polyfit() parameter expresses the degree of the polynomial fit.)

The vector output of `polyfit()` is used as input to `poly1d()`, which calculates the actual y axis data points. The call to `plot()` creates the trendline on the scatterplot. You can see a typical result of this example in Figure 11-7.

```
In [7]: import numpy as np
        import matplotlib.pyplot as plt
        import matplotlib.pylab as plb
        %matplotlib inline

        x1 = 15 * np.random.rand(50)
        x2 = 15 * np.random.rand(50) + 15
        x3 = 30 * np.random.rand(30)
        x = np.concatenate((x1, x2, x3))

        y1 = 15 * np.random.rand(50)
        y2 = 15 * np.random.rand(50) + 15
        y3 = 30 * np.random.rand(30)
        y = np.concatenate((y1, y2, y3))

        color_array = ['b'] * 50 + ['g'] * 50 + ['r'] * 25
        plt.scatter(x, y, s=[90], marker='*', c=color_array)
        z = np.polyfit(x, y, 1)
        p = np.poly1d(z)
        plb.plot(x, p(x), 'm-')

        plt.show()
```

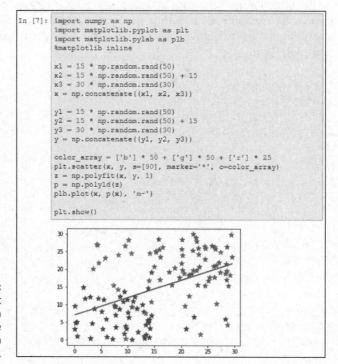

FIGURE 11-7:
Scatterplot trendlines can show you the general data direction.

Plotting Time Series

Nothing is truly static. When you view most data, you see an instant of time — a snapshot of how the data appeared at one particular moment. Of course, such views are both common and useful. However, sometimes you need to view data as it moves through time — to see it as it changes. Only by viewing the data as it changes can you expect to understand the underlying forces that shape it. The following sections describe how to work with data on a time-related basis.

Representing time on axes

Many times, you need to present data over time. The data could come in many forms, but generally you have some type of time tick (one unit of time), followed by one or more features that describe what happens during that particular tick. The following example shows a simple set of days and sales on those days for a particular item in whole (integer) amounts.

```python
import pandas as pd
import matplotlib.pyplot as plt
import datetime as dt
%matplotlib inline

start_date = dt.datetime(2018, 7, 30)
end_date = dt.datetime(2018, 8, 5)
daterange = pd.date_range(start_date, end_date)
sales = (np.random.rand(len(daterange)) * 50).astype(int)
df = pd.DataFrame(sales, index=daterange,
                  columns=['Sales'])

df.loc['Jul 30 2018':'Aug 05 2018'].plot()
plt.ylim(0, 50)
plt.xlabel('Sales Date')
plt.ylabel('Sale Value')
plt.title('Plotting Time')
plt.show()
```

The example begins by creating a DataFrame to hold the information. The source of the information could be anything, but the example generates it randomly. Notice that the example creates a date_range to hold the starting and ending date time frame for easier processing using a for loop.

An essential part of this example is the creation of individual rows. Each row has an actual time value so that you don't lose information. However, notice that the index (row_s.name property) is a string. This string should appear in the form that you want the dates to appear when presented in the plot.

Using loc[] lets you select a range of dates from the total number of entries available. Notice that this example uses only some of the generated data for output. It then adds some amplifying information about the plot and displays it onscreen. The call to plot() must specify the x and y values in this case or you get an error. Figure 11-8 show typical output from the randomly generated data.

```
In [8]:  import pandas as pd
         import matplotlib.pyplot as plt
         import datetime as dt

         start_date = dt.datetime(2018, 7, 29)
         end_date = dt.datetime(2018, 8, 7)
         daterange = pd.date_range(start_date, end_date)
         sales = (np.random.rand(len(daterange)) * 50).astype(int)
         df = pd.DataFrame(sales, index=daterange,
                           columns=['Sales'])

         df.loc['Jul 30 2018':'Aug 05 2018'].plot()
         plt.ylim(0, 50)
         plt.xlabel('Sales Date')
         plt.ylabel('Sale Value')
         plt.title('Plotting Time')
         plt.show()
```

FIGURE 11-8:
Use line graphs to
show the flow of
data over time.

Plotting trends over time

As with any other data presentation, sometimes you really can't see what direction the data is headed in without help. The following example starts with the plot from the previous section and adds a trendline to it:

```
import numpy as np
import pandas as pd
import matplotlib.pyplot as plt
import datetime as dt
%matplotlib inline

start_date = dt.datetime(2018, 7, 29)
end_date = dt.datetime(2018, 8, 7)
daterange = pd.date_range(start_date, end_date)
sales = (np.random.rand(len(daterange)) * 50).astype(int)
df = pd.DataFrame(sales, index=daterange,
                  columns=['Sales'])

lr_coef = np.polyfit(range(0, len(df)), df['Sales'], 1)
lr_func = np.poly1d(lr_coef)
```

```
trend = lr_func(range(0, len(df)))
df['trend'] = trend
df.loc['Jul 30 2018':'Aug 05 2018'].plot()

plt.xlabel('Sales Date')
plt.ylabel('Sale Value')
plt.title('Plotting Time')
plt.legend(['Sales', 'Trend'])
plt.show()
```

REMEMBER

The "Showing correlations" section, earlier in this chapter, shows how most people add a trendline to their graph. In fact, this is the approach that you often see used online. You'll also notice that a lot of people have trouble using this approach in some situations. This example takes a slightly different approach by adding the trendline directly to the DataFrame. If you print df after the call to df['trend'] = trend, you see trendline data similar to the values shown here:

	Sales	trend
2018-07-29	6	18.890909
2018-07-30	13	20.715152
2018-07-31	38	22.539394
2018-08-01	22	24.363636
2018-08-02	40	26.187879
2018-08-03	39	28.012121
2018-08-04	36	29.836364
2018-08-05	21	31.660606
2018-08-06	7	33.484848
2018-08-07	49	35.309091

Using this approach makes it ultimately easier to plot the data. You call plot() only once and avoid relying on the MatPlotLib, pylab, as shown in the example in the "Showing correlations" section. The resulting code is simpler and less likely to cause the issues you see online.

When you plot the initial data, the call to plot() automatically generates a legend for you. MatPlotLib doesn't automatically add the trendline, so you must also create a new legend for the plot. Figure 11-9 shows typical output from this example using randomly generated data.

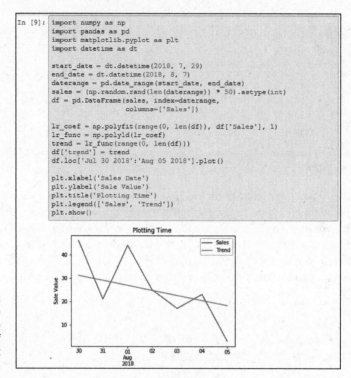

```
In [9]: import numpy as np
        import pandas as pd
        import matplotlib.pyplot as plt
        import datetime as dt

        start_date = dt.datetime(2018, 7, 29)
        end_date = dt.datetime(2018, 8, 7)
        daterange = pd.date_range(start_date, end_date)
        sales = (np.random.rand(len(daterange)) * 50).astype(int)
        df = pd.DataFrame(sales, index=daterange,
                          columns=['Sales'])

        lr_coef = np.polyfit(range(0, len(df)), df['Sales'], 1)
        lr_func = np.poly1d(lr_coef)
        trend = lr_func(range(0, len(df)))
        df['trend'] = trend
        df.loc['Jul 30 2018':'Aug 05 2018'].plot()

        plt.xlabel('Sales Date')
        plt.ylabel('Sale Value')
        plt.title('Plotting Time')
        plt.legend(['Sales', 'Trend'])
        plt.show()
```

FIGURE 11-9:
Add a trendline to show the average direction of change in a chart or graph.

Plotting Geographical Data

Knowing where data comes from or how it applies to a specific place can be important. For example, if you want to know where food shortages have occurred and plan how to deal with them, you need to match the data you have to geographical locations. The same holds true for predicting where future sales will occur. You may find that you need to use existing data to determine where to put new stores. Otherwise, you could put a store in a location that won't receive much in the way of sales, and the effort will lose money rather than make it. The following sections describe how to work with Basemap to interact with geographical data.

WARNING

You must shut the Notebook environment down before you make any changes to it or else conda will complain that some files are in use. To shut the Notebook environment down, close and halt the kernel for any Notebook files you have open and then press Ctrl+C in the Notebook terminal window. Wait a few seconds before you attempt to do anything to give the files time to close properly.

Using an environment in Notebook

Some of the packages you install have a tendency to also change your Notebook environment by installing other packages that may not work well with your baseline setup. Consequently, you see problems with code that functioned earlier. Normally, these problems consist mostly of warning messages, such as deprecation warnings as discussed in the "Dealing with deprecated library issues" section, later in this chapter. In some cases, however, the changed packages can also tweak the output you obtain from code. Perhaps a newer package uses an updated algorithm or interacts with the code differently. When you have a package, such as Basemap, that makes changes to the overall baseline configuration and you want to maintain your current configuration, you need to set up an environment for it. An environment keeps your baseline configuration intact but also allows the new package to create the environment it needs to execute properly. The following steps help you create the Basemap environment used for this chapter:

1. **Open an Anaconda Prompt.**

   Notice that the prompt shows the location of your folder on your system, but that it's preceded by (base). The (base) indicator tells you that you're in your baseline environment — the one you want to preserve.

2. **Type** conda create -n Basemap python=3 anaconda=5.2.0 **and press Enter.**

   This action creates a new Basemap environment. This new environment will use Python 3.6 and Anaconda 5.2.0. You get precisely the same baseline as you've been using so far.

3. **Type** source activate Basemap **if you're using OS X or Linux or** activate Basemap **if you're using Windows and press Enter.**

   You have now changed over to the Basemap environment. Notice that the prompt no longer says (base), it says (Basemap) instead.

4. **Follow the instructions in the "Getting the Basemap toolkit" section to install your copy of Basemap.**

5. **Type** Jupyter Notebook **and press Enter.**

   You see Notebook start, but it uses the Basemap environment, rather than the baseline environment. This copy of Notebook works precisely the same as any other copy of Notebook that you've used. The only difference is the environment in which it operates.

REMEMBER

This same technique works for any special package that you want to install. You should reserve it for packages that you don't intend to use every day. For example, this book uses Basemap for just one example, so it's appropriate to create an environment for it.

After you have finished using the Basemap environment, type **deactivate** at the prompt and press Enter. You see the prompt change back to (base).

Getting the Basemap toolkit

Before you can work with mapping data, you need a library that supports the required mapping functionality. A number of such packages are available, but the easiest to work with and install is the Basemap Toolkit. You can obtain this toolkit from https://matplotlib.org/basemap/users/intro.html. (Make sure you close Notebook and stop the server before you proceed in this section to avoid file access errors.) However, the easiest method is to use the conda tool from the Anaconda Prompt to enter the following commands:

```
conda install -c conda-forge basemap=1.1.0
conda install -c conda-forge basemap-data-hires
conda install -c conda-forge proj4=5.2.0
```

The site does include supplementary information about the toolkit, so you may want to visit it anyway. Unlike some other packages, this one does include instructions for Mac, Windows, and Linux users. In addition, you can obtain a Windows-specific installer. Make sure to also check out the usage video at http://nbviewer. ipython.org/github/mqlaql/geospatial-data/blob/master/Geospatial-Data-with-Python.ipynb.

You need the following code to use the toolkit once you have it installed:

```
import numpy as np
import matplotlib.pyplot as plt
from mpl_toolkits.basemap import Basemap
%matplotlib inline
```

Dealing with deprecated library issues

One of the major advantages of working with Python is the huge number of packages that it supports. Unfortunately, not every package receives updates quickly enough to avoid using deprecated features in other packages. A *deprecated feature* is one that still exists in the target package, but the developers of that package plan to remove it in an upcoming update. Consequently, you receive a deprecated package warning when you run your code. Even though the deprecation warning doesn't keep your code from running, it does tend to make people leery of your application. After all, no one wants to see what appears to be an error message as part of the output. The fact that Notebook displays these messages in light red by default doesn't help matters.

Unfortunately, your copy of the Basemap toolkit may produce a deprecated feature warning message, so this section tells you how to overcome this issue. You can discover more about the potential issues you see at https://github.com/ matplotlib/basemap/issues/382. These messages look something like this:

```
C:\Users\Luca\Anaconda3\lib\site-packages\mpl_toolkits
\basemap\__init__.py:1708: MatplotlibDeprecationWarning:
The axesPatch function was deprecated in version 2.1.
Use Axes.patch instead.
  limb = ax.axesPatch

C:\Users\Luca\Anaconda3\lib\site-packages\mpl_toolkits
\basemap\__init__.py:1711: MatplotlibDeprecationWarning:
The axesPatch function was deprecated in version 2.1. Use
Axes.patch instead.
  if limb is not ax.axesPatch:
```

That looks like a lot of really terrifying text, but these messages point out two issues. The first is that the problem is in MatPlotLib and it revolves about the axesPatch call. The messages also tell you that this particular call is deprecated starting with version 2.1. Use this code to check your version of MatPlotLib:

```
import matplotlib
print(matplotlib.__version__)
```

If you installed Anaconda using the instructions in Chapter 3, you see that you have MatPlotLib 2.2.2 as a minimum. Consequently, one way to deal with this problem is to downgrade your copy of MatPlotLib by using the following command at the Anaconda Prompt:

```
conda install -c conda-forge matplotlib=2.0.2
```

The problem with this approach is that it can also cause problems for any code that uses the newer features found in MatPlotLib 2.2.2. It's not optimal, but if you use Basemap in your application a lot, it might be a practical solution.

A better solution is to simply admit that the problem exists by documenting it as part of your code. Documenting the problem and its specific cause makes it easier to check for the problem later after a package update. To do this, you add the two lines of code shown here:

```
import warnings
warnings.filterwarnings("ignore")
```

The call to `filterwarnings()` performs the specified action, which is `"ignore"` in this case. To cancel the effects of filtering the warnings, you call `resetwarnings()`. Notice that the `module` attribute is the same as the source of the problems in the warning messages. You can also define a broader filter by using the `category` attribute. This particular call is narrow, affecting only one module.

Using Basemap to plot geographic data

Now that you have a good installation of Basemap, you can do something with it. The following example shows how to draw a map and place pointers to specific locations on it:

```
austin = (-97.75, 30.25)
hawaii = (-157.8, 21.3)
washington = (-77.01, 38.90)
chicago = (-87.68, 41.83)
losangeles = (-118.25, 34.05)


m = Basemap(projection='merc',llcrnrlat=10,urcrnrlat=50,
            llcrnrlon=-160,urcrnrlon=-60)

m.drawcoastlines()
m.fillcontinents(color='lightgray',lake_color='lightblue')
m.drawparallels(np.arange(-90.,91.,30.))
m.drawmeridians(np.arange(-180.,181.,60.))
m.drawmapboundary(fill_color='aqua')

m.drawcountries()

x, y = m(*zip(*[hawaii, austin, washington,
                chicago, losangeles]))
m.plot(x, y, marker='o', markersize=6,
       markerfacecolor='red', linewidth=0)

plt.title("Mercator Projection")
plt.show()
```

The example begins by defining the longitude and latitude for various cities. It then creates the basic map. The `projection` parameter defines the basic map appearance. The next four parameters, `llcrnrlat`, `urcrnrlat`, `llcrnrlon`, and `urcrnrlon` define the sides of the map. You can define other parameters, but these parameters generally create a useful map.

The next set of calls defines the map particulars. For example, drawcoastlines() determines whether the coastlines are highlighted to make them easy to see. To make landmasses easy to discern from water, you want to call fillcontinents() with the colors of your choice. When working with specific locations, as the example does, you want to call drawcountries() to ensure that the country boundaries appear on the map. At this point, you have a map that's ready to fill in with data.

In this case, the example creates x and y coordinates using the previously stored longitude and latitude values. It then plots these locations on the map in a contrasting color so that you can easily see them. The final step is to display the map, as shown in Figure 11-10.

```
In [13]: austin = (-97.75, 30.25)
         hawaii = (-157.8, 21.3)
         washington = (-77.01, 38.90)
         chicago = (-87.68, 41.83)
         losangeles = (-118.25, 34.05)


         m = Basemap(projection='merc',llcrnrlat=10,urcrnrlat=50,
                     llcrnrlon=-160,urcrnrlon=-60)

         m.drawcoastlines()
         m.fillcontinents(color='lightgray',lake_color='lightblue')
         m.drawparallels(np.arange(-90.,91.,30.))
         m.drawmeridians(np.arange(-180.,181.,60.))
         m.drawmapboundary(fill_color='aqua')

         m.drawcountries()

         x, y = m(*zip(*[hawaii, austin, washington,
                       chicago, losangeles]))
         m.plot(x, y, marker='o', markersize=6,
               markerfacecolor='red', linewidth=0)

         plt.title("Mercator Projection")
         plt.show()
```

Mercator Projection

FIGURE 11-10:
Maps can illustrate data in ways other graphics can't.

Visualizing Graphs

A *graph* is a depiction of data showing the connections between data points using lines. The purpose is to show that some data points relate to other data points, but not all the data points that appear on the graph. Think about a map of a subway system. Each of the stations connects to other stations, but no single station connects to all the stations in the subway system. Graphs are a popular data science topic because of their use in social media analysis. When performing social media analysis, you depict and analyze networks of relationships, such as friends or business connections, from social hubs such as Facebook, Google+, Twitter, or LinkedIn.

REMEMBER

The two common depictions of graphs are *undirected*, where the graph simply shows lines between data elements, and *directed*, where arrows added to the line show that data flows in a particular direction. For example, consider a depiction of a water system. The water would flow in just one direction in most cases, so you could use a directed graph to depict not only the connections between sources and targets for the water but also to show water direction by using arrows. The following sections help you understand the two types of graphs better and show you how to create them.

Developing undirected graphs

As previously stated, an undirected graph simply shows connections between nodes. The output doesn't provide a direction from one node to the next. For example, when establishing connectivity between web pages, no direction is implied. The following example shows how to create an undirected graph:

```
import networkx as nx
import matplotlib.pyplot as plt
%matplotlib inline

G = nx.Graph()
H = nx.Graph()
G.add_node(1)
G.add_nodes_from([2, 3])
G.add_nodes_from(range(4, 7))
H.add_node(7)
G.add_nodes_from(H)

G.add_edge(1, 2)
G.add_edge(1, 1)
G.add_edges_from([(2,3), (3,6), (4,6), (5,6)])
H.add_edges_from([(4,7), (5,7), (6,7)])
G.add_edges_from(H.edges())

nx.draw_networkx(G)
plt.show()
```

In contrast to the canned example found in the "Using NetworkX basics" section of Chapter 8, this example builds the graph using a number of different techniques. It begins by importing the Networkx package you use in Chapter 8. To create a new undirected graph, the code calls the `Graph()` constructor, which can take a number of input arguments to use as attributes. However, you can build a perfectly usable graph without using attributes, which is what this example does.

The easiest way to add a node is to call `add_node()` with a node number. You can also add a list, dictionary, or `range()` of nodes using `add_nodes_from()`. In fact, you can import nodes from other graphs if you want.

REMEMBER

Even though the nodes used in the example rely on numbers, you don't have to use numbers for your nodes. A node can use a single letter, a string, or even a date. Nodes do have some restrictions. For example, you can't create a node using a Boolean value.

Nodes don't have any connectivity at the outset. You must define connections (edges) between them. To add a single edge, you call `add_edge()` with the numbers of the nodes that you want to add. As with nodes, you can use `add_edges_from()` to create more than one edge using a list, dictionary, or another graph as input. Figure 11-11 shows the output from this example (your output may differ slightly but should have the same connections).

```
In [12]: import networkx as nx
         import matplotlib.pyplot as plt
         %matplotlib inline

         G = nx.Graph()
         H = nx.Graph()
         G.add_node(1)
         G.add_nodes_from([2, 3])
         G.add_nodes_from(range(4, 7))
         H.add_node(7)
         G.add_nodes_from(H)

         G.add_edge(1, 2)
         G.add_edge(1, 1)
         G.add_edges_from([(2,3), (3,6), (4,6), (5,6)])
         H.add_edges_from([(4,7), (5,7), (6,7)])
         G.add_edges_from(H.edges())

         nx.draw_networkx(G)
         plt.show()
```

FIGURE 11-11: Undirected graphs connect nodes together to form patterns.

Developing directed graphs

You use directed graphs when you need to show a direction, say from a start point to an end point. When you get a map that shows you how to get from one specific point to another, the starting node and ending node are marked as such and the lines between these nodes (and all the intermediate nodes), show direction.

TIP

Your graphs need not be boring. You can dress them up in all sorts of ways so that the viewer gains additional information in different ways. For example, you can create custom labels, use specific colors for certain nodes, or rely on color to help people see the meaning behind your graphs. You can also change edge line weight and use other techniques to mark a specific path between nodes as the better one to choose. The following example shows many (but not nearly all) the ways in which you can dress up a directed graph and make it more interesting:

```
import networkx as nx
import matplotlib.pyplot as plt
%matplotlib inline

G = nx.DiGraph()

G.add_node(1)
G.add_by nodes_from([2, 3])
G.add_nodes_from(range(4, 6))
G.add_path([6, 7, 8])

G.add_edge(1, 2)
G.add_edges_from([(1,4), (4,5), (2,3), (3,6), (5,6)])

colors = ['r', 'g', 'g', 'g', 'g', 'm', 'm', 'r']
labels = {1:'Start', 2:'2', 3:'3', 4:'4',
          5:'5', 6:'6', 7:'7', 8:'End'}
sizes = [800, 300, 300, 300, 300, 600, 300, 800]

nx.draw_networkx(G, node_color=colors, node_shape='D',
                 with_labels=True, labels=labels,
                 node_size=sizes)
plt.show()
```

The example begins by creating a directional graph using the `DiGraph()` constructor. You should note that the NetworkX package also supports `MultiGraph()` and `MultiDiGraph()` graph types. You can see a listing of all the graph types at `https://networkx.lanl.gov/reference/classes.html`.

Adding nodes is much like working with an undirected graph. You can add single nodes using add_node() and multiple nodes using add_nodes_from(). The add_path() call lets you create nodes and edges at the same time. The order of nodes in the call is important. The flow from one node to another is from left to right in the list supplied to the call.

REMEMBER

Adding edges is much the same as working with an undirected graph, too. You can use add_edge() to add a single edge or add_edges_from() to add multiple edges at one time. However, the order of the node numbers is important. The flow goes from the left node to the right node in each pair.

This example adds special node colors, labels, shape (only one shape is used), and sizes to the output. You still call on draw_networkx() to perform the task. However, adding the parameters shown changes the appearance of the graph. Note that you must set with_labels to True in order to see the labels provided by the labels parameter. Figure 11-12 shows the output from this example.

```
In [13]: import networkx as nx
         import matplotlib.pyplot as plt
         %matplotlib inline

         G = nx.DiGraph()

         G.add_node(1)
         G.add_nodes_from([2, 3])
         G.add_nodes_from(range(4, 6))
         G.add_path([6, 7, 8])

         G.add_edge(1, 2)
         G.add_edges_from([(1,4), (4,5), (2,3), (3,6), (5,6)])

         colors = ['r', 'g', 'g', 'g', 'g', 'm', 'm', 'r']
         labels = {1:'Start', 2:'2', 3:'3', 4:'4',
                   5:'5', 6:'6', 7:'7', 8:'End'}
         sizes = [800, 300, 300, 300, 300, 600, 300, 800]

         nx.draw_networkx(G, node_color=colors, node_shape='D',
                          with_labels=True, labels=labels,
                          node_size=sizes)
         plt.show()
```

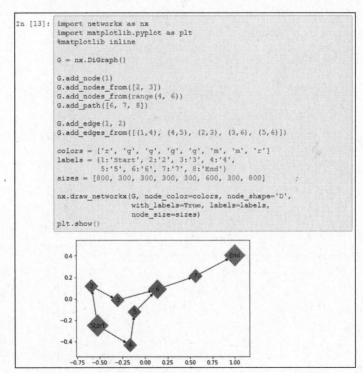

FIGURE 11-12: Use directed graphs to show direction between nodes.

4

Wrangling Data

Chapter **12**

Stretching Python's Capabilities

I f you've gone through the previous chapters, by this point you've dealt with all the basic data loading and manipulation methods offered by Python. Now it's time to start using some more complex instruments for data wrangling (or munging) and for machine learning. The final step of most data science projects is to build a data tool able to automatically summarize, predict, and recommend directly from your data.

Before taking that final step, you still have to process your data by enforcing transformations that are even more radical. That's the *data wrangling* or *data munging* part, where sophisticated transformations are followed by visual and statistical explorations, and then again by further transformations. In the following sections, you learn how to handle huge streams of text, explore the basic characteristics of a dataset, optimize the speed of your experiments, compress data and create new synthetic features, generate new groups and classifications, and detect unexpected or exceptional cases that may cause your project to go wrong.

From here onward, you use the Scikit-learn package more (which means knowing more about it — the full documentation appears at https://scikit-learn.org/stable/documentation.html). The Scikit-learn package offers a single repository containing almost all the tools that you need to be a data scientist and for your data science project to be successful. In this chapter, you discover important characteristics of Scikit-learn, structured in modules, classes, and functions, and some advanced Python time savers for improving performance with big unstructured data and highly time-consuming computational operations.

REMEMBER

You don't have to type the source code for this chapter in by hand. In fact, it's a lot easier if you use the downloadable source (see the Introduction for download instructions). The source code for this chapter appears in the `P4DS4D2_12_Stretching_Pythons_Capabilities.ipynb` source code file.

Playing with Scikit-learn

Sometimes the best way to discover how to use something is to spend time playing with it. The more complex a tool, the more important play becomes. Given the complex math tasks you perform using Scikit-learn, playing becomes especially important. The following sections use the idea of playing with Scikit-learn to help you discover important concepts in using Scikit-learn to perform amazing feats of data science work.

Understanding classes in Scikit-learn

Understanding how classes work is an important prerequisite for being able to use the Scikit-learn package appropriately. Scikit-learn is the package for machine learning and data science experimentation favored by most data scientists. It contains a wide range of well-established learning algorithms, error functions, and testing procedures.

At its core, Scikit-learn features some base classes on which all the algorithms are built. Apart from `BaseEstimator`, the class from which all other classes inherit, there are four class types covering all the basic machine-learning functionalities:

>> Classifying

>> Regressing

>> Grouping by clusters

>> Transforming data

Even though each base class has specific methods and attributes, the core functionalities for data processing and machine learning are guaranteed by one or more series of methods and attributes called interfaces. The interfaces provide a uniform Application Programming Interface (API) to enforce similarity of methods and attributes between all the different algorithms present in the package. There are four Scikit-learn object-based interfaces:

>> estimator: For fitting parameters, learning them from data, according to the algorithm

>> predictor: For generating predictions from the fitted parameters

>> transformer: For transforming data, implementing the fitted parameters

>> model: For reporting goodness of fit or other score measures

The package groups the algorithms built on base classes and one or more object interfaces into modules, each module displaying a specialization in a particular type of machine-learning solution. For example, the linear_model module is for linear modeling, and metrics is for score and loss measure.

To find a specific algorithm in Scikit-learn, you must first find the module containing the same kind of algorithm that interests you, and then select it from the list of contents of the module. The algorithm is typically a class itself, whose methods and attributes are already known because they're common to other algorithms in Scikit-learn.

TIP

Getting accustomed to the Scikit-learn class approach may take some time. However, the API is the same for all the tools available in the package, so learning one class necessarily tells you about all the other classes. The best approach is to learn one class completely and then apply what you know to other classes.

Defining applications for data science

Figuring out ways to use data science to obtain constructive results is important. For example, you can apply the estimator interface to a

>> **Classification problem:** Guessing that a new observation is from a certain group

>> **Regression problem:** Guessing the value of a new observation

It works with the method fit(X, y) where X is the bidimensional array of predictors (the set of observations to learn) and y is the target outcome (another array, unidimensional).

By applying `fit`, the information in X is related to y, so that, knowing some new information with the same characteristics of X, it's possible to guess y correctly. In the process, some parameters are estimated internally by the `fit` method. Using `fit` makes it possible to distinguish between parameters, which are learned, and hyperparameters, which instead are fixed by you when you instantiate the learner.

Instantiation involves assigning a Scikit-learn class to a Python variable. In addition to hyperparameters, you can also fix other working parameters, such as requiring normalization or setting a random seed to reproduce the same results for each call, given the same input data.

Here is an example with linear regression, a very basic and common machine learning algorithm. You upload some data to use this example from the examples that Scikit-learn provides. The Boston dataset, for instance, contains predictor variables that the example code can match against house prices, which helps build a predictor that can calculate the value of a house given its characteristics.

```
from sklearn.datasets import load_boston
boston = load_boston()
X, y = boston.data,boston.target
print("X:%s y:%s" % (X.shape, y.shape))
```

The returned dimensions for the X and y variables are

```
X:(506, 13) y:(506,)
```

The output specifies that both arrays have the same number of rows and that X has 13 features. The `shape` method performs array analysis and reports the arrays' dimensions.

TIP

The number of X rows must equal those in y. You also ensure that X and y correspond, because learning from data happens when the algorithm matches the rows of X with the corresponding element of y. If you randomize the two arrays, no learning is possible.

REMEMBER

The characteristics of X, expressed as X's columns, are called variables (a more statistical term) or features (a term more related to machine learning).

After importing the `LinearRegression` class, you can instantiate a variable called `hypothesis` and set a parameter indicating the algorithm to standardize (that is, to set mean zero and unit standard deviation for all the variables, a statistical operation for having all the variables at a similar level) before estimating the parameters to learn.

```
from sklearn.linear_model import LinearRegression
hypothesis = LinearRegression(normalize=True)
hypothesis.fit(X, y)
print(hypothesis.coef_)
```

Afterwards, the coefficients of the linear regression hypothesis are printed:

```
[-1.07170557e-01  4.63952195e-02  2.08602395e-02
  2.68856140e+00 -1.77957587e+01  3.80475246e+00
  7.51061703e-04 -1.47575880e+00  3.05655038e-01
 -1.23293463e-02 -9.53463555e-01  9.39251272e-03
 -5.25466633e-01]
```

After fitting, `hypothesis` holds the learned parameters, and you can visualize them using the `coef_` method, which is typical of all the linear models (where the model output is a summation of variables weighted by coefficients). You can also call this fitting activity training (as in, "training a machine learning algorithm").

REMEMBER

A *hypothesis* is a way to describe a learning algorithm trained with data. The hypothesis defines a possible representation of y given X that you test for validity. Therefore, it's a hypothesis in both scientific and machine learning language.

Apart from the estimator class, the predictor and the model object classes are also important. The predictor class, which predicts the probability of a certain result, obtains the result of new observations using the `predict` and `predict_proba` methods, as in this script:

```
import numpy as np
new_observation = np.array([1, 0, 1, 0, 0.5, 7, 59,
                            6, 3, 200, 20, 350, 4],
                           dtype=float).reshape(1, -1)
print(hypothesis.predict(new_observation))
```

The single observation is thus converted into a prediction:

```
[25.8972784]
```

TIP

Make sure that new observations have the same feature number and order as in the training X; otherwise, the prediction will be incorrect.

The class model provides information about the quality of the fit using the `score` method, as shown here:

```
hypothesis.score(X, y)
```

The quality is expressed as a float number:

```
0.7406077428649427
```

In this case, `score` returns the coefficient of determination R^2 of the prediction. R^2 is a measure ranging from 0 to 1, comparing our predictor to a simple mean. Higher values show that the predictor is working well. Different learning algorithms may use different scoring functions. Please consult the online documentation of each algorithm or ask for help on the Python console:

```
help(LinearRegression)
```

The transform class applies transformations derived from the fitting phase to other data arrays. `LinearRegression` doesn't have a transform method, but most preprocessing algorithms do. For example, `MinMaxScaler`, from the Scikit-learn `preprocessing` module, can transform values in a specific range of minimum and maximum values, learning the transformation formula from an example array.

```
from sklearn.preprocessing import MinMaxScaler
scaler = MinMaxScaler(feature_range=(0, 1))
scaler.fit(X)
print(scaler.transform(new_observation))
```

Running the code returns transformed values for the observations:

```
[ 0.01116872  0.          0.01979472  0.
  0.23662551  0.65893849  0.57775489  0.44288845
  0.08695652  0.02480916  0.78723404  0.88173887
  0.06263797]
```

In this case, the code applies the `min` and `max` values learned from X to the `new_observation` variable and returns a transformation.

Performing the Hashing Trick

Scikit-learn provides you with most of the data structures and functionality you need to complete your data science project. You can even find classes for the trickiest and most advanced problems.

For instance, when dealing with text, one of the most useful solutions provided by the Scikit-learn package is the hashing trick. You discover how to work with text by using the bag of words model (as shown in the "Using the Bag of Words Model and Beyond" section of Chapter 8) and weighting them with the Term Frequency times Inverse Document Frequency (TF-IDF) transformation. All these powerful transformations can operate properly only if all your text is known and available in the memory of your computer.

A more serious data science challenge is to analyze online-generated text flows, such as from social networks or large, online text repositories. This scenario poses quite a challenge when trying to turn the text into a data matrix suitable for analysis. When working through such problems, knowing the hashing trick can give you quite a few advantages by helping you

» Handle large data matrices based on text on the fly

» Fix unexpected values or variables in your textual data

» Build scalable algorithms for large collections of documents

Using hash functions

Hash functions can transform any input into an output whose characteristics are predictable. Usually they return a value where the output is bound at a specific interval — whose extremities range from negative to positive numbers or just span through positive numbers. You can imagine them as enforcing a standard on your data — no matter what values you provide, they always return a specific data product.

Their most useful hash function characteristic is that, given a certain input, they always provide the same numeric output value. Consequently, they're called deterministic functions. For example, input a word like *dog* and the hashing function always returns the same number.

In a certain sense, hash functions are like a secret code, transforming everything into numbers. Unlike secret codes, however, you can't convert the hashed code to its original value. In addition, in some rare cases, different words generate the same hashed result (also called a hash collision).

Demonstrating the hashing trick

There are many hash functions, with MD5 (often used to check file integrity, because you can hash entire files) and SHA (used in cryptography) being the most popular. Python possesses a built-in hash function named hash that you can use to compare data objects before storing them in dictionaries. For instance, you can test how Python hashes its name:

```
print(hash('Python'))
```

The command returns a large integer number:

```
-1126740211494229687
```

TECHNICAL STUFF

The Python session on your computer may return a different value than the one shown on the preceding line. Don't worry — the built-in hash functions aren't always consistent across computers. When you need consistent output, rely on the Scikit-learn hash functions instead because the output is consistent across machines.

A Scikit-learn hash function can also return an index in a specific positive range. You can obtain something similar using a built-in hash by employing standard division and its remainder:

```
print(abs(hash('Python')) % 1000)
```

This time the resulting hash is an integer number with fewer numbers:

```
687
```

When you ask for the remainder of the absolute number of the result from the hash function, you get a number that never exceeds the value you used for the division. To see how this technique works, pretend that you want to transform a text string from the Internet into a numeric vector (a feature vector) so that you can use it for starting a machine-learning project. A good strategy for managing this data science task is to employ one-hot encoding, which produces a bag of words. Here are the steps for one-hot encoding a string ("Python for data science") into a vector.

1. Assign an arbitrary number to each word, for instance, Python=0 for=1 data=2 science=3.

2. Initialize the vector, counting the number of unique words that you assigned a code in Step 1.

3. Use the codes assigned in Step 1 as indexes for populating the vector with values, assigning a 1 where there is a coincidence with a word existing in the phrase.

The resulting feature vector is expressed as the sequence [1,1,1,1] and made of exactly four elements. You have started the machine-learning process, telling the program to expect sequences of four text features, when suddenly a new phrase arrives and you must convert the following text into a numeric vector as well: "Python for machine learning". Now you have two new words — "machine learning" — to work with. The following steps help you create the new vectors:

1. Assign these new codes: machine=4 learning=5. This is called *encoding*.

2. Enlarge the previous vector to include the new words: [1,1,1,1,0,0].

3. Compute the vector for the new string: [1,1,0,0,1,1].

One-hot encoding is quite optimal because it creates efficient and ordered feature vectors.

```
from sklearn.feature_extraction.text import *
oh_enconder = CountVectorizer()
oh_enconded = oh_enconder.fit_transform([
'Python for data science','Python for machine learning'])

print(oh_enconder.vocabulary_)
```

The command returns a dictionary containing the words and their encodings:

```
{'python': 4, 'for': 1, 'data': 0, 'science': 5,
'machine': 3, 'learning': 2}
```

Unfortunately, one-hot encoding fails and becomes difficult to handle when your project experiences a lot of variability with regard to its inputs. This is a common situation in data science projects working with text or other symbolic features where flow from the Internet or other online environments can suddenly create or add to your initial data. Using hash functions is a smarter way to handle unpredictability in your inputs:

1. Define a range for the hash function outputs. All your feature vectors will use that range. The example uses a range of values from 0 to 24.

2. Compute an index for each word in your string using the hash function.

3. Assign a unit value to vector's positions according to word indexes.

In Python, you can define a simple hashing trick by creating a function and checking the results using the two test strings:

```
string_1 = 'Python for data science'
string_2 = 'Python for machine learning'

def hashing_trick(input_string, vector_size=20):
    feature_vector = [0] * vector_size
```

```
        for word in input_string.split(' '):
            index = abs(hash(word)) % vector_size
            feature_vector[index] = 1
    return feature_vector
```

Now you can test both strings.

```
print(hashing_trick(
        input_string='Python for data science',
    vector_size=20))
```

Here is the first string encoded as a vector:

```
[0,0,0,0,0,1,1,0,0,0,0,0,0,0,1,0,0,0,0,1]
```

As before, your results may not precisely match those in the book because hashes may not match across machines. The code now prints the second string encoded:

```
print(hashing_trick(
        input_string='Python for machine learning',
    vector_size=20))
```

Here's the result for the second string:

```
[0,0,0,0,0,1,1,1,0,0,0,0,0,0,0,0,0,0,0,0]
```

When viewing the feature vectors, you should notice that:

>> You don't know where each word is located. When it's important to be able to reverse the process of assigning words to indexes, you must store the relationship between words and their hashed value separately (for example, you can use a dictionary where the keys are the hashed values and the values are the words).

>> For small values of the vector_size function parameter (for example, vector_size=10), many words overlap in the same positions in the list representing the feature vector. To keep the overlap to a minimum, you must create hash function boundaries that are greater than the number of elements you plan to index later.

The feature vectors in this example are made mostly of zero entries, representing a waste of memory when compared to the more memory-efficient one-hot-encoding. One of the ways in which you can solve this problem is to rely on sparse matrices, as described in the next section.

Working with deterministic selection

Sparse matrices are the answer when dealing with data that has few values, that is, when most of the matrix values are zeroes. Sparse matrices store just the coordinates of the cells and their values, instead of storing the information for all the cells in the matrix. When an application requests data from an empty cell, the sparse matrix will return a zero value after looking for the coordinates and not finding them. Here's an example vector:

```
[1,0,0,0,0,1,0,0,0,0,0,0,0,0,0,0,1,0,1,0]
```

The following code turns it into a sparse matrix.

```
from scipy.sparse import csc_matrix
print csc_matrix([1, 0, 0, 0, 0, 1, 0, 0, 0, 0, 0, 0, 0,
                  0, 0, 0, 1, 0, 1, 0])
```

Here is the representation provided by the csc_matrix:

```
(0, 0)      1
(0, 5)      1
(0, 16)     1
(0, 18)     1
```

Notice that the data representation is in coordinates (expressed in a tuple of row and column index) and the cell value.

The package SciPy offers a large variety of sparse matrix structures — each one storing the data in a different way and each one performing in a different way. (Some are good with slicing; some others are better for computations.) Usually the csc_matrix (a compressed matrix based on rows) is a good choice because most Scikit-learn algorithms accept it as input and it's optimal for matrix operations.

As a data scientist, you don't have to worry about programming your own version of the hashing trick unless you would like some special implementation of the idea. Scikit-learn offers HashingVectorizer, a class that rapidly transforms any collection of text into a sparse data matrix using the hashing trick. Here's an example script that replicates the previous example:

```
import sklearn.feature_extraction.text as txt
htrick = txt.HashingVectorizer(n_features=20,
                        binary=True, norm=None)
hashed_text = htrick.transform(['Python for data science',
                        'Python for machine learning'])
hashed_text
```

Python reports the size of the sparse matrix and a count of the stored elements present in it:

```
<2x20 sparse matrix of type '<class 'numpy.float64'>'
with 8 stored elements in Compressed Sparse Row format>
```

As soon as new text arrives, CountVectorizer transforms the text based on the previous encoding schema where the new words weren't present; hence, the result is simply an empty vector of zeros. You can check this by transforming the sparse matrix into a normal, dense one using todense:

```
oh_enconder.transform(['New text has arrived']).todense()
```

As expected, the printed matrix is empty:

```
matrix([[0, 0, 0, 0, 0, 0]], dtype=int64)
```

Contrast the output from CountVectorizer with HashingVectorizer, which always provides a place for new words in the data matrix:

```
htrick.transform(['New text has arrived']).todense()
```

The matrix populated by HashingVectorizer represents the new words:

```
matrix([[1., 0., 0., 1., 0., 0., 0., 0., 0., 0., 0., 0., 1.,
         0., 0., 0., 0., 0., 0., 1.]])
```

At worst, a word settles in an already occupied position, causing two different words to be treated as the same one by the algorithm (which won't noticeably degrade the algorithm's performances).

TIP

HashingVectorizer is the perfect function to use when your data can't fit into memory and its features aren't fixed. In the other cases, consider using the more intuitive CountVectorizer.

Considering Timing and Performance

As the book introduces more and more complex themes, such as Scikit-learn machine-learning classes and SciPy sparse matrices, you may start to wonder how all this processing might influence application speed. The increased processing requirements affect both running time and available memory.

Managing the best use of machine resources is indeed an art, the art of optimization, and it requires time to master. However, you can start immediately becoming proficient in it by doing some accurate speed measurement and realizing what your problems really are. Profiling the time that operations require, measuring how much memory adding more data takes, or performing a transformation on your data can help you to spot the bottlenecks in your code and start looking for alternative solutions.

As described in Chapter 5, Jupyter is the perfect environment for experimenting, tweaking, and improving your code. Working on blocks of code, recording the results and outputs, and writing additional notes and comments will help your data science solutions take shape in a controlled and reproducible way.

Benchmarking with timeit

While working through the hashing trick example in the "Performing the Hashing Trick" section, earlier in this chapter, you compare two alternatives for encoding textual information into a data matrix that can address different needs:

>> CountVectorizer: Optimally encodes text into a data matrix but cannot address subsequent novelties in text.

>> HashingVectorizer: Provides flexibility in situations when it is likely that the application will receive new data, but is less optimal than techniques based on hashing functions.

Although their advantages are quite clear in terms of how they handle the data, you may wonder what impact using one or the other has on your data processing in terms of speed and memory feasibility.

Concerning speed, Jupyter offers an easy, out-of-the-box solution, the line magic %timeit and the cell magic %%timeit:

>> %timeit: Calculates the best performance time for an instruction.

>> %%timeit: Calculates the best time performance for all the instructions in a cell, apart from the one placed on the same cell line as the cell magic (which could therefore be an initialization instruction).

Both magic commands report the best performance in r trials repeated for n loops. When you add the −r and −n parameters, the notebook chooses the number automatically in order to provide a fast answer.

Here is an example of determining the time required to assign a list 10**6 ordinal values by using list comprehension:

```
%timeit l = [k for k in range(10**6)]
```

The reported timing is:

```
109 ms ± 11.8 ms per loop
(mean ± std. dev. of 7 runs, 10 loops each)
```

The result for the list comprehension can be tested by incrementing both the sample performance and repetitions of the test:

```
%timeit -n 20 -r 5 l = [k for k in range(10**6)]
```

```
After a while, the timing is reported:109 ms ± 5.43 ms per loop
(mean ± std. dev. of 5 runs, 20 loops each)
```

As a comparison, you can check the time required to assign the values in a for loop. Since the for loop requires an entire cell, the example uses the cell magic, %%timeit, call. Notice that the first line that assigns the value of 10**6 to a variable is not considered in the performance.

```
%%timeit
l = list()
for k in range(10**6):
    l.append(k)
```

The resulting timing is

```
198 ms ± 6.62 ms per loop
(mean ± std. dev. of 7 runs, 10 loops each)
```

The results show that list comprehension is about 50 percent faster than using a for loop. You can then repeat the test using different text encoding strategies:

```
import sklearn.feature_extraction.text as txt
htrick = txt.HashingVectorizer(n_features=20,
                               binary=True,
                               norm=None)
oh_enconder = txt.CountVectorizer()
texts = ['Python for data science',
         'Python for machine learning']
```

After performing initial loading of the classes and instantiating them, you can test the two solutions:

```
%timeit oh_enconded = oh_enconder.fit_transform(texts)
```

Here is the timing for the word encoder based on the CountVectorizer:

```
1.15 ms ± 22.5 µs per loop
(mean ± std. dev. of 7 runs, 1000 loops each)
```

You now run the test on the HashingVectorizer:

```
%timeit hashing = htrick.transform(texts)
```

And obtain the following much better timing (µs [microseconds] are smaller than ms [milliseconds]):

```
186 µs ± 13 µs per loop
(mean ± std. dev. of 7 runs, 10000 loops each)
```

The hashing trick is faster than one hot encoder, and it's possible to explain the difference by noting that the latter is an optimized algorithm that keeps track of how the words are encoded, something that the hashing trick doesn't do.

Jupyter is the best environment to benchmark the speed of your data science solution code. If you'd like to track performance on the command line or in a script running from an IDE, you can import the timeit class and use the timeit function for tracking performance of the command by providing the input parameter as a string.

If your command needs variables, classes, or functions that aren't available in the base Python (such as the Scikit-learn classes), you can provide them as a second input parameter. You formulate a string in which Python imports all the necessary objects from the main environment, as shown in the following example:

```
import timeit
cumulative_time = timeit.timeit(
    "hashing = htrick.transform(texts)",
    "from __main__ import htrick, texts",
    number=10000)
print(cumulative_time / 10000.0)
```

USING THE PREFERRED INSTALLER PROGRAM (PIP) AND CONDA

Python provides a huge number of packages that you can install. Many of these packages come as separate, downloadable modules. Some of them have an executable suitable for a platform such as Windows, which means you can easily install the package. However, many other packages rely on **pip**, the preferred installer program, which is a feature that you can access directly from the command line.

To use pip, you open the Anaconda Prompt. If you need to install a package from scratch, such as NumPy, you type **pip install numpy**, and the software will download the package as well as all the related packages that it needs to work, and will install everything. You can even install a specific version by typing, for example, **pip install –U numpy==1.14.5**, or simply update the package to its most recent version if is already installed: **pip install –U numpy**.

If you installed Anaconda, , you can use conda instead of pip, which is even more efficient when installing because it sets all the other packages to the right version for your newly installed Python package (which implies that it can install, upgrade or even downgrade existing packages on your system). Using conda for installing a new package is achieved from the Anaconda Prompt, as well, by entering **conda install numpy**. The software analyzes your system, reports the changes, and then asks whether it should proceed. Press y if you want to proceed with the installation. You also use conda to update existing packages (enter **conda update numpy**) or the entire system (enter **conda update --all)**.

This book uses Jupyter as its environment. Installing and upgrading while using Jupyter is a bit complicated. Jake VanderPlas from the University of Washington wrote a very informative post about this issue, which you can find at `https://jakevdp.github. io/blog/2017/12/05/installing-python-packages-from-jupyter/`. The article proposes a few ways to handle package installation and upgrading while using the Jupyter interface. At the beginning, until you gain confidence and experience, the best option is to install and update your system first and then run Jupyter, making the installation much easier and smoother.

Working with the memory profiler

As you've seen when testing your application code for performance (speed) characteristics, you can obtain analogous information about memory usage. Keeping track of memory consumption could tell you about possible problems in the way data is processed or transmitted to the learning algorithms. The `memory_profiler` package implements the required functionality. This package is not provided as a default Python package and it requires installation. Use the following command to install the package directly from a cell of your Jupyter notebook, as explained by Jake VanderPlas's post described in the "Using the preferred installer program (pip) and conda" sidebar:

```
import sys
!{sys.executable} -m pip install memory_profiler
```

Use the following command for each Jupyter Notebook session you want to monitor:

```
%load_ext memory_profiler
```

After performing these tasks, you can easily track how much memory a command consumes:

```
hashing = htrick.transform(texts)
%memit dense_hashing = hashing.toarray()
```

The reported peak memory and increment tell you about memory usage:

```
peak memory: 90.42 MiB, increment: 0.09 MiB
```

Obtaining a complete overview of memory consumption is possible by saving a notebook cell to disk and then profiling it using the line magic %mprun on an externally imported function. (The line magic works only by operating with external Python scripts.) Profiling produces a detailed report, command by command, as shown in the following example:

```
%%writefile example_code.py
def comparison_test(text):
    import sklearn.feature_extraction.text as txt
    htrick = txt.HashingVectorizer(n_features=20,
                                   binary=True,
                                   norm=None)
    oh_enconder = txt.CountVectorizer()
    oh_enconded = oh_enconder.fit_transform(text)
    hashing = htrick.transform(text)
    return oh_enconded, hashing

from example_code import comparison_test
text = ['Python for data science',
        'Python for machine learning']
%mprun -f comparison_test comparison_test(text)
```

REDUCING MEMORY USAGE AND COMPUTING FAST

You use NumPy `arrays` or pandas `DataFrames` when working with data. However, even if they appear as different data structures: one focuses on storing data as a matrix and the other on handling complex datasets stored in different ways — `DataFrames` rely on NumPy `arrays`. Understanding how `arrays` work and are used by pandas allows you to reduce memory usage and achieve faster computations.

NumPy `arrays` are a tool for handling data by using contiguous memory blocks to store the values. Because the data appears in the same area of computer memory, Python can retrieve the data faster and slice it more easily. It's the same principle as disk fragmentation: If your data is scattered on disk, it occupies more space and requires more handling time.

Depending on your needs, you can order array data by rows (the default choice of both NumPy and the C/C++ programming language) or columns. Computer memory stores cells one after the other in a line. Consequently, you can record your array row after row, allowing fast processing by rows, or column by column, allowing faster processing by columns. All these details, though hidden from your eyes, are crucial because they render working with NumPy `arrays` fast and efficient for data science (which uses numeric matrices and often computes information by rows). This is why all Scikit-learn algorithms expect a NumPy `array` as an input and why NumPy `arrays` have a fixed data type (they can be only of the same type as the data sequence; they can't vary).

pandas `DataFrames` are just well-arranged collections of NumPy `arrays`. Your variables in `DataFrame`, depending on the type, are compacted in an `array`. For instance, all your integer variables are together in an *IntBlock*, all your float data in a *FloatBlock*, and the rest in an *ObjectBlock*. This means that when you want to operate on a single variable, you are actually operating on all the variables. Consequently, if you have an operation to apply, it's better to apply it to all variables of the same type simultaneously. In addition, this also means that working with string variables is incredibly expensive in terms of memory and computations. Even if you store something as simple as a short series of color names in a variable, it will require the use of a complete string (at least 50 bytes) and handling it will be quite cumbersome using the NumPy engine. As suggested in Chapter 7, you can transform your string data in categorical variables; by doing so, behind the scenes, strings are transformed into numbers. In this way, you greatly reduce the memory usage and increase the speed you experience when manipulating the data.

You will get an output similar to this one (the output appears in a separate window at the bottom of the Notebook display by default):

```
Line # Mem usage Increment Line Contents
================================================
     1   94.8 MiB   94.8 MiB def comparison_test(text):
     2   94.8 MiB    0.0 MiB     import...
     3   94.8 MiB    0.0 MiB     htrick = ...
     4   94.8 MiB    0.0 MiB              ...
     5   94.8 MiB    0.2 MiB              ...
     6   94.8 MiB    0.0 MiB     oh_encoder = ...
     7   94.8 MiB    0.0 MiB     oh_encoded = ...
     8   94.8 MiB    0.0 MiB     hashing = ...
     9   94.8 MiB    0.0 MiB     return ...
```

The resulting report details the memory usage from every line in the function, pointing out the major increments.

Running in Parallel on Multiple Cores

Most computers today are multicore (two or more processors in a single package), some with multiple physical CPUs. One of the most important limitations of Python is that it uses a single core by default. (It was created in a time when single cores were the norm.)

Data science projects require quite a lot of computations. In particular, a part of the scientific aspect of data science relies on repeated tests and experiments on different data matrices. Don't forget that working with huge data quantities means that most time-consuming transformations repeat observation after observation (for example, identical and not related operations on different parts of a matrix).

Using more CPU cores accelerates a computation by a factor that almost matches the number of cores. For example, having four cores would mean working at best four times faster. You don't receive a full fourfold increase because there is overhead when starting a parallel process — new running Python instances have to be set up with the right in-memory information and launched; consequently, the improvement will be less than potentially achievable but still significant. Knowing how to use more than one CPU is therefore an advanced but incredibly useful skill for increasing the number of analyses completed, and for speeding up your operations both when setting up and when using your data products.

REMEMBER

Multiprocessing works by replicating the same code and memory content in various new Python instances (the workers), calculating the result for each of them, and returning the pooled results to the main original console. If your original instance already occupies much of the available RAM memory, it won't be possible to create new instances, and your machine may run out of memory.

Performing multicore parallelism

To perform multicore parallelism with Python, you integrate the Scikit-learn package with the joblib package for time-consuming operations, such as replicating models for validating results or for looking for the best hyperparameters. In particular, Scikit-learn allows multiprocessing when

>> **Cross-validating:** Testing the results of a machine-learning hypothesis using different training and testing data

>> **Grid-searching:** Systematically changing the hyperparameters of a machine-learning hypothesis and testing the consequent results

>> **Multilabel prediction:** Running an algorithm multiple times against multiple targets when there are many different target outcomes to predict at the same time

>> **Ensemble machine-learning methods:** Modeling a large host of classifiers, each one independent from the other, such as when using RandomForest-based modeling

You don't have to do anything special to take advantage of parallel computations — you can activate parallelism by setting the n_jobs parameter to a number of cores more than 1 or by setting the value to –1, which means you want to use all the available CPU instances.

WARNING

If you aren't running your code from the console or from a Jupyter Notebook, it is extremely important that you separate your code from any package import or global variable assignment in your script by using the if __name__=='__main__': command at the beginning of any code that executes multicore parallelism. The if statement checks whether the program is directly run or is called by an already-running Python console, avoiding any confusion or error by the multiparallel process (such as recursively calling the parallelism).

Demonstrating multiprocessing

It's a good idea to use a notebook when you run a demonstration of how multiprocessing can really save you time during data science projects. Using Jupyter provides the advantage of using the `%timeit` magic command for timing execution. You start by loading a multiclass dataset, a complex machine learning algorithm (the Support Vector Classifier, or SVC), and a cross-validation procedure for estimating reliable resulting scores from all the procedures. You find details about all these tools later in the book. The most important thing to know is that the procedures become quite large because the SVC produces 10 models, which it repeats 10 times each using cross-validation, for a total of 100 models.

```python
from sklearn.datasets import load_digits
digits = load_digits()
X, y = digits.data,digits.target
from sklearn.svm import SVC
from sklearn.model_selection import cross_val_score

%timeit single_core = cross_val_score(SVC(), X, y, \
                                      cv=20, n_jobs=1)
```

As a result, you get the recorded average running time for a single core:

```
18.2 s ± 265 ms per loop
(mean ± std. dev. of 7 runs, 1 loop each)
```

After this test, you need to activate the multicore parallelism and time the results using the following commands:

```python
%timeit multi_core = cross_val_score(SVC(), X, y, \
                                     cv=20, n_jobs=-1)
```

Running on multiple cores allows for a better average time:

```
10.8 s ± 137 ms per loop
(mean ± std. dev. of 7 runs, 1 loop each)
```

The example machine demonstrates a positive advantage using multicore processing, despite using a small dataset where Python spends most of the time starting consoles and running a part of the code in each one. This overhead, a few seconds, is still significant given that the total execution extends for a handful of seconds. Just imagine what would happen if you worked with larger sets of data — your execution time could be easily cut by two or three times.

Although the code works fine with Jupyter, putting it down in a script and asking Python to run it in a console or using an IDE may cause errors because of the internal operations of a multicore task. The solution, as mentioned before, is to put all the code under an `if` statement, which checks whether the program started directly and wasn't called afterward. Here's an example script:

```
from sklearn.datasets import load_digits
from sklearn.svm import SVC
from sklearn.cross_validation import cross_val_score
if __name__ == '__main__':
        digits = load_digits()
        X, y = digits.data,digits.target
        multi_core = cross_val_score(SVC(), X, y,
                                        cv=20, n_jobs=-1)
```

Chapter **13**

Exploring Data Analysis

Data science relies on complex algorithms for building predictions and spotting important signals in data, and each algorithm presents different strong and weak points. In short, you select a range of algorithms, you have them run on the data, you optimize their parameters as much as you can, and finally you decide which one will best help you build your data product or generate insight into your problem.

It sounds a little bit automatic and, partially, it is, thanks to powerful analytical software and scripting languages like Python. Learning algorithms are complex, and their sophisticated procedures naturally seem automatic and a bit opaque to you. However, even if some of these tools seem like black or even magic boxes, keep this simple acronym in mind: GIGO. GIGO stands for "Garbage In/Garbage Out." It has been a well-known adage in statistics (and computer science) for a long time. No matter how powerful the machine learning algorithms you use, you won't obtain good results if your data has something wrong in it.

Exploratory Data Analysis (EDA) is a general approach to exploring datasets by means of simple summary statistics and graphic visualizations in order to gain a deeper understanding of data. EDA helps you become more effective in the subsequent data analysis and modeling. In this chapter, you discover all the necessary and indispensable basic descriptions of the data and see how those descriptions can help you decide how to proceed using the most appropriate data transformation and solutions.

REMEMBER

You don't have to type the source code for this chapter manually. In fact, it's a lot easier if you use the downloadable source. The source code for this chapter appears in the `P4DS4D2_13_Exploring_Data_Analysis.ipynb` source code file. (See the Introduction for details on where to locate this file.)

The EDA Approach

EDA was developed at Bell Labs by John Tukey, a mathematician and statistician who wanted to promote more questions and actions on data based on the data itself (the exploratory motif) in contrast to the dominant confirmatory approach of the time. A confirmatory approach relies on the use of a theory or procedure — the data is just there for testing and application. EDA emerged at the end of the 70s, long before the big data flood appeared. Tukey could already see that certain activities, such as testing and modeling, were easy to make automatic. In one of his famous writings, Tukey said:

"The only way humans can do BETTER than computers is to take a chance of doing WORSE than them."

This statement explains why, as a data scientist, your role and tools aren't limited to automatic learning algorithms but also to manual and creative exploratory tasks. Computers are unbeatable at optimizing, but humans are strong at discovery by taking unexpected routes and trying unlikely but in the end very effective solutions.

If you've been through the examples in the previous chapters, you have already worked on quite a bit of data, but using EDA is a bit different because it checks beyond the basic assumptions about data workability, which actually comprises the Initial Data Analysis (IDA). Up to now, the book has shown how to

>> Complete observations or mark missing cases by appropriate features

>> Transform text or categorical variables

>> Create new features based on domain knowledge of the data problem

>> Have at hand a numeric dataset where rows are observations and columns are variables

EDA goes further than IDA. It's moved by a different attitude: going beyond basic assumptions. With EDA, you

>> Describe of your data

>> Closely explore data distributions

>> Understand the relations between variables

>> Notice unusual or unexpected situations

>> Place the data into groups

>> Notice unexpected patterns within groups

>> Take note of group differences

REMEMBER

You will read a lot in the following pages about how EDA can help you learn about variable distribution in your dataset. *Variable distribution* is the list of values you find in that variable compared to their *frequency,* that is, how often they occur. Being able to determine variable distribution tells you a lot about how a variable could behave when fed into a machine learning algorithm and, thus, help you take appropriate steps to have it perform well in your project.

Defining Descriptive Statistics for Numeric Data

The first actions that you can take with the data are to produce some synthetic measures to help figure out what is going in it. You acquire knowledge of measures such as maximum and minimum values, and you define which intervals are the best place to start.

During your exploration, you use a simple but useful dataset that is used in previous chapters, the Fisher's Iris dataset. You can load it from the Scikit-learn package by using the following code:

```
from sklearn.datasets import load_iris
iris = load_iris()
```

Having loaded the Iris dataset into a variable of a custom Scikit-learn class, you can derive a NumPy nparray and a pandas DataFrame from it:

```
import pandas as pd
import numpy as np
```

```
print('Your pandas version is: %s' % pd.__version__)
print('Your NumPy version is %s' % np.__version__)
from sklearn.datasets import load_iris
iris = load_iris()
iris_nparray = iris.data

iris_dataframe = pd.DataFrame(iris.data, columns=iris.
    feature_names)
iris_dataframe['group'] = pd.Series([iris.target_names[k] for k
    in iris.target], dtype="category")



Your pandas version is: 0.23.3
Your NumPy version is 1.14.5
```

REMEMBER

NumPy, Scikit-learn, and especially pandas are packages under constant development, so before you start working with EDA, it's a good idea to check the product version numbers. Using an older or newer version could cause your output to differ from that shown in the book or cause some commands to fail. For this edition of the book, use pandas version 0.23.3 and NumPy version 1.14.5.

TIP

This chapter presents a series of pandas and NumPy commands that help you explore the structure of data. Even though applying single explorative commands grants you more freedom in your analysis, it's nice to know that you can obtain most of these statistics using the describe method applied to your pandas DataFrame: such as, print iris_dataframe.describe(), when you're in a hurry in your data science project.

Measuring central tendency

Mean and median are the first measures to calculate for numeric variables when starting EDA. They can provide you with an estimate when the variables are centered and somehow symmetric.

Using pandas, you can quickly compute both means and medians. Here is the command for getting the mean from the Iris DataFrame:

```
print(iris_dataframe.mean(numeric_only=True))
```

Here is the resulting output for the mean statistic:

```
sepal length (cm) 5.843333
sepal width (cm) 3.054000
```

```
petal length (cm) 3.758667
petal width (cm) 1.198667
```

Similarly, here is the command that will output the median:

```
print(iris_dataframe.median(numeric_only=True))
```

```
You then obtain the median estimates for all the variables:sepal
    length (cm) 5.80
sepal width (cm) 3.00
petal length (cm) 4.35
petal width (cm) 1.30
```

The median provides the central position in the series of values. When creating a variable, it is a measure less influenced by anomalous cases or by an asymmetric distribution of values around the mean. What you should notice here is that the means are not centered (no variable is zero mean) and that the median of petal length is quite different from the mean, requiring further inspection.

When checking for central tendency measures, you should:

» Verify whether means are zero

» Check whether they are different from each other

» Notice whether the median is different from the mean

Measuring variance and range

As a next step, you should check the variance by using its square root, the standard deviation. The standard deviation is as informative as the variance, but comparing to the mean is easier because it's expressed in the same unit of measure. The variance is a good indicator of whether a mean is a suitable indicator of the variable distribution because it tells you how the values of a variable distribute around the mean. The higher the variance, the farther you can expect some values to appear from the mean.

```
print(iris_dataframe.std())
```

The printed output for each variable:

```
sepal length (cm) 0.828066
sepal width (cm) 0.433594
```

```
petal length (cm) 1.764420
petal width (cm) 0.763161
```

In addition, you also check the range, which is the difference between the maximum and minimum value for each quantitative variable, and it is quite informative about the difference in scale among variables.

```
print(iris_dataframe.max(numeric_only=True)
      - iris_dataframe.min(numeric_only=True))
```

Here you can find the output of the preceding command:

```
sepal length (cm)    3.6
sepal width (cm)     2.4
petal length (cm)    5.9
petal width (cm)     2.4
```

Note the standard deviation and the range in relation to the mean and median. A standard deviation or range that's too high with respect to the measures of centrality (mean and median) may point to a possible problem, with extremely unusual values affecting the calculation or an unexpected distribution of values around the mean.

Working with percentiles

Because the median is the value in the central position of your distribution of values, you may need to consider other notable positions. Apart from the minimum and maximum, the position at 25 percent of your values (the lower quartile) and the position at 75 percent (the upper quartile) are useful for determining the data distribution, and they are the basis of an illustrative graph called a *boxplot*, which is one of the topics discuss in this chapter.

```
print(iris_dataframe.quantile([0,.25,.50,.75,1]))
```

In Figure 13-1, you can see the output as a matrix — a comparison that uses quartiles for rows and the different dataset variables as columns. So, the 25-percent quartile for sepal length (cm) is 5.1, which means that 25 percent of the dataset values for this measure are less than 5.1.

```
In [8]: print(iris_dataframe.quantile([0,.25,.50,.75,1]))

      sepal length (cm)  sepal width (cm)  petal length (cm)  petal width (cm)
0.00               4.3               2.0                1.00               0.1
0.25               5.1               2.8                1.60               0.3
0.50               5.8               3.0                4.35               1.3
0.75               6.4               3.3                5.10               1.8
1.00               7.9               4.4                6.90               2.5
```

REMEMBER

The difference between the upper and lower percentile constitutes the interquartile range (IQR) which is a measure of the scale of variables that are of highest interest. You don't need to calculate it, but you will find it in the boxplot because it helps to determinate the plausible limits of your distribution. What lies between the lower quartile and the minimum, and the upper quartile and the maximum, are exceptionally rare values that can negatively affect the results of your analysis. Such rare cases are outliers — and they're the topic of Chapter 16.

Defining measures of normality

The last indicative measures of how the numeric variables used for these examples are structured are skewness and kurtosis:

» *Skewness* defines the asymmetry of data with respect to the mean. If the skew is negative, the left tail is too long and the mass of the observations are on the right side of the distribution. If it is positive, it is exactly the opposite.

» *Kurtosis* shows whether the data distribution, especially the peak and the tails, are of the right shape. If the kurtosis is above zero, the distribution has a marked peak. If it is below zero, the distribution is too flat instead.

Although reading the numbers can help you determine the shape of the data, taking notice of such measures presents a formal test to select the variables that may need some adjustment or transformation in order to become more similar to the Gaussian distribution. Remember that you also visualize the data later, so this is a first step in a longer process.

REMEMBER

The normal, or Gaussian, distribution is the most useful distribution in statistics thanks to its frequent recurrence and particular mathematical properties. It's essentially the foundation of many statistical tests and models, with some of them, such as the linear regression, widely used in data science. In a Gaussian distribution, mean and median have the same values, the values are symmetrically distributed around the mean (it has the shape of a bell), and its standard deviation points out the distance from the mean where the distribution curve changes from being concave to convex (it is called the inflection point). All these characteristics make the Gaussian distribution a special distribution, and they can be leveraged for statistical computations.

TIP

You seldom encounter a Gaussian distribution in your data. Even if the Gaussian distribution is important for its statistical properties, in reality you'll have to handle completely different distributions, hence the need for EDA and measures such as skewness and kurtosis.

As an example, a previous illustration in this chapter shows that the petal length feature presents differences between the mean and the median (see "Measuring variance and range," earlier in this chapter). In this section, you test the same example for skewness and kurtosis in order to determine whether the variable requires intervention.

When performing the skewness and kurtosis tests, you determine whether the p-value is less than or equal 0.05. If so, you have to reject normality (your variable distributed as a Gaussian distribution), which implies that you could obtain better results if you try to transform the variable into a normal one. The following code shows how to perform the required test:

```
from scipy.stats import skew, skewtest
variable = iris_dataframe['petal length (cm)']
s = skew(variable)
zscore, pvalue = skewtest(variable)
print('Skewness %0.3f z-score %0.3f p-value %0.3f'
    % (s, zscore, pvalue))
```

Here are the skewness scores you get:

```
Skewness -0.272 z-score -1.398 p-value 0.162
```

You can perform another test for kurtosis, as shown in the following code:

```
from scipy.stats import kurtosis, kurtosistest
variable = iris_dataframe['petal length (cm)']
k = kurtosis(variable)
zscore, pvalue = kurtosistest(variable)
print('Kurtosis %0.3f z-score %0.3f p-value %0.3f'
    % (k, zscore, pvalue))
```

Here are the kurtosis scores you obtain:

```
Kurtosis -1.395 z-score -14.811 p-value 0.000
```

The test results tell you that the data is slightly skewed to the left, but not enough to make it unusable. The real problem is that the curve is much too flat to be bell shaped, so you should investigate the matter further.

TIP

It's a good practice to test all variables for skewness and kurtosis automatically. You should then proceed to inspect those whose values are the highest visually. Non-normality of a distribution may also conceal different issues, such as outliers to groups that you can perceive only by a graphical visualization.

Counting for Categorical Data

The Iris dataset is made of four metric variables and a qualitative target outcome. Just as you use means and variance as descriptive measures for metric variables, so do frequencies strictly relate to qualitative ones.

Because the dataset is made up of metric measurements (width and lengths in centimeters), you must render it qualitative by dividing it into bins according to specific intervals. The pandas package features two useful functions, cut and qcut, that can transform a metric variable into a qualitative one:

» cut expects a series of edge values used to cut the measurements or an integer number of groups used to cut the variables into equal-width bins.

» qcut expects a series of percentiles used to cut the variable.

You can obtain a new categorical DataFrame using the following command, which concatenates a binning (see the "Understanding binning and discretization" section of Chapter 9 for details) for each variable:

```
pcts = [0, .25, .5, .75, 1]
iris_binned = pd.concat(
    [pd.qcut(iris_dataframe.iloc[:,0], pcts, precision=1),
     pd.qcut(iris_dataframe.iloc[:,1], pcts, precision=1),
     pd.qcut(iris_dataframe.iloc[:,2], pcts, precision=1),
     pd.qcut(iris_dataframe.iloc[:,3], pcts, precision=1)],
    join='outer', axis = 1)
```

TIP

This example relies on binning. However, it could also help to explore when the variable is above or below a singular hurdle value, usually the mean or the median. In this case, you set pd.qcut to the 0.5 percentile or pd.cut to the mean value of the variable.

REMEMBER

Binning transforms numerical variables into categorical ones. This transformation can improve your understanding of data and the machine-learning phase that follows by reducing the noise (outliers) or nonlinearity of the transformed variable.

Understanding frequencies

You can obtain a frequency for each categorical variable of the dataset, both for the predictive variable and for the outcome, by using the following code:

```
print(iris_dataframe['group'].value_counts())
```

The resulting frequencies show that each group is of the same size:

```
virginica    50
versicolor   50
setosa       50
```

You can try also computing frequencies for the binned petal length that you obtained from the previous paragraph:print(iris_binned['petal length (cm)'].value_counts())

In this case, binning produces different groups:

```
(0.9, 1.6]   44
(4.4, 5.1]   41
(5.1, 6.9]   34
(1.6, 4.4]   31
```

This example provides you with some basic frequency information as well, such as the number of unique values in each variable and the mode of the frequency (top and freq rows in the output).

```
print(iris_binned.describe())
```

Figure 13-2 shows the binning description.

FIGURE 13-2:
Descriptive
statistics for the
binning.

```
In [14]:  print(iris_binned.describe())

            sepal length (cm) sepal width (cm) petal length (cm) petal width (cm)
count                     150              150               150              150
unique                      4                4                 4                4
top                (4.2, 5.1]       (1.9, 2.8]        (0.9, 1.6]       (0.0, 0.3]
freq                       41               47                44               41
```

Frequencies can signal a number of interesting characteristics of qualitative features:

- » The mode of the frequency distribution that is the most frequent category

- » The other most frequent categories, especially when they are comparable with the mode (bimodal distribution) or if there is a large difference between them

- » The distribution of frequencies among categories, if rapidly decreasing or equally distributed

- » Rare categories

Creating contingency tables

By matching different categorical frequency distributions, you can display the relationship between qualitative variables. The `pandas.crosstab` function can match variables or groups of variables, helping to locate possible data structures or relationships.

In the following example, you check how the outcome variable is related to petal length and observe how certain outcomes and petal binned classes never appear together. Figure 13-3 shows the various iris types along the left side of the output, followed by the output as related to petal length.

```
print(pd.crosstab(iris_dataframe['group'],
                  iris_binned['petal length (cm)']))
```

FIGURE 13-3:
A contingency table based on groups and binning.

```
In [15]: print(pd.crosstab(iris_dataframe['group'],
                  iris_binned['petal length (cm)']))

petal length (cm)  (0.9, 1.6]  (1.6, 4.4]  (4.4, 5.1]  (5.1, 6.9]
group
setosa                     44           6           0           0
versicolor                  0          25          25           0
virginica                   0           0          16          34
```

Creating Applied Visualization for EDA

Up to now, the chapter has explored variables by looking at each one separately. Technically, if you've followed along with the examples, you have created a *univariate* (that is, you've paid attention to stand-alone variations of the data only) description of the data. The data is rich in information because it offers a perspective that goes beyond the single variable, presenting more variables with their reciprocal variations. The way to use more of the data is to create a *bivariate* (seeing how couples of variables relate to each other) exploration. This is also the basis for complex data analysis based on a *multivariate* (simultaneously considering all the existent relations between variables) approach.

If the univariate approach inspected a limited number of descriptive statistics, then matching different variables or groups of variables increases the number of possibilities. Such exploration overloads the data scientist with different tests and bivariate analysis. Using visualization is a rapid way to limit test and analysis to only interesting traces and hints. Visualizations, using a few informative graphics, can convey the variety of statistical characteristics of the variables and their reciprocal relationships with greater ease.

Inspecting boxplots

Boxplots provide a way to represent distributions and their extreme ranges, signaling whether some observations are too far from the core of the data — a problematic situation for some learning algorithms. The following code shows how to create a basic boxplot using the Iris dataset:

```
boxplots = iris_dataframe.boxplot(fontsize=9)
```

In Figure 13-4, you see the structure of each variable's distribution at its core, represented by the 25° and 75° percentile (the sides of the box) and the median (at the center of the box). The lines, the so-called whiskers, represent 1.5 times the IQR from the box sides (or by the distance to the most extreme value, if within 1.5 times the IQR). The boxplot marks every observation outside the whisker (deemed an unusual value) by a sign.

FIGURE 13-4:
A boxplot arranged by variables.

Boxplots are also extremely useful for visually checking group differences. Note in Figure 13-5 how a boxplot can hint that the three groups, setosa, versicolor, and virginica, have different petal lengths, with only partially overlapping values at the fringes of the last two of them.

```
import matplotlib.pyplot as plt
boxplots = iris_dataframe.boxplot(
                            column='petal length (cm)',
                            by='group', fontsize=10)
plt.suptitle("")
plt.show()
```

```
In [17]: import matplotlib.pyplot as plt
         boxplots = iris_dataframe.boxplot(column='petal length (cm)',
                                           by='group', fontsize=10)
         plt.suptitle("")
         plt.show()
```

FIGURE 13-5:
A boxplot of petal
length arranged
by groups.

Performing t-tests after boxplots

After you have spotted a possible group difference relative to a variable, a t-test
(you use a t-test in situations in which the sampled population has an exact normal distribution) or a one-way Analysis Of Variance (ANOVA) can provide you
with a statistical verification of the significance of the difference between the
groups' means.

```
from scipy.stats import ttest_ind

group0 = iris_dataframe['group'] == 'setosa'
group1 = iris_dataframe['group'] == 'versicolor'
group2 = iris_dataframe['group'] == 'virginica'
variable = iris_dataframe['petal length (cm)']

print('var1 %0.3f var2 %03f' % (variable[group1].var(),
                                variable[group2].var()))

var1 0.221 var2 0.304588
```

The t-test compares two groups at a time, and it requires that you define whether
the groups have similar variance or not. Therefore, it is necessary to calculate the
variance beforehand, like this:

```
variable = iris_dataframe['sepal width (cm)']
t, pvalue = ttest_ind(variable[group1], variable[group2],
                      axis=0, equal_var=False)
print('t statistic %0.3f p-value %0.3f' % (t, pvalue))
```

The resulting t statistic and its p-values are

```
t statistic -3.206 p-value 0.002
```

You interpret the `pvalue` as the probability that the calculated t statistic differ-ence is just due to chance. Usually, when it is below 0.05, you can confirm that the groups' means are significantly different.

You can simultaneously check more than two groups using the one-way ANOVA test. In this case, the `pvalue` has an interpretation similar to the t-test:

```
from scipy.stats import f_oneway
variable = iris_dataframe['sepal width (cm)']
f, pvalue = f_oneway(variable[group0],
                     variable[group1],
                     variable[group2])
print('One-way ANOVA F-value %0.3f p-value %0.3f'
      % (f,pvalue))
```

The result from the ANOVA test is

```
One-way ANOVA F-value 47.364 p-value 0.000
```

Observing parallel coordinates

Parallel coordinates can help spot which groups in the outcome variable you could easily separate from the other. It is a truly multivariate plot, because at a glance it represents all your data at the same time. The following example shows how to use parallel coordinates.

```
from pandas.plotting import parallel_coordinates
iris_dataframe['group'] = iris.target
iris_dataframe['labels'] = [iris.target_names[k]
                   for k in iris_dataframe['group']]
pll = parallel_coordinates(iris_dataframe, 'labels')
```

As shown in Figure 13-6, on the abscissa axis you find all the quantitative vari-ables aligned. On the ordinate, you find all the observations, carefully represented as parallel lines, each one of a different color given its ownership to a different group.

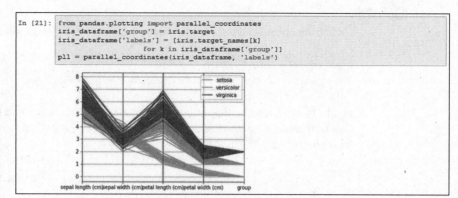

FIGURE 13-6:
Parallel
coordinates
anticipate
whether groups
are easily
separable.

```
In [21]: from pandas.plotting import parallel_coordinates
         iris_dataframe['group'] = iris.target
         iris_dataframe['labels'] = [iris.target_names[k]
                     for k in iris_dataframe['group']]
         pll = parallel_coordinates(iris_dataframe, 'labels')
```

If the parallel lines of each group stream together along the visualization in a separate part of the graph far from other groups, the group is easily separable. The visualization also provides the means to assert the capability of certain features to separate the groups.

Graphing distributions

You usually render the information that boxplot and descriptive statistics provide into a curve or a histogram, which shows an overview of the complete distribution of values. The output shown in Figure 13-7 represents all the distributions in the dataset. Different variable scales and shapes are immediately visible, such as the fact that petals' features display two peaks.

```
cols = iris_dataframe.columns[:4]
densityplot = iris_dataframe[cols].plot(kind='density')
```

FIGURE 13-7:
Features'
distribution and
density.

```
In [22]: cols = iris_dataframe.columns[:4]
         densityplot = iris_dataframe[cols].plot(kind='density')
```

Histograms present another, more detailed, view over distributions:

```
variable = iris_dataframe['petal length (cm)']
single_distribution = variable.plot(kind='hist')
```

Figure 13-8 shows the histogram of petal length. It reveals a gap in the distribution that could be a promising discovery if you can relate it to a certain group of Iris flowers.

FIGURE 13-8:
Histograms can detail better distributions.

Plotting scatterplots

In scatterplots, the two compared variables provide the coordinates for plotting the observations as points on a plane. The result is usually a cloud of points. When the cloud is elongated and resembles a line, you can deduce that the variables are correlated. The following example demonstrates this principle:

```
palette = {0: 'red', 1: 'yellow', 2:'blue'}
colors = [palette[c] for c in iris_dataframe['group']]
simple_scatterplot = iris_dataframe.plot(
                kind='scatter', x='petal length (cm)',
                y='petal width (cm)', c=colors)
```

This simple scatterplot, represented in Figure 13-9, compares length and width of petals. The scatterplot highlights different groups using different colors. The elongated shape described by the points hints at a strong correlation between the two observed variables, and the division of the cloud into groups suggests a possible separability of the groups.

Because the number of variables isn't too large, you can also generate all the scatterplots automatically from the combination of the variables. This representation is a matrix of scatterplots. The following example demonstrates how to create one:

FIGURE 13-9:
A scatterplot
reveals how two
variables relate to
each other.

```
from pandas.plotting import scatter_matrix
palette = {0: "red", 1: "yellow", 2: "blue"}
colors = [palette[c] for c in iris_dataframe['group']]
matrix_of_scatterplots = scatter_matrix(
    iris_dataframe, figsize=(6, 6),
    color=colors, diagonal='kde')
```

In Figure 13-10, you can see the resulting visualization for the Iris dataset. The diagonal representing the density estimation can be replaced by a histogram using the parameter diagonal='hist'.

FIGURE 13-10:
A matrix of
scatterplots
displays more
information at
one time.

Understanding Correlation

Just as the relationship between variables is graphically representable, it is also measurable by a statistical estimate. When working with numeric variables, the estimate is a correlation, and the Pearson's correlation is the most famous. The Pearson's correlation is the foundation for complex linear estimation models. When you work with categorical variables, the estimate is an association, and the chi-square statistic is the most frequently used tool for measuring association between features.

Using covariance and correlation

Covariance is the first measure of the relationship of two variables. It determines whether both variables have a coincident behavior with respect to their mean. If the single values of two variables are usually above or below their respective averages, the two variables have a positive association. It means that they tend to agree, and you can figure out the behavior of one of the two by looking at the other. In such a case, their covariance will be a positive number, and the higher the number, the higher the agreement.

If, instead, one variable is usually above and the other variable usually below their respective averages, the two variables are negatively associated. Even though the two disagree, it's an interesting situation for making predictions, because by observing the state of one of them, you can figure out the likely state of the other (albeit they're opposite). In this case, their covariance will be a negative number.

A third state is that the two variables don't systematically agree or disagree with each other. In this case, the covariance will tend to be zero, a sign that the variables don't share much and have independent behaviors.

Ideally, when you have a numeric target variable, you want the target variable to have a high positive or negative covariance with the predictive variables. Having a high positive or negative covariance among the predictive variables is a sign of information redundancy. *Information redundancy* signals that the variables point to the same data — that is, the variables are telling us the same thing in slightly different ways.

Computing a covariance matrix is straightforward using pandas. You can immediately apply it to the DataFrame of the Iris dataset as shown here:

```
iris_dataframe.cov()
```

The matrix in Figure 13-11 shows variables present on both rows and columns. By observing different row and column combinations, you can determine the value of covariance between the variables chosen. After observing these results, you can immediately understand that little relationship exists between sepal length and sepal width, meaning that they're different informative values. However, there could be a special relationship between petal width and petal length, but the example doesn't tell what this relationship is because the measure is not easily interpretable.

FIGURE 13-11: A covariance matrix of Iris dataset.

```
In [26]:  iris_dataframe.cov()
```

Out[26]:

	sepal length (cm)	sepal width (cm)	petal length (cm)	petal width (cm)	group
sepal length (cm)	0.685694	-0.039268	1.273682	0.516904	0.530872
sepal width (cm)	-0.039268	0.188004	-0.321713	-0.117981	-0.148993
petal length (cm)	1.273682	-0.321713	3.113179	1.296387	1.371812
petal width (cm)	0.516904	-0.117981	1.296387	0.582414	0.597987
group	0.530872	-0.148993	1.371812	0.597987	0.671141

The scale of the variables you observe influences covariance, so you should use a different, but standard, measure. The solution is to use correlation, which is the covariance estimation after having standardized the variables. Here is an example of obtaining a correlation using a simple pandas method:

```
iris_dataframe.corr()
```

You can examine the resulting correlation matrix in Figure 13-12:

FIGURE 13-12: A correlation matrix of Iris dataset.

```
In [27]:  iris_dataframe.corr()
```

Out[27]:

	sepal length (cm)	sepal width (cm)	petal length (cm)	petal width (cm)	group
sepal length (cm)	1.000000	-0.109369	0.871754	0.817954	0.782561
sepal width (cm)	-0.109369	1.000000	-0.420516	-0.356544	-0.419446
petal length (cm)	0.871754	-0.420516	1.000000	0.962757	0.949043
petal width (cm)	0.817954	-0.356544	0.962757	1.000000	0.956464
group	0.782561	-0.419446	0.949043	0.956464	1.000000

Now that's even more interesting, because correlation values are bound between values of −1 and +1, so the relationship between petal width and length is positive and, with a 0.96, it is almost the maximum possible.

You can compute covariance and correlation matrices also by means of NumPy commands, as shown here:

```
covariance_matrix = np.cov(iris_nparray, rowvar=0)
correlation_matrix = np.corrcoef(iris_nparray, rowvar=0)
```

REMEMBER

In statistics, this kind of correlation is a *Pearson correlation*, and its coefficient is a *Pearson's r*.

TIP

Another nice trick is to square the correlation. By squaring it, you lose the sign of the relationship. The new number tells you the percentage of the information shared by two variables. In this example, a correlation of 0.96 implies that 96 percent of the information is shared. You can obtain a squared correlation matrix using this command: `iris_dataframe.corr()**2`.

TECHNICAL STUFF

Something important to remember is that covariance and correlation are based on means, so they tend to represent relationships that you can express using linear formulations. Variables in real-life datasets usually don't have nice linear formulations. Instead they are highly nonlinear, with curves and bends. You can rely on mathematical transformations to make the relationships linear between variables anyway. A good rule to remember is to use correlations only to assert relationships between variables, not to exclude them.

Using nonparametric correlation

Correlations can work fine when your variables are numeric and their relationship is strictly linear. Sometimes, your feature could be ordinal (a numeric variable but with orderings) or you may suspect some nonlinearity due to non-normal distributions in your data. A possible solution is to test the doubtful correlations with a nonparametric correlation, such as a Spearman rank-order correlation (which means that it has fewer requirements in terms of distribution of considered variables). A *Spearman correlation* transforms your numeric values into rankings and then correlates the rankings, thus minimizing the influence of any nonlinear relationship between the two variables under scrutiny. The resulting correlation, commonly denoted as *rho*, is to be interpreted in the same way as a Pearson's correlation.

As an example, you verify the relationship between sepals' length and width whose Pearson correlation was quite weak:

```
from scipy.stats import spearmanr
from scipy.stats.stats import pearsonr
a = iris_dataframe['sepal length (cm)']
b = iris_dataframe['sepal width (cm)']
rho_coef, rho_p = spearmanr(a, b)
r_coef, r_p = pearsonr(a, b)
print('Pearson r %0.3f | Spearman rho %0.3f'
      % (r_coef, rho_coef))
```

```
Here is the resulting comparison:Pearson r -0.109 | Spearman rho
   -0.159
```

In this case, the code confirms the weak association between the two variables using the nonparametric test.

Considering the chi-square test for tables

You can apply another nonparametric test for relationship when working with cross-tables. This test is applicable to both categorical and numeric data (after it has been discretized into bins). The chi-square statistic tells you when the table distribution of two variables is statistically comparable to a table in which the two variables are hypothesized as not related to each other (the so-called independence hypothesis). Here is an example of how you use this technique:

```
from scipy.stats import chi2_contingency
table = pd.crosstab(iris_dataframe['group'],
                    iris_binned['petal length (cm)'])
chi2, p, dof, expected = chi2_contingency(table.values)
print('Chi-square %0.2f p-value %0.3f' % (chi2, p))
```

The resulting chi-square statistic is

```
Chi-square 212.43 p-value 0.000
```

As seen before, the p-value is the chance that the chi-square difference is just by chance. The high chi-square value and the significant p-value are signaling that the petal length variable can be effectively used for distinguishing between Iris groups.

REMEMBER

The larger the chi-square value, the greater the probability that two variables are related, yet, the chi-square measure value depends on how many cells the table has. Do not use the chi-square measure to compare different chi-square tests unless you know that the tables in comparison are of the same shape.

TIP

The chi-square is particularly interesting for assessing the relationships between binned numeric variables, even in the presence of strong nonlinearity that can fool Person's r. Contrary to correlation measures, it can inform you of a possible association, but it won't provide clear details of its direction or absolute magnitude.

Modifying Data Distributions

As a by-product of data exploration, in an EDA phase you can do the following:

» Obtain new feature creation from the combination of different but related variables

» Spot hidden groups or strange values lurking in your data

» Try some useful modifications of your data distributions by binning (or other discretizations such as binary variables)

When performing EDA, you need to consider the importance of data transformation in preparation for the learning phase, which also means using certain mathematical formulas. Most machine learning algorithms work best when the Pearson's correlation is maximized between the variables you have to predict and the variable you use to predict them. The following sections present an overview of the most common procedures used during EDA in order to enhance the relationship between variables. The data transformation you choose depends on the actual distribution of your data, therefore it's not something you decide beforehand; rather, you discover it by EDA and multiple testing. In addition, these sections highlight the need to match the transformation process to the mathematical formula you use.

Using different statistical distributions

During data science practice, you'll meet with a wide range of different distributions — with some of them named by probabilistic theory, others not. For some distributions, the assumption that they should behave as a normal distribution may hold, but for others, it may not, and that could be a problem depending on what algorithms you use for the learning process. As a general rule, if your model is a linear regression or part of the linear model family because it boils down to a summation of coefficients, then both variable standardization and distribution transformation should be considered.

REMEMBER

Apart from the linear models, many other machine learning algorithms are actually indifferent to the distribution of the variables you use. However, transforming the variables in your dataset in order to render their distribution more Gaussian-like could result in positive effects.

Creating a Z-score standardization

In your EDA process, you may have realized that your variables have different scales and are heterogeneous in their distributions. As a consequence of your analysis, you need to transform the variables in a way that makes them easily comparable:

```
from sklearn.preprocessing import scale
variable = iris_dataframe['sepal width (cm)']
stand_sepal_width = scale(variable)
```

Some algorithms will work in unexpected ways if you don't rescale your variables using standardization. As a rule of thumb, pay attention to any linear models, cluster analysis, and any algorithm that claims to be based on statistical measures.

Transforming other notable distributions

When you check variables with high skewness and kurtosis for their correlation, the results may disappoint you. As you find out earlier in this chapter, using a nonparametric measure of correlation, such as Spearman's, may tell you more about two variables than Pearson's r may tell you. In this case, you should transform your insight into a new, transformed feature:

```
from scipy.stats.stats import pearsonr
tranformations = {'x': lambda x: x,
                  '1/x': lambda x: 1/x,
                  'x**2': lambda x: x**2,
                  'x**3': lambda x: x**3,
                  'log(x)': lambda x: np.log(x)}
a = iris_dataframe['sepal length (cm)']
b = iris_dataframe['sepal width (cm)']
for transformation in tranformations:
    b_transformed =  tranformations[transformation](b)
    pearsonr_coef, pearsonr_p = pearsonr(a, b_transformed)
    print('Transformation: %s \t Pearson\'s r: %0.3f'
          % (transformation, pearsonr_coef))


Transformation: x        Pearson's r: -0.109
Transformation: x**2     Pearson's r: -0.122
Transformation: x**3     Pearson's r: -0.131
Transformation: log(x)   Pearson's r: -0.093
Transformation: 1/x      Pearson's r:  0.073
```

In exploring various possible transformations, using a `for` loop may tell you that a power transformation will increase the correlation between the two variables, thus increasing the performance of a linear machine learning algorithm. You may also try other, further transformations such as square root `np.sqrt(x)`, exponential `np.exp(x)`, and various combinations of all the transformations, such as log inverse `np.log(1/x)`.

TIP

Transforming a variable using the logarithmic transformation sometimes presents difficulties because it won't work for negative or zero values. You need to rescale the values of the variable so that the minimum value is 1. You can achieve that using some functions from the NumPy package: `np.log(x + np.abs(np.min(x)) + 1)`.

Chapter **14**

Reducing Dimensionality

Big data is defined as a collection of datasets so huge that the data becomes difficult to process using traditional techniques. The manipulation of big data differentiates statistical problems, which are based on small samples, from data science problems. You typically use traditional statistical techniques on small problems and data science techniques on big problems.

Data may be viewed as big because it consists of many examples, and this is the first kind of big that spontaneously comes to mind. Analyzing a database of millions of customers and interacting with them all simultaneously is really challenging, but that isn't the only possible perspective of big data. Another view of big data is data dimensionality, which refers to how many aspects of the cases an application tracks. Data with high dimensionality may offer many features (variables) — often hundreds or thousands of them. And that may turn into a real problem. Even if you're observing only a few cases for a short time, dealing with too many features can make most analysis intractable.

The complexity of working with so many dimensions drives the necessity for various data techniques to filter the information — keeping the data that seems to solve the problem better. The filter reduces dimensionality by removing redundant information in high-dimension datasets. The focus in this chapter is on reducing data dimensions when the data has too many repetitions of the same information. You can view this reduction as a kind of information compression, which is similar to compressing files on a hard disk in order to save space.

You don't have to type the source code for this chapter manually. In fact, it's a lot easier if you use the downloadable source (see the Introduction for download instructions). The source code for this chapter appears in the P4DS4D2_14_Reducing_Dimensionality.ipynb source code file.

Understanding SVD

The core of data reduction magic lies in an operation of linear algebra called Singular Value Decomposition (SVD). *SVD* is a mathematical method that takes data as input in the form of a single matrix and gives back three resulting matrices that, multiplied together, return the original input matrix. (You can find a short introduction to SVD at https://machinelearningmastery.com/singular-value-decomposition-for-machine-learning/.) The formula of SVD is

M = U * s * Vh

Here is a short explanation of the letters used in the equation:

>> **U:** Contains all the information about the rows (observations)

>> **Vh:** Contains all the information about the columns (features)

>> **s:** Records the SVD process (a type of log record)

Creating three matrices out of one seems counterproductive when the goal is to reduce data dimensions. When using SVD, you seem to be generating more data, not reducing it. However, SVD conceals the magic in the process, because as it builds these new matrices, it separates the information regarding the rows from the columns of the original matrix. As a result, it compresses all the valuable information into the first columns of the new matrices.

The resulting matrix s shows how the compression happened. The sum of all the values in s tells you how much information was previously stored in your original matrix, and each value in r reports how much data has accumulated in each respective column of U and Vh.

To understand how this all works, you need to look at individual values. For instance, if the sum of s is 100 and the first value of s is 99, that means that 99 percent of the information is now stored in the first column of U and Vh. Therefore, you can happily discard all the remaining columns after the first column without losing any important information for your data science knowledge discovery process.

Looking for dimensionality reduction

It's time to see how Python can help you reduce data complexity. The following example demonstrates a method for reducing your big data. You can use this technique in many other interesting applications, too.

```
import numpy as np
A = np.array([[1, 3, 4], [2, 3, 5], [1, 2, 3], [5, 4, 6]])
print(A)
```

The code prints matrix A, which appears in the following examples:

```
[[1 3 4]
 [2 3 5]
 [1 2 3]
 [5 4 6]]
```

Matrix, A contains the data you want to reduce. A is made of four observations containing three features each. Using the module linalg from NumPy, you can access the svd function that exactly splits your original matrix into three variables: U, s, and Vh.

```
U, s, Vh = np.linalg.svd(A, full_matrices=False)
print(np.shape(U), np.shape(s), np.shape(Vh))
print(s)
```

The output enumerates the shapes of U, s, and Vh, respectively, and prints the content of the s variable:

```
(4, 3) (3,) (3, 3)
[12.26362747 2.11085464 0.38436189]
```

Matrix U, representing the rows, has four row values. Matrix Vh is a square matrix, and its three rows represent the original columns. Matrix s is a diagonal matrix. A diagonal matrix contains zeros in every element but its diagonal. The length of its diagonal is exactly that of the three original columns. Inside s, you find that most of the values are in the first elements, indicating that the first column is what holds the most information (about 83 percent), the second has some values (about 14 percent), and the third contains the residual values. To obtain these percentages, you add the three values together to obtain 14.758844 and then use that number to divide the individual columns. For example, 12.26362747 / 14.758844 is 0.8309341483655495 or about 83 percent.

You can check whether the SVD keeps its promises by viewing the example output. The example reconstructs the original matrix using the dot NumPy function to multiply U, s (diagonal), and Vh. The dot function performs matrix multiplication, which is a multiplication procedure slightly different from the arithmetic one. Here is an example of a full matrix reconstruction:

```
print(np.dot(np.dot(U, np.diag(s)), Vh))
```

The code prints the reconstructed original matrix A:

```
[[ 1.  3.  4.]
 [ 2.  3.  5.]
 [ 1.  2.  3.]
 [ 5.  4.  6.]]
```

The reconstruction is perfect, but clearly you need to keep the same number of components in the resulting matrix U as variables as appeared in the original dataset. No dimensionality reduction really happened, you just restructured data in a way that makes the new variables uncorrelated (and this is useful for clustering algorithms, as you discover in Chapter 15).

TIP

When working with SVD, you usually care about the resulting matrix U, the matrix representing the rows, because it is a replacement of your initial dataset.

Now it's time to play with the results a little and obtain some real reduction. For example, you might want to see what happens when you exclude the third column from matrix U, the less important of the three. The following example shows what happens when you cut the last column from all three matrices.

```
print np.round(np.dot(np.dot(U[:,:2], np.diag(s[:2])),
               Vh[:2,:]),1) # k=2 reconstruction
```

The code prints the reconstruction of the original matrix using the first two components:

```
[[ 1. 2.8 4.1]
 [ 2. 3.2 4.8]
 [ 1. 2. 3. ]
 [ 5. 3.9 6. ]]
```

The output is almost perfect. It means that you could drop the last component and use U as a perfect substitute for the original dataset. There are a few decimal points of difference. To take the example further, the following code removes both the second and third columns from matrix U:

```
print np.round(np.dot(np.dot(U[:,:1], np.diag(s[:1])),
               Vh[:1,:]),1) # k=1 reconstruction
```

Here is the reconstruction of the original matrix using a single component:

```
[[ 2.1 2.5 3.7]
 [ 2.6 3.1 4.6]
 [ 1.6 1.8 2.8]
 [ 3.7 4.3 6.5]]
```

Now there are more errors. Some elements of the matrix are missing more than a few decimal points. However, you can see that most of the numeric information is intact, and you could safely use matrix U in place of your initial data. Just imagine the potential of using such a technique on a larger matrix, one with hundreds of columns that you can first transform into a U matrix and then safely drop most of the columns.

TIP

One of the difficult issues to consider is determining how many columns to keep. Creating a cumulated sum of the diagonal matrix s (using the NumPy cumsum function is perfect for this task) is useful for keeping track of how information is expressed, and by how many columns. As a general rule, you should consider solutions maintaining from 70 to 99 percent of the original information; however, that's not a strict rule — it really depends on how important it is for you to be able to reconstruct the original dataset.

Using SVD to measure the invisible

A property of SVD is to compress the original data at such a level and in such a smart way that, in certain situations, the technique can really create new meaningful and useful features, not just compressed variables. Therefore, you could have used the three columns of the U matrix in the previous example as new features.

If your data contains hints and clues about a hidden cause or motif, an SVD can put them together and offer you proper answers and insights. That is especially true when your data is made up of interesting pieces of information like the ones in the following list:

>> **Text in documents hints at ideas and meaningful categories.** Just as you can make up your mind about treated themes by reading blogs and newsgroups, so also can SVD help you deduce a meaningful classification of groups of documents or the specific topics being written about in each of them.

>> **Reviews of specific movies or books hint at your personal preferences and at larger product categories.** So if you say that you loved the original *Star Trek* series collection on a rating site, it becomes easy to determine what you like in terms of other films, consumer products, or even personality types.

An example of a method based on SVD is Latent Semantic Indexing (LSI), which has been successfully used to associate documents and words on the basis of the idea that words, though different, tend to have the same meaning when placed in similar contexts. This type of analysis suggests not only synonymous words but also higher grouping concepts. For example, an LSI analysis on some sample sports news may group together baseball teams of the Major League based solely on the co-occurrence of team names in similar articles, without any previous knowledge of what a baseball team or the Major League are.

Performing Factor Analysis and PCA

SVD operates directly on the numeric values in data, but you can also express data as a relationship between variables. Each feature has a certain variation. You can calculate the variability as the variance measure around the mean. The more the variance, the more the information contained inside the variable. In addition, if you place the variable into a set, you can compare the variance of two variables to determine whether they correlate, which is a measure of how strongly they have similar values.

Checking all the possible correlations of a variable with the others in the set, you can discover that you may have two types of variance:

>> **Unique variance:** Some variance is unique to the variable under examination. It cannot be associated to what happens to any other variable.

>> **Shared variance:** Some variance is shared with one or more other variables, creating redundancy in the data. Redundancy implies that you can find the same information, with slightly different values, in various features and across many observations.

Of course, the next step is to determine the reason for shared variance. Trying to answer such a question, as well as determining how to deal with unique and shared variances, led to the creation of factor analysis and principal component analysis (commonly referred to as PCA).

Considering the psychometric model

Long before many machine learning algorithms were thought up, *psychometrics*, the discipline in psychology that is concerned with psychological measurement, tried to find a statistical solution to effectively measure dimensions in personality. Our personality, as with other aspects of ourselves, is not directly measurable.

For example, it isn't possible to measure precisely how much a person is introverted or intelligent. Questionnaires and psychological tests only hint at these values.

Psychologists knew of SVD and tried to apply it to the problem. Shared variance attracted their attention: If some variables are almost the same, they should have the same root cause, they thought. Psychologists created *factor analysis* to perform this task and instead of applying SVD directly to data, they applied it to a newly created matrix tracking the common variance, in the hope of condensing all the information and recovering new useful features called *factors*.

Looking for hidden factors

A good way to show how to use factor analysis is to start with the Iris dataset:

```
from sklearn.datasets import load_iris
from sklearn.decomposition import FactorAnalysis
iris = load_iris()
X = iris.data
Y = iris.target
cols = [s[:12].strip() for s in iris.feature_names]
factor = FactorAnalysis(n_components=4).fit(X)
```

After loading the data and storing all the predictive features, the `FactorAnalysis` class is initialized with a request to look for four factors. The data is then fitted. You can explore the results by observing the `components_` attribute, which returns an array containing measures of the relationship between the newly created factors, placed in rows, and the original features, placed in columns:

```
import pandas as pd
print(pd.DataFrame(factor.components_, columns=cols))
```

In the output you find how the factors produced by the code, indicated in the rows, relate to the original variables depicted on the columns. You can interpret the numbers as if they were correlations:

	sepal length	sepal width	petal length	petal width
0	0.707227	-0.153147	1.653151	0.701569
1	0.114676	0.159763	-0.045604	-0.014052
2	-0.000000	0.000000	0.000000	0.000000
3	-0.000000	0.000000	0.000000	-0.000000

At the intersection of each factor and feature, a positive number indicates that a positive proportion exists between the two; a negative number points out that they diverge and that one is contrary to the other. In the test on the Iris dataset, for example, the resulting factors should be a maximum of 2, not 4, because only two factors have significant connections with the original features. You can use these two factors as new variables in your project because they reflect an unseen but important feature that the previously available data only hinted at.

TIP

You'll have to test different values of n_components because you can't know how many factors exist in the data. If the algorithm is required for more factors than exist, it will generate factors with low or zero values in the components_ array.

Using components, not factors

If an SVD could be successfully applied to the common variance, you might wonder why you can't apply it to all the variances. Using a slightly modified starting matrix, all the relationships in the data could be reduced and compressed in a similar way to how SVD does it. The results of this process, which are quite similar to SVD, are called *principal components analysis* (PCA). The newly created features are named *components.* In contrast to factors, components aren't described as the root cause of the data structure but are just restructured data, so you can view them as a big, smart summation of selected variables.

For data science applications, PCA and SVD are quite similar. However, PCA isn't affected by the scale of the original features (because it works on correlation measures that are all bound between −1 and +1 values) and PCA focuses on rebuilding the relationship between the variables, thus offering different results from SVD.

Achieving dimensionality reduction

The procedure to obtain a PCA is quite similar to the factor analysis. The difference is that you don't specify the number of components to extract. You decide later how many components to keep after checking the explained_variance_ratio_ attribute, which provides quantification (in percentage) of the informative value of each extracted component. The following example shows how to perform this task:

```
from sklearn.decomposition import PCA
import pandas as pd
pca = PCA().fit(X)
```

```
print('Explained variance by each component: %s'
      % pca.explained_variance_ratio_)
print(pd.DataFrame(pca.components_,
                   columns=iris.feature_names))
```

In the output, you can observe how the initial variance of the dataset distributes across the components (for instance, here the first component accounts for 92.5 percent of the variance initially present in the dataset) and the resulting PCA matrix of components, where each component (displayed in the rows) relates to each original variable (placed on the columns):

```
     Explained variance by each component:
       [0.92461621 0.05301557 0.01718514 0.00518309]
     sepal length  sepal width  petal length  petal width
0        0.361590    -0.082269      0.856572     0.358844
1        0.656540     0.729712     -0.175767    -0.074706
2       -0.580997     0.596418      0.072524     0.549061
3        0.317255    -0.324094     -0.479719     0.751121
```

In this decomposition of the Iris dataset, the vector array provided by explained_ variance_ratio_ indicates that most of the information is concentrated into the first component (92.5 percent). You saw this same sort of result after the factor analysis. It's therefore possible to reduce the entire dataset to just two components, providing a reduction of noise and redundant information from the original dataset.

Squeezing information with t-SNE

Because SVD and PCA reduce data complexity, you can use the reduced dimensions for visualization. However, often PCA scatter plots aren't helpful for visualization because you need more plots to see how examples relate to each other. Therefore, scientists created algorithms for *nonlinear dimensionality reduction* (also called *manifold learning*), such as t-SNE, to visualize relations in complex datasets of hundreds of variables using simple bidimensional scatter plots.

The t-SNE algorithm starts by randomly projecting the data into the indicated number of dimensions (usually two for a bidimensional representation) as points. Then, in a series of iterations, the algorithm tries to push points that refer to similar examples in the dataset (similarity is calculated using probability) together and push points that are too different from each other apart. After a few iterations, similar points should arrange themselves in clusters separated from the other points. This arrangement helps represent data as a plot, and you inspect it to gain insight about the data and its meaning.

This example uses the handwritten number dataset in Scikit-learn. The dataset contains the grayscale images of handwritten numbers represented as an 8-x-8 matrix of values ranging from zero to one. (They are shades, where zero is pure black, and one is white.)

```
from sklearn.datasets import load_digits
digits = load_digits()
X = digits.data
ground_truth = digits.target
```

After loading the dataset, you run the t-SNE algorithm to squeeze the data:

```
from sklearn.manifold import TSNE
tsne = TSNE(n_components=2,
            init='pca',
            random_state=0,
            perplexity=50,
            early_exaggeration=25,
            n_iter=300)
Tx = tsne.fit_transform(X)
```

This example sets the initial `perplexity`, `early_exaggeration` and `n_iter` parameters, which contribute to the quality of the ending representation. You can try different values of these parameters and obtain slightly different solutions. When the dataset is reduced, you can plot it and place the original number label to the area of the plot where most of the similar examples are, as follows:

```
import numpy as np
import matplotlib.pyplot as plt
plt.xticks([], [])
plt.yticks([], [])
for target in np.unique(ground_truth):
    selection = ground_truth==target
    X1, X2 = Tx[selection, 0], Tx[selection, 1]
    c1, c2 = np.median(X1), np.median(X2)
    plt.plot(X1, X2, 'o', ms=5)
    plt.text(c1, c2, target, fontsize=18)
```

In Figure 14-1 you see the resulting plot, which reveals how some handwritten numbers such as zero, six, or four are easily distinguishable from others, whereas numbers such as three and nine (or five and eight) could be more easily misinterpreted.

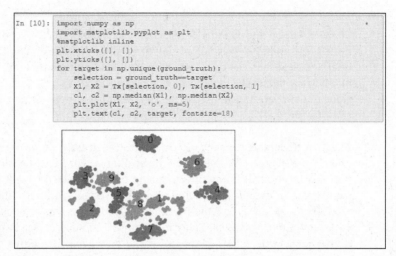

```
In [10]: import numpy as np
         import matplotlib.pyplot as plt
         %matplotlib inline
         plt.xticks([], [])
         plt.yticks([], [])
         for target in np.unique(ground_truth):
             selection = ground_truth==target
             X1, X2 = Tx[selection, 0], Tx[selection, 1]
             c1, c2 = np.median(X1), np.median(X2)
             plt.plot(X1, X2, 'o', ms=5)
             plt.text(c1, c2, target, fontsize=18)
```

FIGURE 14-1:
The resulting projection of the handwritten data by the t-SNE algorithm.

Understanding Some Applications

Understanding the algorithms that compose the family of SVD-derived data decomposition techniques is complex because of its mathematical complexity and its numerous variants (such as Factor, PCA, and SVD). A few examples will help you understand the best ways to employ these powerful data science tools. In the following paragraphs, you work with algorithms you likely seen in action when

» Performing a search of images on a search engine or publishing an image on a social network

» Automatically labeling blog posts or questions to Q&A websites

» Receiving purchase recommendations on e-commerce websites

Recognizing faces with PCA

The following example shows how to use facial images to explain how social networks tag images with the appropriate label or name.

```
from sklearn.datasets import fetch_olivetti_faces
dataset = fetch_olivetti_faces(shuffle=True,
                                random_state=101)
train_faces = dataset.data[:350,:]
test_faces  = dataset.data[350:,:]
train_answers = dataset.target[:350]
test_answers = dataset.target[350:]
```

The example begins by importing the Olivetti faces dataset, a set of images readily available from Scikit-learn. For this experiment, the code divides the set of labeled images into a training and a test set. You need to pretend that you know the labels of the training set but don't know anything about the test set. As a result, you want to associate images from the test set to the most similar image from the training set.

The Olivetti dataset consists of 400 photos taken from 40 people (so there are 10 photos of each person). Even though the photos represent the same person, each photo is taken at different times during the day, with different light and facial expressions or details (for example, with glasses and without). The images are 64 x 64 pixels, so unfolding the pixels into features creates a dataset made of 400 cases and 4,096 variables. You can obtain additional dataset information using: print(dataset.DESCR), as shown in the downloadable source code. For additional information about the dataset refer to AT&T Laboratories Cambridge web pages: https://www.cl.cam.ac.uk/research/dtg/attarchive/facedatabase.html. The following code snippet transforms and reduces the images using a PCA algorithm from Scikit-learn:

```
from sklearn.decomposition import RandomizedPCA
n_components = 25
Rpca = PCA(svd_solver='randomized',
           n_components=n_components,
           whiten=True)
Rpca.fit(train_faces)
print('Explained variance by %i components: %0.3f'
 % (n_components, np.sum(Rpca.explained_variance_ratio_)))
compressed_train_faces = Rpca.transform(train_faces)
compressed_test_faces  = Rpca.transform(test_faces)
```

When executed, the run outputs the proportion of variance retained by the first 25 components of the resulting PCA:Explained variance by 25 components: 0.794.

The RandomizedPCA class is an approximate PCA version, which works better when the dataset is large (many rows and variables). The decomposition creates 25 new variables (n_components parameter) and whitening (whiten=True), thus removing some constant noise (created by textual and photo granularity) from images. The resulting decomposition uses 25 components, which is about 80 percent of information held in 4,096 features.

```
import matplotlib.pyplot as plt
%matplotlib inline

photo = 17
```

```
print('The represented person is subject %i'
      % test_answers[photo])
plt.subplot(1, 2, 1)
plt.axis('off')
plt.title('Unknown photo '+str(photo)+' in test set')
plt.imshow(test_faces[photo].reshape(64,64),
           cmap=plt.cm.gray, interpolation='nearest')
plt.show()
```

Figure 14-2 represents subject number 34, whose photo number 17 has been chosen as the test set.

```
In [14]:   import matplotlib.pyplot as plt
           %matplotlib inline

           photo = 17
           print('We are looking for face id=%i'
                 % test_answers[photo])
           plt.subplot(1, 2, 1)
           plt.axis('off')
           plt.title('Unknown face '+str(photo)+' in test set')
           plt.imshow(test_faces[photo].reshape(64,64),
                      cmap=plt.cm.gray, interpolation='nearest')

           We are looking for face id=34

Out[14]:   <matplotlib.image.AxesImage at 0xb94f9b0>

                       Unknown face 17 in test set
```

After test set decomposition, the example takes the data relative only to photo 17 and subtracts it from the decomposition of the training set. Now the training set is made of differences with respect to the example photo. The code squares them (to remove negative values) and sums them by row, which results in a series of summed errors. The most similar photos are the ones with the least-squared errors, the ones whose differences are the least.

```
mask = compressed_test_faces[photo,]
squared_errors = np.sum((compressed_train_faces
                         - mask)**2, axis=1)
minimum_error_face = np.argmin(squared_errors)
most_resembling = list(np.where(squared_errors < 20)[0])
print('Best resembling subject in training set: %i'
      % train_answers[minimum_error_face])
```

The preceding code returns the code number of the best resembling person in the dataset, which effectively corresponds with the code of the subject chosen from the test set:

```
Best resembling subject in training set: 34
```

You check the work done by the code by displaying photo 17 from the test set next to the top three images from the training set that best resemble it (as shown in Figure 14-3):

```python
import matplotlib.pyplot as plt
plt.subplot(2, 2, 1)
plt.axis('off')
plt.title('Unknown face '+str(photo)+' in test set')
plt.imshow(test_faces[photo].reshape(64, 64),
           cmap=plt.cm.gray,
           interpolation='nearest')
for k,m in enumerate(most_resembling[:3]):
    plt.subplot(2, 2, 2+k)
    plt.title('Match in train set no. '+str(m))
    plt.axis('off')
    plt.imshow(train_faces[m].reshape(64, 64),
               cmap=plt.cm.gray,
               interpolation='nearest')
plt.show()
```

FIGURE 14-3:
The output shows the results that resemble the test image.

Even though the most similar photo from the training data it is just a differently scaled version of the one in the test set, the other two photos are displaying a different pose of the same person present in the test photo 17. This example using PCA, starting from an example image, accurately finds other photos of the very same person from a set of image.

Extracting topics with NMF

Textual data is another field of application for the family of data reduction algorithms. The idea that prompted such application is that if a group of people talks or writes about something, they tend to use words from a limited set because they refer or relate to the same topic; they share some meaning or are part of the same group. Consequently, if you have a collection of texts and don't know what topics the text references, you can reverse the previous reasoning — you can simply look for groups of words that tend to associate together, so the group newly formed by dimensionality reduction hints at the topics you'd like to know about.

This is a perfect application for the SVD family, because by reducing the number of columns, the features (in a document, the words are the features) will gather in dimensions, and you can discover the topics by checking high-scoring words. SVD and PCA provide features to relate both positively and negatively with the newly created dimensions. So a resulting topic may be expressed by the presence of a word (high positive value) or by the absence of it (high negative value), making interpretation both tricky and counterintuitive for humans. Luckily, Scikit-learn includes the Non-Negative Matrix Factorization (NMF) decomposition class, which allows an original feature to relate only positively with the resulting dimensions.

This example begins by loading the 20newsgroups dataset, selecting only the posts regarding objects for sale and automatically removing headers, footers, and quotes.

```
from sklearn.datasets import fetch_20newsgroups
dataset = fetch_20newsgroups(shuffle=True,
            categories = ['misc.forsale'],
            remove=('headers', 'footers', 'quotes'),
            random_state=101)
print('Posts: %i' % len(dataset.data))
```

The code loads the dataset and prints the number of posts it contains:

```
Posts: 585
```

The TfidVectorizer class is imported and set up to remove stop words (common words such as *the* or *and*) and keep only distinctive words, producing a matrix whose columns point to distinct words.

```
from sklearn.feature_extraction.text import TfidfVectorizer
from sklearn.decomposition import NMF

vectorizer = TfidfVectorizer(max_df=0.95, min_df=2,
                             stop_words='english')
tfidf = vectorizer.fit_transform(dataset.data)
n_topics = 5
nmf = NMF(n_components=n_topics,
          random_state=101).fit(tfidf)
```

REMEMBER

Term frequency-inverse document frequency (Tf-idf) is a simple calculation based on the frequency of a word in document. It's weighted by word rarity in the available documents. Weighting words is an effective way to rule out words that can't help you to classify or to identify the document when processing text. For example, you can eliminate common parts of speech or other common words.

As with other algorithms from the sklearn.decomposition module, the n_components parameter indicates the number of desired components. If you'd like to look for more topics, you use a higher number. As the required number of topics increases, the reconstruction_err_ method reports lower error rates. It's up to you to decide when to stop given the trade-off between more time spent on computations and more topics.

The last part of the script outputs the resulting five topics. By reading the printed words, you can decide on the meaning of the extracted topics, thanks to product characteristics (for instance, the words *drive, hard, card,* and *floppy* refer to computers) or the exact product (for instance, *comics, car, stereo, games*).

```
feature_names = vectorizer.get_feature_names()
n_top_words = 15
for topic_idx, topic in enumerate(nmf.components_):
    print('Topic #%d:' % (topic_idx+1),)
    topics = topic.argsort()[:-n_top_words - 1:-1]
    print(' '.join([feature_names[i] for i in topics]))
```

The topics appear in order, accompanied by their most representative keywords. You can explore the resulting model by looking into the attribute components_ from the trained NMF model. It consists of a NumPy ndarray holding positive values for words connected to the topic. By using the argsort method, you can get the indexes of the top associations, whose high values indicate that they are the most representative words. This code extracts the indexes of the top representative words for the topic 1:

```
print(nmf.components_[0,:].argsort()[:-n_top_words-1:-1])
```

The output is a list of indexes, each one corresponding to a word:

```
[2463 740 2200 2987 2332 853 3727 3481 2251 2017 556 842
 2829 2826 2803]
```

Decoding the words' indexes creates readable strings by calling them from the array derived from the `get_feature_names` method applied to the `TfidfVectorizer` that was previously fitted. In the following snippet, you see how to extract the word related to the 2463 index, the top explicative word of the topic 1:

```
word_index = 2463
print(vectorizer.get_feature_names()[word_index])
```

The word related to the 2463 index is "offer":

```
offer
```

Recommending movies

Other interesting applications for data reduction are systems that generate recommendations for things you may like to buy or know more about. You likely see recommenders in action on most e-commerce websites after logging-in and visiting some product pages. As you browse, you rate items or put them in your electronic basket. Based on these actions and those of other customers, you see other buying opportunities (this method is *collaborative filtering*).

You can implement collaborative recommendations based on simple means or frequencies calculated on other customers' set of purchased items or on ratings using SVD. This approach helps you reliably generate recommendations even in the case of products the vendor seldom sells or that are quite new to users. For this example, you use a well-known database created by the MovieLens website, collected from its users' ratings of a movie they liked or disliked. Because this is an external dataset, you first have to download it from its Internet location at http:// files.grouplens.org/datasets/movielens/ml-1m.zip. After downloading the database, you have to extract it into your Python working directory. You discover your working directory using these commands:

```
import os
print(os.getcwd())
```

Take note of the displayed directory and extract the `ml-1m` database there. Then execute the following code.

```python
import pandas as pd
from scipy.sparse import csr_matrix
users = pd.read_table('ml-1m/users.dat', sep='::',
        header=None, names=['user_id', 'gender',
        'age', 'occupation', 'zip'], engine='python')
ratings = pd.read_table('ml-1m/ratings.dat', sep='::',
         header=None, names=['user_id', 'movie_id',
         'rating', 'timestamp'], engine='python')
movies = pd.read_table('ml-1m/movies.dat', sep='::',
        header=None, names=['movie_id', 'title',
        'genres'], engine='python')
MovieLens = pd.merge(pd.merge(ratings, users), movies)
```

Using `pandas`, the code loads the different datatables and then merges them on the basis of the features with the same name (the `user_id` and `movie_id` variables).

```python
ratings_mtx_df = MovieLens.pivot_table(values='rating',
        index='user_id', columns='title', fill_value=0)
movie_index = ratings_mtx_df.columns
```

`pandas` will also help create a datatable crossing information in rows about users and in columns about movie titles. A movie index will keep track about what movie each column represents.

```python
from sklearn.decomposition import TruncatedSVD
recom = TruncatedSVD(n_components=15, random_state=101)
R = recom.fit_transform(ratings_mtx_df.values.T)
```

The `TruncatedSVD` class reduces the datatable to ten components. This class offers a more scalable algorithm than SciPy's `linalg.svd` used in earlier examples. `TruncatedSVD` computes result matrices of exactly the shape you decide by the `n_components` parameter (the full resulting matrices are not calculated), resulting in a faster output and less memory usage.

By calculating the `Vh` matrix, you can reduce the ratings of different but similar users (each user's scores are expressed by row) into compressed dimensions that reconstruct general tastes and preferences. Please also notice that because you're interested in the `Vh` matrix (the columns/movies reduction) but the algorithm provides you with only the `U` matrix (the decomposition based on rows), you need to input the transposition of the datatable (by transposition columns become rows and you obtain `TruncatedSVD` output, which is the `Vh` matrix). You now look for a specific movie:

```
movie = 'Star Wars: Episode V \
- The Empire Strikes Back (1980)'
movie_idx = list(movie_index).index(movie)
print("movie index: %i" %movie_idx)
print(R[movie_idx])
```

The output points out the index of a *Star Wars* episode and its SVD coordinates:

```
movie index: 3154
[184.72254552 -17.77612872 47.33450866 51.4664494
  47.92058216 17.65033116 14.3574635 -12.82219207
  17.51347857 5.46888807 7.5430805 -0.57117869
 -30.74032355 2.4088565 -22.50368497]
```

Using the movie label, you can find out what column the movie is in (column index 3154 in this case) and print the values of the 10 components. This sequence provides the movie profile. You now try getting all the movies with scores similar to the target movie and highly correlated with it. A good strategy is to calculate a correlation matrix of all movies, get the slice related to your movie, and find out inside it what are the most related (characterized by high positive correlation — say at least 0.98) movie titles using indexing as shown in the following code:

```
import numpy as np
correlation_matrix = np.corrcoef(R)
P = correlation_matrix[movie_idx]
print(list(movie_index[(P > 0.985) & (P < 1.0)]))
```

The code will return names of films most similar to your movie; they are intended as suggestions based on a preference for that film.

```
['Raiders of the Lost Ark (1981)',
 'Star Wars: Episode IV - A New Hope (1977)',
 'Star Wars: Episode V - The Empire Strikes Back (1980)',
 'Star Wars: Episode VI - Return of the Jedi (1983)',
 'Terminator, The (1984)']
```

Star Wars fans would like quite a few titles, such as *Star Wars Episodes IV* and *VI* (of course). In addition, fans might like *Raiders of the Lost Ark*, because of the actor Harrison Ford, main character in all these films.

REMEMBER

SVD will always find the best way to relate a row or column in your data, discovering complex interactions or relations you didn't imagine before. You don't need to imagine anything in advance; it's fully a data-driven approach.

Chapter **15**

Clustering

O ne of the basic abilities that humans have exercised since primitive times is to divide the known world into separate classes where individual objects share common features deemed important by the classifier. Starting with primitive cave dwellers classifying the natural world they lived in, distinguishing plants and animals useful or dangerous for their survival, we arrive at modern times in which marketing departments classify consumers into target segments and then act with proper marketing plans.

Classifying is crucial to our process of building new knowledge because, by gathering similar objects, we can:

» Mention all the items in a class by the same denomination

» Summarize relevant features by an exemplificative class type

» Associate particular actions or recall specific knowledge automatically

Dealing with big data streams today requires the same classificatory ability, but on a different scale. To spot unknown groups of signals present in the data, we need specialized algorithms that are both able to learn how to assign examples to certain given classes (the *supervised* approach) and to spot new interesting classes that we weren't aware of (*unsupervised* learning).

Even though your main routine as a data scientist will be to put into practice your predictive skills, you'll also have to provide useful insight into possible novel information present in your data. For example, you'll often need to locate new features in order to strengthen the predictive power of your models, find an easy way to make complex comparisons inside the data, and discover communities in social networks.

A data-driven approach to classification, called *clustering,* will prove to be of great help in achieving success for your data project when you need to provide new insights from scratch and you lack labeled data or you want to create new labels for it.

Clustering techniques are a set of *unsupervised classification* methods that can create meaningful classes by directly processing your data, without any previous knowledge or hypothesis about the groups that may be present. If all supervised algorithms need labeled examples (class labels), unsupervised ones can figure out by themselves what the most appropriate labels could be.

TIP

Clustering can help you to summarize huge quantities of data. It is an effective technique for presenting data to a nontechnical audience and for feeding a supervised algorithm with group variables, thus providing them with concentrated, significant information.

There are a few kinds of clustering techniques. You can distinguish between them using the guidelines in the following list:

>> Assigning every example to a unique group (partitioning) or to multiple ones (fuzzy clustering)

>> Determining the heuristic — that is, the rule of thumb — that they use to figure out whether an example is part of a group

>> Specifying how they quantify the difference between observations, that is, the so-called distance measure

Most of the time you use *partition-clustering techniques* (a data point can be part of only one group, so the groups don't overlap; their membership is distinct) and among partitioning methods, you use K-means the most. In addition, other useful methods are mentioned in this chapter, which are based on agglomerative methods and on data density.

Agglomerative methods set data into clusters based on a distance measure. *Data density approaches* take advantage of the idea that groups are very dense and continuous, so if you notice a decrease in density when exploring a part of a group of points, it could mean that you arrived at one of its borders.

TIP

Because you normally don't know what you're looking for, different methods can provide you with different solutions and points of view on the data. The secret of a successful clustering is to try as many of the recipes as possible, compare the results, and try to find a reason why you can consider certain observations as a group in respect to others.

REMEMBER

You don't have to type the source code for this chapter manually. In fact, it's a lot easier if you use the downloadable source (see the Introduction for download instructions). The source code for this chapter appears in the P4DS4D2_15_Clustering.ipynb source code file.

Clustering with K-means

K-means is an iterative algorithm that has become very popular in machine learning because of its simplicity, speed, and scalability to a large number of data points. The K-means algorithm relies on the idea that there are a specific number of data groups, called *clusters.* Each data group is scattered around a central point with which they share some key characteristics.

You can actually imagine the central point of a cluster, called a *centroid,* as a sun. The data points distribute around the centroid like planets. As star systems are separated by the void of space, clusters are also expected to clearly separate from each other, so, as groups of points they are both internally homogeneous and different from each other.

REMEMBER

The K-means algorithm expects to find clusters in your data. Therefore, it will find them even when none exist. It's important to check inside the groups to determine whether the group is a true gold nugget.

Given such assumptions, all you have to do is to specify the number of groups you expect (you can use a guess or try a number of possible desirable solutions), and the K-means algorithm will look for them, using a heuristic in order to recover the position of the central points.

The cluster centroids should be evident by their different characteristics and positions from each other. Even if you start by randomly guessing where they could be, in the end, after a few corrections, you always find them by using the many data points that gravitate around them.

Understanding centroid-based algorithms

The procedure for finding the centroids is straightforward:

1. Guess a K number of clusters.

   K centroids are picked randomly from your data points or chosen so that they are placed in your data in very distant positions from each other. All the other points are assigned to their nearest centroid based on the Euclidean distance.

2. Form the initial clusters.

3. Reiterate the clusters until you notice that your solution doesn't change anymore.

   You recalculate the centroids as an average of all the points present in the group. All the data points are reassigned to the groups based on the distance from the new centroids.

The iterative process of assigning cases to the most plausible centroid and then averaging the assigned ones to find a new centroid will slowly shift the centroid position toward the areas where most data points gravitate. The result is that you end up with the true centroid position.

The procedure has only two weak points that you need to consider. First, you choose the initial centroids randomly, which means that you could start from a bad starting point. As a result, the iterative process will stop at some unlikely solution — for example, having a centroid in the middle of two groups. To ensure that your solution is the most probable, you have to try the algorithm a few times and track the results. The more often you try, the more likely you are to confirm the right solution. The Python Scikit-learn implementation of K-means will do that for you, so you just have to decide how many times you intend to try. (The trade-off is that more iterations produce better results, but each iteration consumes valuable time.)

The second weak point is due to the distance that K-means uses, the *Euclidean distance*, which is the distance between two points on a plane (a concept that you likely studied at school). In a K-means application, each data point is a vector of features, so when comparing the distance of two points, you do the following:

1. Create a list containing the differences of the elements in the two vectors.

2. Square all the elements of the difference vector.

3. Calculate the square root of the summed elements.

You can try a simple example in Python. Pretend that you have two points, A and B, and they have three numeric features. If A and B are the data representation of two persons, their distinguishing features could be measured in height (cm), weight (kg), and age (years), as shown in the following code:

```
import numpy as np
A = np.array([165, 55, 70])
B = np.array([185, 60, 30])
```

The following example shows how to calculate the differences between the three elements, square all the resulting elements, and determine the square root of the summed squared values:

```
D = (A - B)
D = D**2
D = np.sqrt(np.sum(D))
print(D)

45.0
```

In the end, the Euclidean distance is really just a big sum. When the variables making up the difference vector are significantly different in scale from each other (in this example, the height could have been expressed in meters), you end up with a distance dominated by the elements with the largest scale. It is very important to rescale the variables so that they use a similar scale before applying the K-means algorithm. You can use a fixed range or a statistical normalization with zero mean and unit variance to achieve this goal.

Another problem that may arise is due to correlation between variables, causing redundancy of information. If two variables are highly correlated, that means that a part of their information content is repeated. Replication implies counting the same information more than once in the summation used to calculate the distance. If you're not aware of the correlation issue, some variables will dominate your distance measure calculation — a situation that may lead to not finding the useful clusters that you want. The solution is to remove the correlation thanks to a dimensionality reduction algorithm such as Principle Component Analysis (PCA). It is up to you to remember to evaluate scale and correlation before employing K-means and other clustering techniques using the Euclidean distance measure.

Creating an example with image data

An example with image data demonstrates how to apply the tool and how to get insight from clusters. An ideal example is clustering the handwritten digits dataset provided by the Scikit-learn package. Hand-written numbers are naturally different from each other — they possess variability in that there are several ways to write certain numbers. Of course, we all have different writing styles, so it is natural that each person's numbers differ slightly. The following code shows how to import the image data.

```
from sklearn.datasets import load_digits
digits = load_digits()
X = digits.data
ground_truth = digits.target
```

The example begins by importing the digits dataset from Scikit-learn and assigning the data to a variable. It then stores the labels in another variable for later verification. The next step is to process the data using a PCA.

```
from sklearn.decomposition import PCA
from sklearn.preprocessing import scale
pca = PCA(n_components=30)
Cx = pca.fit_transform(scale(X))
print('Explained variance %0.3f'
        % sum(pca.explained_variance_ratio_))

Explained variance 0.893
```

By applying a PCA on scaled data, the code addresses the problems of scale and correlation. Even though PCA can recreate the same number of variables as in the input data, the example code drops a few using the n_components parameter. The decision to use 30 components, as compared to the original 64 variables, allows the example to retain most of the original information (about 90 percent of the original variation in data) and simplify the dataset by removing correlation and reducing redundant variables and their noise.

TIP

The remainder of the chapter uses the Cx dataset. If you need to run single, isolated code examples from the chapter, you need to run the code presented earlier in this paragraph first.

In this example, the PCA-transformed data appears in the Cx variable. After importing the KMeans class, the code defines its main parameters:

» n_clusters is the K number of centroids to find.

» n_init is the number of times to try the K-means with different starting centroids. The code needs to test the procedure a sufficient number of times, such as 10, as shown here.

```
from sklearn.cluster import KMeans
clustering = KMeans(n_clusters=10,
                        n_init=10, random_state=1)
clustering.fit(Cx)
```

After creating the parameters, the clustering class is ready for use. You can apply the `fit()` method to the `Cx` dataset, which produces a scaled and dimensionally reduced dataset.

Looking for optimal solutions

As mentioned in the previous section, the example is clustering ten different numbers. It's time to start checking the solution with K = 10 first. The following code compares the previous clustering result to the *ground truth* — the true labels — in order to determine whether there is any correspondence.

```
import numpy as np
import pandas as pd
ms = np.column_stack((ground_truth,clustering.labels_))
df = pd.DataFrame(ms,
                  columns = ['Ground truth','Clusters'])
pd.crosstab(df['Ground truth'], df['Clusters'],
            margins=True)
```

Converting the solution, given by the `labels` variable internal to the `clustering` class, into a pandas `DataFrame` allows it to apply a cross-tabulation and compare the original labels with the labels derived from clustering. You can observe the results in Figure 15-1. Because rows represent ground truth, you can look for numbers whose majority of observations are split among different clusters. These observations are the handwritten examples that are more difficult to figure out by K-means.

Notice how numbers such as six or zero are concentrated into a single major cluster, whereas others, such as three, nine and many examples from five and eight, tend to gather into the same group, cluster 1. Cluster 9 consists of a single number four (an example that's so different from all others that that it has its own cluster). From such a discovery, you can deduce that certain handwritten numbers are easy to guess, while others aren't.

TIP

Cross-tabulation has been particularly useful in this example because you can compare the clustering result to the ground truth. However, in many clustering applications, you won't have any ground truth to compare with. In such cases, representing the variables' values using the cluster centroids you found is particularly useful. You can use descriptive statistics to perform this task by applying the mean or the median, as described in Chapter 13, on each cluster and comparing the different descriptive stats between clusters.

```
In [5]: import numpy as np
        import pandas as pd
        ms = np.column_stack((ground_truth,clustering.labels_))
        df = pd.DataFrame(ms,
                        columns = ['Ground truth','Clusters'])
        pd.crosstab(df['Ground truth'], df['Clusters'],
                    margins=True)

Out[5]:
```

Clusters	0	1	2	3	4	5	6	7	8	9	All
Ground truth											
0	177	0	0	1	0	0	0	0	0	0	178
1	0	27	0	0	0	1	0	96	58	0	182
2	1	141	6	0	1	0	0	24	4	0	177
3	0	1	160	0	7	8	0	7	0	0	183
4	0	0	0	157	4	2	0	2	7	9	181
5	0	0	39	2	0	137	2	2	0	0	182
6	1	0	0	0	0	0	174	5	1	0	181
7	0	0	0	0	157	1	0	1	3	17	179
8	1	1	46	0	2	7	2	103	12	0	174
9	0	0	144	0	8	4	0	2	19	3	180
All	180	170	395	160	179	160	178	242	104	29	1797

FIGURE 15-1: Cross-tabulation of ground truth and K-means clusters.

Another observation you can make is that even though there are just ten numbers in this example, there are more types of handwritten forms of each, hence the necessity of finding more clusters. Of course, the problem is to determine just how many clusters you need.

You use inertia to measure the viability of a cluster. *Inertia* is the sum of all the differences between every cluster member and its centroid. If the examples in the group are similar to the centroid, the difference is small and so is the inertia. Inertia as an individual measure reveals little. Moreover, when comparing inertia from different clusters in general, you notice that the more groups you have, the less the inertia. You want to compare the inertia of a cluster solution with the previous cluster solution. This comparison provides you with the rate of change, a more interpretable measure. To obtain the inertia rate of change in Python, you will have to create a loop. Try progressive cluster solutions inside the loop, recording their values. Here is a script for the handwritten digit example:

```
import numpy as np
inertia = list()
for k in range(1,21):
    clustering = KMeans(n_clusters=k,
                        n_init=10, random_state=1)
    clustering.fit(Cx)
    inertia.append(clustering.inertia_)
delta_inertia = np.diff(inertia) * -1
```

You use the `inertia` variable inside the clustering class after fitting the clustering. The inertia variable is a list containing the rate of change of inertia between a solution and the previous one. Here is some code that prints a line graph of the rate of change, as depicted by Figure 15-2.

```python
import matplotlib.pyplot as plt
%matplotlib inline
plt.figure()
x_range = [k for k in range(2, 21)]
plt.xticks(x_range)
plt.plot(x_range, delta_inertia, 'ko-')
plt.xlabel('Number of clusters')
plt.ylabel('Rate of change of inertia')
plt.show()
```

When examining `inertia`'s rate of change, look for jumps in the rate itself. If the rate jumps up, it means that adding a cluster more than the previous solution brings much more benefit than expected; if it jumps down instead, you're likely forcing a cluster more than necessary. All the cluster solutions before a jump down may be a good candidate, according to the principle of parsimony (the jump signals a sophistication in our analysis, but the right solutions are usually the simplest). In the example, there are quite a few jumps at k=7, 9, 11, 14, 17 but k=17 seems to be the most promising peak because of a rate of change much higher with respect to the descending trend.

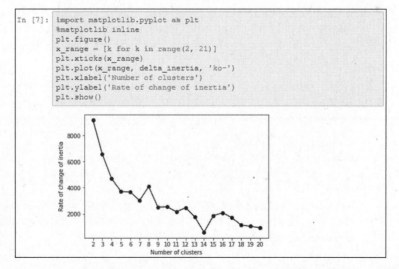

FIGURE 15-2: Rate of change of inertia for solutions up to k=20.

REMEMBER

The rate of change in inertia will provide you with just a few tips where there could be good cluster solutions. It is up to you to decide which to pick if you need to get some extra insight on data. If, instead, clustering is just a step in a complex data science project, you don't need to spend much effort in looking for an optimal number of clusters; you just pass a solution featuring enough clusters to the next machine learning algorithm and let it decide for the best.

Clustering big data

K-means is a way to reduce the complexity of your data by summarizing the many examples in your dataset. To perform this task, you load the data into your computer's memory, and that won't always be feasible, especially if you are working with big data. Scikit-learn offers an alternative way to apply K-means; the `Mini-BatchKMeans` is a variant that can progressively cluster separated chunks of data. In fact, a batch learning procedure usually processes the data part by part. There are only two differences between the standard K-means function and `MiniBatchKMeans`:

>> You cannot automatically test different starting centroids unless you try running the analysis again.

>> The analysis will start when there is a batch made of at least a minimum number of cases. This value is usually set to 100 (but the more cases there are, the better the result) by the `batch_size` parameter.

A simple demonstration on the previous handwritten dataset shows how effective and easy it is to use the `MiniBatchKMeans` clustering class. First, the example runs a test on the K-means algorithm on all the data available and records the inertia of the solution:

```
k = 10
clustering = KMeans(n_clusters=k,
                    n_init=10, random_state=1)
clustering.fit(Cx)
kmeans_inertia = clustering.inertia_
print("K-means inertia: %0.1f" % kmeans_inertia)
```

Take note that the resulting inertia is 58253.3. The example then tests the same data and number of clusters by fitting a `MiniBatchKMeans` clustering by small separate batches of 100 examples:

```
from sklearn.cluster import MiniBatchKMeans
batch_clustering = MiniBatchKMeans(n_clusters=k,
                                   random_state=1)
```

```
batch = 100
for row in range(0, len(Cx), batch):
    if row+batch < len(Cx):
        feed = Cx[row:row+batch,:]
    else:
        feed = Cx[row:,:]
    batch_clustering.partial_fit(feed)
batch_inertia = batch_clustering.score(Cx) * -1

print("MiniBatchKmeans inertia: %0.1f" % batch_inertia)
```

This script iterates through the indexes of the previously scaled and PCA simplified dataset (Cx), creating batches of 100 observations each. Using the partial_fit method, it fits a K-means clustering on each batch, using the centroids found by the previous call. The algorithm stops when it runs out of data. Using the score method on all the data available, it then reports its inertia for a 10-clusters solution. Now the reported inertia is 64633.6. Note that MiniBatchKmeans results in a higher inertia than the standard algorithm. Though the difference is minimal, the fitted solution is pejorative, thus you should reserve this approach for those times when you really cannot work with in-memory datasets.

Performing Hierarchical Clustering

If the K-means algorithm is concerned with centroids, hierarchical (also known as agglomerative) clustering tries to link each data point, by a distance measure, to its nearest neighbor, creating a cluster. Reiterating the algorithm using different linkage methods, the algorithm gathers all the available points into a rapidly diminishing number of clusters, until in the end all the points reunite into a single group.

The results, if visualized, will closely resemble the biological classifications of living beings that you may have studied in school or seen on posters at the local natural history museum, an upside-down tree whose branches are all converging into a trunk. Such a figurative tree is a *dendrogram*, and you see it used in medical and biological research. Scikit-learn implementation of agglomerative clustering does not offer the possibility of depicting a dendrogram from your data because such a visualization technique works fine with only a few cases, whereas you can expect to work on many examples.

Compared to K-means, agglomerative algorithms are more cumbersome and do not scale well to large datasets. Agglomerative algorithms are more suitable for statistical studies (they can be easily found in natural sciences, archeology, and sometimes psychology and economics). These algorithms do offer the advantage of creating a complete range of nested cluster solutions, so you just need to pick the right one for your purpose.

To use agglomerative clustering effectively, you have to know about the different linkage methods (the heuristics for clustering) and the distance metrics. There are three linkage methods:

>> **Ward:** Tends to look for spherical clusters, very cohesive inside and extremely differentiated from other groups. Another nice characteristic is that the method tends to find clusters of similar size. It works only with the Euclidean distance.

>> **Complete:** Links clusters using their furthest observations, that is, their most dissimilar data points. Consequently, clusters created using this method tend to be comprised of highly similar observations, making the resulting groups quite compact.

>> **Average:** Links clusters using their centroids and ignoring their boundaries. The method creates larger groups than the complete method. In addition, the clusters can be of different sizes and shapes, contrary to the Ward's solutions. Consequently, this approach sees successful use in the field of biological sciences, easily catching natural diversity.

There are also three distance metrics:

>> **Euclidean (euclidean or l2):** As seen in K-means.

>> **Manhattan (manhattan or l1):** Similar to Euclidean, but the distance is calculated by summing the absolute value of the difference between the dimensions. In a map, if the Euclidean distance is the shortest route between two points, the Manhattan distance implies moving straight, first along one axis and then along the other — as a car in the city would, reaching a destination by driving along city blocks (the distance is also known as city block distance).

>> **Cosine (cosine):** A good choice when there are too many variables and you worry that some variable may not be significant (being just noise). Cosine distance reduces noise by taking the shape of the variables, more than their values, into account. It tends to associate observations that have the same maximum and minimum variables, regardless of their effective value.

Using a hierarchical cluster solution

If your dataset doesn't contain too many observations, it's worth trying agglomerative clustering with all the combinations of linkage and distance and then comparing the results carefully. In clustering, you rarely already know the right answers, and agglomerative clustering can provide you with another useful potential solution. For example, you can recreate the previous analysis with K-means and handwritten digits, using the ward linkage and the Euclidean distance as follows (the output appears in Figure 15-3):

```
from sklearn.cluster import AgglomerativeClustering
Hclustering = AgglomerativeClustering(n_clusters=10,
                               affinity='euclidean',
                               linkage='ward')
Hclustering.fit(Cx)
ms = np.column_stack((ground_truth,Hclustering.labels_))
df = pd.DataFrame(ms,
              columns = ['Ground truth','Clusters'])
pd.crosstab(df['Ground truth'],
        df['Clusters'], margins=True)
```

```
In [10]: from sklearn.cluster import AgglomerativeClustering

         Hclustering = AgglomerativeClustering(n_clusters=10,
                                        affinity='euclidean',
                                        linkage='ward')
         Hclustering.fit(Cx)

         ms = np.column_stack((ground_truth,Hclustering.labels_))
         df = pd.DataFrame(ms,
                       columns = ['Ground truth','Clusters'])
         pd.crosstab(df['Ground truth'],
                 df['Clusters'], margins=True)
```

Out[10]:

Clusters	0	1	2	3	4	5	6	7	8	9	All
Ground truth											
0	0	0	0	0	0	178	0	0	0	0	178
1	1	27	154	0	0	0	0	0	0	0	182
2	0	165	10	0	1	0	1	0	0	0	177
3	0	4	13	0	0	0	166	0	0	0	183
4	1	0	4	0	1	0	0	14	0	161	181
5	168	1	0	1	0	0	11	0	0	1	182
6	0	0	1	180	0	0	0	0	0	0	181
7	1	0	1	0	0	0	0	8	169	0	179
8	2	4	167	0	0	0	1	0	0	0	174
9	3	0	29	1	0	0	143	4	0	0	180
All	176	201	379	182	2	178	322	26	169	162	1797

FIGURE 15-3:
Cross-tabulation of ground truth and Ward's agglomerative clusters.

The results, in this case, are slightly better than K-means, although, you may have noticed that completing the analysis using this approach certainly takes longer than using K-means. When working with a large number of observations, the computations for a hierarchical cluster solution may take hours to complete, making this solution less feasible. You can get around the time issue by using a two-phase clustering, which is faster and provides you with a hierarchical solution even when you are working with large datasets.

Using a two-phase clustering solution

To implement the two-phase clustering solution, you process the original observations using K-means with a large number of clusters. A good rule of thumb is to take the square root of the number of observations and use that figure; moreover, you always have to keep the number of clusters from exceeding the range of 100–200 for the second phase, based on hierarchical clustering, to work well. The following example uses 50 clusters.

```
from sklearn.cluster import KMeans
clustering = KMeans(n_clusters=50,
                    n_init=10,
                    random_state=1)
clustering.fit(Cx)
```

At this point, the tricky part is to keep track of what case has been assigned to what cluster derived from K-means. We use a dictionary for such a purpose.

```
Kx = clustering.cluster_centers_
Kx_mapping = {case:cluster for case,
    cluster in enumerate(clustering.labels_)}
```

The new dataset is Kx, which is made up of the cluster centroids that the K-means algorithm has discovered. You can think of each cluster as a well-represented summary of the original data. If you cluster the summary now, it will be almost the same as clustering the original data.

```
from sklearn.cluster import AgglomerativeClustering
Hclustering = AgglomerativeClustering(n_clusters=10,
                                      affinity='cosine',
                                      linkage='complete')
Hclustering.fit(Kx)
```

You now map the results to the centroids you originally used so that you can easily determine whether a hierarchical cluster is made of certain K-means centroids. The result consists of the observations making up the K-means clusters having those centroids.

```
H_mapping = {case:cluster for case,
    cluster in enumerate(Hclustering.labels_)}
final_mapping = {case:H_mapping[Kx_mapping[case]]
    for case in Kx_mapping}
```

Now you can evaluate the solution you obtained using a similar confusion matrix as you did before for both K-means and hierarchical clustering (see Figure 15-4 for the results).

```
ms = np.column_stack((ground_truth,
  [final_mapping[n] for n in range(max(final_mapping)+1)]))
df = pd.DataFrame(ms,
                  columns = ['Ground truth','Clusters'])
pd.crosstab(df['Ground truth'],
            df['Clusters'], margins=True)
```

```
In [15]:  ms = np.column_stack((ground_truth,
            [final_mapping[n] for n in range(max(final_mapping)+1)]))
          df = pd.DataFrame(ms,
                            columns = ['Ground truth','Clusters'])
          pd.crosstab(df['Ground truth'],
                      df['Clusters'], margins=True)
```

Out[15]:

Clusters	0	1	2	3	4	5	6	7	8	9	All
Ground truth											
0	0	0	0	0	0	0	178	0	0	0	178
1	1	59	27	0	0	95	0	0	0	0	182
2	0	11	160	0	1	4	0	0	0	1	177
3	2	1	3	0	167	4	0	0	0	6	183
4	1	1	0	0	0	3	4	15	154	3	181
5	169	0	0	0	11	2	0	0	0	0	182
6	1	0	0	177	0	1	2	0	0	0	181
7	0	0	3	0	0	66	0	26	0	84	179
8	0	23	3	0	51	92	0	0	0	5	174
9	3	18	0	1	140	6	0	2	0	10	180
All	177	113	196	178	370	273	184	43	154	109	1797

FIGURE 15-4: Cross-tabulation of ground truth and two-step clustering.

The solution you obtain is somehow analogous to the previous solutions. The result proves that this approach is a viable method for handling large datasets or even big data datasets, reducing them to a smaller representations and then operating with less scalable clustering, but more varied and precise techniques.

The two-phase approach also presents another advantage because it operates well with noisy or outlying data — the initial K-means phase filters out such problems well and relegates them to separate cluster solutions.

Discovering New Groups with DBScan

Both K-means and agglomerative clustering, especially if you are using the Ward's linkage criteria, will produce cohesive groups, similar to bubbles, equally spread in all directions. Reality can sometimes produce complex and unsettling results — groups may have strange forms far from the canonical bubble. The Scikit-learns's datasets module (see `http://scikit-learn.org/stable/modules/clustering.html` for an overview) offers a wide range of mind-teasing shapes that you can't successfully crunch using either K-means or agglomerative clustering: large circles containing smaller ones, interleaved small circles, and spiraling Swiss roll datasets (named after the sponge cake roll because of how the data points are arranged).

DBScan is another clustering algorithm based on a smart intuition that can solve even the most difficult problems. DBScan relies on the idea that clusters are dense, so to start exploring the data space in every direction and mark a cluster boundary when the density decreases should be sufficient. Areas of the data space with insufficient density of points are just considered empty, and all the points there are noise or *outliers*, that is, points characterized by unusual or strange values.

DBScan is more complex and requires more running time than K-means (but it is faster than agglomerative clustering). It automatically guesses the number of clusters and points out strange data that doesn't easily fit into any class. This makes DBScan different from the previous algorithms that try to force every observation into a class.

Replicating the handwritten digit clustering requires just a few lines of Python code:

```
from sklearn.cluster import DBSCAN
DB = DBSCAN(eps=3.7, min_samples=15)
DB.fit(Cx)
```

Using DBScan, you won't have to set a K number of expected clusters; the algorithm will find them by itself. Apparently, the lack of a K number seems to simplify the usage of DBScan; in reality, the algorithm requires you to fix two essential parameters, `eps` and `min_sample`, in order to work properly:

>> eps: The maximum distance between two observations that allows them to be part of the same neighborhood.

>> min_sample: The minimum number of observations in a neighborhood that transform them into a core point.

The algorithm works by walking around the data and building clusters by linking observations arranged into neighborhoods. A *neighborhood* is a small cluster of data points all within a distance value of eps. If the number of points in the neighborhood is less than the number min_sample, then DBScan doesn't form the neighborhood.

No matter what the shape of the cluster, DBScan links all the neighborhoods together if they are near enough (under the distance value of eps). When no more neighborhoods are within reach, DBScan tries to aggregate to group even single data points, if they are within eps distance. The data points that aren't associated with any group are treated as noisy points (being too particular to be part of a group).

TIP

Try many values of eps and min_sample. The resulting clusters may also change drastically with respect to the values set into these two parameters. Start with a low number of min_samples. Using a lower number allows many neighborhoods to cluster together. The default number 5 is fine. Then try different numbers for eps, starting from 0.1 upward. Don't be disappointed if you can't get a viable result initially — keep trying different combinations.

Getting back to the example, after this brief explanation of DBScan details, some data exploration can allow you to observe the results under the right point of view. First, count the clusters:

```
from collections import Counter
print('No. clusters: %i' % len(np.unique(DB.labels_)))
print(Counter(DB.labels_))

ms = np.column_stack((ground_truth, DB.labels_))
df = pd.DataFrame(ms,
                  columns = ['Ground truth', 'Clusters'])
pd.crosstab(df['Ground truth'],
            df['Clusters'], margins=True)
```

Almost half the observations are assigned to the cluster labeled –1, which represents the noise (noise is defined as examples that are too unusual to group). Given the number of dimensions (30 uncorrelated variables from a PCA analysis) in the data and its high variability (they are handwritten samples), many cases do not naturally fall together into the same group. Figure 15-5 shows the output from this example.

```
No. clusters: 12
Counter({-1: 836, 6: 182, 0: 172, 2: 159, 1: 156, 4: 119,
         5: 77, 3: 28, 10: 21, 7: 18, 8: 16, 9: 13})
```

```
In [17]:  from collections import Counter
          print('No. clusters: %i' % len(np.unique(DB.labels_)))
          print(Counter(DB.labels_))

          ms = np.column_stack((ground_truth, DB.labels_))
          df = pd.DataFrame(ms,
                            columns = ['Ground truth', 'Clusters'])

          pd.crosstab(df['Ground truth'],
                      df['Clusters'], margins=True)
```

No. clusters: 12
Counter({-1: 829, 6: 183, 0: 172, 1: 159, 2: 158, 4: 119, 5: 80, 3: 27, 10: 21, 8: 19, 7: 17, 9: 13})

Out[17]:

Clusters	-1	0	1	2	3	4	5	6	7	8	9	10	All
Ground truth													
0	6	172	0	0	0	0	0	0	0	0	0	0	178
1	68	0	88	0	26	0	0	0	0	0	0	0	182
2	143	0	2	0	0	0	0	0	0	19	13	0	177
3	75	0	4	0	0	0	0	104	0	0	0	0	183
4	84	0	0	0	0	0	80	0	17	0	0	0	181
5	157	0	0	1	0	0	0	3	0	0	0	21	182
6	23	0	1	157	0	0	0	0	0	0	0	0	181
7	60	0	0	0	0	119	0	0	0	0	0	0	179
8	110	0	63	0	1	0	0	0	0	0	0	0	174
9	103	0	1	0	0	0	0	76	0	0	0	0	180
All	829	172	159	158	27	119	80	183	17	19	13	21	1797

FIGURE 15-5: Cross-tabulation of ground truth and DBScan.

REMEMBER

The strength of DBScan is to provide reliable, consistent clusters. DBScan isn't forced, as are K-means and agglomerative clustering, to reach a solution with a certain number of clusters, even when such a solution does not exist.

Chapter **16**

Detecting Outliers in Data

E rrors happen when you least expect, and that's also true in regard to your data. In addition, data errors are difficult to spot, especially when your dataset contains many variables of different types and scale. Data errors can take a number of forms. For example, the values may be systematically missing on certain variables, erroneous numbers could appear here and there, and the data could include outliers. A red flag has to be raised when:

» Missing values on certain groups of cases or variables imply that some specific cause is generating the error.

» Erroneous values depend on how the application has produced or manipulated the data. For instance, you need to know whether the application has obtained data from a measurement instrument. External conditions and human error can affect the reliability of instruments.

» The case is apparently valid, but quite different from the usual values that characterize that variable. When you can't explain the reason for the difference, you could be observing an outlier.

Among the illustrated errors, the trickiest problem to solve is when your dataset has outliers, because you don't always have a unique definition of outliers, or a clear reason to have them in your data. As a result, much is left to your investigation and evaluation.

You don't have to type the source code for this chapter manually. In fact, it's a lot easier if you use the downloadable source (see the Introduction for download instructions). The source code for this chapter appears in the P4DS4D2_16_Detecting_Outliers.ipynb source code file.

Considering Outlier Detection

As a general definition, *outliers* are data that differ significantly (they're distant) from other data in a sample. The reason they're distant is that one or more values are too high or too low when compared to the majority of the values. They could also display an almost unique combination of values. For instance, if you are analyzing records of students enlisted in a university, students who are too young or too old may catch you attention. Students studying unusual mixes of different subjects would also require scrutiny.

Outliers skew your data distributions and affect all your basic central tendency statistics. Means are pushed upward or downward, influencing all other descriptive measures. An outlier will always inflate variance and modify correlations, so you may obtain incorrect assumptions about your data and the relationships between variables.

This simple example can display the effect (on a small scale) of a single outlier with respect to more than one thousand regular observations:

```
import matplotlib.pyplot as plt
plt.style.use('seaborn-whitegrid')
%matplotlib inline

import numpy as np
from scipy.stats.stats import pearsonr
np.random.seed(101)
normal = np.random.normal(loc=0.0, scale= 1.0, size=1000)
print('Mean: %0.3f Median: %0.3f Variance: %0.3f' %
                        (np.mean(normal),
                         np.median(normal),
                         np.var(normal)))
```

Using the NumPy random generator, the example creates the variable named normal, which contains 1000 observation derived from a standard normal distribution.

Basic descriptive statistics (mean, median, variance) do not show anything unexpected. Here is the resulting mean, median, and variance:

```
Mean: 0.026 Median: 0.032 Variance: 1.109
```

Now we change a single value by inserting an outlying value:

```
outlying = normal.copy()
outlying[0] = 50.0
print('Mean: %0.3f Median: %0.3f Variance: %0.3f' %
                          (np.mean(outlying),
                           np.median(outlying),
                           np.var(outlying)))

print('Pearson''s correlation: %0.3f p-value: %0.3f' %
                          pearsonr(normal,outlying))
```

You can call this new variable outlying and put an outlier into it (at index 0, you have a positive value of 50.0). Now you obtain much different descriptive statistics:

```
Mean: 0.074 Median: 0.032 Variance: 3.597
Pearsons correlation coefficient: 0.619 p-value: 0.000
```

Now, statistics show that the mean has a value three times higher than before, and so does variance. Only the median, which relies on position (it tells you the value occupying the middle position when all the observations are arranged in order) is not affected by the change.

More significant, the correlation of the original variable and the outlying variable is quite far from being +1.0 (the correlation value of a variable in respect of itself), indicating that the measure of linear relationship between the two variables has been seriously damaged.

Finding more things that can go wrong

Outliers do not simply shift key measures in your explorative statistics — they also change the structure of the relationships between variables in your data. Outliers can affect machine learning algorithms in two ways:

>> Algorithms based on coefficients may take the wrong coefficient in order to minimize their inability to understand the outlying cases. Linear models are a clear example (they are sums of coefficients), but they are not the only ones.

Outliers can also influence tree-based learners such as Adaboost or Gradient Boosting Machines.

>> Because algorithms learn from data samples, outliers may induce the algorithm to overweight the likelihood of extremely low or high values given a certain variable configuration.

Both situations limit the capacity of a learning algorithm to generalize well to new data. In other words, they make your learning process overfit to the present dataset.

There are a few remedies for outliers — some of them require that you modify your present data and others that you choose a suitable error function for your machine learning algorithm. (Some algorithms offer you the possibility of choosing a different error function as a parameter when setting up the learning procedure.)

REMEMBER

Most machine learning algorithms can accept different error functions. The error function is important because it helps the algorithm to learn by understanding errors and enforcing adjustments in the learning process, but some error functions are extremely sensitive to outliers, while others are quite resistant to them. For instance, a squared error measure tends to emphasize outliers because errors deriving from examples with large values are squared, thus becoming even more prominent.

Understanding anomalies and novel data

Because outliers occur as mistakes or in extremely rare cases, detecting an outlier is never an easy job; it is, however, an important one for obtaining effective results from your data science project. In certain fields, detecting anomalies is itself the purpose of data science: fraud detection in insurance and banking, fault detection in manufacturing, system monitoring in health and other critical applications, and event detection in security systems and for early warning.

An important distinction is when you look for existing outliers in data, or when you check for any new data containing anomalies with respect to existing cases. Maybe you spent a lot of time cleaning your data or you developed a machine learning application based on available data, so it would be critical to figure out whether the new data is similar to the old data and whether the algorithms will continue working well in classification or prediction.

In such cases, data scientists instead talk of novelty detection, because they need to know how well the new data resembles the old. Being exceptionally new is considered an anomaly: Novelty may conceal a significant event or may risk preventing an algorithm from working properly because machine learning heavily relies on learning from past examples and it may not generalize to completely novel cases. When working with new data, you should retrain the algorithm.

Experience teaches that the world is rarely stable. Sometimes novelties do naturally appear because the world is so mutable. Consequently, your data changes over time in unexpected ways, in both target and predictor variables. This phenomenon is called *concept drift.* The term *concept* refers to your target and *drift* to the source data used to perform a prediction that moves in a slow but uncontrollable way, like a boat drifting because of strong tides. When considering a data science model, you distinguish between different concept drift and novelties situations:

>> **Physical:** Face or voice recognition systems, or even climate models, never really change. Don't expect novelties, but check for outliers that result from data problems, such as erroneous measurements.

>> **Political and economic:** These models sometimes change, especially in the long run. You have to keep an eye out for long-term effects that start slowly and then propagate and consolidate, rendering your models ineffective.

>> **Social behavior:** Social networks and the language you use everyday change over time. Expect novelties to appear and take precautionary steps; otherwise, your model will suddenly deteriorate and turn unusable.

>> **Search engine data, banking, and e-commerce fraud schemes:** These models change quite often. You need to exercise extra care in checking for the appearance of novelties, telling you to train a new model to maintain accuracy.

>> **Cyber security threats and advertising trends:** These models change continuously. Spotting novelties is the norm, and reusing the same models over a long time is a hazard.

Examining a Simple Univariate Method

When looking for outliers, a good way to start, no matter how many variables you have in your data, is to look at every single variable by itself, using both graphical and statistical inspection. This is the univariate approach, which allows you to spot an outlier given an incongruous value on a variable. The pandas package can make spotting outliers quite easy thanks to

>> A straightforward describe method that informs you on mean, variance, quartiles, and extremes of your numeric values for each variable

>> A system of automatic boxplot visualizations

Using both techniques in tandem makes it easy to know when you have outliers and where to look for them. The diabetes dataset, from the Scikit-learn datasets module, is a good example to start with.

```
from sklearn.datasets import load_diabetes
diabetes = load_diabetes()
X,y = diabetes.data, diabetes.target
```

After these commands, all the data is contained in the X variable, a NumPy ndarray. The example then transforms it into a pandas DataFrame and asks for some descriptive statistics (see the output in Figure 16-1):

```
import pandas as pd
pd.options.display.float_format = '{:.2f}'.format
df = pd.DataFrame(X)
df.describe()
```

```
In [5]: import pandas as pd
        pd.options.display.float_format = '{:.2f}'.format
        df = pd.DataFrame(X)
        df.describe()
```

Out[5]:

	0	1	2	3	4	5	6	7	8	9
count	442.00	442.00	442.00	442.00	442.00	442.00	442.00	442.00	442.00	442.00
mean	-0.00	0.00	-0.00	0.00	-0.00	0.00	-0.00	0.00	-0.00	-0.00
std	0.05	0.05	0.05	0.05	0.05	0.05	0.05	0.05	0.05	0.05
min	-0.11	-0.04	-0.09	-0.11	-0.13	-0.12	-0.10	-0.08	-0.13	-0.14
25%	-0.04	-0.04	-0.03	-0.04	-0.03	-0.03	-0.04	-0.04	-0.03	-0.03
50%	0.01	-0.04	-0.01	-0.01	-0.00	-0.00	-0.01	-0.00	-0.00	-0.00
75%	0.04	0.05	0.03	0.04	0.03	0.03	0.03	0.03	0.03	0.03
max	0.11	0.05	0.17	0.13	0.15	0.20	0.18	0.19	0.13	0.14

FIGURE 16-1: Descriptive statistics for a DataFrame.

You can spot the problematic variables by looking at the extremities of the distribution (the maximum value of a variable). For example, you must consider whether the minimum and maximum values lie respectively far from the 25th and 75th percentile. As shown in the output, many variables have suspiciously large maximum values. A boxplot analysis will clarify the situation. The following command creates the boxplot of all variables shown in Figure 16-2.

```
fig, axes = plt.subplots(nrows=1, ncols=1,
                            figsize=(10, 5))
df.boxplot(ax=axes);
```

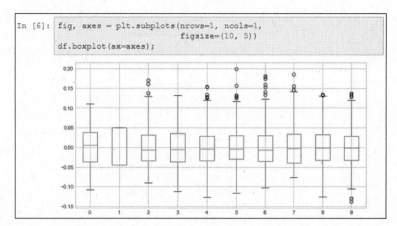

```
In [6]: fig, axes = plt.subplots(nrows=1, ncols=1,
                                  figsize=(10, 5))
        df.boxplot(ax=axes);
```

FIGURE 16-2:
Boxplots.

Boxplots generated from `pandas` `DataFrame` will have whiskers set to plus or minus 1.5 IQR (*interquartile range* or the distance between the lower and upper quartile) with respect to the upper and lower side of the box (the upper and lower quartiles). This boxplot style is called the Tukey boxplot (from the name of statistician John Tukey, who created and promoted it among statisticians together with other explanatory data techniques) and it allows a visualization of the presence of cases outside the whiskers. (All points outside these whiskers are deemed outliers.)

Leveraging on the Gaussian distribution

Another effective check for outliers in your data is accomplished by leveraging the normal distribution. Even if your data isn't normally distributed, standardizing it will allow you to assume certain probabilities of finding anomalous values. For instance, 99.7% of values found in a standardized normal distribution should be inside the range of +3 and −3 standard deviations from the mean, as shown in the following code.

```
from sklearn.preprocessing import StandardScaler
Xs = StandardScaler().fit_transform(X)
# .any(1) method will avoid duplicating
df[(np.abs(Xs)>3).any(1)]
```

In Figure 16-3, you see the results depicting the rows in the dataset featuring some possibly outlying values.

The Scikit-learn module provides an easy way to standardize your data and to record all the transformations for later use on different datasets. This means that all your data, no matter whether it's for machine learning training or for performance test purposes, is standardized in the same way.

```
In [7]:   from sklearn.preprocessing import StandardScaler
          Xs = StandardScaler().fit_transform(X)
          # .any(1) method will avoid duplicating
          df[(np.abs(Xs)>3).any(1)]

Out[7]:
```

	0	1	2	3	4	5	6	7	8	9
58	0.04	-0.04	-0.06	0.04	0.01	-0.06	0.18	-0.08	-0.00	-0.05
123	0.01	0.05	0.03	-0.00	0.15	0.20	-0.06	0.19	0.02	0.07
216	0.01	0.05	0.04	0.05	0.05	0.07	-0.07	0.15	0.05	0.05
230	-0.04	0.05	0.07	-0.06	0.15	0.16	0.00	0.07	0.05	0.07
256	-0.05	-0.04	0.16	-0.05	-0.03	-0.02	-0.05	0.03	0.03	0.01
260	0.04	-0.04	-0.01	-0.06	0.01	-0.03	0.15	-0.08	-0.08	-0.02
261	0.05	-0.04	-0.04	0.10	0.04	-0.03	0.18	-0.08	-0.01	0.02
269	0.01	-0.04	-0.03	-0.03	0.04	-0.01	0.16	-0.08	-0.01	-0.04
322	0.02	0.05	0.06	0.06	0.02	-0.04	-0.09	0.16	0.13	0.08
336	-0.02	-0.04	0.09	-0.04	0.09	0.09	-0.06	0.15	0.08	0.05
367	-0.01	0.05	0.17	0.01	0.03	0.03	-0.02	0.03	0.03	0.03
441	-0.05	-0.04	-0.07	-0.08	0.08	0.03	0.17	-0.04	-0.00	0.00

FIGURE 16-3:
Reporting possibly outlying examples.

TIP

The 68-95-99.7 rule says that in a standardized normal distribution, 68 percent of values are within one standard deviation, 95 percent are within two standard deviations, and 99.7 percent are within three. When working with skewed data, the 68-95-99.7 rule may not hold true, and in such an occurrence, you may need some more conservative estimate, such as Chebyshev's inequality. *Chebyshev's inequality* relies on a formula that says that for k standard deviations around the mean, no more cases than a percentage of $1/k^2$ should be over the mean. Therefore, at seven standard deviations around the mean, your probability of finding a legitimate value is at most two percent, no matter what the distribution is (two percent is a low probability; your case could be deemed almost certainly an outlier).

TIP

Chebyshev's inequality is conservative. A high probability of being an outlier corresponds to seven or more standard deviations away from the mean. Use it when it may be costly to deem a value an outlier when it isn't. For all other applications, the 68-95-99.7 rule will suffice.

Making assumptions and checking out

Having found some possible univariate outliers, you now have to decide how to deal with them. If you completely distrust the outlying cases, under the assumption that they were unfortunate errors or mistakes, you could just delete them. (In Python, you can just deselect them using fancy indexing.)

TIP

Modifying the values in your data or deciding to exclude certain values is a decision to make after you understand why there are some outliers in your data. You can rule out unusual values or cases for which you presume that some error in measurement has occurred, in recording or previous handling of the data. If instead you realize that the outlying case is a legitimate, though rare, one, the best approach would be to underweight it (if your learning algorithms use weight for the observations) or to increase the size of your data sample.

In our case, deciding to keep the data and having standardized it, we could just cap the outlying values by using a simple multiplier of the standard deviation:

```
Xs_capped = Xs.copy()
o_idx = np.where(np.abs(Xs)>3)
Xs_capped[o_idx] = np.sign(Xs[o_idx]) * 3
```

In the proposed code, the sign function from NumPy recovers the sign of the outlying observation (+1 or −1), which is then multiplied by the value of 3 and then assigned to the respective data point recovered by a Boolean indexing of the standardized array.

This approach does have a limitation. Being the standard deviation used both for high and low values, it implies symmetry in your data distribution, an assumption often unverified in real data. As an alternative, you can use a bit more sophisticated approach called winsorizing. When using *winsorizing*, the values deemed outliers are clipped to the value of specific percentiles that act as value limits (usually the fifth percentile for the lower bound, the 95th for the upper):

```
from scipy.stats.mstats import winsorize
Xs_winsorized = winsorize(Xs, limits=(0.05, 0.95))
```

In this way, you create a different hurdle value for larger and smaller values — taking into account any asymmetry in the data distribution. Whatever you decide for capping (by standard deviation or by winsorizing), your data is now ready for further processing and analysis.

Finally, an alternative, automatic solution is to let Scikit-learn automatically transform your data and clip outliers by using the RobustScaler, a scaler based on the IQR (as in the boxplot previously discussed in this chapter):

```
from sklearn.preprocessing import RobustScaler
Xs_rescaled = RobustScaler().fit_transform(Xs)
```

Developing a Multivariate Approach

Working on single variables allows you to spot a large number of outlying observations. However, outliers do not necessarily display values too far from the norm. Sometimes outliers are made of unusual combinations of values in more variables. They are rare, but influential, combinations that can especially trick machine learning algorithms.

In such cases, the precise inspection of every single variable won't suffice to rule out anomalous cases from your dataset. Only a few selected techniques, taking in consideration more variables at a time, will manage to reveal problems in your data.

The presented techniques approach the problem from different points of view:

>> Dimensionality reduction

>> Density clustering

>> Nonlinear distribution modeling

Using these techniques allows you to compare their results, taking notice of the recurring signals on particular cases — sometimes already located by the univariate exploration, sometimes as yet unknown.

Using principal component analysis

Principal component analysis can completely restructure the data, removing redundancies and ordering newly obtained components according to the amount of the original variance that they express. This type of analysis offers a synthetic and complete view over data distribution, making multivariate outliers particularly evident.

The first two components, being the most informative in term of variance, can depict the general distribution of the data if visualized. The output provides a good hint at possible evident outliers.

The last two components, being the most residual, depict all the information that could not be otherwise fitted by the PCA method. They can also provide a suggestion about possible but less evident outliers.

```
from sklearn.decomposition import PCA
from sklearn.preprocessing import scale
from pandas.plotting import scatter_matrix
```

```
pca = PCA()
Xc = pca.fit_transform(scale(X))

first_2 = sum(pca.explained_variance_ratio_[:2]*100)
last_2 = sum(pca.explained_variance_ratio_[-2:]*100)

print('variance by the components 1&2: %0.1f%%' % first_2)
print('variance by the last components: %0.1f%%' % last_2)

df = pd.DataFrame(Xc, columns=['comp_' + str(j)
                               for j in range(10)])
fig, axes = plt.subplots(nrows=1, ncols=2,
                         figsize=(15, 5))
first_two = df.plot.scatter(x='comp_0', y='comp_1',
                            s=50,. grid=True, c='Azure',
                            edgecolors='DarkBlue',
                            ax=axes[0])
last_two  = df.plot.scatter(x='comp_8', y='comp_9',
                            s=50, grid=True, c='Azure',
                            edgecolors='DarkBlue',
                            ax=axes[1])

plt.show()
```

Figure 16-4 shows two scatterplots of the first and last components. The output also reports the variance explained by the first two components (half of the informative content of the dataset) of the PCA and by the last two ones:

```
variance by the components 1&2: 55.2%
variance by the last components: 0.9%
```

Pay particular attention to the data points along the axis (where the x axis defines the independent variable and the y axis defines the dependent variable). You can see a possible threshold to use for separating regular data from suspect data.

Using the two last components, you can locate a few points to investigate using the threshold of −0.3 for the tenth component and of −1.0 for the ninth. All cases below these values are possible outliers (see Figure 16-5).

```
outlying = (Xc[:,-1] > 0.3) | (Xc[:,-2] > 1.0)
df[outlying]
```

```
first_2 = sum(pca.explained_variance_ratio_[:2]*100)
last_2  = sum(pca.explained_variance_ratio_[-2:]*100)

print('variance by the components 1&2: %0.1f%%' % first_2)
print('variance by the last components: %0.1f%%' % last_2)

df = pd.DataFrame(Xc, columns=['comp_' + str(j)
                               for j in range(10)])

fig, axes = plt.subplots(nrows=1, ncols=2,
                         figsize=(15, 5))
first_two = df.plot.scatter(x='comp_0', y='comp_1',
                            s=50, grid=True, c='Azure',
                            edgecolors='DarkBlue',
                            ax=axes[0])
last_two  = df.plot.scatter(x='comp_8', y='comp_9',
                            s=50, grid=True, c='Azure',
                            edgecolors='DarkBlue',
                            ax=axes[1])

plt.show()
```

```
variance by the components 1&2: 55.2%
variance by the last components: 0.9%
```

FIGURE 16-4: The first two and last two components from the PCA.

```
In [12]:  outlying = (Xc[:,-1] > 0.3) | (Xc[:,-2] > 1.0)
          df[outlying]

Out[12]:
```

	comp_0	comp_1	comp_2	comp_3	comp_4	comp_5	comp_6	comp_7	comp_8	comp_9
23	3.77	-1.76	1.09	0.72	-0.64	1.90	0.56	1.09	0.44	0.50
58	-2.65	2.23	2.79	-0.63	0.26	-0.13	1.44	0.67	1.01	-0.21
110	-2.04	-0.76	0.74	-1.93	-0.07	0.24	-1.75	-0.41	0.47	0.31
169	2.35	0.15	-0.13	1.19	-0.64	0.64	2.65	-0.31	0.22	0.50
254	3.82	-1.03	1.06	0.44	0.27	0.86	0.97	0.66	0.43	0.33
322	4.52	-2.24	-0.14	0.85	-0.47	0.73	1.28	0.34	1.39	0.38
323	3.87	-0.69	0.26	-0.58	-0.97	0.76	1.79	0.36	0.69	0.40
353	0.98	1.61	-1.16	1.14	-0.36	1.46	2.53	0.90	-0.02	0.50
371	2.11	-0.28	0.64	-0.65	-0.36	-0.26	2.22	1.09	0.07	0.35
394	2.24	-1.13	0.51	1.54	-1.30	-0.12	2.28	-0.10	0.40	0.43

FIGURE 16-5: The possible outlying cases spotted by PCA.

Using cluster analysis for spotting outliers

Outliers are isolated points in the space of variables, and DBScan is a clustering algorithm that links dense data parts together and marks the too-sparse parts. DBScan is therefore an ideal tool for an automated exploration of your data for possible outliers to verify.

Here is an example of how you can use DBScan for outlier detection:

```
from sklearn.cluster import DBSCAN
DB = DBSCAN(eps=2.5, min_samples=25)
DB.fit(Xc)

from collections import Counter
print(Counter(DB.labels_))
df[DB.labels_==-1]
```

However, `DBSCAN` requires two parameters, `eps` and `min_samples`. These two parameters require multiple tries to locate the right values, making using the parameters a little tricky.

As hinted in the previous chapter, start with a low value of `min_samples` and try growing the values of `eps` from 0.1 upward. After every trial with modified parameters, check the situation by counting the number of observations in the class −1 inside the attribute `labels`, and stop when the number of outliers seems reasonable for a visual inspection.

TIP

There will always be points on the fringe of the dense parts' distribution, so it's hard to provide you with a threshold for the number of cases that might be classified in the −1 class. Normally, outliers should not be more than 5 percent of cases, so use this indication as a generic rule of thumb.

The output from the previous example will report to you how many examples are in the −1 group, which the algorithm considers not part of the main cluster, and the list of the cases that are part of it.

TIP

It is less automated, but you can also use the K-means clustering algorithm for outlier detection. You first run a cluster analysis with a reasonable enough number of clusters. (You can try different solutions if you're not sure.) Then you look for clusters featuring just a few examples (or maybe a single one); they are probably outliers because they appear as small, distinct clusters that are separate from the large clusters that contain the majority of examples.

Automating detection with Isolation Forests

Random Forests and Extremely Randomized Trees are powerful machine learning techniques that are illustrated in Chapter 20 of the book. They work by dividing your dataset into smaller sets based on certain variable values to make it easier to predict the classification or regression on each smaller subset (a *divide et impera* solution).

IsolationForest is an algorithm that takes advantage of the fact that an outlier is easier to separate from majority cases based on differences between its values or combination of values. The algorithm keeps track of how long it takes to separate a case from the others and get it into its own subset. The less effort it takes to separate it, the more likely the case is an outlier. As a measure of such effort, IsolationForest produces a distance measurement (the shorter the distance, the more likely the case that it's an outlier).

TIP

When your machine learning algorithms are in production, a trained Isolation-Forest can act as a sanity check because many machine learning algorithms cannot cope with outlying and novel examples.

To set IsolationForest to catch outliers, all you have to decide is the level of contamination, which is the percentage of cases considered outliers based on the distance measurement. You decide such a percentage based on your experience and expectation of data quality. Executing the following script create a working IsolationForest:

```
from sklearn.ensemble import IsolationForest
auto_detection = IsolationForest(max_samples=50,
                                 contamination=0.05,
                                 random_state=0)
auto_detection.fit(Xc)
evaluation = auto_detection.predict(Xc)
df[evaluation==-1]
```

The output reports the list of the cases suspected of being outliers. In addition, the algorithm is trained to recognize what normal dataset examples. When you provide new cases to the dataset and you evaluate them using the trained IsolationForest, you can immediately spot whether something is wrong with your new data.

REMEMBER

IsolationForest.is a computationally intensive algorithm. Performing an analysis on a large dataset takes a long time and a lot of memory.

5

Learning from Data

Chapter **17**

Exploring Four Simple and Effective Algorithms

I n this new part of the book, you start to explore all the algorithms and tools necessary for learning from data (training a model with data) and being capable of predicting a numeric estimate (for example, house pricing) or a class (for instance, the species of an Iris flower) given any new example that you didn't have before. In this chapter, you start with the simplest algorithms and work toward those that are more complex. The four algorithms in this chapter represent a good starting point for any data scientist.

REMEMBER

You don't have to type the source code for this chapter manually. In fact, it's a lot easier if you use the downloadable source (see the Introduction for download instructions). The source code for this chapter appears in the P4DS4D2_17_ Exploring_Four_Simple_and_Effective_Algorithms.ipynb **source code file.**

Guessing the Number: Linear Regression

Regression has a long history in statistics, from building simple but effective linear models of economic, psychological, social, or political data, to hypothesis testing for understanding group differences, to modeling more complex problems with ordinal values, binary and multiple classes, count data, and hierarchical relationships. It's also a common tool in data science, a Swiss Army knife of machine learning that you can use for every problem. Stripped of most of its statistical properties, data science practitioners perceive linear regression as a simple, understandable, yet effective algorithm for estimations, and, in its logistic regression version, for classification as well.

Defining the family of linear models

Linear regression is a statistical model that defines the relationship between a target variable and a set of predictive features. It does so by using a formula of the following type:

$$y = bx + a.$$

You can translate this formula into something readable and useful for many problems. For instance, if you're trying to guess your sales based on historical results and available data about advertising expenditures, the same preceding formula becomes

$$sales = b * (advertising\ expenditure) + a$$

REMEMBER

CONSIDERING SIMPLE AND COMPLEX

Simple and *complex* aren't absolute terms in machine learning; their meaning is relative to the data problem you're facing. Some algorithms are simple summations while others require complex calculations and data manipulations (and Python deals with both the simple and complex algorithms for you). The data makes the difference. As a good practice, test multiple models, starting with the basic ones. You may discover that a simple solution performs better in many cases. For example, you may want to keep things simple and use a linear model instead of a more sophisticated approach and get more solid results. This is in essence what is implied by the "no free lunch" theorem: No one approach suits all problems, and even the most simple solution may hold the key to solving an important problem.

The "no free lunch" theorem by David Wolpert and William Macready states that "any two optimization algorithms are equivalent when their performance is averaged across all possible problems." If the algorithms are equivalent in the abstract, no one is superior to the other unless proved in a specific, practical problem. See the discussion at http://www.no-free-lunch.org/ for more details about no-free-lunch theorems; two of them are actually used for machine learning.

TIP

Memories from your high school algebra and geometry tell you that the formulation y=bx+a is a line in a coordinate plane made of an x axis (the abscissa) and a y axis (the ordinate). Most machine learning mathematics is actually high school level, and Python can handle them nicely for you, too.

You can demystify the formula by explaining its components: a is the value of the intercept (the value of y when x is zero) and b is a coefficient that expresses the slope of the line (the relationship between x and y). If b is positive, y increases and decreases as x increases and decreases — when b is negative, y behaves in the opposite manner. You can understand b as the unit change in y given a unit change in x. When the value of b is near zero, the effect of x on y is slight, but if the value of b is high, either positive or negative, the effect of changes in x on y are great.

Linear regression, therefore, can find the best $y = bx + a$ and represent the relationship between your target variable, y, with respect to your predictive feature, x. Both a (alpha) and b (beta coefficient) are estimated on the basis of the data, and they are found using the linear regression algorithm so that the difference between all the real y target values and all the y values derived from the linear regression formula are the minimum possible.

You can express this relationship graphically as the sum of the square of all the vertical distances between all the data points and the regression line. Such a sum is always the minimum possible when you calculate the regression line correctly using an estimation called ordinary least squares, which is derived from statistics or the equivalent gradient descent, a machine learning method. The differences between the real y values and the regression line (the predicted y values) are defined as residuals (because they are what are left after a regression: the errors).

Using more variables

When using a single variable for predicting y, you use simple linear regression, but when working with many variables, you use multiple linear regression. When you have many variables, their scale isn't important in creating precise linear regression predictions. But a good habit is to standardize X because the scale of the variables is quite important for some variants of regression (that you see later on) and it is insightful for your understanding of data to compare coefficients according to their impact on y.

The following example relies on the Boston dataset from Scikit-learn. It tries to guess Boston housing prices using a linear regression. The example also tries to determine which variables influence the result more, so the example standardizes the predictors.

```
from sklearn.datasets import load_boston
from sklearn.preprocessing import scale
boston = load_boston()
X = scale(boston.data)
y = boston.target
```

The regression class in Scikit-learn is part of the `linear_model` module. Having previously scaled the X variable, you have no other preparations or special parameters to decide when using this algorithm.

```
from sklearn.linear_model import LinearRegression
regression = LinearRegression(normalize=True)
regression.fit(X, y)
```

Now that the algorithm is fitted, you can use the `score` method to report the R^2 measure, which is a measure that ranges from 0 to 1 and points out how using a particular regression model is better in predicting y than using a simple mean would be. (The act of *fitting* creates a line or curve that best matches the data points provided by the data; you fit the line or curve to the data points in order to perform various tasks, such as predictions, based on the trends or patterns produced by the data.) You can also see R^2 as being the quantity of target information explained by the model (the same as the squared correlation), so getting near 1 means being able to explain most of the y variable using the model.

```
print(regression.score(X, y))
```

Here is the resulting score:

```
0.740607742865
```

In this case, R^2 on the previously fitted data is about 0.74, a good result for a simple model. You can interpret the R^2 score as the percentage of information present in the target variable that has been explained by the model using the predictors. A score of 0.74, therefore, means that the model has fit the larger part of the information you wanted to predict and that only 26 percent of it remains unexplained.

REMEMBER

Calculating R^2 on the same set of data used for the training is considered reasonable in statistics when using linear models. In data science and machine learning, it's always the correct practice to test scores on data that has not been used for training. Algorithms of greater complexity can memorize the data better than they learn from it, but this statement can be also true sometimes for simpler models, such as linear regression.

To understand what drives the estimates in the multiple regression model, you have to look at the `coefficients_` attribute, which is an array containing the regression beta coefficients. The coefficients are the numbers estimated by the linear regression model in order to effectively transform the input variables in the formula into the target y prediction. Printing at the same time, the `boston.DESCR` attribute helps you understand which variable the coefficients reference. The `zip` function will generate an iterable of both attributes, and you can print it for reporting.

```
print([a + ':' + str(round(b, 2)) for a, b in zip(
    boston.feature_names, regression.coef_,)])
```

The reported variables and their rounded coefficients (b values, or slopes, as described in the "Defining the family of linear models" section, earlier in this chapter) are

```
['CRIM:-0.92', 'ZN:1.08', 'INDUS:0.14', 'CHAS:0.68',
 'NOX:-2.06', 'RM:2.67', 'AGE:0.02', 'DIS:-3.1', 'RAD:2.66',
 'TAX:-2.08', 'PTRATIO:-2.06', 'B:0.86', 'LSTAT:-3.75']
```

`DIS` is the weighted distances to five employment centers. It shows the major absolute unit change. For example, in real estate, a house that's too far from people's interests (such as work) lowers the value. As a contrast, `AGE` and `INDUS`, with both proportions describing building age and showing whether nonretail activities are available in the area, don't influence the result as much because the absolute value of their beta coefficients is lower than `DIS`.

Understanding limitations and problems

Although linear regression is a simple yet effective estimation tool, it has quite a few problems. The problems can reduce the benefit of using linear regressions in some cases, but it really depends on the data. You determine whether any problems exist by employing the method and testing its efficacy. Unless you work hard on data (see Chapter 19), you may encounter these limitations:

» Linear regression can model only quantitative data. When modeling categories as response, you need to modify the data into a logistic regression.

» If data is missing and you don't deal with it properly, the model stops working. It's important to impute the missing values or, using the value of zero for the variable, to create an additional binary variable pointing out that a value is missing.

» Also, outliers are quite disruptive for a linear regression because linear regression tries to minimize the square value of the residuals, and outliers have big residuals, forcing the algorithm to focus more on them than on the mass of regular points.

» The relation between the target and each predictor variable is based on a single coefficient — there isn't an automatic way to represent complex relations like a parabola (there is a unique value of x maximizing y) or exponential growth. The only way you can manage to model such relations is to use mathematical transformations of x (and sometimes y) or add new variables. Chapter 19 explores both the use of transformations and the addition of variables.

» The greatest limitation is that linear regression provides a summation of terms, which can vary independently of each other. It's hard to figure out how to represent the effect of certain variables that affect the result in very different ways according to their value. A solution is to create *interaction terms,* that is, to multiply two or more variables to create a new variable; however, doing so requires that you know what variables to multiply and that you create the new variable before running the linear regression. In short, you can't easily represent complex situations with your data, just simple ones.

Moving to Logistic Regression

Linear regression is well suited for estimating values, but it isn't the best tool for predicting the class of an observation. In spite of the statistical theory that advises against it, you can actually try to classify a binary class by scoring one class as 1, and the other as 0. The results are disappointing most of the time, so the statistical theory wasn't wrong!

The fact is that linear regression works on a continuum of numeric estimates. In order to classify correctly, you need a more suitable measure, such as the probability of class ownership. Thanks to the following formula, you can transform a linear regression numeric estimate into a probability that is more apt to describe how a class fits an observation:

probability of a class = exp(r) / (1+exp(r))

r is the regression result (the sum of the variables weighted by the coefficients) and exp is the exponential function. exp(r) corresponds to Euler's number e elevated to the power of r. A linear regression using such a formula (also called a link function) for transforming its results into probabilities is a logistic regression.

Applying logistic regression

Logistic regression is similar to linear regression, with the only difference being the y data, which should contain integer values indicating the class relative to the observation. Using the Iris dataset from the Scikit-learn `datasets` module, you can use the values 0, 1, and 2 to denote three classes that correspond to three species:

```
from sklearn.datasets import load_iris
iris = load_iris()
X = iris.data[:-1,:],
y = iris.target[:-1]
```

To make the example easier to work with, leave a single value out so that later you can use this value to test the efficacy of the logistic regression model on it.

```
from sklearn.linear_model import LogisticRegression
logistic = LogisticRegression()
logistic.fit(X, y)
single_row_pred = logistic.predict(
    iris.data[-1, :].reshape(1, -1))
single_row_pred_proba = logistic.predict_proba(
    iris.data[-1, :].reshape(1, -1))
print ('Predicted class %s, real class %s'
    % (single_row_pred, iris.target[-1]))
print ('Probabilities for each class from 0 to 2: %s'
    % single_row_pred_proba)
```

The preceding code snippet outputs the following:

```
Predicted class [2], real class 2
Probabilities for each class from 0 to 2:
  [[ 0.00168787  0.28720074  0.71111138]]
```

In contrast to linear regression, logistic regression doesn't just output the resulting class (in this case, the class 2) but also estimates the probability of the observation's being part of all three classes. Based on the observation used for prediction, logistic regression estimates a probability of 71 percent of its being from class 2 — a high probability, but not a perfect score, therefore leaving a margin of uncertainty.

TIP

Using probabilities lets you guess the most probable class, but you can also order the predictions with respect to being part of that class. This is especially useful for medical purposes: Ranking a prediction in terms of likelihood with respect to others can reveal what patients are at most risk of getting or already having a disease.

Considering when classes are more

The previous problem, logistic regression, automatically handles a multiple class problem (it started with three iris species to guess). Most algorithms provided by Scikit-learn that predict probabilities or a score for class can automatically handle multiclass problems using two different strategies:

>> **One versus rest:** The algorithm compares every class with all the remaining classes, building a model for every class. If you have ten classes to guess, you have ten models. This approach relies on the OneVsRestClassifier class from Scikit-learn.

>> **One versus one:** The algorithm compares every class against every individual remaining class, building a number of models equivalent to n * (n–1) / 2, where n is the number of classes. If you have ten classes, you have 45 models, 10 * (10 – 1) / 2. This approach relies on the OneVsOneClassifier class from Scikit-learn.

In the case of logistic regression, the default multiclass strategy is the one versus rest. The example in this section shows how to use both the strategies with the handwritten digit dataset, containing a class for numbers from 0 to 9. The following code loads the data and places it into variables:

```
from sklearn.datasets import load_digits
digits = load_digits()
train = range(0, 1700)
test = range(1700, len(digits.data))
X = digits.data[train]
y = digits.target[train]
tX = digits.data[test]
ty = digits.target[test]
```

The observations are actually a grid of pixel values. The grid's dimensions are 8 pixels by 8 pixels. To make the data easier to learn by machine learning algorithms, the code aligns them into a list of 64 elements. The example reserves a part of the available examples for a test.

```
from sklearn.multiclass import OneVsRestClassifier
from sklearn.multiclass import OneVsOneClassifier
OVR = OneVsRestClassifier(LogisticRegression()).fit(X, y)
OVO = OneVsOneClassifier(LogisticRegression()).fit(X, y)
print('One vs rest accuracy: %.3f' % OVR.score(tX, ty))
print('One vs one accuracy: %.3f' % OVO.score(tX, ty))
```

The performances of the two multiclass strategies are

```
One vs rest accuracy: 0.938
One vs one accuracy: 0.969
```

The two multiclass classes `OneVsRestClassifier` and `OneVsOneClassifier` operate by incorporating the estimator (in this case, `LogisticRegression`). After incorporation, they usually work just like any other learning algorithm in Scikit-learn. Interestingly, the one-versus-one strategy obtained the highest accuracy thanks to its high number of models in competition.

Making Things as Simple as Naïve Bayes

You might wonder why anyone would name an algorithm Naïve Bayes. The naïve part comes from its formulation; it makes some extreme simplifications to standard probability calculations. The reference to Bayes in its name relates to the Reverend Bayes and his theorem on probability.

Reverend Thomas Bayes (1701–1761) was an English statistician and a philosopher who formulated his theorem during the first half of the eighteenth century. The theorem was never published while he was alive. It has deeply revolutionized the theory of probability by introducing the idea of conditional probability — that is, probability conditioned by evidence.

Of course, it helps to start from the beginning — probability itself. *Probability* tells you the likelihood of an event and is expressed in a numeric form. The probability of an event is measured in the range from 0 to 1 (from 0 percent to 100 percent) and it's empirically derived from counting the number of times the specific event happened with respect to all the events. You can calculate it from data!

When you observe events (for example, when a feature has a certain characteristic), and you want to estimate the probability associated with the event, you count the number of times the characteristic appears in the data and divide that figure by the total number of observations available. The result is a number ranging from 0 to 1, which expresses the probability.

When you estimate the probability of an event, you tend to believe that you can apply the probability in each situation. The term for this belief is *a priori* because it constitutes the first estimate of probability with regard to an event (the one that comes to mind first). For example, if you estimate the probability of an unknown person's being a female, you might say, after some counting, that it's 50 percent, which is the prior, or the first, probability that you will stick with.

The prior probability can change in the face of evidence, that is, something that can radically modify your expectations. For example, the evidence of whether a person is male or female could be that the person's hair is long or short. You can estimate having long hair as an event with 35 percent probability for the general population, but within the female population, it's 60 percent. If the percentage is higher in the female population, contrary to the general probability (the prior for having long hair), that should be some useful information that you can use.

Imagine that you have to guess whether a person is male or female and the evidence is that the person has long hair. This sounds like a predictive problem, and in the end, this situation is really similar to predicting a categorical variable from data: We have a target variable with different categories and you have to guess the probability of each category on the basis of evidence, the data. Reverend Bayes provided a useful formula:

$$P(A|B) = P(B|A)*P(A) / P(B)$$

The formula looks like statistical jargon and is a bit counterintuitive, so it needs to be explained in depth. Reading the formula using the previous example as input makes the meaning behind the formula quite a bit clearer:

>> P(A|B) is the probability of being a female (event A) given long hair (evidence B). This part of the formula defines what you want to predict. In short, it says to predict y given x where y is an outcome (male or female) and x is the evidence (long or short hair).

>> P(B|A) is the probability of having long hair when the person is a female. In this case, you already know that it's 60 percent. In every data problem, you can obtain this figure easily by simple cross-tabulation of the features against the target outcome.

>> P(A) is the probability of being a female, a 50 percent general chance (a prior).

>> P(B) is the probability of having long hair, which is 35 percent (another prior).

TIP

When reading parts of the formula such as P(A|B), you should read them as follows: probability of A given B. The | symbol translates as given. A probability expressed in this way is a conditional probability, because it's the probability of A conditioned by the evidence presented by B. In this example, plugging the numbers into the formula translates into: 60% * 50% / 35% = 85.7%.

Therefore, getting back to the previous example, even if being a female is a 50 percent probability, just knowing evidence like long hair takes it up to 85.7 percent, which is a more favorable chance for the guess. You can be more confident in guessing that the person with long hair is a female because you have a bit less than a 15 percent chance of being wrong.

Finding out that Naïve Bayes isn't so naïve

Naïve Bayes, leveraging the simple Bayes' rule, takes advantage of all the evidence available in order to modify the prior base probability of your predictions. Because your data contains so much evidence — that is, it has many features — the data makes a big sum of all the probabilities derived from a simplified Naïve Bayes formula.

REMEMBER

As discussed in the "Guessing the number: linear regression" section, earlier in this chapter, summing variables implies that the model takes them as separate and unique pieces of information. But this isn't true in reality, because applications exist in a world of interconnections, with every piece of information connecting to many other pieces. Using one piece of information more than once means giving more emphasis to that particular piece.

Because you don't know (or simply ignore) the relationships between each piece of evidence, you probably just plug all of them in to Naïve Bayes. The simple and naïve move of throwing everything that you know at the formula works well indeed, and many studies report good performance despite the fact that you make a naïve assumption. It's okay to use everything for prediction, even though it seems as though it shouldn't be okay given the strong association between variables. Here are some of the ways in which you commonly see Naïve Bayes used:

- >> Building spam detectors (catching all annoying e-mails in your inbox)

- >> Sentiment analysis (guessing whether a text contains positive or negative attitudes with respect to a topic, and detecting the mood of the speaker)

- >> Text-processing tasks such as spell correction, or guessing the language used to write or classify the text into a larger category

Naïve Bayes is also popular because it doesn't need as much data to work. It can naturally handle multiple classes. With some slight variable modifications (transforming them into classes), it can also handle numeric variables. Scikit-learn provides three Naïve Bayes classes in the `sklearn.naive_bayes` module:

- >> `MultinomialNB`: Uses the probabilities derived from a feature's presence. When a feature is present, it assigns a certain probability to the outcome, which the textual data indicates for the prediction.

- >> `BernoulliNB`: Provides the multinomial functionality of Naïve Bayes, but it penalizes the absence of a feature. It assigns a different probability when the feature is present than when it's absent. In fact, it treats all features as dichotomous variables (the distribution of a dichotomous variable is a Bernoulli distribution). You can also use it with textual data.

> » GaussianNB: Defines a version of Naïve Bayes that expects a normal distribution of all the features. Hence, this class is suboptimal for textual data in which words are sparse (use the multinomial or Bernoulli distributions instead). If your variables have positive and negative values, this is the best choice.

Predicting text classifications

Naïve Bayes is particularly popular for document classification. In textual problems, you often have millions of features involved, one for each word spelled correctly or incorrectly. Sometimes the text is associated with other nearby words in *n-grams*, that is, sequences of consecutive words. Naïve Bayes can learn the textual features quickly and provide fast predictions based on the input.

This section tests text classifications using the binomial and multinomial Naïve Bayes models offered by Scikit-learn. The examples rely on the 20newsgroups dataset, which contains a large number of posts from 20 kinds of newsgroups. The dataset is divided into a training set, for building your textual models, and a test set, which is comprised of posts that temporarily follow the training set. You use the test set to test the accuracy of your predictions:

```
from sklearn.datasets import fetch_20newsgroups
newsgroups_train = fetch_20newsgroups(
            subset='train', remove=('headers', 'footers',
                                    'quotes'))
newsgroups_test = fetch_20newsgroups(
            subset='test', remove=('headers', 'footers',
                                    'quotes'))
```

After loading the two sets into memory, you import the two Naïve Bayes models and instantiate them. At this point, you set alpha values, which are useful for avoiding a zero probability for rare features (a zero probability would exclude these features from the analysis). You typically use a small value for alpha, as shown in the following code:

```
from sklearn.naive_bayes import BernoulliNB, MultinomialNB
Bernoulli = BernoulliNB(alpha=0.01)
Multinomial = MultinomialNB(alpha=0.01)
```

In Chapter 12, you use the hashing trick to model textual data without fear of encountering new words when using the model after the training phase. You can use two different hashing tricks, one counting the words (for the multinomial approach) and one recording whether a word appeared in a binary variable (the binomial approach). You can also remove *stop words*, that is, common words found in the English language, such as *a, the, in,* and so on.

```
import sklearn.feature_extraction.text as txt
multinomial = txt.HashingVectorizer(stop_words='english',
                                    binary=False, norm=None)
binary = txt.HashingVectorizer(stop_words='english',
                               binary=True, norm=None)
```

At this point, you can train the two classifiers and test them on the test set, which is a set of posts that temporarily appear after the training set. The test measure is accuracy, which is the percentage of right guesses that the algorithm makes.

```
import numpy as np
target = newsgroups_train.target
target_test = newsgroups_test.target
multi_X = np.abs(
    multinomial.transform(newsgroups_train.data))
multi_Xt = np.abs(
    multinomial.transform(newsgroups_test.data))
bin_X = binary.transform(newsgroups_train.data)
bin_Xt = binary.transform(newsgroups_test.data)

Multinomial.fit(multi_X, target)
Bernoulli.fit(bin_X, target)

from sklearn.metrics import accuracy_score
from sklearn.metrics import accuracy_score
for name, model, data in [('BernoulliNB', Bernoulli, bin_Xt),
                          ('MultinomialNB', Multinomial, multi_Xt)]:
    accuracy = accuracy_score(y_true=target_test,
                              y_pred=model.predict(data))
    print ('Accuracy for %s: %.3f' % (name, accuracy))
```

The reported accuracies for the two Naïve Bayes models are

```
Accuracy for BernoulliNB: 0.570
Accuracy for MultinomialNB: 0.651
```

You might notice that it won't take long for both models to train and report their predictions on the test set. Consider that the training set is made up of more than 11,000 posts containing 300,000 words, and the test set contains about 7,500 other posts.

```
print('number of posts in training: %i'
    % len(newsgroups_train.data))
D={word:True for post in newsgroups_train.data
    for word in post.split(' ')}
print('number of distinct words in training: %i'
    % len(D))
print('number of posts in test: %i'
    % len(newsgroups_test.data))
```

Running the code returns all these useful text statistics:

```
number of posts in training: 11314
number of distinct words in training: 300972
number of posts in test: 7532
```

Learning Lazily with Nearest Neighbors

K-Nearest Neighbors (KNN) is not about building rules from data based on coefficients or probability. KNN works on the basis of similarities. When you have to predict something like a class, it may be the best to find the most similar observations to the one you want to classify or estimate. You can then derive the answer you need from the similar cases.

Observing how many observations are similar doesn't imply learning something, but rather measuring. Because KNN isn't learning anything, it's considered lazy, and you'll hear it referenced as a lazy learner or an instance-based learner. The idea is that similar premises usually provide similar results, and it's important not to forget to get such low-hanging fruit before trying to climb the tree!

The algorithm is fast during training because it only has to memorize data about the observations. It actually calculates more during predictions. When there are too many observations, the algorithm can become slow and memory consuming. You're best advised not to use it with big data or it may take almost forever to predict anything! Moreover, this simple and effective algorithm works better when you have distinct data groups without too many variables involved because the algorithm is also sensitive to the dimensionality curse.

The curse of dimensionality happens as the number of variables increases. Consider a situation in which you're measuring the distance between observations and, as the space becomes larger and larger, it becomes difficult to find real neighbors — a problem for KNN, which sometimes mistakes a far observation for a near one. Rendering the idea is just like playing chess on a multidimensional chessboard. When playing on the classic 2-D board, most pieces are near and you can more easily spot opportunities and menaces for your pawns when you have 32 pieces and 64 positions. However, when you start playing on a 3-D board, such as those found in some sci-fi films, your 32 pieces can become lost in 512 possible positions. Now just imagine playing with a 12-D chessboard. You can easily misunderstand what is near and what is far, which is what happens with KNN.

TIP

You can still make KNN smart in detecting similarities between observations by removing redundant information and simplifying the data dimensionality using data the reduction techniques, as explained in Chapter 14.

Predicting after observing neighbors

For an example showing how to use KNN, you can start with the digit dataset again. KNN is particularly useful, just like Naïve Bayes, when you have to predict many classes, or in situations that would require you to build too many models or rely on a complex model.

```
from sklearn.datasets import load_digits
from sklearn.decomposition import PCA
digits = load_digits()
train = range(0, 1700)
test = range(1700, len(digits.data))
pca = PCA(n_components = 25)
pca.fit(digits.data[train])
X = pca.transform(digits.data[train])
y = digits.target[train]
tX = pca.transform(digits.data[test])
ty = digits.target[test]
```

KNN is an algorithm that's quite sensitive to outliers. Moreover, you have to rescale your variables and remove some redundant information. In this example, you use PCA. Rescaling is not necessary because the data represents pixels, which means that it's already scaled.

TIP

You can avoid the problem with outliers by keeping the neighborhood small, that is, by not looking too far for similar examples.

TIP

Knowing the data type can save you a lot of time and many mistakes. For example, in this case, you know that the data represents pixel values. Doing EDA (as described in Chapter 13) is always the first step and can provide you with useful insights, but getting additional information about how the data was obtained and what the data represents is also a good practice and can be just as useful.

To see this task in action, you reserve cases in tX and try a few cases that KNN won't look up when looking for neighbors.

```
from sklearn.neighbors import KNeighborsClassifier
kNN = KNeighborsClassifier(n_neighbors=5, p=2)
kNN.fit(X, y)
```

KNN uses a distance measure to determine which observations to consider as possible neighbors for the target case. You can easily change the predefined distance using the p parameter:

» When p is 2, use the Euclidean distance (discussed as part of the clustering topic in Chapter 15).

» When p is 1, use the Manhattan distance metric, which is the absolute distance between observations. In a 2-D square, when you go from one corner to the opposite one, the Manhattan distance is the same as walking the perimeter, whereas Euclidean is like walking on the diagonal. Although the Manhattan distance isn't the shortest route, it's a more realistic measure than Euclidean distance, and it's less sensitive to noise and high dimensionality.

Usually, the Euclidean distance is the right measure, but sometimes it can give you worse results, especially when the analysis involves many correlated variables. The following code shows that the analysis seems fine with it.

```
print('Accuracy: %.3f' % kNN.score(tX,ty) )
print('Prediction: %s Actual: %s'
      % (kNN.predict(tX[-15:,:]),ty[-15:]))
```

The code returns the accuracy and a sample of the predictions you can compare with the actual values in order to spot differences:

```
Accuracy: 0.990
Prediction: [2 2 5 7 9 5 4 8 1 4 9 0 8 9 8]
    Actual: [2 2 5 7 9 5 4 8 8 4 9 0 8 9 8]
```

Choosing your k parameter wisely

A critical parameter that you have to define in KNN is k. As k increases, KNN considers more points for its predictions, and the decisions are less influenced by noisy instances that could exercise an undue influence. Your decisions are based on an average of more observations, and they become more solid. When the k value you use is too large, you start considering neighbors that are too far, sharing less and less with the case you have to predict.

It's an important trade-off. When the value of k is less, you consider a more homogeneous pool of neighbors but can more easily make an error by taking the few similar cases for granted. When the value of k is more, you consider more cases at a higher risk of observing neighbors that are too far or that are outliers. Getting back to the previous example with handwritten digit data, you can experiment with changing the k value, as shown in the following code:

```
for k in [1, 5, 10, 50, 100, 200]:
    kNN = KNeighborsClassifier(n_neighbors=k).fit(X, y)
    print('for k = %3i accuracy is %.3f'
          % (k, kNN.score(tX, ty))
```

After running this code, you get an overview of what happens when k changes and determine the value of k that best fits the data:

```
for k =   1 accuracy is 0.979
for k =   5 accuracy is 0.990
for k =  10 accuracy is 0.969
for k =  50 accuracy is 0.959
for k = 100 accuracy is 0.959
for k = 200 accuracy is 0.907
```

Through experimentation, you find that setting n_neighbors (the parameter representing k) to 5 is the optimum choice, resulting in the highest accuracy. Using just the nearest neighbor (n_neighbors =1) isn't a bad choice, but setting the value above 5 instead brings decreasing results in the classification task.

TIP

As a rule of thumb, when your dataset doesn't have many observations, set k as a number near the squared number of available observations. However, there is no general rule, and trying different k values is always a good way to optimize your KNN performance. Always start from low values and work toward higher values.

Chapter **18**

Performing Cross-Validation, Selection, and Optimization

Machine learning algorithms can indeed learn from data. For instance, the four algorithms presented in the previous chapter, although quite simple, can effectively estimate a class or a value after being presented with examples associated with outcomes. It is all a matter of learning by induction, which is the process of extracting general rules from specific examples. From childhood, humans commonly learn by seeing examples, deriving some general rules or ideas from them, and then successfully applying the derived rule to new situations as we grow up. For example, if we see someone being burned after touching fire, we understand that fire is dangerous, and we don't need to touch it ourselves to know that.

Learning by example using machine algorithms has pitfalls. Here are a few issues that might arise:

> » There aren't enough examples to make a judgment about a rule, no matter what machine learning algorithm you are using.

» The machine learning application is presented with the wrong examples and consequently cannot reason correctly.

» Even when the application sees enough right examples, it still can't figure out rules because they're too complex. Sir Isaac Newton, the father of modern physics, narrated the story that he was inspired by the fall of an apple from a tree in his formulation of gravity. Unfortunately, deriving a universal law from a series of observations is not an automatic consequence for most of us and the same applies to algorithms.

It's important to consider these pitfalls when delving into machine learning. The quantity of data, its quality, and the characteristics of the learning algorithm decide whether a machine learning application can generalize well to new cases. If anything is wrong with any of them, they can pose some serious limits. As a data science practitioner, you must recognize and learn to avoid these types of pitfalls in your data science experiments.

REMEMBER

You don't have to type the source code for this chapter manually. In fact, it's a lot easier if you use the downloadable source (see the Introduction for download instructions). The source code for this chapter appears in the P4DS4D2_18_Performing_Cross_Validation_Selection_and_Optimization. ipynb source code file.

Pondering the Problem of Fitting a Model

Fitting a model implies learning from data a representation of the rules that generated the data in the first place. From a mathematical perspective, fitting a model is analogous to guessing an unknown function of the kind you faced in high school, such as, y=4x^2+2x, just by observing its y results. Therefore, under the hood, you expect that machine learning algorithms generate mathematical formulations by determining how reality works based on the examples provided.

Demonstrating whether such formulations are real is beyond the scope of data science. What is most important is that they work by producing exact predictions. For example, even though you can describe much of the physical world using mathematical functions, you often can't describe social and economic dynamics this way — but people try guessing them anyway.

To summarize, as a data scientist, you should always strive to approximate the real, unknown functions underlying the problems you face using the best information available. The result of your work is evaluated based on your capacity to predict specific outcomes (the target outcome) given certain premises (the data) thanks to a useful range of algorithms (the machine learning algorithms).

Earlier in the book, you see something akin to a real function or law when the book presents linear regression, which has its own formulation. The linear formula $y = Bx + a$, which mathematically represents a line on a plane, can often approximate training data well, even if the data is not representing a line or something similar to a line. As with linear regression, all other machine learning algorithms have an internal formulation themselves (and some, such as neural networks, even require you to define their formulation from scratch). The linear regression's formulation is one of the simplest ones; formulations from other learning algorithms can appear quite complex. You don't need to know exactly how they work. You do need to have an idea of how complex they are, whether they represent a line or a curve, and whether they can sense outliers or noisy data. When planning to learn from data, you should address these problematic aspects based on the formulation you intend to use:

1. Whether the learning algorithm is the best one that can approximate the unknown function that you imagine behind the data you are using. In order to make such a decision, you must consider the learning algorithm's formulation performance on the data at hand and compare it with other, alternative formulations from other algorithms.

2. Whether the specific formulation of the learning algorithm is too simple, with respect to the hidden function, to make an estimate (this is called a bias problem).

3. Whether the specific formulation of the learning algorithm is too complex, with respect to the hidden function to be guessed (leading to the variance problem).

REMEMBER

Not all algorithms are suitable for every data problem. If you don't have enough data or the data is full of erroneous information, it may be too difficult for some formulations to figure out the real function.

Understanding bias and variance

If your chosen learning algorithm can't learn properly from data and is not performing well, the cause is bias or variance in its estimates.

» **Bias:** Given the simplicity of formulation, your algorithm tends to overestimate or underestimate the real rules behind the data and is systematically wrong in certain situations. Simple algorithms have high bias; having few internal parameters, they tend to represent only simple formulations well.

» **Variance:** Given the complexity of formulation, your algorithm tends to learn too much information from the data and detect rules that don't exist, which causes its predictions to be erratic when faced with new data. You can think of variance as a problem connected to memorization. Complex algorithms can memorize data features thanks to the algorithms' high number of internal parameters. However, memorization doesn't imply any understanding about the rules.

Bias and variance depend on the complexity of the formulation at the core of the learning algorithm with respect to the complexity of the formulation that is presumed to have generated the data you are observing. However, when you consider a specific problem using the available data rules, you're better off having high bias or variance when

» **You have few observations:** Simpler algorithms perform better, no matter what the unknown function is. Complex algorithms tend to learn too much from data, estimating with inaccuracy.

» **You have many observations:** Complex algorithms always reduce variance. The reduction occurs because even complex algorithms can't learn all that much from data, so they learn just the rules, not any erratic noise.

» **You have many variables:** Provided that you also have many observations, simpler algorithms tend to find a way to approximate even complex hidden functions.

Defining a strategy for picking models

When faced with a machine learning problem, you usually know little about the problem and don't know whether a particular algorithm will manage it well. Consequently, you don't really know whether the source of a problem is caused by bias or variance — although you can usually use the rule of thumb that if an algorithm is simple, it will have high bias, and if it is complex, it will have high variance. Even when working with common, well-documented data science applications, you'll notice that what works in other situations (as described in academic and industry papers) often doesn't operate very well for your own application because the data is different.

You can summarize this situation using the famous no-free-lunch theorem of the mathematician David Wolpert: Any two machine learning algorithms are equivalent in performance when tested across all possible problems. Consequently, it isn't possible to say that one algorithm is always better than another; it can be better than another one only when used to solve specific problems. You can view the concept in another way: For every problem, there is never a fixed recipe! The best and only strategy is just to try everything you can and verify the results using a controlled scientific experiment. Using this approach ensures that what seems to work is what really works and, most important, what will keep on working with new data. Although you may have more confidence when using some learners over others, you can never tell what machine learning algorithm is the best before trying it and measuring its performance on your problem.

At this point, you must consider a critical, yet underrated, aspect to ensure the success of your data project. For a best model and greatest results, it's essential to define an evaluation metric that distinguishes a good model from a bad one with respect to the business or scientific problem that you want to solve. In fact, for some projects, you may need to avoid predicting negative cases when they are positive; for others, you may want to absolutely spot all the positive ones; and for still others, all you need to do is order them so that positive ones come before the negative ones and you don't need to check them all.

By picking an algorithm, you automatically also pick an optimization process ruled by an evaluation metric that reports its performance to the algorithm so that the algorithm can better adjust its parameters. For instance, when using a linear regression, the metric is the mean squared error given by the vertical distance of the observations from the regression line. Therefore, it's automatic, and you can more easily accept the algorithm performance provided by such a default evaluation metric.

Apart from accepting the default metric, some algorithms do let you choose a preferred evaluation function. In other cases, when you can't point out a favorite evaluation function, you can still influence the existing evaluation metric by appropriately fixing some of its hyperparameters, thus optimizing the algorithm indirectly for another, different, metric.

Before starting to train your data and create predictions, always consider what could be the best performance measure for your project. Scikit-learn offers access to a wide range of measures for both classification and regression problems. The `sklearn.metrics` module allows you to call the optimization procedures using a simple string or by calling an error function from its modules. Table 18-1 shows the measures commonly used for regression problems.

TABLE 18-1

Regression Evaluation Measures

Callable String	Function
mean_absolute_error	sklearn.metrics.mean_absolute_error
mean_squared_error	sklearn.metrics.mean_squared_error
r2	sklearn.metrics.r2_score

The r2 string specifies a statistical measure for linear regression called R^2 (R squared). It expresses how the model compares in predictive power with respect to a simple mean. Machine learning applications seldom use this measure because it doesn't explicitly report errors made by the model, although high R^2 values imply fewer errors; more viable metrics for regression models are the mean squared errors and the mean absolute errors.

Squared errors penalize extreme values more, whereas absolute error weights all the errors the same. So it is really a matter of considering the trade-off between reducing the error on extreme observations as much as possible (squared error) or trying to reduce the error for the majority of the observations (absolute error). The choice you make depends on the application. When extreme values represent critical situations for your application, a squared error measure is better. However, when your concern is to minimize the common and usual observations, as often happens in forecasting sales problems, you should use a mean absolute error as the reference. The choices are even for complex classification problems, as you can see in Table 18-2.

TABLE 18-2

Classification Evaluation Measures

Callable String	Function
accuracy	sklearn.metrics.accuracy_score
precision	sklearn.metrics.precision_score
recall	sklearn.metrics.recall_score
f1	sklearn.metrics.f1_score
roc_auc	sklearn.metrics.roc_auc_score

Accuracy is the simplest error measure in classification, counting (as a percentage) how many of the predictions are correct. It takes into account whether the machine learning algorithm has guessed the right class. This measure works with both binary and multiclass problems. Even though it's a simple measure, optimizing accuracy may cause problems when an imbalance exists between classes.

For example, it could be a problem when the class is frequent or preponderant, such as in fraud detection, where most transactions are actually legitimate with respect to a few criminal transactions. In such situations, machine learning algorithms optimized for accuracy tend to guess in favor of the preponderant class and be wrong most of time with the minor classes, which is an undesirable behavior for an algorithm that you expect to guess all the classes correctly, not just a few selected ones.

Precision and recall, and their conjoint optimization by F1 score, can solve problems not addressed by accuracy. Precision is about being precise when guessing. It tracks the percentage of times, when forecasting a class, that a class was right. For example, you can use precision when diagnosing cancer in patients after evaluating data about their exams. Your precision in this case is the percentage of patients who really have cancer among those diagnosed with cancer. Therefore, if you have diagnosed ten ill patients and nine are truly ill, your precision is 90 percent.

You face different consequences when you don't diagnose cancer in a patient who has it or you do diagnose it in a healthy patient. Precision tells just a part of the story, because there are patients with cancer that you have diagnosed as healthy, and that's a terrible problem. The recall measure tells the second part of the story. It reports, among an entire class, your percentage of correct guesses. For example, when reviewing the previous example, the recall metric is the percentage of patients that you correctly guessed have cancer. If there are 20 patients with cancer and you have diagnosed just 9 of them, your recall will be 45 percent.

When using your model, you can be accurate but still have low recall, or have a high recall but lose accuracy in the process. Fortunately, precision and recall can be maximized together using the F1 score, which uses the formula: `F1 = 2 * (precision * recall) / (precision + recall)`. Using the F1 score ensures that you always get the best precision and recall combined.

Receiver Operating Characteristic Area Under Curve (ROC AUC) is useful when you want to order your classifications according to their probability of being correct. Therefore, when optimizing ROC AUC in the previous example, the learning algorithm will first try to order (sort) patients starting from those most likely to have cancer to those least likely to have cancer. The ROC AUC is higher when the ordering is good and low when it is bad. If your model has a high ROC AUC, you need to check the most likely ill patients. Another example is in a fraud detection problem, when you want to order customers according to the risk of being fraudulent. If your model has a good ROC AUC, you need to check just the riskiest customers closely.

Dividing between training and test sets

Having explored how to decide among the different error metrics for classification and regression, the next step in the strategy for choosing the best model is to experiment and evaluate the solutions by viewing their ability to generalize to new cases. As an example of correct procedures for experimenting with machine learning algorithms, begin by loading the Boston dataset (a popular example dataset created in the 1970s), which consists of Boston housing prices, various house characteristic measurements, and measures of the residential area where each house is located.

```
from sklearn.datasets import load_boston
boston = load_boston()
X, y = boston.data, boston.target
```

Notice that the dataset contains more than 500 observations and 13 features. The target is a price measure, so you decide to use linear regression and to optimize the result using the mean squared error. The objective is to ensure that a linear regression is a good model for the Boston dataset and to quantify how good it is using the mean squared error (which lets you compare it with alternative models).

```
from sklearn.linear_model import LinearRegression
from sklearn.metrics import mean_squared_error
regression = LinearRegression()
regression.fit(X,y)
print('Mean squared error: %.2f' % mean_squared_error(
    y_true=y, y_pred=regression.predict(X)))
```

The resulting mean square error generated by the commands is

```
Mean squared error: 21.90
```

After having fitted the model with the data (which is called the training data because it provides examples to learn from), the `mean_squared_error` error function reports the data prediction error. The mean squared error is 21.90, apparently a good measure but calculated directly on the training set, so you cannot be sure if it could work as well with new data (machine learning algorithms are both good at learning and at memorizing from examples).

Ideally, you need to perform a test on data that the algorithm has never seen in order to exclude any memorization. Only in this way can you discover whether your algorithm will work well when new data arrives. To perform this task, you wait for new data, make the predictions on it, and then compare the predictions to reality. But, performing the task this way may take a long time and could become both risky and expensive, depending on the type of problem you want to solve using machine learning (for example, some applications such as cancer detection can be incredibly risky to experiment with because lives are at a stake).

Luckily, you have another way to obtain the same result. To simulate having new data, you can divide the observations into test and training cases. It's quite common in data science to have a test size of 25–30 percent of the available data and to train the predictive model using the remaining 70–75 percent. Here is an example of how you can achieve data partitioning in Python:

```
from sklearn.model_selection import train_test_split
X_train, X_test, y_train, y_test = train_test_split(
    X, y, test_size=0.30, random_state=5)
```

print(X_train.shape, X_test.shape)The code prints the resulting shapes of the training and test sets, with the former being 70 percent of the initial dataset size and the latter just 30 percent:

```
(354, 13) (152, 13)
```

The example separates training and test X and y variables into distinct variables using the `train_test_split` function. The `test_size` parameter indicates a test set made of 30 percent of the available observations. The function always chooses the test sample randomly. Now you can use the training set for training:

```
regression.fit(X_train,y_train)
print('Train mean squared error: %.2f' % mean_squared_error(
    y_true=y_train, y_pred=regression.predict(X_train)))
```

The output shows the training set's mean squared error:

```
Train mean squared error: 19.07
```

At this point, you fit the model again and the code reports a new training error of 19.07, which is somehow different from before. However, the error you really have to refer to comes from the test set you reserved.

```
print('Test mean squared error: %.2f' % mean_squared_error(
    y_true=y_test, y_pred=regression.predict(X_test)))
```

After running the evaluation on the test set, you get its error value:

```
Test mean squared error: 30.70
```

When you the estimate the error on the test set, the results show that the reported value is 30.70. What a difference, indeed! Somehow, the estimate on the training set was too optimistic. Using the test set, while more realistic in error estimation, really makes your result depend on a small portion of the data. If you change that small portion, the test result will also change. Here is an example:

```
from sklearn.model_selection import train_test_split
X_train, X_test, y_train, y_test = train_test_split(
    X, y, test_size=0.30, random_state=6)
regression.fit(X_train,y_train)
print('Train mean squared error: %.2f' % mean_squared_error(
    y_true=y_train, y_pred=regression.predict(X_train)))
print('Test mean squared error: %.2f' % mean_squared_error(
    y_true=y_test, y_pred=regression.predict(X_test)))
```

You get a new report of the errors in the train and test sets:

```
Train mean squared error: 19.48
Test mean squared error: 28.33
```

What you have experienced in this section is a common problem with machine learning algorithms. You know that each algorithm has a certain bias or variance in predicting an outcome; the problem is that you can't estimate its impact for sure. Moreover, if you have to make choices with regard to the algorithm, you can't be sure of which decision might be the most effective one.

Using training data is always unsuitable when evaluating algorithm performance because the learning algorithm can actually predict the training data better. This is especially true when an algorithm has a low bias because of its complexity. In this case, you can expect a lower error when predicting the training data, which means that you get an overly optimistic result that doesn't compare it fairly with other algorithms (which may have a different bias/variance profile), nor are the results useful for this example's evaluation. By using the test data, you actually reduce the training examples (which may cause the algorithm to perform less well), but in exchange, you get a more reliable and comparable error estimate.

Cross-Validating

If test sets provide unstable results because of sampling, the solution is to systematically sample a certain number of test sets and then average the results. It's a statistical approach (to observe many results and take an average of them), and that's the basis of cross-validation. The recipe is straightforward:

1. Divide your data into folds (each *fold* is a container that holds an even distribution of the cases), usually 10, but fold sizes of 3, 5, and 20 are viable alternative options.

2. Hold out one fold as a test set and use the others as training sets.

3. Train and record the test set result. If you have little data, it's better to use a larger number of folds, because the quantity of data and the use of additional folds positively affects the quality of training.

4. Perform Steps 2 and 3 again, using each fold in turn as a test set.

5. Calculate the average and the standard deviation of all the folds' test results. The average is a reliable estimator of the quality of your predictor. The standard deviation will tell you the predictor reliability (if it is too high, the cross-validation error could be imprecise). Expect that predictors with high variance will have a high cross-validation standard deviation.

Even though this technique may appear complicated, Scikit-learn handles it using the functions in the `sklearn.model_selection` module.

Using cross-validation on k folds

To run cross-validation, you first have to initialize an iterator. KFold is the iterator that implements k folds cross-validation. There are other iterators available from the `sklearn.model_selection` module, mostly derived from the statistical practice, but KFold is the most widely used in data science practice.

KFold requires you to specify specify the `n_splits` number (the number of folds to generate), and indicate whether you want to shuffle the data (by using the `shuffle` parameter). As a rule, the higher the expected variance, the more that increasing the number of splits improves the mean estimate. It's a good idea to shuffle the data because ordered data can introduce confusion into the learning processes for some algorithms if the first observations are different from the last ones.

After setting KFold, call the `cross_val_score` function, which returns an array of results containing a score (from the scoring function) for each cross-validation fold. You have to provide `cross_val_score` with your data (both X and y) as an input, your estimator (the regression class), and the previously instantiated KFold iterator (as the cv parameter). In a matter of a few seconds or minutes, depending on the number of folds and data processed, the function returns the results.

You average these results to obtain a mean estimate, and you can also compute the standard deviation to check how stable the mean is.

```
from sklearn.model_selection import cross_val_score, KFold
import numpy as np
crossvalidation = KFold(n_splits=10, shuffle=True,
    random_state=1)
scores = cross_val_score(regression, X, y,
    scoring='neg_mean_squared_error', cv=crossvalidation,
    n_jobs=1)
print('Folds: %i, mean squared error: %.2f std: %.2f' %
    (len(scores),np.mean(np.abs(scores)),np.std(scores)))
```

Here is the result:

```
Folds: 10, mean squared error: 23.76 std: 12.13
```

TIP

Cross-validating can work in parallel because no estimate depends on any other estimate. You can take advantage of the multiple cores present on your computer by setting the parameter n_jobs=-1.

Sampling stratifications for complex data

Cross-validation folds are decided by random sampling. Sometimes it may be necessary to track if and how much of a certain characteristic is present in the training and test folds in order to avoid malformed samples. For instance, the Boston dataset has a binary variable (a feature that has a value of 1 or 0) indicating whether the house bounds the Charles River. This information is important to understand the value of the house and determine whether people would like to spend more for it. You can see the effect of this variable using the following code.

```
%matplotlib inline
import pandas as pd
df = pd.DataFrame(X, columns=boston.feature_names)
df['target'] = y
df.boxplot('target', by='CHAS', return_type='axes');
```

A boxplot, represented in Figure 18-1, reveals that houses on the river tend to have values higher than other houses. Of course, there are expensive houses all around Boston, but you have to keep an eye about how many river houses you are analyzing because your model has to be general for all of Boston, not just Charles River houses.

```
In [8]:  %matplotlib inline
         import pandas as pd
         df = pd.DataFrame(X, columns=boston.feature_names)
         df['target'] = y
         df.boxplot('target', by='CHAS', return_type='axes');
```

FIGURE 18-1:
Boxplot of the
target outcome,
grouped by CHAS.

In similar situations, when a characteristic is rare or influential, you can't be sure when it's present in the sample because the folds are created in a random way. Having too many or too few of a particular characteristic in each fold implies that the machine learning algorithm may derive incorrect rules.

The StratifiedKFold class provides a simple way to control the risk of building malformed samples during cross-validation procedures. It can control the sampling so that certain features, or even certain outcomes (when the target classes are extremely unbalanced), will always be present in your folds in the right proportion. You just need to point out the variable you want to control by using the y parameter, as shown in the following code.

```
from sklearn.model_selection import StratifiedShuffleSplit
from sklearn.metrics import mean_squared_error
strata = StratifiedShuffleSplit(n_splits=3,
                                test_size=0.35,
                                random_state=0)
scores = list()
for train_index, test_index in strata.split(X, X[:,3]):
    X_train, X_test = X[train_index], X[test_index]
    y_train, y_test = y[train_index], y[test_index]
    regression.fit(X_train, y_train)
    scores.append(mean_squared_error(y_true=y_test,
                        y_pred=regression.predict(X_test)))
print('%i folds cv mean squared error: %.2f std: %.2f' %
    (len(scores),np.mean(np.abs(scores)),np.std(scores)))
```

The result from the 3-fold stratified cross-validation is

```
3 folds cv mean squared error: 24.30 std: 3.99
```

Although the validation error is similar, by controlling the CHAR variable, the standard error of the estimates decreases, making you aware that the variable was influencing the previous cross-validation results.

Selecting Variables Like a Pro

Selecting the right variables can improve the learning process by reducing the amount of noise (useless information) that can influence the learner's estimates. Variable selection, therefore, can effectively reduce the variance of predictions. In order to involve just the useful variables in training and leave out the redundant ones, you can use these techniques:

>> **Univariate approach:** Select the variables most related to the target outcome.

>> **Greedy or backward approach:** Keep only the variables that you can remove from the learning process without damaging its performance.

Selecting by univariate measures

If you decide to select a variable by its level of association with its target, the class SelectPercentile provides an automatic procedure for keeping only a certain percentage of the best, associated features. The available metrics for association are

>> f_regression: Used only for numeric targets and based on linear regression performance.

>> f_classif: Used only for categorical targets and based on the Analysis of Variance (ANOVA) statistical test.

>> chi2: Performs the chi-square statistic for categorical targets, which is less sensible to the nonlinear relationship between the predictive variable and its target.

TIP

When evaluating candidates for a classification problem, f_classif and chi2 tend to provide the same set of top variables. It's still a good practice to test the selections from both the association metrics.

Apart from applying a direct selection of the top percentile associations, Select-Percentile can also rank the best variables to make it easier to decide at what percentile to exclude a feature from participating in the learning process. The class SelectKBest is analogous in its functionality, but it selects the top k variables, where k is a number, not a percentile.

```
from sklearn.feature_selection import SelectPercentile
from sklearn.feature_selection import f_regression
Selector_f = SelectPercentile(f_regression, percentile=25)
Selector_f.fit(X, y)
for n,s in zip(boston.feature_names,Selector_f.scores_):
    print('F-score: %3.2f\t for feature %s ' % (s,n))
```

After a few iterations, the code prints the following results:

```
F-score: 88.15      for feature CRIM
F-score: 75.26      for feature ZN
F-score: 153.95     for feature INDUS
F-score: 15.97      for feature CHAS
F-score: 112.59     for feature NOX
F-score: 471.85     for feature RM
F-score: 83.48      for feature AGE
F-score: 33.58      for feature DIS
F-score: 85.91      for feature RAD
F-score: 141.76     for feature TAX
F-score: 175.11     for feature PTRATIO
F-score: 63.05      for feature B
F-score: 601.62     for feature LSTAT
```

Using the level of association output (higher values signal more association of a feature with the target variable) helps you to choose the most important variables for your machine learning model, but you should watch out for these possible problems:

>> Some variables with high association could also be highly correlated, introducing duplicated information, which acts as noise in the learning process.

>> Some variables may be penalized, especially binary ones (variables indicating a status or characteristic using the value 1 when it is present, 0 when it is not). For example, notice that the output shows the binary variable CHAS as the least associated with the target variable (but you know from previous examples that it's influential from the cross-validation phase).

TIP

The univariate selection process can give you a real advantage when you have a huge number of variables to select from and all other methods turn computationally infeasible. The best procedure is to reduce the value of SelectPercentile by half or more of the available variables, reduce the number of variables to a manageable number, and consequently allow the use of a more sophisticated and more precise method such as a greedy selection.

Using a greedy search

When using a univariate selection, you have to decide for yourself how many variables to keep: Greedy selection automatically reduces the number of features involved in a learning model on the basis of their effective contribution to the performance measured by the error measure. The RFECV class, fitting the data, can provide you with information on the number of useful features, point them out to you, and automatically transform the X data, by the method transform, into a reduced variable set, as shown in the following example:

```
from sklearn.feature_selection import RFECV
selector = RFECV(estimator=regression,
                 cv=10,
                 scoring='neg_mean_squared_error')
selector.fit(X, y)
print("Optimal number of features : %d"
      % selector.n_features_)The example outputs an optimal
   number of features for the problem:Optimal number of
   features: 6
```

Obtaining an index to the optimum variable set is possible by calling the attribute support_ from the RFECV class after you fit it:

```
print(boston.feature_names[selector.support_])
```

The command prints the list containing the features:

```
['CHAS' 'NOX' 'RM' 'DIS' 'PTRATIO' 'LSTAT']
```

Notice that CHAS is now included among the most predictive features, which contrasts with the result from the univariate search in the previous section. The RFECV method can detect whether a variable is important, no matter whether it is binary, categorical, or numeric, because it directly evaluates the role played by the feature in the prediction.

REMEMBER

The RFECV method is certainly more efficient, when compared to the univariate approach, because it considers highly correlated features and is tuned to optimize the evaluation measure (which usually is not Chi-square or F-score). Being a greedy process, it's somehow computationally demanding and may only approximate the best set of predictors.

TIP

As RFECV learns the best set of variables from data, the selection may overfit, which is what happens with all other machine learning algorithms. Trying RFECV on different samples of the training data can confirm the best variables to use.

Pumping Up Your Hyperparameters

As a last example for this chapter, you can see the procedures for searching for the optimal hyperparameters of a machine learning algorithm in order to achieve the best possible predictive performance. Actually, much of the performance of your algorithm has already been decided by

>> **The choice of the algorithm:** Not every machine learning algorithm is a good fit for every type of data, and choosing the right one for your data can make the difference.

>> **The selection of the right variables:** Predictive performance is increased dramatically by feature creation (new created variables are more predictive than old ones) and feature selection (removing redundancies and noise).

Fine-tuning the correct hyperparameters could provide even better predictive generalizability and pump up your results, especially in the case of complex algorithms that don't work well using the out-of-the-box default settings.

REMEMBER

Hyperparameters are parameters that you have to decide by yourself, since an algorithm can't learn them automatically from data. As with all other aspects of the learning process that involve a decision by the data scientist, you have to make your choices carefully after evaluating the cross-validated results.

The Scikit-learn sklearn.grid_search module specializes in hyperparameters optimization. It contains a few utilities for automating and simplifying the process of searching for the best values of hyperparameters. The code in the following paragraphs provides an illustration of the correct procedures, starting from uploading the Iris dataset into memory:

```
import numpy as np
from sklearn.datasets import load_iris
```

```
iris = load_iris()
X, y = iris.data, iris.target
```

The example prepares to perform its task by loading the Iris dataset and the NumPy library. At this point, the example can optimize a machine learning algorithm for predicting Iris species.

Implementing a grid search

The best way to verify the best hyperparameters for an algorithm is to test them all and then pick the best combination. This means, in the case of complex settings of multiple parameters, that you have to run hundreds, if not thousands, of slightly differently tuned models. *Grid searching* is a systematic search method that combines all the possible combinations of the hyperparameters into individual sets. It's a time-consuming technique. However, grid searching provides one of the best ways to optimize a machine learning application that could have many working combinations, but just a single best one. Hyperparameters that have many acceptable solutions (called *local minima*) may trick you into thinking that you have found the best solution when you could actually improve their performance.

TIP

Grid searching is like throwing a net into the sea. It's better to use a large net at first, one that has loose meshes. The large net helps you understand where there are schools of fish in the sea. After you know where the fish are, you can use a smaller net with tight meshes to get the fish that are in the right places. In the same way, when performing grid searching, you start first with a grid search with a few sparse values to test (the loose meshes). After you understand which hyperparameter values to explore (the schools of fish), you can perform a more thorough search. In this way, you also minimize the risk of overfitting by cross-validating too many variables because as a general principle in machine learning and scientific experimentation, the more things you try, the greater the chances that some fake good result will appear.

TIP

Grid searching is easy to perform as a parallel task because the results of a tested combination of hyperparameters are independent from the results of the others. Using a multicore computer at its full power requires that you change n_jobs to −1 when instantiating any of the grid search classes from Scikit-learn.

TECHNICAL
STUFF

You have options other than grid searching. Scikit-learn implements a random search algorithm as an alternative to using a grid search. There are other optimization techniques based on Bayesian optimization or on nonlinear optimization techniques such as the Nelder–Mead method, which aren't implemented in the data science packages that you're using in Python now.

In the example for demonstrating how to implement a grid search effectively, you use one of the previously seen simple algorithms, the K-neighbors classifier:

```
from sklearn.neighbors import KNeighborsClassifier
classifier = KNeighborsClassifier(n_neighbors=5,
    weights='uniform', metric= 'minkowski', p=2)
```

The K-neighbors classifier has quite a few hyperparameters that you can set for optimal performance:

>> The number of neighbor points to consider in the estimate

>> How to weight each of them

>> What metric to use for finding the neighbors

Using a range of possible values for all the parameters, you can easily realize that you're going to test a large number of models — exactly 40 in this case:

```
grid = {'n_neighbors': range(1,11),
        'weights': ['uniform', 'distance'], 'p': [1,2]}
print ('Number of tested models: %i'
    % np.prod([len(grid[element]) for element in grid]))
score_metric = 'accuracy'
```

The code multiplies the number of all the parameters you test and prints the result:

```
Number of tested models: 40
```

To set the instructions for the search, you have to build a Python dictionary whose keys are the names of the parameters, and the dictionary's values are lists of the values you want to test. For instance, the example records a range of 1 to 10 for the hyperparameter n_neighbors using the range(1,11) iterator, which produces the sequence of numbers during the grid search.

Before starting, you also figure out what the cross-validation score is with a "vanilla" model, a model with the following default parameters:

```
from sklearn.model_selection import cross_val_score
print('Baseline with default parameters: %.3f'
        % np.mean(cross_val_score(classifier, X, y,
                cv=10, scoring=score_metric, n_jobs=1)))
```

```
You take note of the result to determine the increase provided
    by optimizing the parameters: Baseline with default
    parameters: 0.967
```

Using the accuracy metric (the percentage of exact answers), the example first tests the baseline, which consists of the algorithm's default parameters (also explicated when instantiating the `classifier` variable with its class). It's difficult to improve an already high accuracy of 0.967 (or 96.7 percent), but the search will locate the answer using a tenfold cross-validation.

```
from sklearn.model_selection import GridSearchCV
search = GridSearchCV(estimator=classifier,
                      param_grid=grid,
                      scoring=score_metric,
                      n_jobs=1,
                      refit=True,
                      return_train_score=True,
                      cv=10)
search.fit(X,y)
```

After being instantiated with the learning algorithm, the search dictionary, the scoring metric, and the cross-validation folds, the `GridSearch` class operates with the `fit` method. Optionally, after the grid search ended, it refits the model with the best found parameter combination (`refit=True`), allowing it to immediately start predicting by using the `GridSearch` class itself. Finally, you print the resulting best parameters and the score of the best combination:

```
print('Best parameters: %s' % search.best_params_)
print('CV Accuracy of best parameters: %.3f' %
      search.best_score_)
```

```
Here are the printed values:Best parameters: {'n_neighbors': 9,
    'weights': 'uniform',
                  'p': 1}
CV Accuracy of best parameters: 0.973
```

When the search is completed, you can inspect the results using the `best_params_` and `best_score:_` attributes. The best accuracy found was 0.973, an improvement over the initial baseline. You can also inspect the complete sequence of obtained cross-validation scores and their standard deviation:

```
print(search.cv_results_)
```

By looking through the large number of tested combinations, you notice that more than a few obtained the score of 0.973 when the combinations had nine or ten neighbors. To better understand how the optimization works with respect to the number of neighbors used by your algorithm, you can launch a Scikit-learn class for visualization. The `validation_curve` method provides you with detailed information about how `train` and `validation` behave when used with different `n_neighbors` hyperparameters.

```
from sklearn.model_selection import validation_curve
model = KNeighborsClassifier(weights='uniform',
                             metric= 'minkowski', p=1)
train, test = validation_curve(model, X, y,
                               param_name='n_neighbors',
                               param_range=range(1, 11),
                               cv=10, scoring='accuracy',
                               n_jobs=1)
```

The `validation_curve` class provides you with two arrays containing the results arranged with the parameters values on the rows and the cross-validation folds on the columns.

```
import matplotlib.pyplot as plt
mean_train = np.mean(train,axis=1)
mean_test  = np.mean(test,axis=1)
plt.plot(range(1,11), mean_train,'ro--', label='Training')
plt.plot(range(1,11), mean_test,'bD-.', label='CV')
plt.grid()
plt.xlabel('Number of neighbors')
plt.ylabel('accuracy')
plt.legend(loc='upper right', numpoints= 1)
plt.show()
```

Projecting the row means creating a graphic visualization, as shown in Figure 18-2, which helps you understand what is happening with the learning process.

You can obtain two pieces of information from the visualization:

» The peak cross-validation accuracy using nine neighbors is higher than the training score. The training score should always be better than any cross-validation score. The higher score points out that the example overfitted the cross-validation and luck played a role in getting such a good cross-validation score.

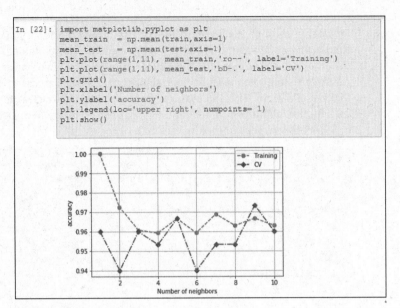

```
In [22]:  import matplotlib.pyplot as plt
          mean_train  = np.mean(train,axis=1)
          mean_test   = np.mean(test,axis=1)
          plt.plot(range(1,11), mean_train,'ro--', label='Training')
          plt.plot(range(1,11), mean_test,'bD-.', label='CV')
          plt.grid()
          plt.xlabel('Number of neighbors')
          plt.ylabel('accuracy')
          plt.legend(loc='upper right', numpoints= 1)
          plt.show()
```

FIGURE 18-2:
Validation curves.

>> The second peak of cross-validation accuracy, at five neighbors, is near the lowest results. Well-scoring areas usually surround optimum values, so this peak is a bit suspect.

Based on the visualization, you should accept the nine- neighbors solution (it is the highest and it is indeed surrounded by other acceptable solutions). As an alternative, given that nine neighbors is a solution on the limit of the search, you could instead launch a new grid search, extending the limit to a higher number of neighbors (above ten) in order to verify whether the accuracy stabilizes, decreases, or even improves.

TIP

It is part of the data science process to query, test, and query again. Even though Python and its packages offer you many automated processes in data learning and discovering, it is up to you to ask the right questions and to check whether the answers are the best ones by using statistical tests and visualizations.

Trying a randomized search

Grid searching, though exhaustive, is indeed a time-consuming activity. It's prone to overfitting the cross-validation folds when you have few observations in your dataset and you extensively search for an optimization. Instead, an interesting alternative option is to try a randomized search. In this case, you define a grid search to test only some of the combinations, picked at random.

Even though it may sound like betting on blind luck, a grid search is actually quite useful because it's inefficient — if you pick enough random combinations, you have a high statistical probability of finding an optimum hyperparameter combination, without risking overfitting at all. For instance, in the previous example, the code tested 40 different models using a systematic search. Using a randomized search, you can reduce the number of tests by 75 percent, to just 10 tests, and reach the same level of optimization!

Using a randomized search is straightforward. You import the class from the `grid_search` module and input the same parameters as the `GridSearchCV`, adding a `n_iter` parameter that indicates how many combinations to sample. As a rule of thumb, you choose from a quarter or a third of the total number of hyperparameter combinations:

```
from sklearn.model_selection import RandomizedSearchCV
random_search = RandomizedSearchCV(estimator=classifier,
                param_distributions=grid, n_iter=10,
    scoring=score_metric, n_jobs=1, refit=True, cv=10, )
random_search.fit(X, y)
```

Having completed the search using the same technique as before, you can explore the results by outputting the best scores and parameters:

```
print('Best parameters: %s' % random_search.best_params_)
print('CV Accuracy of best parameters: %.3f' %
      random_search.best_score_)The resulting search ends with
  the following best parameters and score:Best parameters: {'n_
  neighbors': 9, 'weights': 'distance',
                'p': 2}
Accuracy of best parameters: 0.973
```

From the reported results, it appears that a random search can actually obtain results similar to a much more CPU-expensive grid search.

Chapter 19

Increasing Complexity with Linear and Nonlinear Tricks

Previous chapters introduce you to some of the simplest, yet effective, machine learning algorithms, such as linear and logistic regression, Naïve Bayes, and K-Nearest Neighbors (KNN). At this point, you can successfully complete a regression or classification project in data science. This chapter explores even more complex and powerful machine learning techniques including the following: reasoning on how to enhance your data; improving your estimates by regularization; and learning from big data by breaking it into manageable chunks.

This chapter also introduces you to the support vector machine (SVM), a powerful family of algorithms for classification and regression. The chapter touches on neural networks as well. Both SVMs and neural networks can perform the most difficult data problems in data science. Initially introduced a few years ago as a replacement for neural networks, neural networks and tree ensembles have recently overtaken SVMs again (the topic of Chapter 20, "Understanding the Power of the Many") as the state-of-the-art predictive tool. Neural networks have a long history, but only in the last five years have they improved to the point of becoming an indispensable tool for predictions based on images and text. Given the complexity of both regression and classification using advanced techniques, quite a few pages are devoted to SVM and some to neural networks, but increasing your understanding of both strategies is definitely worth the time and effort.

REMEMBER

You don't have to type the source code for this chapter manually. In fact, it's a lot easier if you use the downloadable source (see the Introduction for download instructions). The source code for this chapter appears in the `P4DS4D2_19_ Increasing_Complexity.ipynb` source code file. You can also plot some of the complex drawings illustrating SVM algorithms by running the code in the `P4DS4D2_19_Representing_SVM_boundaries.ipynb` source file.

Using Nonlinear Transformations

Linear models, such as linear and logistic regression, are actually linear combinations that sum your features (weighted by learned coefficients) and provide a simple but effective model. In most situations, they offer a good approximation of the complex reality they represent. Even though they're characterized by a high bias, using a large number of observations can improve their coefficients and make them more competitive when compared to complex algorithms.

However, they can perform better when solving certain problems if you pre-analyze the data using the Exploratory Data Analysis (EDA) approach. After performing the analysis, you can transform and enrich the existing features by

>> Linearizing the relationships between features and the target variable using transformations that increase their correlation and make their cloud of points in the scatterplot more similar to a line.

>> Making variables interact by multiplying them so that you can better represent their conjoint behavior.

>> Expanding the existing variables using the polynomial expansion in order to represent relationships more realistically (such as ideal point curves, when there is a peak in the variable representing a maximum, akin to a parabola).

Doing variable transformations

An example is the best way to explain the kind of transformations you can successfully apply to data to improve a linear model. The example in this section, and the "Regularizing Linear Models" and "Fighting with Big Data Chunk by Chunk" sections that follow, relies on the Boston dataset. The problem relies on regression, and the data originally has ten variables to explain the different housing prices in Boston during the 1970s. The dataset also has implicit ordering. Fortunately, order doesn't influence most algorithms because they learn the data as a whole. When an algorithm learns in a progressive manner, ordering can interfere with effective model building. By using seed (to fix a preordinated sequence of random numbers) and shuffle from the random package (to shuffle the index), you can reindex the dataset.

```
From sklearn.datasets import load_boston
import random
from random import shuffle

boston = load_boston()
random.seed(0) # Creates a replicable shuffling
new_index = list(range(boston.data.shape[0]))
shuffle(new_index) # shuffling the index
X, y = boston.data[new_index], boston.target[new_index]
print(X.shape, y.shape, boston.feature_names)
```

In the code, random.seed(0) creates a replicable shuffling operation, and shuffle(new_index) creates the new shuffled index used to reorder the data. After that, the code prints the X and y shapes as well as the list of dataset variable names:

```
(506, 13) (506,) ['CRIM' 'ZN' 'INDUS' 'CHAS' 'NOX' 'RM' 'AGE'
    'DIS' 'RAD' 'TAX' 'PTRATIO'  'B' 'LSTAT']
```

TIP

You can find out more detail about the meaning of the variables present in the Boston dataset by issuing the following command: print(boston.DESCR). You see the output of this command in the downloadable source code.

Converting the array of predictors and the target variable into a pandas DataFrame helps support the series of explorations and operations on data. Moreover, although Scikit-learn requires an ndarray as input, it will also accept DataFrame objects.

```
import pandas as pd
df = pd.DataFrame(X,columns=boston.feature_names)
df['target'] = y
```

The best way to spot possible transformations is by graphical exploration, and using a scatterplot can tell you a lot about two variables. You need to make the relationship between the predictors and the target outcome as linear as possible, so you should try various combinations, such as the following:

```
ax = df.plot(kind='scatter', x='LSTAT', y='target', c='b')
```

In Figure 19-1, you see a representation of the resulting scatterplot. Notice that you can approximate the cloud of points by using a curved line rather than a straight line. In particular, when LSTAT is around 5, the target seems to vary between values of 20 to 50. As LSTAT increases, the target decreases to 10, reducing the variation.

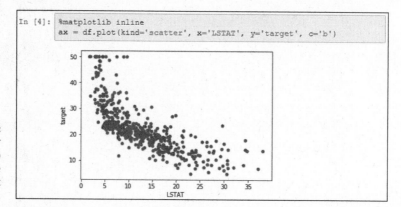

FIGURE 19-1:
Nonlinear
relationship
between variable
LSTAT and target
prices.

Logarithmic transformation can help in such conditions. However, your values should range from zero to one, such as percentages, as demonstrated in this example. In other cases, other useful transformations for your x variable could include $x{**}2$, $x{**}3$, $1/x$, $1/x{**}2$, $1/x{**}3$, and sqrt(x). The key is to try them and test the result. As for testing, you can use the following script as an example:

```
import numpy as np
from sklearn.feature_selection import f_regression
single_variable = df['LSTAT'].values.reshape(-1, 1)
F, pval = f_regression(single_variable, y)
print('F score for the original feature %.1f' % F)
F, pval = f_regression(np.log(single_variable),y)
print('F score for the transformed feature %.1f' % F)
```

The code prints the F score, a measure to evaluate how a feature is predictive in a machine learning problem, both the original and the transformed feature. The score for the transformed feature is a great improvement over the untransformed one.

```
F score for the original feature 601.6
F score for the transformed feature 1000.2
```

The `F score` is useful for variable selection. You can also use it to assess the usefulness of a transformation because both `f_regression` and `f_classif` are themselves based on linear models, and are therefore sensitive to every effective transformation used to make variable relationships more linear.

Creating interactions between variables

In a linear combination, the model reacts to how a variable changes in an independent way with respect to changes in the other variables. In statistics, this kind of model is a *main effects model*.

REMEMBER

The Naïve Bayes classifier makes a similar assumption for probabilities, and it also works well with complex text problems.

Even though machine learning works by using approximations and a set of independent variables can make your predictions work well in most situations, sometimes you may miss an important part of the picture. You can easily catch this problem by depicting the variation in your target associated with the conjoint variation of two or more variables in two simple and straightforward ways:

>> **Existing domain knowledge of the problem:** For instance, in the car market, having a noisy engine is a nuisance in a family car but considered a plus for sports cars (car aficionados want to hear that you have an ultra-cool and expensive car). By knowing a consumer preference, you can model a noise level variable and a car type variable together to obtain exact predictions using a predictive analytic model that guesses the car's value based on its features.

>> **Testing combinations of different variables:** By performing group tests, you can see the effect that certain variables have on your target variable. Therefore, even without knowing about noisy engines and sports cars, you could have caught a different average of preference level when analyzing your dataset split by type of cars and noise level.

The following example shows how to test and detect interactions in the Boston dataset. The first task is to load a few helper classes, as shown here:

```
from sklearn.linear_model import LinearRegression
from sklearn.model_selection import cross_val_score, KFold
regression = LinearRegression(normalize=True)
crossvalidation = KFold(n_splits=10, shuffle=True,
                        random_state=1)
```

The code reinitializes the pandas DataFrame using only the predictor variables. A for loop matches the different predictors and creates a new variable containing each interaction. The mathematical formulation of an interaction is simply a multiplication.

```
df = pd.DataFrame(X,columns=boston.feature_names)
baseline = np.mean(cross_val_score(regression, df, y,
                                   scoring='r2',
                                   cv=crossvalidation))
interactions = list()
for var_A in boston.feature_names:
    for var_B in boston.feature_names:
        if var_A > var_B:
            df['interaction'] = df[var_A] * df[var_B]
            cv = cross_val_score(regression, df, y,
                                 scoring='r2',
                                 cv=crossvalidation)
            score = round(np.mean(cv), 3)
            if score > baseline:
                interactions.append((var_A, var_B, score))
print('Baseline R2: %.3f' % baseline)
print('Top 10 interactions: %s' % sorted(interactions,
                                   key=lambda x :x[2],
                                   reverse=True)[:10])
```

The code starts by printing the baseline R^2 score for the regression; then it reports the top ten interactions whose addition to the mode increase the score:

```
Baseline R2: 0.716
Top 10 interactions: [('RM', 'LSTAT', 0.79), ('TAX', 'RM',
   0.782), ('RM', 'RAD', 0.778), ('RM', 'PTRATIO', 0.766), ('RM',
   'INDUS', 0.76), ('RM', 'NOX', 0.747), ('RM', 'AGE', 0.742),
   ('RM', 'B', 0.738), ('RM', 'DIS', 0.736), ('ZN', 'RM', 0.73)]
```

The code tests the specific addition of each interaction to the model using a 10 folds cross-validation. (The "Cross-Validating" section of Chapter 18 tells you more about working with folds.) The code records the change in the R^2 measure into a stack (a simple list) that an application can order and explore later.

The baseline score is 0.699, so a reported improvement of the stack of interactions to 0.782 looks quite impressive. It's important to know how this improvement is made possible. The two variables involved are RM (the average number of rooms) and LSTAT (the percentage of lower-status population). A plot will disclose the case about these two variables:

```
colors = ['b' if v > np.mean(y) else 'r' for v in y]
scatter = df.plot(kind='scatter', x='RM', y='LSTAT',
                    c=colors)
```

The scatterplot in Figure 19-2 clarifies the improvement. In a portion of houses at the center of the plot, it's necessary to know both LSTAT and RM in order to correctly separate the high-value houses from the low-value houses; therefore, an interaction is indispensable in this case.

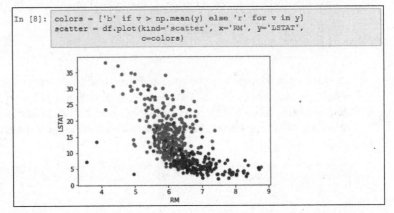

FIGURE 19-2:
Combined variables LSTAT and RM help to separate high from low prices.

Adding interactions and transformed variables leads to an extended linear regression model, a polynomial regression. Data scientists rely on testing and experimenting to validate an approach to solving a problem, so the following code slightly modifies the previous code to redefine the set of predictors using interactions and quadratic terms by squaring the variables:

```
polyX = pd.DataFrame(X,columns=boston.feature_names)
cv = cross_val_score(regression, polyX, y,
                        scoring='neg_mean_squared_error',
                        cv=crossvalidation)
baseline = np.mean(cv)
improvements = [baseline]
for var_A in boston.feature_names:
    polyX[var_A+'^2'] = polyX[var_A]**2
    cv = cross_val_score(regression, polyX, y,
                            scoring='neg_mean_squared_error',
                            cv=crossvalidation)
    improvements.append(np.mean(cv))
    for var_B in boston.feature_names:
        if var_A > var_B:
```

```
        poly_var = var_A + '*' + var_B
        polyX[poly_var] = polyX[var_A] * polyX[var_B]
        cv = cross_val_score(regression, polyX, y,
                        scoring='neg_mean_squared_error',
                        cv=crossvalidation)
        improvements.append(np.mean(cv))
```

```
import matplotlib.pyplot as plt
plt.figure()
plt.plot(range(0,92),np.abs(improvements),'-')
plt.xlabel('Added polynomial features')
plt.ylabel('Mean squared error')
plt.show()
```

To track improvements as the code adds new, complex terms, the example places values in the `improvements` list. Figure 19-3 shows a graph of the results that demonstrates some additions are great because the squared error decreases, and other additions are terrible because they increase the error instead.

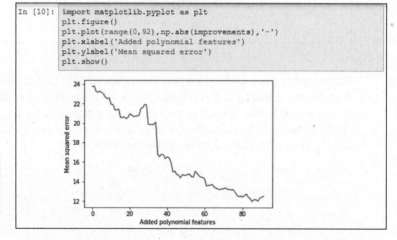

FIGURE 19-3:
Adding polynomial features increases the predictive power.

Of course, instead of unconditionally adding all the generated variables, you could perform an ongoing test before deciding to add a quadratic term or an interaction, checking by cross validation if each addition is really useful for your predictive purposes. This example is a good foundation for checking other ways of controlling the existing complexity of your datasets or the complexity that you have to induce with transformation and feature creation in the course of data exploration efforts. Before moving on, you check both the shape of the actual dataset and its cross-validated mean squared error.

```
print('New shape of X:', np.shape(polyX))
crossvalidation = KFold(n_splits=10, shuffle=True,
                        random_state=1)
cv = cross_val_score(regression, polyX, y,
                     scoring='neg_mean_squared_error',
                     cv=crossvalidation)
print('Mean squared error: %.3f' % abs(np.mean(cv)))
```

Even though the mean squared error is good, the ratio between 506 observations and 104 features isn't all that good because the number of observations may not be enough for a correct estimate of the coefficients.

```
New shape of X: (506, 104)
Mean squared error: 12.514
```

As a rule of thumb, divide the number of observations by the number of coefficients. The code should have at least 10 to 20 observations for every coefficient you want to estimate in linear models. However, experience shows that having at least 30 of them is better.

Regularizing Linear Models

Linear models have a high bias, but as you add more features, more interactions, and more transformations, they start gaining adaptability to the data characteristics and memorizing power for data noise, thus increasing the variance of their estimates. Trading higher variance for less bias isn't always the best choice, but, as mentioned earlier, sometimes it's the only way to increase the predictive power of linear algorithms.

You can introduce L1 and L2 regularization as a way to control the trade-off between bias and variance in favor of an increased generalization capability of the model. When you introduce one of the regularizations, an additive function that depends on the complexity of the linear model penalizes the optimized cost function. In linear regression, the cost function is the squared error of the predictions, and the cost function is penalized using a summation of the coefficients of the predictor variables.

If the model is complex but the predictive gain is little, the penalization forces the optimization procedure to remove the useless variables, or to reduce their impact on the estimate. The regularization also acts on highly correlated features — attenuating or excluding their contribution, thus stabilizing the results and reducing the consequent variance of the estimates:

>> **L1 (also called Lasso):** Shrinks some coefficients to zero, making your coefficients sparse. It performs variable selection.

>> **L2 (also called Ridge):** Reduces the coefficients of the most problematic features, making them smaller, but seldom equal to zero. All coefficients keep participating in the estimate, but many become small and irrelevant.

REMEMBER

You can control the strength of the regularization using a hyperparameter, usually a coefficient itself, often called alpha. When alpha approaches 1.0, you have stronger regularization and a greater reduction of the coefficients. In some cases, the coefficients are reduced to zero. Don't confuse alpha with C, a parameter used by `LogisticRegression` and by support vector machines, because C is 1/alpha, so it can be greater than 1. Smaller C numbers actually correspond to more regularization, exactly the opposite of alpha.

TIP

Regularization works because it is the sum of the coefficients of the predictor variables, therefore it's important that they're on the same scale or the regularization may find it difficult to converge, and variables with larger absolute coefficient values will greatly influence it, generating an infective regularization. It's good practice to standardize the predictor values or bind them to a common min-max, such as the $[-1, +1]$ range. The following sections demonstrate various methods of using both L1 and L2 regularization to achieve various effects.

Relying on Ridge regression (L2)

The first example uses the L2 type regularization, reducing the strength of the coefficients. The `Ridge` class implements L2 for linear regression. Its usage is simple; it presents just the parameter alpha to fix. `Ridge` also has another parameter, `normalize`, that automatically normalizes the inputted predictors to zero mean and unit variance.

```
from sklearn.model_selection import GridSearchCV
from sklearn.linear_model import Ridge
ridge = Ridge(normalize=True)
search_grid = {'alpha':np.logspace(-5,2,8)}
search = GridSearchCV(estimator=ridge,
                      param_grid=search_grid,
                      scoring='neg_mean_squared_error',
                      refit=True, cv=10)
search.fit(polyX,y)
print('Best parameters: %s' % search.best_params_)
score = abs(search.best_score_)
print('CV MSE of best parameters: %.3f' % score)
```

After searching for the best alpha parameter, the resulting best model is

```
Best parameters: {'alpha': 0.001}
CV MSE of best parameters: 11.630
```

TIP

A good search space for the alpha value is in the range np.logspace(-5,2,8). Of course, if the resulting optimum value is on one of the extremities of the tested range, you need to enlarge the range and retest.

REMEMBER

The polyX and y variables used for the examples in this section and the sections that follow are created as part of the example in the "Creating interactions between variables" section, earlier in this chapter. If you haven't worked through that section, the examples in this section will fail to work properly.

Using the Lasso (L1)

The second example uses the L1 regularization, the Lasso class, whose principal characteristic is to reduce the effect of less useful coefficients down toward zero. This action enforces sparsity in the coefficients, with just a few having values above zero. The class uses the same parameters of the Ridge class that are demonstrated in the previous section.

```
from sklearn.linear_model import Lasso
lasso = Lasso(normalize=True,tol=0.05, selection='random')
search_grid = {'alpha':np.logspace(-2,3,8)}
search = GridSearchCV(estimator=lasso,
                      param_grid=search_grid,
                      scoring='neg_mean_squared_error',
                      refit=True, cv=10)
search.fit(polyX,y)
print('Best parameters: %s' % search.best_params_)
score = abs(search.best_score_)
print('CV MSE of best parameters: %.3f' % score)
```

In setting the Lasso, the code uses a less sensitive algorithm (tol=0.05) and a random approach for its optimization (selection='random'). The resulting mean squared error obtained is higher than it is using the L2 regularization:

```
Best parameters: {'alpha': 1e-05}
CV MSE of best parameters: 12.432
```

Leveraging regularization

Because you can indent the sparse coefficients resulting from a L1 regression as a feature selection procedure, you can effectively use the Lasso class for selecting the most important variables. By tuning the alpha parameter, you can select a greater or lesser number of variables. In this case, the code sets the alpha parameter to 0.01, obtaining a much simplified solution as a result.

```
lasso = Lasso(normalize=True, alpha=0.01)
lasso.fit(polyX,y)
print(polyX.columns[np.abs(lasso.coef_)>0.0001].values)
```

The simplified solution is made of a handful of interactions:

```
['CRIM*CHAS' 'ZN*CRIM' 'ZN*CHAS' 'INDUS*DIS' 'CHAS*B'
 'NOX^2' 'NOX*DIS' 'RM^2' 'RM*CRIM' 'RM*NOX' 'RM*PTRATIO'
 'RM*B' 'RM*LSTAT' 'RAD*B' 'TAX*DIS' 'PTRATIO*NOX'
 'LSTAT^2']
```

TIP

You can apply L1-based variable selection automatically to both regression and classification using the RandomizedLasso and RandomizedLogisticRegression classes. Both classes create a series of randomized L1 regularized models. The code keeps track of the resulting coefficients. At the end of the process, the application keeps any coefficients that the class didn't reduce to zero because they're considered important. You can train the two classes using the fit method, but they don't have a predict method, just a transform method that effectively reduces your dataset, just like most classes in the sklearn.preprocessing module.

Combining L1 & L2: Elasticnet

L2 regularization reduces the impact of correlated features, whereas L1 regularization tends to selects them. A good strategy is to mix them using a weighted sum by using the ElasticNet class. You control both L1 and L2 effects by using the same alpha parameter, but you can decide the L1 effect's share by using the l1_ratio parameter. Clearly, if l1_ratio is 0, you have a ridge regression; on the other hand, when l1_ratio is 1, you have a lasso.

```
from sklearn.linear_model import ElasticNet
elastic = ElasticNet(normalize=True, selection='random')
search_grid = {'alpha':np.logspace(-4,3,8),
               'l1_ratio': [0.10 ,0.25, 0.5, 0.75]}
search = GridSearchCV(estimator=elastic,
                      param_grid=search_grid,
```

```
                              scoring='neg_mean_squared_error',
                              refit=True, cv=10)
search.fit(polyX,y)
print('Best parameters: %s' % search.best_params_)
score = abs(search.best_score_)
print('CV MSE of best parameters: %.3f' % score)
```

After a while, you get a result that's quite comparable to L1's:

```
Best parameters: {'alpha': 0.0001, 'l1_ratio': 0.75}
CV MSE of best parameters: 12.581
```

Fighting with Big Data Chunk by Chunk

Up to this point, the book has dealt with small example databases. Real data, apart from being messy, can also be quite big — sometimes so big that it can't fit in memory, no matter what the memory specifications of your machine are.

WARNING

The polyX and y variables used for the examples in the sections that follow are created as part of the example in the "Creating interactions between variables" section, earlier in this chapter. If you haven't worked through that section, the examples in this section will fail to work properly.

Determining when there is too much data

In a data science project, data can be deemed big when one of these two situations occur:

>> It can't fit in the available computer memory.

>> Even if the system has enough memory to hold the data, the application can't elaborate the data using machine learning algorithms in a reasonable amount of time.

Implementing Stochastic Gradient Descent

When you have too much data, you can use the Stochastic Gradient Descent Regressor (SGDRegressor) or Stochastic Gradient Descent Classifier (SGDClassifier) as a linear predictor. The only difference with other methods described earlier in the chapter is that they actually optimize their coefficients using only one observation at a time. It therefore takes more iterations before the code reaches comparable results using a ridge or lasso regression, but it requires much less memory and time.

This is because both predictors rely on Stochastic Gradient Descent (SGD) optimization — a kind of optimization in which the parameter adjustment occurs after the input of every observation, leading to a longer and a bit more erratic journey toward minimizing the error function. Of course, optimizing based on single observations, and not on huge data matrices, can have a tremendous beneficial impact on the algorithm's training time and the amount of memory resources.

When using the SGDs, apart from different cost functions that you have to test for their performance, you can also try using L1, L2, and Elasticnet regularization just by setting the penalty parameter and the corresponding controlling alpha and l1_ratio parameters. Some of the SGDs are more resistant to outliers, such as modified_huber for classification or huber for regression.

REMEMBER

SGD is sensitive to the scale of variables, and that's not just because of regularization, it's because of the way it works internally. Consequently, you must always standardize your features (for instance, by using StandardScaler) or you force them in the range $[0,+1]$ or $[-1,+1]$. Failing to do so will lead to poor results.

TIP

When using SGDs, you'll always have to deal with chunks of data unless you can stretch all the training data into memory. To make the training effective, you should standardize by having the StandardScaler infer the mean and standard deviation from the first available data. The mean and standard deviation of the entire dataset is most likely different, but the transformation by an initial estimate will suffice to develop a working learning procedure.

```
from sklearn.linear_model import SGDRegressor
from sklearn.preprocessing import StandardScaler

SGD = SGDRegressor(loss='squared_loss',
                   penalty='l2',
                   alpha=0.0001,
                   l1_ratio=0.15,
                   max_iter=2000,
                   random_state=1)
scaling = StandardScaler()
scaling.fit(polyX)
scaled_X = scaling.transform(polyX)
cv = cross_val_score(SGD, scaled_X, y,
         scoring='neg_mean_squared_error',
         cv=crossvalidation)
```

```
score = abs(np.mean(cv))
print('CV MSE: %.3f' % score)
```

The resulting mean squared error after running the SGDRegressor is

```
CV MSE: 12.179
```

In the preceding example, you used the `fit` method, which requires that you pre-load all the training data into memory. You can train the model in successive steps by using the `partial_fit` method instead, which runs a single iteration on the provided data, then keeps it in memory and adjusts it when receiving new data. This time, the code uses a higher number of iterations:

```
from sklearn.metrics import mean_squared_error
from sklearn.model_selection import train_test_split

X_tr, X_t, y_tr, y_t = train_test_split(scaled_X, y,
                                        test_size=0.20,
                                        random_state=2)
SGD = SGDRegressor(loss='squared_loss',
                   penalty='l2',
                   alpha=0.0001,
                   l1_ratio=0.15,
                   max_iter=2000,
                   random_state=1)
improvements = list()
for z in range(10000):
    SGD.partial_fit(X_tr, y_tr)
    score = mean_squared_error(y_t, SGD.predict(X_t))
    improvements.append(score)
```

Having kept track of the algorithm's partial improvements during 10000 iterations over the same data, you can produce a graph and understand how the improvements work as shown in the following code. Note that you could have used different data at each step.

```
import matplotlib.pyplot as plt
plt.figure(figsize=(8, 4))
plt.subplot(1,2,1)
range_1 = range(1,101,10)
score_1 = np.abs(improvements[:100:10])
plt.plot(range_1, score_1,'o--')
plt.xlabel('Iterations up to 100')
plt.ylabel('Test mean squared error')
```

```
plt.subplot(1,2,2)
range_2 = range(100,10000,500)
score_2 = np.abs(improvements[100:10000:500])
plt.plot(range_2, score_2,'o--')
plt.xlabel('Iterations from 101 to 5000')
plt.show()
```

As shown in the first of the two panes in Figure 19-4, the algorithm initially starts with a high error rate, but it manages to reduce it in just a few iterations, usually 5–10. After that, the error rate slowly improves by a smaller amount each iteration. In the second pane, you can see that after 1,500 iterations, the error rate reaches a minimum and starts increasing. At that point, you're starting to overfit because data already understands the rules and you're actually forcing the SGD to learn more when nothing is left in the data other than noise. Consequently, it starts learning noise and erratic rules.

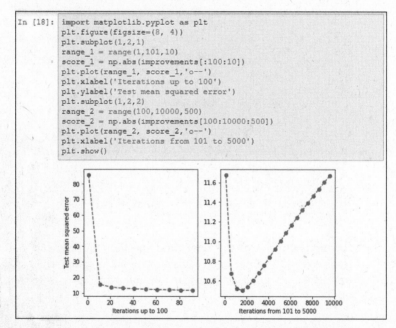

FIGURE 19-4:
A slow descent optimizing squared error.

TIP

Unless you're working with all the data in memory, grid-searching and cross-validating the best number of iterations will be difficult. A good trick is to keep a chunk of training data to use for validation apart in memory or storage. By checking your performance on that untouched part, you can see when SGD learning performance starts decreasing. At that point, you can interrupt data iteration (a method known as early stopping).

Understanding Support Vector Machines

Data scientists deem support vector machines (SVM) to be one of the most complex and powerful machine learning techniques in their toolbox, so you usually find this topic solely in advanced manuals. However, you shouldn't turn away from this great learning algorithm because the Scikit-learn library offers you a wide and accessible range of SVM-supervised classes for regression and classification. You can even access an unsupervised SVM that appears in Chapter 16 (about outliers). When evaluating whether you want to try SVM algorithms as a machine learning solution, consider these main benefits:

>> Comprehensive family of techniques for binary and multiclass classification, regression, and novelty detection

>> Good prediction generator that provides robust handling of overfitting, noisy data, and outliers

>> Successful handling of situations that involve many variables

>> Effective when you have more variables than examples

>> Fast, even when you're working with up to 10,000 training examples

>> Detects nonlinearity in your data automatically, so you don't have to apply complex transformations of your variables

Wow, that sounds great. However, you should also consider a few relevant drawbacks before you jump into importing the SVM module:

>> Performs better when applied to binary classification (which was the initial purpose of SVM), so SVM doesn't work as well on other prediction problems

>> Less effective when you have a lot more variables than examples; you have to look for other solutions like SGD

>> Provides you with only a predicted outcome; you can obtain a probability estimate for each response at the cost of more time-consuming computations

>> Works satisfactorily out of the box, but if you want the best results, you have to spend time experimenting in order to tune the many parameters

Relying on a computational method

Vladimir Vapnik and his colleagues invented SVM in the 1990s while working at AT&T laboratories. SVM gained success thanks to its high performance in many challenging problems for the machine learning community of the time, especially when used to help a computer read handwritten input. Today, data scientists frequently apply SVM to an incredible array of problems, from medical diagnosis to image recognition and textual classification. You'll likely find SVM quite useful for your problems, too!

REMEMBER

The code for this section is relatively long and complex. It appears in the P4DS4D2_19_Representing_SVM_boundaries.ipynb file, along with the outputs described in this section. You should refer to the source code to see how the code generates the figures in this section.

The idea behind SVM is simple, but the mathematical implementation is quite complex and requires many computations to work. This section helps you understand the technology behind the technique — knowing how a tool works always helps you figure out where and how to employ it best. Start considering the problem of separating two groups of data points — stars and squares scattered on two dimensions. It's a classic binary classification problem in which a learning algorithm has to figure out how to separate one class of instances from the other one using the information provided by the data at hand. The first pane in Figure 19-5 shows a representation of a similar problem.

```
ax = plt.subplot(1, 2, 2)
ax.scatter(X[:, 0], X[:, 1],
                edgecolor='black',
                facecolor=colors, s=70);
ax.plot([0.20, 0.25],[-2.3, 2.3],'k--')
ax.text(0.30, 2.1, "A")
ax.plot([-1.80, 1.80],[0.6, -0.7],'k--')
ax.text(-1.75, 0.7, "B")
ax.xlim = (-x_max, + x_max)
ax.ylim = (-y_max, + y_max)
ax.margins(0)
```

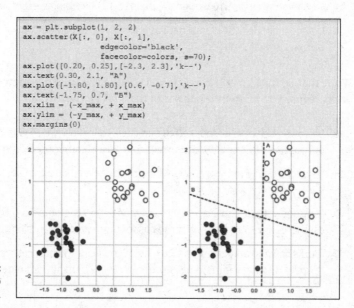

FIGURE 19-5:
Dividing two groups.

If the two groups are separate from one another, you may solve the problem in many different ways just by choosing different separating lines. Of course, you must pay attention to the details and use fine measurements. Even though it may seem like an easy task, you need to consider what happens when the data changes, such as adding more points later. You may not be able to be sure that you chose the right separation line.

The second pane in Figure 19-5 shows two possible solutions, but even more can exist. Both chosen solutions are too near to the existing observations (as shown by the proximity of the lines to the data points), but there is no reason to think that new observations will behave precisely like those shown in the figure. SVM minimizes the risk of choosing the wrong line (as you may have done by selecting solution A or B from Figure 19-6) by choosing the solution characterized by the largest distance from the bordering points of the two groups. Having so much space between groups (the maximum possible) should reduce the chance of picking the wrong solution!

```
ax = plt.subplot(1, 2, 2)
from sklearn.datasets import make_circles

X, y = make_circles(n_samples=50,
                    factor=.3,
                    noise=.1,
                    random_state=1)

X = scale(X)

clf = SVC(kernel='rbf', C=10)
clf.fit(X, y)

colors = ['white' if i==0 else 'blue' for i in y]
ax = plt.scatter(X[:, 0], X[:, 1], edgecolor='black',
                facecolor=colors, s=70);

ax.xlim = (-x_max, + x_max)
ax.ylim = (-y_max, + y_max)

svc_decision_boundaries(clf);
```

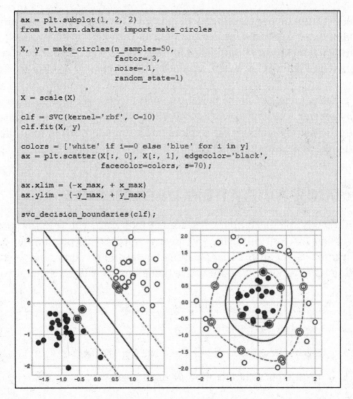

FIGURE 19-6:
A viable SVM solution for the problem of the two groups and more.

The largest distance between the two groups is the *margin*. When the margin is large enough, you can be quite sure that it'll keep working well, even when you have to classify previously unseen data. The margin is determined by the points that are present on the limit of the margin — the *support vectors* (the support vector machines algorithm takes its name from them).

You can see an SVM solution in the first pane in Figure 19-6. The figure shows the margin as a dashed line, the separator as the continuous line, and the support vectors as the circled data points.

Real-world problems don't always provide neatly separable classes, as in this example. However, a well-tuned SVM can withstand some ambiguity (some misclassified points). An SVM algorithm with the right parameters can really do miracles.

REMEMBER

When working with example data, it's easier to look for neat solutions so that the data points can better explain how the algorithm works and you can grasp the core concepts. With real data, though, you need approximations that work. Therefore, you rarely see large and clear margins.

Apart from binary classifications on two dimensions, SVM can also work on complex data. You can consider the data as complex when you have more than two dimensions, or in situations that are similar to the layout depicted in the second pane in Figure 19-6, when separating the groups by a straight line isn't possible.

TECHNICAL STUFF

In the presence of many variables, SVM can use a complex separating plane (the *hyperplane*). SVM also works well when you can't separate classes by a straight line or plane because it can explore nonlinear solutions in multidimensional space thanks to a computational technique called the kernel trick.

Fixing many new parameters

Although SVM is complex, it's a great tool. After you find the most suitable SVM version for your problem, you have to apply it to your data and work a little to optimize some of the many parameters available and improve your results. Setting up a working SVM predictive model involves these general steps:

1. Choose the SVM class you'll use.

2. Train your model with the data.

3. Check your validation error and make it your baseline.

4. Try different values for the SVM parameters.

5. Check whether your validation error improves.

6. Train your model again using the data with the best parameters.

To choose the right SVM class, you have to think about your problem. For example, you could choose a classification (guess a class) or regression (guess a number). When working with a classification, you must consider whether you need to classify just two groups (binary classification) or more than two (multi-class classification). Another important aspect to consider is the quantity of data you have to process. After taking notes of all your requirements on a list, a quick glance at Table 19-1 will help you to narrow your choices.

TABLE 19-1 **The SVM Module of Learning Algorithms**

Class	Characteristic Usage	Key Parameters
sklearn.svm.SVC	Binary and multiclass classification when the number of examples is less than 10,000	C, kernel, degree, gamma
sklearn.svm.NuSVC	Similar to SVC	nu, kernel, degree, gamma
sklearn.svm.LinearSVC	Binary and multiclass classification when the number of examples is more than 10,000; sparse data	Penalty, loss, C
sklearn.svm.SVR	Regression problems	C, kernel, degree, gamma, epsilon
sklearn.svm.NuSVR	Similar to SVR	Nu, C, kernel, degree, gamma
sklearn.svm.OneClassSVM	Outliers detection	nu, kernel, degree, gamma

The first step is to check the number of examples in your data. Having more than 10,000 examples could mean slow and cumbersome computations, but you can still use SVM to obtain acceptable performance for classification problems by using sklearn.svm.LinearSVC. When solving a regression problem, you may find that the LinearSVC isn't fast enough, in which case you use a stochastic solution for SVM (as described in the sections that follow).

TIP

The Scikit-learn SVM module wraps two powerful libraries written in C, libsvm and liblinear. When fitting a model, there is a flow of data between Python and the two external libraries. A cache smooths the data exchange operations. However, if the cache is too small and you have too many data points, the cache becomes a bottleneck! If you have enough memory, it's a good idea to set a cache size greater than the default 200MB (1000MB, if possible) using the SVM class' cache_size parameter. Smaller numbers of examples require only that you decide between classification and regression.

In each case, you'll have two alternative algorithms. For example, for classification, you may use sklearn.svm.SVC or sklearn.svm.NuSVC. The only difference with the Nu version is the parameters it takes and the use of a slightly different algorithm. In the end, it gets basically the same results, so you normally choose the non-Nu version.

After deciding on which algorithm to use, you find that you have a number of parameters from which to choose, and the C parameter is always among them. The C parameter indicates how much the algorithm has to adapt to training points. When C is small, the SVM adapts less to the points and tends to take an average direction, just using a few of the available points and variables. Larger C values tend to force the learning process to follow more of the available training points and to get involved with many variables.

The right C is usually a middle value, and you can find it after a bit of experimentation. If your C is too large, you risk *overfitting*, a situation in which your SVM adapts too much to your data and cannot properly handle new problems. If your C is too small, your prediction will be rougher and imprecise. You'll experience a situation called *underfitting* — your model is too simple for the problem you want to solve.

After deciding the C value to use, the important block of parameters to fix is kernel, degree, and gamma. All three interconnect and their value depends on the kernel specification (for instance, the linear kernel doesn't require degree or gamma, so you can use any value). The kernel specification determines whether your SVM model uses a line or a curve in order to guess the class or the point measure. Linear models are simpler and tend to guess well on new data, but sometimes underperform when variables in the data relate to each other in complex ways. Because you can't know in advance whether a linear model works for your problem, it's good practice to start with a linear kernel, fix its C value, and use that model and its performance as a baseline for testing nonlinear solutions afterward.

Classifying with SVC

It's time to build the first SVM model. Because SVM initially performed so well with handwritten classification, starting with a similar problem is a great idea. Using this approach can give you an idea of how powerful this machine learning technique is. The example uses the digits dataset available from the module datasets in the Scikit-learn package. The digits dataset contains a series of 8-x-8-pixel images of handwritten numbers ranging from 0 to 9.

```
from sklearn import datasets
digits = datasets.load_digits()
X, y = digits.data, digits.target
```

After loading the datasets module, the `load.digits` function imports all the data, from which the example extracts the predictors (digits.data) as X and the predicted classes (`digits.target`) as y.

You can look at what's inside this dataset using the matplotlib functions sub-plot (for creating an array of drawings arranged in two rows of five columns) and imshow (for plotting grayscale pixel values onto an 8-x-8 grid). The code arranges the information inside digits.images as a series of matrices, each one containing the pixel data of a number.

```python
import matplotlib.pyplot as plt
%matplotlib inline

for k,img in enumerate(range(10)):
    plt.subplot(2, 5, k+1)
    plt.imshow(digits.images[img],
            cmap='binary',
            interpolation='none')
plt.show()
```

The code displays the first ten numbers as an example of the data used in the example. You can see the result in Figure 19-7.

FIGURE 19-7: The first ten handwritten digits from the digits dataset.

By observing the data, you can also determine that SVM could guess a particular number by associating a probability with the values of specific pixels in the grid. A number 2 could turn on different pixels than a number 1, or maybe different groups of pixels. Data science involves testing many programming approaches and algorithms before reaching a solid result, but it helps to be imaginative and intuitive in order to determine which approach to try first. In fact, if you explore X, you discover that it's made of exactly 64 variables, each one representing the grayscale value of a single pixel, and that you have plentiful examples — exactly 1,797 cases.

```
print(X[0])
```

The code returns a vector of the first example in the dataset:

```
[ 0.  0.  5. 13.  9.  1.  0.  0.  0.  0. 13. 15. 10. 15.
  5.  0.  0.  3. 15.  2.  0. 11.  8.  0.  0.  4. 12.  0.
  0.  8.  8.  0.  0.  5.  8.  0.  0.  9.  8.  0.  0.  4.
 11.  0.  1. 12.  7.  0.  0.  2. 14.  5. 10. 12.  0.  0.
  0.  0.  6. 13. 10.  0.  0.  0.]
```

If you reprint the same vector as an 8-x-8 matrix, you spot the image of a zero.

```
print(X[0].reshape(8, 8))
```

You interpret the zero values as the color white and the higher values as darker shades of gray:

```
[[ 0.  0.  5. 13.  9.  1.  0.  0.]
 [ 0.  0. 13. 15. 10. 15.  5.  0.]
 [ 0.  3. 15.  2.  0. 11.  8.  0.]
 [ 0.  4. 12.  0.  0.  8.  8.  0.]
 [ 0.  5.  8.  0.  0.  9.  8.  0.]
 [ 0.  4. 11.  0.  1. 12.  7.  0.]
 [ 0.  2. 14.  5. 10. 12.  0.  0.]
 [ 0.  0.  6. 13. 10.  0.  0.  0.]]
```

At this point, you might wonder what to do about labels. You can try getting a count of the labels using the unique function in the NumPy package:

```
np.unique(y, return_counts=True)
```

The output associates the class label (the first number) with its frequency and is worth observing (it is the second row of output):

```
(array([0, 1, 2, 3, 4, 5, 6, 7, 8, 9]),
 array([178, 182, 177, 183, 181, 182, 181, 179, 174, 180],
 dtype=int64))
```

All the class labels present about the same number of examples. That means that your classes are balanced and that the SVM won't be led to think that one class is more probable than any of the others. If one or more of the classes had a significantly different number of cases, you'd face an unbalanced class problem. An unbalanced class scenario requires you to perform an evaluation:

>> Keep the unbalanced class and get predictions biased toward the most frequent classes

>> Establish equality among the classes using weights, which means allowing some observations to count more

>> Use selection to cut some cases from the classes that have too many cases

TIP

An imbalanced class problem requires you to set some additional parameters. `sklearn.svm.SVC` has both a `class_weight` parameter and a `sample_weight` keyword in the `fit` method. The most straightforward and easiest way to solve the problem is to set `class_weight='auto'` when defining your SVC and let the algorithm fix everything by itself.

Now you're ready to test the SVC with the linear kernel. However, don't forget to split your data into training and test sets, or you won't be able to judge the effectiveness of the modeling work. Always use a separate data fraction for performance evaluation or the results will look good at the start but turn worse when adding fresh data.

```
from sklearn.model_selection import train_test_split
from sklearn.model_selection import cross_val_score
from sklearn.preprocessing import MinMaxScaler
X_tr, X_t, y_tr, y_t = train_test_split(X, y,
                                         test_size=0.3,
                                         random_state=0)
```

The `train_test_split` function splits X and y into training and test sets, using the `test_size` parameter value of 0.3 as a reference for the split ratio.

```
scaling = MinMaxScaler(feature_range=(-1, 1)).fit(X_tr)
X_tr = scaling.transform(X_tr)
X_t = scaling.transform(X_t)
```

As a best practice, after splitting the data into training and test parts, you scale the numeric values, first by getting scaling parameters from the training data and then by applying a transformation on both training and test sets.

Another important action to take before feeding the data into an SVM is scaling. *Scaling* transforms all the values to the range between –1 to 1 (or from 0 to 1, if you prefer). Scaling transformation avoids the problem of having some variables influence the algorithm (they may trick it into thinking they are important because they have big values) and it makes the computations exact, smooth, and fast.

The following code fits the training data to an SVC class with a linear kernel. It also cross-validates and tests the results in terms of accuracy (the percentage of numbers correctly guessed).

```
from sklearn.svm import SVC
svc = SVC(kernel='linear',
          class_weight='balanced')
```

The code instructs the SVC to use the linear kernel and to reweight the classes automatically. Reweighting the classes ensures that they remain equally sized after the dataset is split into training and test sets.

```
cv = cross_val_score(svc, X_tr, y_tr, cv=10)
test_score = svc.fit(X_tr, y_tr).score(X_t, y_t)
```

The code then assigns two new variables. Cross-validation performance is recorded by the cross_val_score function, which returns a list with all ten scores after a ten-fold cross-validation (cv=10). The code obtains a test result by using two methods in sequence on the learning algorithm — fit, that fits the model, and score, which evaluates the result on the test set using mean accuracy (mean percentage of correct results among the classes to predict).

```
print('CV accuracy score: %0.3f' % np.mean(cv))
print('Test accuracy score: %0.3f' % (test_score))
```

Finally, the code prints the two variables and evaluates the result. The result is quite good: 97.4 percent correct predictions on the test set:

```
CV accuracy score: 0.983
Test accuracy score: 0.976
```

You might wonder what would happen if you optimize the principal parameter C instead of using the default value of 1.0. The following script provides you with an answer, using gridsearch to look for an optimal value for the C parameter:

```
from sklearn.model_selection  import GridSearchCV
svc = SVC(class_weight='balanced', random_state=1)
search_space = {'C': np.logspace(-3, 3, 7)}
```

```
gridsearch = GridSearchCV(svc,
                          param_grid=search_space,
                          scoring='accuracy',
                          refit=True, cv=10)
gridsearch.fit(X_tr,y_tr)
```

Using GridSearchCV is a little more complex, but it allows you to check many models in sequence. First, you must define a search space variable using a Python dictionary that contains the exploration schedule of the procedure. To define a search space, you create a dictionary (or, if there is more than one dictionary, a dictionary list) for each tested group of parameters. Inside the dictionary, you place the name of the parameters as keys and associate them with a list (or a function generating a list, as in this case) containing the values to test.

TIP

The NumPy logspace function creates a list of seven C values, ranging from 10^-3 to 10^3. This is a computationally expensive number of values to test, but it's also comprehensive, and you can always be safe when you test C and the other SVM parameters using such a range.

You then initialize GridSearchCV, defining the learning algorithm, search space, scoring function, and number of cross-validation folds. The next step is to instruct the procedure, after finding the best solution, to fit the best combination of parameters, so that you can have a ready-to-use predictive model:

```
cv = gridsearch.best_score_
test_score = gridsearch.score(X_t, y_t)
best_c =  gridsearch.best_params_['C']
```

In fact, gridsearch now contains a lot of information about the best score (and best parameters, plus a complete analysis of all the evaluated combinations) and methods, such as score, which are typical of fitted predictive models in Scikit-learn.

```
print('CV accuracy score: %0.3f' % cv)
print('Test accuracy score: %0.3f' % test_score)
print('Best C parameter: %0.1f' % best_c)
```

Here, the code extracts cross-validation and test scores, and outputs the C value related to these best scores:

```
CV accuracy score: 0.989
Test accuracy score: 0.987
Best C parameter: 10.0
```

The last step prints the results and shows that using a C=100 increases performance compared to before, both on the cross-validation and the test set.

Going nonlinear is easy

Having defined a simple linear model as a benchmark for the handwritten digit project, you can now test a more complex hypothesis, and SVM offers a range of nonlinear kernels:

» Polynomial (poly)

» Radial Basis Function (rbf)

» Sigmoid (sigmoid)

» Advanced custom kernels

Even though so many choices exist, you rarely use something different from the radial basis function kernel (rbf for short) because it's faster than other kernels and can approximate almost any nonlinear function.

TECHNICAL STUFF

Here's a basic, practical explanation about how rbf works: It separates the data into many clusters, so it's easy to associate a response to each cluster.

The rbf kernel requires that you set the degree and gamma parameters besides setting C. They're both easy to set (and a good grid search will always find the right value).

The degree parameter has values that begin at 2. It determinates the complexity of the nonlinear function used to separate the points. As a practical suggestion, don't worry too much about degree — test values of 2, 3, and 4 on a grid search. If you notice that the best result has a degree of 4, try shifting the grid range upward and test 3, 4, and 5. Continue proceeding upward as needed, but using a value greater than 5 is rare.

The gamma parameter's role in the algorithm is similar to C (it provides a trade-off between overfit and underfit). It's exclusive of the rbf kernel. High gamma values induce the algorithm to create nonlinear functions that have irregular shapes because they tend to fit the data more closely. Lower values create more regular, spherical functions, ignoring most of the irregularities present in the data.

Now that you know the details of the nonlinear approach, it's time to try rbf on the previous example. Be warned that, given the high number of combinations tested, the computations may take some time to complete, depending on the characteristics of your computer.

```
from sklearn.model_selection import GridSearchCV
svc = SVC(class_weight='balanced', random_state=101)
search_space = [{'kernel': ['linear'],
```

```
                    'C': np.logspace(-3, 3, 7)},
                {'kernel': ['rbf'],
                 'degree':[2, 3, 4],
                 'C':np.logspace(-3, 3, 7),
                 'gamma': np.logspace(-3, 2, 6)}]
gridsearch = GridSearchCV(svc,
                          param_grid=search_space,
                          scoring='accuracy',
                          refit=True, cv=10,
                          n_jobs=-1)
gridsearch.fit(X_tr, y_tr)
cv = gridsearch.best_score_
test_score = gridsearch.score(X_t, y_t)
print('CV accuracy score: %0.3f' % cv)
print('Test accuracy score: %0.3f' % test_score)
```

print('Best parameters: %s' % gridsearch.best_params_)Notice that the only difference in this script is that the search space is more sophisticated. By using a list, you enclose two dictionaries — one containing the parameters to test for the linear kernel and another for the rbf kernel. In this way, you can compare the performance of the two approaches at the same time. The code will take quite a while to run. Afterwards, it will report to you:

```
CV accuracy score: 0.990
Test accuracy score: 0.993
Best parameters: {'C': 1.0, 'degree': 2,
                  'gamma': 0.1, 'kernel': 'rbf'}
```

The results confirm that rbf performs better. However, it's a small margin of victory over the linear models, gained at the expense of more complexity and computational time. In such cases, having more data available could help in determining the better model with greater confidence. Unfortunately, getting more data may be expensive in terms of money and time. When faced with the absence of a clear winning model, the best suggestion is to decide in favor of the simpler model. In this case, the linear kernel is much simpler than rbf.

Performing regression with SVR

Up to now, you have dealt only with classification, but SVM can also handle regression problems. Having seen how a classification works, you don't need to know much more than that the SVM regression class is SVR and there is a new parameter to fix, epsilon. Everything else previous sections discussed for classification works precisely the same with regression.

This example uses a different dataset, a regression dataset. The Boston house price dataset, taken from the StatLib library maintained at Carnegie Mellon University, appears in many machine learning and statistical papers that address regression problems. It has 506 cases and 13 numeric variables (one of which is a 1/0 binary variable).

```
from sklearn.model_selection import train_test_split
from sklearn.model_selection import cross_val_score
from sklearn.model_selection import GridSearchCV
from sklearn.preprocessing import MinMaxScaler
from sklearn.svm import SVR
from sklearn import datasets

boston = datasets.load_boston()
X,y = boston.data, boston.target
X_tr, X_t, y_tr, y_t = train_test_split(X, y,
                                        test_size=0.3,
                                        random_state=0)
scaling = MinMaxScaler(feature_range=(-1, 1)).fit(X_tr)
X_tr = scaling.transform(X_tr)
X_t  = scaling.transform(X_t)
```

The target is the median value of houses occupied by an owner, and you'll try to guess it using SVR (epsilon-Support Vector Regression). In addition to C, kernel, degree, and gamma, SVR also has epsilon. *Epsilon* is a measure of how much error the algorithm considers acceptable. A high epsilon implies fewer support points, while a lower epsilon requires a larger number of support points. In other words, epsilon provides another way to trade-off underfit against overfit.

As a search space for this parameter, experience tells you that the sequence [0, 0.01, 0.1, 0.5, 1, 2, 4] works quite fine. Starting from a minimum value of 0 (when the algorithm doesn't accept any error) and reaching a maximum of 4, you should enlarge the search space only if you notice that higher epsilon values bring better performance.

Having included epsilon in the search space and assigning SVR as a learning algorithm, you can complete the script. Be warned that, given the high number of combinations evaluated, the computations may take quite some time, depending on the characteristics of your computer.

```
svr = SVR()
search_space = [{'kernel': ['linear'],
                 'C': np.logspace(-3, 2, 6),
                 'epsilon': [0, 0.01, 0.1, 0.5, 1, 2, 4]},
```

```
                {'kernel': ['rbf'],
                 'degree':[2, 3],
                 'C':np.logspace(-3, 3, 7),
                 'gamma': np.logspace(-3, 2, 6),
                 'epsilon': [0, 0.01, 0.1, 0.5, 1, 2, 4]}]
gridsearch = GridSearchCV(svr,
                          param_grid=search_space,
                          refit=True,
                          scoring= 'r2',
                          cv=10, n_jobs=-1)
gridsearch.fit(X_tr, y_tr)
cv = gridsearch.best_score_
test_score = gridsearch.score(X_t, y_t)
print('CV R2 score: %0.3f' % cv)
print('Test R2 score: %0.3f' % test_score)
print('Best parameters: %s' % gridsearch.best_params_)
```

The grid search may take a while on your computer. Even though the example uses all the computational power in your system (n_jobs=-1), the computer has to test quite a few combinations; for each kernel, you can figure out how many models it has to compute by multiplying the number of values it has to test for each parameter. For instance for the rbf kernel, it has two values for degree, seven for C, six for gamma, and seven for epsilon, which equates to 2 * 7 * 6 * 7 = 588 models, each one replicated 10 times (because cv=10). That is 5,880 models tested just for the rbf kernel (the code also tests the linear model, which requires 420 tests). Finally, you should get these results:

```
CV R2 score: 0.868
Test R2 score: 0.834
Best parameters: {'C': 1000.0, 'degree': 2, 'epsilon': 2,
                  'gamma': 0.1, 'kernel': 'rbf'}
```

Note that on the error measure, as a regression, the error is calculated using R squared, a measure in the range from 0 to 1 that indicates the model's performance (with 1 being the best possible result to achieve).

Creating a stochastic solution with SVM

Now that you're at the end of the overview of the family of SVM machine learning algorithms, you should see that they're a fantastic tool for a data scientist. Of course, even the best solutions have problems. For example, you might think that the SVM has too many parameters in the SVM. Certainly, the parameters are a nuisance, especially when you have to test so many combinations of them, which can take a lot of CPU time. However, the key problem is the time necessary for training the SVM. You may have noticed that the examples use small datasets with a limited number of variables, and performing some extensive grid searches still takes a lot of time. Real-world datasets are much bigger. Sometimes it may seem to take forever to train and optimize your SVM on your computer.

A possible solution when you have too many cases (a suggested limit is 10,000 examples) is found inside the same SVM module, the LinearSVC class. This algorithm works only with the linear kernel and its focus is to classify (sorry, no regression) large numbers of examples and variables at a higher speed than the standard SVC. Such characteristics make the LinearSVC a good candidate for textual-based classification. LinearSVC has fewer and slightly different parameters to fix than the usual SVM (it's similar to a regression class):

>> C: The penalty parameter. Small values imply more regularization (simpler models with attenuated or set to zero coefficients).

>> loss: A value of l1 (just as in SVM) or l2 (errors weight more, so it strives harder to fit misclassified examples).

>> penalty: A value of l2 (attenuation of less important parameters) or l1 (unimportant parameters are set to zero).

>> dual: A value of true or false. It refers to the type of optimization problem solved and, though it won't change the obtained scoring much, setting the parameter to false results in faster computations than when it is set to true.

The loss, penalty, and dual parameters are also bound by reciprocal constraints, so please refer to Table 19-2 to plan which combination to use in advance.

TABLE 19-2

The Loss, Penalty, and Dual Constraints

Penalty	Loss	Dual
l1	l2	False
l2	l1	True
l2	l2	True; False

The algorithm doesn't support the combination of penalty='l1' and loss='l1'. However, the combination of penalty='l2' and loss='l1' perfectly replicates the SVC optimization approach.

As mentioned previously, LinearSVC is quite fast, and a speed test against SVC demonstrates the level of improvement to expect in choosing this algorithm.

```
from sklearn.datasets import make_classification
from sklearn.model_selection import train_test_split
import numpy as np
X,y = make_classification(n_samples=10**4,
                          n_features=15,
                          n_informative=10,
                          random_state=101)
X_tr, X_t, y_tr, y_t = train_test_split(X, y,
                                        test_size=0.3,
                                        random_state=1)


from sklearn.svm import SVC, LinearSVC
svc = SVC(kernel='linear', random_state=1)
linear = LinearSVC(loss='hinge', random_state=1)

svc.fit(X_tr, y_tr)
linear.fit(X_tr, y_tr)
svc_score = svc.score(X_t, y_t)
libsvc_score = linear.score(X_t, y_t)
print('SVC test accuracy: %0.3f' % svc_score)
print('LinearSVC test accuracy: %0.3f' % libsvc_score)
```

The results are quite similar to SVC:

```
SVC test accuracy: 0.803
LinearSVC test accuracy: 0.804
```

After you create an artificial dataset using make_classfication, the code obtains confirmation of how the two algorithms arrive at almost identical results. At this point, the code tests the speed of the two solutions on the synthetic dataset in order to understand how they scale to use more data.

```
import timeit
X,y = make_classification(n_samples=10**4,
                          n_features=15,
                          n_informative=10,
                          random_state=101)
t_svc = timeit.timeit('svc.fit(X, y)',
                      'from __main__ import svc, X, y',
                      number=1)
```

```
t_libsvc = timeit.timeit('linear.fit(X, y)',
                         'from __main__ import linear, X, y',
                         number=1)
print('best avg secs for SVC: %0.1f' % np.mean(t_svc))
print('best avg secs for LinearSVC: %0.1f' % np.mean(t_libsvc))
```

The example system shows the following result (the output of your system may differ):

```
avg secs for SVC, best of 3: 16.6
avg secs for LinearSVC, best of 3: 0.4
```

Clearly, given the same data quantity, LinearSVC is much faster than SVC. You can calculate its performance ratio as 16.6 / 0.4 = 41.5 times faster than SVC. However, it's important to understand what happens when you increase the size of the sample. For example, here's what happens when you triple the size:

```
avg secs for SVC, best of 3: 162.6
avg secs for LinearSVC, best of 3: 2.6
```

The point here is that the time required for SVC grows faster (9.8 times) than that required by LinearSVC (6.5 times). This is because SVC requires proportionally more time to process the data provided and the time will grow even more as the sample size increases. Here are the results when you have five times more data, highlighting even more differences:

```
avg secs for SVC, best of 3: 539.1
avg secs for LinearSVC, best of 3: 4.5
```

Using SVC with large amounts of data soon becomes unfeasible; LinearSVC should be your choice if you need to work with large data amounts. Yet, even if LinearSVC is quite fast at performing tasks, you may need to classify or regress millions of examples. You need to know whether LinearSVC is still a better choice. You previously saw how the SGD class, using SGDClassifier and SGDRegressor, helps you implement an SVM-type algorithm in situations with millions of data rows without investing too much computational power. All you have to do is to set their loss to 'hinge' for SGDClassifier and to 'epsilon_insensitive' for SGDRegressor (in which case, you have to tune the epsilon parameter).

Another performance and speed test makes the advantages and limitations of using LinearSVC or SGDClassifier clear:

```
from sklearn.datasets import make_classification
from sklearn.model_selection import train_test_split
```

```
from sklearn.model_selection import cross_val_score
from sklearn.svm import LinearSVC
import timeit

from sklearn.linear_model import SGDClassifier
X, y = make_classification(n_samples=10**5,
                           n_features=15,
                           n_informative=10,
                           random_state=101)
X_tr, X_t, y_tr, y_t = train_test_split(X, y,
                                        test_size=0.3,
                                        random_state=1)
```

The sample now is quite big — 100,000 cases. If you have enough memory and a lot of time, you may even want to increase the number of trained cases or the number of features and more extensively test how the two algorithms scale with even bigger data.

```
linear = LinearSVC(penalty='l2',
                   loss='hinge',
                   dual=True,
                   random_state=1)
linear.fit(X_tr, y_tr)
score = linear.score(X_t, y_t)
t = timeit.timeit("linear.fit(X_tr, y_tr)",
        "from __main__ import linear, X_tr, y_tr",
        number=1)
print('LinearSVC test accuracy: %0.3f' % score)
print('Avg time for LinearSVC: %0.1f secs' % np.mean(t))
```

On the test computer, LinearSVC completed its computations on all the rows in about seven seconds:

```
LinearSVC test accuracy: 0.796
Avg time for LinearSVC: 7.4 secs
```

The following code tests SGDClassifier using the same procedure:

```
sgd = SGDClassifier(loss='hinge',
                    max_iter=100,
                    shuffle=True,
                    random_state=101)
sgd.fit(X_tr, y_tr)
score = sgd.score(X_t, y_t)
```

```
t = timeit.timeit("sgd.fit(X_tr, y_tr)",
                  "from __main__ import sgd, X_tr, y_tr",
                  number=1)
print('SGDClassifier test accuracy: %0.3f' % score)
print('Avg time SGDClassifier: %0.1f secs' % np.mean(t))
```

SGDClassifier instead took about a second and a half for processing the same data and obtaining a comparable, score:

```
SGDClassifier test accuracy: 0.796
Avg time SGDClassifier: 1.5 secs
```

TIP

Increasing the n_iter parameter can improve the performance, but it proportionally increases the computation time. Increasing the number of iterations up to a certain value (that you have to find out by test) increases the performance. However, after that value, performance starts to decrease because of overfitting.

Playing with Neural Networks

Starting with the idea of reverse-engineering how a brain processes signals, researchers based neural networks on biological analogies and their components, using brain terms such as *neurons* and *axons* as names. However, you'll discover that neural networks resemble nothing more than a sophisticated kind of linear regression because they are a summation of coefficients multiplied by numeric inputs. You also find that neurons are just where such summations happen.

Even if neural networks don't mimic a brain (they're arithmetic), these algorithms are extraordinarily effective against complex problems such as image and sound recognition, or machine language translation. They also execute quickly when predicting, if you use the right hardware. Well-devised neural networks use the name *deep learning* and are behind powerful tools like Siri and other digital assistants, along with more astonishing machine learning applications as well.

Running deep learning requires special hardware (a computer with a GPU) and installing special frameworks such as Tensorflow (https://www.tensorflow.org/), MXNet (https://mxnet.apache.org/), Pytorch (https://pytorch.org/) or Chainer (https://chainer.org/). This book doesn't delve into complex neural networks but does explore a simpler implementation offered by Scikit-learn instead, which allows you to create neural network quickly and compare them to other machine learning algorithms.

Understanding neural networks

The core neural network algorithm is the neuron (also called a unit). Many neurons arranged in an interconnected structure make up the layers of a neural network, with each neuron linking to the inputs and outputs of other neurons. Thus, a neuron can input features from examples or from the results of other neurons, depending on its location in the neural network.

Contrary to other algorithms, which have a fixed pipeline that determines how algorithms receive and process data, neural networks require you to decide how information flows by fixing the number of units (the neurons) and their distribution in layers. For this reason, setting up neural networks is more an art than a science; you learn from experience how to arrange neurons into layers and obtain the best predictions. In a more detailed view, neurons in a neural network take many weighted values as inputs, sum them, and provide the summation as the result.

REMEMBER

A neural network can process only numeric, continuous information; it can't process qualitative variables (for example, labels indicating a quality such as red, blue, or green in an image). You can process qualitative variables by transforming them into a continuous numeric value, such as a series of binary values

Neurons also provide a more sophisticated transformation of the summation. In observing nature, scientists noticed that neurons receive signals but don't always release a signal of their own. It depends on the amount of signal received. When a neuron in a brain acquires enough stimuli, it fires an answer; otherwise, it remains silent. In a similar fashion, neurons in a neural network, after receiving weighted values, sum them and use an activation function to evaluate the result, which transforms it in a nonlinear way. For instance, the activation function can release a zero value unless the input achieves a certain threshold, or it can dampen or enhance a value by nonlinearly rescaling it, thus transmitting a rescaled signal.

Each neuron in the network receives inputs from the previous layers (when starting, it connects directly with data), weights them, sums them all, and transforms the result using the activation function. After activating, the computed output becomes the input for other neurons or the prediction of the network. Consequently, given a neural network made of a certain number of neurons and layers, what makes this structure efficient in its predictions is the weights used by each neuron for its inputs. Such weights aren't different from the coefficients of a linear regression, and the network learns their value by repeated passes (iterations or epochs) over the examples of the dataset.

Classifying and regressing with neurons

Scikit-learn offers two functions for neural networks:

» MLPClassifier: Implements a multilayer perceptron (MLP) for classification. Its outputs (one or many, depending on how many classes you have to predict) are intended as probabilities of the example being of a certain class.

» MLPRegressor: Implements MLP for regression problems. All its outputs (because it can predict multiple target values at one time) are intended as estimates of the measures to predict.

Because both functions have the exact same parameters, the example delves into a single example for classification, using the handwritten digits as an example of multiclass classification using a MLP. The example starts by importing the necessary packages, loading the dataset into memory, and splitting it into a training and a test set (as the chapter has done when demonstrating support vector machines):

```
from sklearn.model_selection import train_test_split
from sklearn.model_selection import cross_val_score
from sklearn.preprocessing import MinMaxScaler
from sklearn import datasets
from sklearn.neural_network import MLPClassifier
digits = datasets.load_digits()
X, y = digits.data, digits.target
X_tr, X_t, y_tr, y_t = train_test_split(X, y,
                                        test_size=0.3,
                                        random_state=0)
```

Preprocessing the data to feed to the neural network is an important aspect because the operations that neural networks perform under the hood are sensitive to the scale and distribution of data. Consequently, it's good practice to normalize the data by putting its mean to zero and its variance to one, or to rescale it by fixing the minimum and maximum between −1 and +1 or 0 and +1. Experimentation shows which transformation works better for your data, though most people find that rescaling between −1 and +1 works better. This example rescales all the values between −1 and +1.

```
scaling = MinMaxScaler(feature_range=(-1, 1)).fit(X_tr)
X_tr = scaling.transform(X_tr)
X_t = scaling.transform(X_t)
```

TIP

As discussed earlier, it's good practice to define the preprocessing transformations on the training data alone and then apply the learned procedure to the test data. Only in this way can you correctly test how your model works with different data.

To define MLP, you must consider that there are quite a few parameters and if you don't tune them correctly, the results may be disappointing. (MLP is not an algorithm that works out of the box.) For an MLP to work properly, you should first define the architecture of the neurons, setting how many to use for each layer and how many layers to create. (You state the number of neurons for each layer in the `hidden_layer_sizes` parameter.) Then you have to determine the right solver among:

>> **L-BFGS:** Use for small datasets.

>> **Adam:** Use for large datasets.

>> **SGD:** Excels at most problems if you correctly set some special parameters. L-BFGS works for small datasets, Adam for large ones, and SDG can excel at most problems if you set its parameters correctly. SGD's parameters are the learning rate, which can reflect learning speed, and momentum (or Nesterov's momentum), a value that helps the neural network to avoid less useful solutions. When specifying the learning rate, you have to define its starting value (`learning_rate_init`, which is usually around 0.001, but it can be even less) and how the speed changes during training (the `learning_rate` parameter, which can be `'constant'`, `'invscaling'`, or `'adaptive'`).

TIP

Given the complexity of setting the parameters for an SGD solver, you can determine how they work on your data only by testing them in a hyperparameter optimization. Most people prefer to start with an L–BFGS or Adam solver.

Another critical hyperparameter is `max_iter`, the number of iterations, which can lead to completely different results if you set it too low or too high. The default is 200 iterations, but it's always better, after having fixed the other parameters, to try to increase or decrease its number. Finally, shuffling the data (`shuffle=True`) and setting a `random_state` for reproducibility of results are also important. The example code sets 512 nodes on a single layer, relies on the Adam solver, and uses the standard number of iterations (200):

```
nn = MLPClassifier(hidden_layer_sizes=(512, ),
                   activation='relu',
                   solver='adam',
                   shuffle=True,
                   tol=1e-4,
                   random_state=1)
```

```
cv = cross_val_score(nn, X_tr, y_tr, cv=10)
test_score = nn.fit(X_tr, y_tr).score(X_t, y_t)
print('CV accuracy score: %0.3f' % np.mean(cv))
print('Test accuracy score: %0.3f' % (test_score))
```

Using this code, the example successfully classifies handwritten digits by running an MLP whose CV and test score are

```
CV accuracy score: 0.978
Test accuracy score: 0.981
```

The results obtained are a little better than SVC's, yet the increase involves tuning quite a few parameters correctly as well. When using nonlinear algorithms, you can't expect any no-brainer approach, apart from a few decision-tree based solutions, which is the topic of the next chapter.

Chapter **20**

Understanding the Power of the Many

I n this chapter, you go beyond the single machine learning models you've seen until now and explore the power of *ensembles*, which are groups of models that can outperform single models. Ensembles work like the collective intelligence of crowds, using pooled information to make better predictions. The basic idea is that a group of nonperforming algorithms can produce better results than a single well-trained model.

Maybe you've participated in one of those games that ask you to guess the number of sweets in a jar at parties or fairs. Even though a single person has a slim chance of guessing the right number, various experiments have confirmed that if you take the wrong answers of a large number of game participants and average them, you can get close to the right answer! Such incredible shared group knowledge (also known as the wisdom of crowds) is possible because wrong answers tend to distribute around the true one. By taking a mean of these wrong answers, you get almost the right answer.

In data science projects involving complex predictions, you can leverage the wisdom of various machine learning algorithms and become more precise and accurate at predictions than you can when using a single algorithm. This chapter creates a process you can use to leverage the power of many different algorithms to obtain a better single answer.

REMEMBER

You don't have to type the source code for this chapter manually. In fact, it's a lot easier if you use the downloadable source (see the Introduction for download instructions). The source code for this chapter appears in the P4DS4D2_20_Understanding_the_Power_of_the_Many.ipynb file.

Starting with a Plain Decision Tree

Decision trees have long been part of data mining tools. The first models date well before the 1970s. Since then, decision trees have enjoyed popularity in many fields because of their intuitive algorithm, understandable output, and effectiveness with respect to simple linear models. With the introduction of better-performing algorithms, decision trees slowly went out of the machine learning scene for a time, blamed for being too easy to overfit, but they came back in recent years as an essential building block of ensemble algorithms. Today, tree ensembles such as Random Forest or Gradient Boosting Machines are the core of many data science applications and are considered to be state-of-the-art of machine learning tools.

Understanding a decision tree

The basis of decision trees is the idea that you can divide your dataset into smaller and smaller parts using specific rules based on the values of the dataset's features. When dividing the dataset in this way, the algorithm must choose splits that increase the chance of guessing the target outcome correctly, either as a class or as an estimate. Therefore, the algorithm must try to maximize the presence of a certain class or a certain average of values in each split.

As an example of an application and execution of a decision tree, you could try to predict the likelihood of passenger survival from the RMS Titanic, the British passenger liner that sank in the North Atlantic Ocean in April 1912 after colliding with an iceberg. Quite a few datasets are available on the web that pertain to this tragedy at sea. Most notable among them is the one on the Encyclopedia Titanica website (https://www.encyclopedia-titanica.org), which contains articles, biographies, and data. Another is a Kaggle data science competition that has involved tens of thousands of enthusiastic participants (https://www.kaggle.com/c/titanic).

Many Titanic tragedy datasets differ in the data they contain. This chapter's example relies on the Titanic dataset freely granted for use by the Department of Biostatistics at the Vanderbilt University School of Medicine and available for download at http://biostat.mc.vanderbilt.edu/wiki/pub/Main/DataSets/titanic3.csv. This dataset features 1,309 recorded passengers with full stats.

You don't find any of the crew in the dataset because the records focus on the paying passengers to determine whether surviving the disaster is a matter of luck or the place passengers were found on the ship at the time of the collision. The survival rate among passengers was 38.2 percent (500 of 1,309 passengers lost their lives). Based on the passengers' characteristics, the decision tree determines the following:

» Being male changes the likelihood of survival, lowering it from 38.2 percent to 19.1 percent.

» Being male, but being younger than 9.5 years of age, raises the chance of survival to 58.1 percent.

» Being female, regardless of age, implies a survival probability of 72.7 percent.

Using such knowledge, you can easily to build a tree like the one depicted in Figure 20-1. Such visualization (and the visualization of the Iris dataset found later in the chapter) is possible because of the dtreeviz package developed by Prof. Terence Parr from San Francisco University (https://parrt.cs.usfca.edu) and Prince Grover, of the same faculty. If you are interested in creating visualizations of your decision trees, you can get the package and installation guidance at https://github.com/parrt/dtreeviz and read about the development and the functioning of the package in Prof. Parr's blog entry, "How to visualize decision trees," at https://explained.ai/decision-tree-viz.

FIGURE 20-1: A tree model of survival rates from the Titanic disaster.

Notice that the visualized tree looks upside down (with the root at the top and all the branches spreading out from there). It starts at the top using the entire sample. Then it splits on the gender feature, creating two *branches*, one that turns into a *leaf*. A leaf is a terminal segmentation. The diagram classifies the leaf cases by using the most frequent class or by calculating the base probability of cases with the same features as the leaf probability. The second branch is further split by age.

To read the nodes of the tree, consider that the topmost node begins by reporting the rule used to split that node into all the following nodes. You have to start from the top. The tree shown in Figure 20-1 infers that gender is the best predictor, and on the top node, is the is_female variable is in vertical, stacked bars. The left bar is for males and the right bar is for females. At a first glance, you can see that, proportionally, females had a higher survivability because the survived share (the light-green area, which doesn't show in color in the printed book) mostly occupies all the area of the bar.

The tree splits this node in half, separating males from females. You can read the rest of the story told by the tree by observing what happens on the next level. On the second level of the tree representation, on the right, you find a node consisting only of females, and the stacked bars reveal a key insight: almost all the female first- and second-class passengers survived, and about half of the female third-class passengers perished. This insight enables the tree to develop a first rule: Women in first and second class can be classified as survivors because that status is highly likely. As for third class, survival is uncertain, and the tree would need to split again to extract some other insight that the analysis doesn't include.

As for males, the second level shows that age is a criterion that discriminates because males under the age of ten most likely survived, while older males most likely perished. Again, the tree stops, but additional criteria could provide a more precise set of partitioning rules that could explore the probability of surviving the Titanic disaster based on one's own characteristics. From the top-level tree splits, you can see that most of the survivors were women with their children based on the "women and children first" code of conduct applied in situations when life-saving resources are scarce. This code perfectly matches the *Titanic*'s situation because very few lifeboats were available as a result of the owners' belief that the boat was unsinkable. (You can read more speculations about the lifeboats on the History on the Net website at https://www.historyonthenet.com/the-titanic-lifeboats/.)

 In this example tree, every split is binary, but multiple splits are also possible, depending on the tree algorithm. In Scikit-learn, the implemented class DecisionTreeClassifier and DecisionTreeRegressor in the sklearn.tree module are all binary trees. A decision tree can stop splitting the data when:

REMEMBER

>> There are no more cases to split, so the data appears as part of leaf nodes.

>> The rule used to split a leaf has fewer than a predefined number of cases. This action keeps the algorithm from working with leaves that have little representation in general or are more specific than the data you're analyzing, thus preventing overfitting (see Chapter 18) and variance of estimates.

>> One of the resulting leaves has fewer than a predefined number of cases — another sanity check for avoiding inferring general rules without the confidence provided by a good sample size.

TIP

Decision trees tend to overfit the data. By setting the right number for splits and terminal leaves, you can reduce the variance of the estimates. Depending on your starting sample size, a limit of 30 cases is usually a good choice.

Apart from being intuitive, and easy to understand and represent (depending on how many branches and leaves you have in your tree), decision trees offer another strong advantage to the data science practitioner — they don't require any particular data treatment or transformation because they model any nonlinearity using approximations. In fact, they accept any kind of variable, even categorical variables encoded with arbitrary codes for the represented classes. In addition, decision trees handle missing cases. All you need to do is to assign missing cases an unlikely value, such as an extreme or a negative value (depending on your data distribution of non-missing cases). Finally, decision trees are also incredibly resistant to outliers.

Creating trees for different purposes

Data scientists call trees that specialize in guessing *classes* (the attributes, qualities, or traits that identify groups) classification trees; trees that work with estimation instead are known as regression trees. Here's a classification problem, using the Fisher's Iris dataset (you first use this dataset in the "Defining Descriptive Statistics for Numeric Data" section of Chapter 13):

```
from sklearn.datasets import load_iris
iris = load_iris()
X, y = iris.data, iris.target
features = iris.feature_names
```

After loading the data into X, which contains predictors, and y, which holds the classifications, you can define a cross-validation for checking the results using decision trees:

```
from sklearn.model_selection import cross_val_score
from sklearn.model_selection import KFold
```

```
crossvalidation = KFold(n_splits=5,
                        shuffle=True,
                        random_state=1)
```

Using the `DecisionTreeClassifier` class, you define `max_depth` inside an iterative loop to experiment with the effect of increasing the complexity of the resulting tree. The expectation is to reach an ideal point quickly and then witness decreasing cross-validation performance because of overfitting:

```
import numpy as np
from sklearn import tree
for depth in range(1,10):
    tree_classifier = tree.DecisionTreeClassifier(
        max_depth=depth, random_state=0)
    if tree_classifier.fit(X,y).tree_.max_depth < depth:
        break
    score = np.mean(cross_val_score(tree_classifier,
                                    X, y,
                                    scoring='accuracy',
                                    cv=crossvalidation))
    print('Depth: %i Accuracy: %.3f' % (depth,score))
```

The code will iterate through deeper trees until the tree won't expand anymore, and then the code will report the cross-validation score for accuracy:

```
Depth: 1 Accuracy: 0.580
Depth: 2 Accuracy: 0.913
Depth: 3 Accuracy: 0.920
Depth: 4 Accuracy: 0.940
Depth: 5 Accuracy: 0.920
```

The best solution is a tree with four splits because, when growing further, the tree starts overfitting. Figure 20-2 shows the complexity of the resulting tree, which provides another insightful visualization obtained using the dtreeviz package. Visualizing helps show that you can easily distinguish the Setosa species from the others. Discriminating between Versicolor and Virginica requires carefully segmenting along both petal width and length measures.

To obtain an effective reduction and simplification, you can set `min_samples_split` to 30 and avoid terminal leaves that are too small by setting `min_samples_leaf` to 10. This setting prunes the small terminal leaves in the new resulting tree, diminishing cross-validation accuracy but increasing simplicity and the generalization power of the solution.

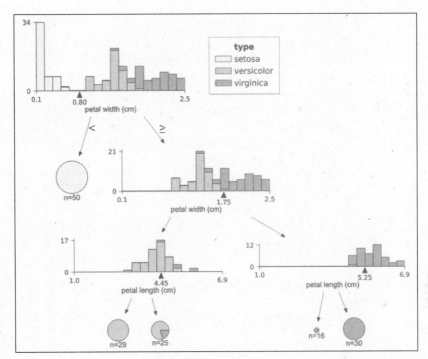

FIGURE 20-2:
A tree model of the Iris dataset using a depth of four splits.

```
tree_classifier = tree.DecisionTreeClassifier(
    min_samples_split=30, min_samples_leaf=10,
    random_state=0)
tree_classifier.fit(X,y)
score = np.mean(cross_val_score(tree_classifier, X, y,
                                scoring='accuracy',
                                cv=crossvalidation))
```

print('Accuracy: %.3f' % score)

```
The reported cross-validation accuracy is less than the
    previously obtained score because focusing on a simpler tree
    structure implies forcing some underfitting to the data
    problem:Accuracy: 0.913
```

Similarly, by using the DecisionTreeRegressor class, you can model a regression problem, such as the Boston house price dataset (you first use this dataset in the "Defining applications for data science" section of Chapter 12). When dealing with a regression tree, the terminal leaves offer the average of the cases as the prediction output.

```
from sklearn.datasets import load_boston
boston = load_boston()
X, y = boston.data, boston.target
features = boston.feature_names

from sklearn.tree import DecisionTreeRegressor
regression_tree = tree.DecisionTreeRegressor(
    min_samples_split=30, min_samples_leaf=10,
    random_state=0)
regression_tree.fit(X,y)
score = np.mean(cross_val_score(regression_tree,
                X, y,
                scoring='neg_mean_squared_error',
                cv=crossvalidation))
print('Mean squared error: %.3f' % abs(score))
```

The cross-validated mean squared error for the Boston house price dataset is

```
Mean squared error: 22.593
```

Making Machine Learning Accessible

Random Forest is a classification and regression algorithm developed by Leo Breiman and Adele Cutler that uses a large number of decision tree models to provide precise predictions by reducing both the bias and variance of the estimates. When you aggregate many models together to produce a single prediction, the result is an *ensemble of models.* Random Forest isn't just an ensemble model, it's also a simple and effective algorithm to use as an out-of-the-box algorithm. It makes machine learning accessible to nonexperts. The Random Forest algorithm uses these steps to perform its predictions:

1. Create a large number of decision trees, each one different from the other, based on different subsets of observations and variables.

2. Bootstrap the dataset of observations for each tree (sampled from the original data with replacement). The same observation can appear multiple times in the same dataset.

3. Randomly select and use only a part of the variables for each tree.

4. Estimate the performance for each tree using the observations excluded by sampling (the Out Of Bag, or OOB, estimate).

5. Obtain the final prediction, which is the average for regression estimates or the most frequent class for prediction, after all the trees have been fitted and used for prediction.

You can reduce bias by using these steps, because the decision trees have a good fit on data and, by relying on complex splits, can approximate even the most complex relationships between predictors and predicted outcome. Decision trees can produce a great variance of estimates, but you reduce this variance by averaging many trees. Noisy predictions, due to variance, tend to distribute evenly above and below the correct value that you want to predict — and when averaged together, they tend to cancel each other, leaving, as a result, a more correct average prediction.

Leo Breiman derived the idea for Random Forest from the bagging technique. Scikit-learn has a bagging class for both regression (BaggingRegressor) and classifying (BaggingClassifier) that you can use with any other predictor you prefer to pick from Scikit-learn modules. The max_samples and max_features parameters let you decide the proportion of cases and variables to sample (not bootstrapped, but sampled, so you can use a case only once) for building each model of the ensemble. The n_estimators parameter decides the total number of models in the ensemble. Here's an example that loads the handwritten digit dataset (used for demonstrations later with other ensemble algorithms) and then fits the model by bagging:

```python
from sklearn.datasets import load_digits
digit = load_digits()
X, y = digit.data, digit.target
```

```python
from sklearn.ensemble import BaggingClassifier
from sklearn.tree import DecisionTreeClassifier
from sklearn.model_selection import cross_val_score
from sklearn.model_selection import KFold
tree_classifier = DecisionTreeClassifier(random_state=0)
crossvalidation = KFold(n_splits=5, shuffle=True,
                        random_state=1)
bagging = BaggingClassifier(tree_classifier,
                            max_samples=0.7,
                            max_features=0.7,
                            n_estimators=300)
scores = np.mean(cross_val_score(bagging, X, y,
                                 scoring='accuracy',
                                 cv=crossvalidation))
print ('Accuracy: %.3f' % scores)
```

Here's the cross-validated accuracy for the bagging applied to the handwritten dataset:

```
Accuracy: 0.967
```

In bagging, as in Random Forest, the more models in the ensemble, the better. You run little risk of overfitting because every model is different from the others, and errors tend to spread around the real value. Adding more models just adds stability to the result.

Another characteristic of the algorithm is that it permits estimation of variable importance while taking the presence of all the other predictors into account. In this way, you can determine which feature is important for predicting a target given the set of features that you have; also, you can use the importance estimate as a guideline for variable selection.

REMEMBER

In contrast to single decision trees, you can't easily visualize or understand Random Forest, making it act as a black box (a *black box* is a transformation that doesn't reveal its inner workings; all you see are its inputs and outputs). Given its opacity, importance estimation is the only way to understand how the algorithm works with respect to the features.

Importance estimation in a Random Forest is obtained in a straightforward way. After building each tree, the code fills each variable in turn with junk data and the example records how much the predictive power decreases. If the variable is important, crowding it with casual data harms the prediction; otherwise, the predictions are left almost unchanged and the variable is deemed unimportant.

Working with a Random Forest classifier

The example Random Forest classifier keeps using the previously loaded digit dataset:

```
X, y = digit.data, digit.target
from sklearn.ensemble import RandomForestClassifier
from sklearn.model_selection import cross_val_score
from sklearn.model_selection import KFold
crossvalidation = KFold(n_splits=5, shuffle=True,
                        random_state=1)
RF_cls = RandomForestClassifier(n_estimators=300,
                                random_state=1)
score = np.mean(cross_val_score(RF_cls, X, y,
                                scoring='accuracy',
                                cv=crossvalidation))
print('Accuracy: %.3f' % score)
```

The cross-validated accuracy reported by this code for the Random Forest is an improvement over the bagging method tested in the previous section:

```
Accuracy: 0.977
```

Just setting the number of estimators is sufficient for most problems you encounter, and setting it correctly is a matter of using the highest number possible given the time and resource constraints of the host computer. You can demonstrate this by calculating and drawing a validation curve for the algorithm.

```
from sklearn.model_selection import validation_curve
param_range = [10, 50, 100, 200, 300, 500, 800, 1000, 1500]
crossvalidation = KFold(n_splits=3,
                        shuffle=True,
                        random_state=1)
RF_cls = RandomForestClassifier(n_estimators=300,
                                random_state=0)
train_scores, test_scores = validation_curve(RF_cls, X, y,
                                'n_estimators',
                                param_range=param_range,
                                cv=crossvalidation,
                                scoring='accuracy')
mean_test_scores = np.mean(test_scores, axis=1)
```

```
import matplotlib.pyplot as plt
plt.plot(param_range, mean_test_scores,
         'bD-.', label='CV score')
plt.grid()
plt.xlabel('Number of estimators')
plt.ylabel('accuracy')
plt.legend(loc='lower right', numpoints= 1)
plt.show()
```

Figure 20-3 shows the results provided by the preceding code. The more estimators, the better the results. However, at a certain point the gain becomes minimal indeed.

Working with a Random Forest regressor

RandomForestRegressor works in a similar way as the Random Forest for classification, using exactly the same parameters:

```
X, y = boston.data, boston.target
from sklearn.ensemble import RandomForestRegressor
from sklearn.model_selection import cross_val_score
```

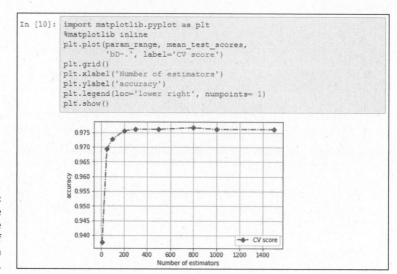

FIGURE 20-3:
Verifying the
impact of the
number of
estimators on
Random Forest.

```
from sklearn.model_selection import KFold
RF_rg = RandomForestRegressor (n_estimators=300,
                                random_state=1)
crossvalidation = KFold(n_splits=5, shuffle=True,
                        random_state=1)
score = np.mean(cross_val_score(RF_rg, X, y,
                    scoring='neg_mean_squared_error',
                    cv=crossvalidation))
print('Mean squared error: %.3f' % abs(score))
```

Here is the resulting cross-validated mean squared error:

```
Mean squared error: 12.028
```

REMEMBER

The Random Forest uses decision trees. Decision trees segment the dataset into small partitions, called leaves, when estimating regression values. The Random Forest takes the average of the values in each leaf to create a prediction. Using this procedure causes extreme and high values to disappear from predictions because of the averaging used for each leaf of the forest, producing dumped values instead of much higher or much lower values.

Optimizing a Random Forest

Random Forest models are out-of-box algorithms that can work quite well without optimization or worrying about overfitting. (The more estimators you use, the better the output, depending on your resources.) You can always improve performance by removing redundant and less informative variables, fixing a minimum leaf size, and defining a sampling number that avoids having too many correlated predictors in the sample. The following example shows how to perform these tasks:

```
from sklearn.ensemble import RandomForestClassifier
from sklearn.model_selection import KFold
X, y = digit.data, digit.target
crossvalidation = KFold(n_splits=5, shuffle=True,
                        random_state=1)
RF_cls = RandomForestClassifier(random_state=1)
scorer = 'accuracy'
```

Using the handwritten digit dataset and a first default classifier, you can optimize both max_features and min_samples_leaf. When optimizing max_features, you use preconfigured options (auto for all features, sqrt or log2 functions applied to the number of features) and integrate them using small feature numbers and a value of 1/3 of the features. Selecting the right number of features to sample tends to reduce the number of times when correlated and similar variables are picked together, thus increasing the predictive performances.

There is a statistical reason to optimize min_samples_leaf. Using leaves with few cases often corresponds to overfitting to very specific data combinations. You need to have at least 30 observations to achieve a minimal statistical confidence that data patterns correspond to real and general rules:

```
from sklearn.model_selection import GridSearchCV
max_features = [X.shape[1]//3, 'sqrt', 'log2', 'auto']
min_samples_leaf = [1, 10, 30]
n_estimators = [50, 100, 300]
search_grid =  {'n_estimators':n_estimators,
                'max_features': max_features,
                'min_samples_leaf': min_samples_leaf}
search_func = GridSearchCV(estimator=RF_cls,
                           param_grid=search_grid,
                           scoring=scorer,
                           cv=crossvalidation)
search_func.fit(X, y)
best_params = search_func.best_params_
best_score = search_func.best_score_
print('Best parameters: %s' % best_params)
print('Best accuracy: %.3f' % best_score)
```

The best parameters and best accuracy obtained are then reported, highlighting that the parameters to act on is the number of trees:

```
Best parameters: {'max_features': 'sqrt',
                  'min_samples_leaf': 1,
                  'n_estimators': 100}
Best accuracy: 0.978
```

Boosting Predictions

Gathering different tree models is not the only ensemble technique possible. In fact, another machine learning technique, called *boosting,* uses ensembles effectively. In boosting, you grow many trees sequentially. Each tree tries to build a model that successfully predicts what trees that were built before it weren't able to forecast. The technique pools subsequent models together and uses a weighted average or a weighted majority vote on the final prediction.

The following sections present two boosting applications, adaboost and gradient boosting machines. You can use all boosting algorithms for both regression and classification. The examples in these sections start working with classification. The multilabel dataset of handwritten digits is, as it was with Random Forest, a good place to start.

If you have already loaded the data using `load_digits` into the variable `digit`, you just need to reassign the X and y variables as follows:

```
X, y = digit.data, digit.target
```

Knowing that many weak predictors win

`AdaBoostClassifier` fits sequential weak predictors. It's used by default when working with decision trees, but you can choose other algorithms by changing the `base_estimator` parameter. Weak predictors are usually machine learning predictors that don't perform well because they have too much variance or bias, so they perform slightly better than chance. The classic example of a weak learner is the decision stump, which is a decision tree grown to only one level. Usually, decision trees are the best-performing option in boosting, so you can safely use the default learner and concentrate on two important parameters to obtain good predictions: n_estimators and `learning_rate`.

`learning_rate` determines how each weak predictor contributes to the final result. A high learning rate requires few `n_estimators` before converging to an optimal solution, but it likely won't be the best solution possible. A low learning rate takes longer to train because it requires more predictors before reaching a solution. In addition, it also overfits more slowly.

TIP

Contrary to bagging, boosting can overfit if you use too many estimators. A cross-validation is always helpful in finding the correct number, keeping in mind that lower learning rates take longer to overfit, so picking an almost optimal value using a loose grid search is easier.

```
from sklearn.ensemble import AdaBoostClassifier
from sklearn.model_selection import cross_val_score
from sklearn.model_selection import KFold
ada = AdaBoostClassifier(n_estimators=1000,
                         learning_rate=0.01,
                         random_state=1)
crossvalidation = KFold(n_splits=5, shuffle=True,
                        random_state=1)
score = np.mean(cross_val_score(ada, X, y,
                                scoring='accuracy',
                                cv=crossvalidation))
print('Accuracy: %.3f' % score)
```

After running the code, you get the cross-validated accuracy:

```
Accuracy: 0.754
```

This example uses the default estimator, which is a full-blown decision tree. If you'd like to try a stump (which needs more estimators), you should instantiate the Ada-BoostClassifier with `base_estimator=DecisionTreeClassifier(max_depth=1)`.

Setting a gradient boosting classifier

The Gradient Boosting Machine (GBM) performs much better than the Adaboost boosting technique, the first boosting algorithm ever created. In particular, GBM uses an optimization computation for weighting the subsequent estimators. As with the example in the preceding section, the following example uses the digit dataset and explores some extra parameters available in GBM:

```
X, y = digit.data, digit.target
crossvalidation = KFold(n_splits=5,
                        shuffle=True,
                        random_state=1)
```

Apart from the learning rate and the number of estimators, which are key parameters for optimal learning without overfitting, you must provide values for subsample and max_depth. subsample introduces subsampling into the training (so that the training is done on a different dataset every time), as is done in bagging. max_depth defines the maximum level of the built trees. It's usually a good practice to start with three levels, but more levels may be necessary for modeling complex data.

```python
from sklearn.ensemble import GradientBoostingClassifier
from sklearn.model_selection import cross_val_score
GBC = GradientBoostingClassifier(n_estimators=300,
                                 subsample=1.0,
                                 max_depth=2,
                                 learning_rate=0.1,
                                 random_state=1)
score = np.mean(cross_val_score(GBC, X, y,
                                scoring='accuracy',
                                cv=crossvalidation))
print('Accuracy: %.3f' % score)
```

On the very same problem you tested before, the GradientBoostingClassifier results in the following accuracy score after running the code:

```
Accuracy: 0.972
```

Running a gradient boosting regressor

Creating a gradient boosting regressor doesn't present particular differences from creating the classifier. The main difference is the presence of multiple loss functions that you can use (contrast this with GradientBoostingClassifier, which has only the deviance loss, analogous to the cost function of a logistic regression).

```python
X, y = boston.data, boston.target
from sklearn.ensemble import GradientBoostingRegressor
from sklearn.model_selection import cross_val_score
from sklearn.model_selection import KFold
GBR = GradientBoostingRegressor(n_estimators=1000,
                                subsample=1.0,
                                max_depth=3,
                                learning_rate=0.01,
                                random_state=1)
crossvalidation = KFold(n_splits=5,
                        shuffle=True,
                        random_state=1)
```

```
score = np.mean(cross_val_score(GBR,
                                X, y,
                                scoring='neg_mean_squared_error',
                                cv=crossvalidation))
print('Mean squared error: %.3f' % abs(score))
```

After running the code, you get the mean squared error for the regression, which is much better than the corresponding one by a Random Forest:

```
Mean squared error: 10.094
```

The example trains a GradientBoostingRegressor using the default ls value for the loss parameter, which is analogous to a linear regression. Here are some other choices:

>> quantile: This guesses a particular quantile that you specify using the alpha parameter (usually it's 0.5, which is the median).

>> lad (least absolute deviation): This choice is highly robust to outliers; it tends to ordinally rank correctly the predictions.

>> huber: This creates a combination of ls and lad. It requires that you fix the alpha parameter.

Using GBM hyperparameters

GBM models are quite sensitive to overfitting when you have too many sequential estimators and the model starts fitting the noise in the data. It's important to check the efficiency of the coupled values of the number of estimators and the learning rate. The following example uses the Boston dataset of housing prices:

```
X, y = boston.data, boston.target
from sklearn.model_selection import KFold
crossvalidation = KFold(n_splits=5, shuffle=True,
                        random_state=1)
GBR = GradientBoostingRegressor(n_estimators=1000,
                                subsample=1.0,
                                max_depth=3,
                                learning_rate=0.01,
                                random_state=1)
```

Optimization may take some time because of the computational burden required by the GBM algorithms, especially if you decide to test high values of max_depth.

TIP

A good strategy is to keep the learning rate fixed and try to optimize `subsample` and `max_depth` with respect to `n_estimators` (keeping in mind that high values of `max_depth` usually imply a lesser number of estimators). After you find the optimum values for `subsample` and `max_depth`, you can start searching for further optimization of `n_estimators` and `learning_rate`.

```python
from sklearn import grid_search
from sklearn.model_selection import GridSearchCV
subsample = [1.0, 0.9]
max_depth = [2, 3, 5]
n_estimators = [500 , 1000, 2000]
search_grid =  {'subsample': subsample,
                'max_depth': max_depth,
                'n_estimators': n_estimators}
search_func = GridSearchCV(estimator=GBR,
             param_grid=search_grid,
             scoring='neg_mean_squared_error',
             cv=crossvalidation)
search_func.fit(X,y)

best_params = search_func.best_params_
best_score = abs(search_func.best_score_)
print('Best parameters: %s' % best_params)
print('Best mean squared error: %.3f' % best_score)
```

After running the optimization, you can examine the resulting best mean squared error and notice how it improved running the algorithm by the default parameters. (Gradient Boosting always require some parameter tuning in order to return the best results.)

```
Best parameters: {'max_depth': 3,
                  'n_estimators': 2000,
                  'subsample': 0.9}
Best mean squared error: 9.324
```

6

The Part of Tens

Chapter **21**

Ten Essential Data Resources

I n reading this book, you discover quite a lot about data science and Python. Before your head explodes from all the new knowledge you gain, it's important to realize that this book is really just the tip of the iceberg. Yes, there really is more information available out there, and that's what this chapter is all about. The following sections introduce you to a wealth of data science resource collections that you really need to make the best use of your new knowledge.

In this case, a resource collection is simply a listing of really cool links with some text to tell you why they're so great. In some cases, you gain access to articles about data science; in other cases, you're exposed to new tools. In fact, data science is such a huge topic that you could easily find more resources than those discussed here, but the following sections provide a good place to start.

REMEMBER

As with anything else on the Internet, links break, sites go out of business, and new sites take their place. If you find that a link is broken, please let me know about it at John@JohnMuellerBooks.com.

Discovering the News with Subreddit

The data science field changes constantly for a number of reasons, including the addition of new algorithms and techniques, as well as the use of ever larger datasets from an increasingly diverse set of sources. Consequently, you need a news source, such as Subreddit (https://www.reddit.com/r/datascience/) to obtain the latest information and stay ahead of your competitors. These blog posts often contain the latest techniques as well, ensuring that after you get up to speed on data science, you can stay that way. In addition, you find topics that are essential for your career, such as finding the range of data science salaries. This site also provides Python-specific information at https://www.reddit.com/r/Python/ and data science news at https://www.reddit.com/r/datasciencenews/.

Getting a Good Start with KDnuggets

Learning about data mining and data science is a process. KDnuggets breaks down the learning process into a series of steps at https://www.kdnuggets.com/faq/learning-data-mining-data-science.html. Each step gives you an overview of what you should be doing and why. You also find links to a variety of resources online to make the learning process considerably easier. Even though the site emphasizes the use of R, Python, and SQL (in that order) to perform data science tasks, the steps will actually work for any of a number of approaches that you might take.

REMEMBER

As with any other learning experience, a procedure like the one shown on the KDnuggets site will work for some people and not others. Everyone learns a little differently. Don't be afraid to improvise. The resources on this site might provide insights into other things that you can do to make your learning process easier.

Locating Free Learning Resources with Quora

Resisting the word *free* is really hard, especially when it comes to education, which normally costs many thousands of dollars. The Quora site at https://www.quora.com/What-are-the-best-free-resources-to-learn-data-science provides a listing of the best no-cost learning resources for data science.

Most of the links take on a question format, such as, "How do I become a data scientist?" The question-and-answer format is helpful because you might be asking the questions that the site answers. The resulting list of sites, courses, and resources are introductory, for the most part, but they are a good way to get started working in the data science field.

TIP

A few of the links go to prestigious institutions such as Harvard. The link gives you access to course materials such as lecture videos and blackboards. However, you don't get the actual course free of charge. If you want the benefits of the course, you still need to pay for it. Even so, just by viewing the course materials, you can obtain a lot of useful data science knowledge.

Gaining Insights with Oracle's Data Science Blog

Major vendors can offer you significant amounts of useful information. Of course, you need to keep the source of this information in mind because it can be quite biased. The Oracle Data Science Blog (https://www.datascience.com/blog) provides you with a considerable amount of information — everything from the latest data analysis techniques to the methods you can use to reduce costs. In addition, you find category-specific information based on

>> Best practices

>> Data science education

>> Use cases

>> Data science as a platform

Accessing the Huge List of Resources on Data Science Central

Many of the resources you find online cover mainstream topics. Data Science Central (https://www.datasciencecentral.com/) provides access to a relatively large number of data science experts who tell you about the most obscure facts of data science. One of the more interesting blog posts appears at https://www.datasciencecentral.com/profiles/blogs/huge-trello-list-of-great-data-science-resources.

This resource points you to a Trello list (https://trello.com/) of some truly amazing resources. Navigating the huge list can be a bit difficult, but the process is aided by the treelike structure that Trello provides for organizing information.

You want to meander through this sort of list when you have time and simply want to see what is available. The categories include the following (with possibly more by the time you read this book):

>> Data news

>> Data business people track

>> Data journalist track

>> Data padawan track

>> Data scientist track

>> Statistics

>> R

>> Python

>> Big data and other tools

>> Data

>> Others

Learning New Tricks from the Aspirational Data Scientist

The Aspirational Data Scientist (https://newdatascientist.blogspot.com/) blog site offers an amazing array of essays on various data science topics. The author splits the posts into these areas: data science commentary; online course reviews; becoming a data scientist.

Data science attracts practitioners from all sorts of existing fields. The site seems mainly devoted to serving the needs of social scientists moving into the data science field. In fact, the most interesting post that appears at https://newdatascientist.blogspot.com/p/useful-links.html provides a list of resources to help the social scientist move into the data scientist field. The list of resources is organized by author, so you may find names that you already recognize as potential informational resources.

TIP

As with any other resource, even if an article is meant for one audience, it often serves the needs of another audience with equal ease. Even if you aren't a social scientist, you might find that the articles contain helpful information as you progress on the road to fully discovering the wonders of data science.

Obtaining the Most Authoritative Sources at Udacity

Even with the right connections online and a good search engine, trying to find just the right resource can be hard. U Climb Higher has published a list of 24 data science resources at `https://blog.udacity.com/2014/12/24-data-science-resources-keep-finger-pulse.html` that's guaranteed to help keep your finger on the pulse of new strategies and technologies. This resource broaches the following topics: trends and happenings; places to learn more about data science; joining a community; data science news; people who really know data science well; all the latest research.

Receiving Help with Advanced Topics at Conductrics

The Conductrics site (`https://conductrics.com/`) as a whole is devoted to selling products that help you perform various data science tasks. However, the site includes a blog that contains a couple of useful blog posts that answer the sorts of advanced questions you might find it difficult to get answered elsewhere. The two posts appear at `https://conductrics.com/data-science-resources/` and `https://conductrics.com/data-science-resources-2`.

The author of the blog posts, Matt Gershoff, makes it clear that the listings are the result of answering people's questions in the past. The list is huge, which is why it appears in two posts rather than one, so Matt must answer many questions. The list focuses mostly on machine learning rather than hardware or specific coding issues. Therefore, you can expect to see entries for topics such as Latent Semantic Indexing (LSI); Single Value Decomposition (SVD); Linear Discriminant Analysis (LDA); nonparametric Bayesian approaches; statistical machine translation; Reinforcement Learning (RL); Temporal Difference (TD) learning; context bandits.

TIP

The list goes on and on. Many of these entries won't make much sense to you right now unless you're already heavily involved in data science. However, the authors write many of the articles in a way that helps you pick up the information even if you aren't completely familiar with it. In most cases, your best course of action is to at least scan the article to see whether you can understand it. If the article starts to make sense, read it in detail. Otherwise, hold on to the article reference for later use. You might be surprised to discover that the article you can't completely understand today becomes something you understand with ease tomorrow.

Obtaining the Facts of Open Source Data Science from Masters

Many organizations now focus on open source for data science solutions. The focus has become so prevalent that you can now get an Open Source Data Science Masters (OSDSM) education at http://datasciencemasters.org/. The emphasis is on providing you with the materials that are normally lacking from a purely academic education. In other words, the site provides pointers to courses that fill in gaps in your education so that you become more marketable in today's computing environment. The various links provide you with access to online courses, books, and other resources that help you gain a better understanding of just how OSDSM works.

Zeroing In on Developer Resources with Jonathan Bower

More than a few interesting resources appear on GitHub (https://github.com/), a site devoted to collaboration, code review, and code management. One of the sites you need to check out is Jonathan Bower's listing of data science resources at https://github.com/jonathan-bower/DataScienceResources. The majority of these resources will appeal to the developer, but just about anyone can benefit from them. You find resources categorized into the following topics:

>> Data science, getting started

>> Data pipeline and tools

>> Product

>> Career resources

>> Open source data science resources

The hierarchical formatting of the various topics makes finding just what you need easier. Each major category divides into a list of topics. Within each topic, you find a list of resources that apply to that topic. For example, within Data Pipeline & Tools, you find Python, which includes a link for Anyone Can Code. This is one of the most usable sites in the list.

Chapter **22**

Ten Data Challenges You Should Take

D ata science is all about working with data. While working through this book, you have used a number of datasets, including the toy datasets that come with the Scikit-learn library. Of course, these datasets are all great for getting you started, but just as a runner wouldn't stop after conquering the local fun run, so you need to start training for data science marathons by working with larger datasets.

This chapter introduces you to a number of challenging datasets that can help you become a world-class data scientist. By combining what you discover in this book with these new datasets, you can learn how to do amazing things. In fact, some people may view you as a bit of a magician as you pull seemingly impossible data patterns out of your hat. Each of the following datasets provides you with specific skills and helps you achieve different goals.

REMEMBER

You can find a wealth of datasets on the Internet. However, not every dataset is created equal, and you need to choose your challenges with care. These ten datasets provide well-known functionality, often provide you with tutorials, and appear in scientific papers. These three features make these datasets stand apart from the competition. Yes, other good datasets are available, but these ten datasets provide skills needed to conquer even bigger challenges, such as that database lurking on your company server.

Meeting the Data Science London + Scikit-learn Challenge

You use Scikit-learn quite a bit while using this book, so you may already understand it a bit. The Kaggle competition at https://www.kaggle.com/c/data-science-london-Scikit-learn (the current competition ended in December 2014, but there should be others) provides a practice ground for trying, sharing, and creating examples using the Scikit-learn classification algorithms. All the tools for the previous competition are still in place, and it's still well worth exploring. The goal is to try, create, and share examples of using Scikit-learn's classification capabilities. You can find the data used for the competition at https://www.kaggle.com/c/data-science-london-scikit-learn/data. The rules appear at https://www.kaggle.com/c/data-science-london-scikit-learn/rules, and you can discover how Kaggle evaluates your submissions at https://www.kaggle.com/c/data-science-london-scikit-learn/details/evaluation.

Of course, you might not have any desire to compete. Looking at the leaderboard (https://www.kaggle.com/c/data-science-london-scikit-learn/leaderboard) may keep you from seriously considering actual competition because the contest has attracted serious data scientists. However, you can still enjoy taking a chance at figuring out how to solve a challenging data problem and learn something new in the meanwhile, without needing to submit a solution of yours to the leaderboard.

REMEMBER

Because this site builds on knowledge you already have from the book, it's actually the best place to begin building new skills. That's why this site appears first in the chapter: You can get a good start using other datasets with techniques you already know.

Predicting Survival on the Titanic

You work with the Titanic data to some extent in the book (Chapters 6 and 20) by using Titanic.csv and Titanic3.csv from the Vanderbilt University School of Medicine. This challenge is actually much easier than the one described in the previous section because Kaggle designed it for the beginner. You can find it at https://www.kaggle.com/c/titanic. The data model, found at https://www.kaggle.com/c/titanic/data, is different from the one in the book, but the concepts are the same. You can find the rules for this competition at https://www.kaggle.com/c/titanic/rules and the method of evaluation at https://www.kaggle.com/c/titanic#evaluation.

You can find the leaderboard for this competition at `https://www.kaggle.com/c/titanic/leaderboard`. The number of people who have already achieved what amounts to a perfect score should fill you with confidence.

The biggest challenge in this case is that the dataset is quite small and requires that you create new features in order to obtain an accurate score. The competition helps you apply the skills you learn in the "Considering the Art of Feature Creation" section of Chapter 9 and see demonstrated in Chapter 19.

Finding a Kaggle Competition that Suits Your Needs

Competitions are great at helping you think through solutions in an environment in which others are doing the same. In the real world, you may find yourself pitted against competition on a regular basis, so competitions provide good experiences in thinking critically and quickly. They also present you with an opportunity to learn from others. The best place to find such competitions is on the Kaggle site at `https://www.kaggle.com/competitions`.

This site will help you locate any past or present Kaggle competition. To find a present competition, click the Active Competitions link. To find a past competition, click the All Competitions link. All the datasets are freely available, so you have a chance to try your skills against any real-world scenario you might want to select. The Kaggle community will provide you with plenty of tutorials, benchmarks, and beat-the-benchmarks posts.

You don't have to select an ongoing competition. For example, you might see a past competition that meets a need and try that instead (benefitting from the published solutions). If you take an active competition you can post your questions on the forum and have some of the most skilled data scientists in the world answer your questions and doubts. Because of the great number of competitions on this site, it's likely that you'll find a competition that will suit your interests!

It's interesting to note that the Kaggle competitions come from companies that don't normally have access to data scientists, so you really are working in a real world environment. You can also use this site to locate a potential job. Just go to `https://www.kaggle.com/jobs` by clicking the Jobs link on the main page.

Honing Your Overfit Strategies

The Madelon Data Set at `https://archive.ics.uci.edu/ml/datasets/Madelon` is an artificial dataset containing a two-class classification problem with continuous input variables. This NIPS 2003 feature selection challenge will seriously test your skills in cross-validating models. The main emphasis of this challenge is to devise strategies for avoiding overfit — an issue that you first confront in the "Finding more things that can go wrong" section of Chapter 16. You find overfit issues mentioned in Chapters 18, 19, and 20 as well. To obtain the dataset, contact Isabelle Guyon at the address found in the Source section of the page at `https://archive.ics.uci.edu/ml/datasets/Madelon`.

TIP

This particular dataset attracted the attention of a number of people who created papers about it. The best papers appear in the book *Feature Extraction, Foundations and Applications* at `https://www.springer.com/us/book/9783540354871`. You can also download an associated technical report from `https://clopinet.com/isabelle/Projects/ETH/TM-fextract-class.pdf`. The Advances in Neural Information Processing Systems 17 (NIPS 2004) at `https://papers.nips.cc/book/advances-in-neural-information-processing-systems-17-2004` also contains useful links to papers that will help you with this particular dataset.

Trudging Through the MovieLens Dataset

The MovieLens site (`https://movielens.org/`) is all about helping you find a movie you might like. After all, with millions of movies out there, finding something new and interesting could take time that you don't want to spend. The setup works by asking you to input ratings for movies you already know about. The MovieLens site then makes recommendations for you based on your ratings. In short, your ratings teach an algorithm what to look for, and then the site applies this algorithm to the entire dataset.

You can obtain the MovieLens dataset at `https://grouplens.org/datasets/movielens/`. The interesting thing about this site is that you can download all or part of the dataset based on how you want to interact with it. You can find downloads in the following sizes:

>> 100,000 ratings from 1,000 users on 1,700 movies

>> 1 million ratings from 6,000 users on 4,000 movies

>> 10 million ratings and 100,000 tag applications applied to 10,000 movies by 72,000 users

>> 20 million ratings and 465,000 tag applications applied to 27,000 movies by 138,000 users

>> MovieLens's latest dataset in small or full sizes (the full size contained 21,000,000 ratings and 470,000 tag applications applied to 27,000 movies by 230,000 users as of this writing but will increase in size with time)

This dataset presents you with an opportunity to work with user-generated data using both supervised and unsupervised techniques. The large datasets present special challenges that only big data can provide. You can find some starter information for working with supervised and unsupervised techniques in Chapters 15 and 19.

Getting Rid of Spam E-mails

Everyone wants to get rid of spam e-mail — those time wasters that contain everything from invitations to join in a fantastic new venture to pornography. Of course, the best way to accomplish the task is to create an algorithm to do the sorting for you. However, you need to train the algorithm to perform its work, which is where the Spambase Data Set comes into play. You can find the Spambase Data Set at https://archive.ics.uci.edu/ml/datasets/Spambase.

This collection of spam e-mails came from postmasters and individuals who had filed spam reports. It also includes nonspam e-mail from various sources to allow the creation of filters that let good e-mails through. This is a complex challenge dealing with textual data and complex, different targets.

TIP

You can find a number of papers that cite this particular dataset. The following list provides a quick overview of the pertinent papers and their host sites:

>> Los Alamos National Laboratory Stability of Unstable Learning Algorithms (http://rexa.info/paper/a2734ae038cae7393159934e860c24a52dc2754d)

>> Modeling for Optimal Probability Prediction (http://rexa.info/paper/6311 97638c7e0317c98e1a8d98e5fce8921aa758)

>> Visualization and Data Mining in an 3-D Immersive Environment: Summer Project 2003 (http://rexa.info/paper/48d6beec2a36a87d9d88b6de85dd 85a75e5ed24d)

>> Online Policy Adaptation for Ensemble Classifiers (http://rexa.info/paper/ 3cb3fbd5512e3cd12111b598fece53fcb42c484b)

Working with Handwritten Information

Pattern recognition, especially working with handwritten information, is an important data science task. The Mixed National Institute of Standards and Technology (MNIST) dataset of handwritten digits at http://yann.lecun.com/exdb/mnist/ provides a training set of 60,000 examples, and a test set of 10,000 examples. This is a subset of the original National Institute of Standards and Technology (NIST) dataset found at https://srdata.nist.gov/gateway/gateway?keyword=handwriting+recognition. It's a good dataset to use to learn how to work with handwritten data without having to perform a lot of preprocessing at the outset.

TIP

The dataset appears in four files. The two training and two test files contain images and labels. You need all four files in order to create a complete dataset for working with digits. A potential problem in working with the MNIST dataset is that the image files aren't in a particular format. The format used for storing the images appears at the bottom of the page. Of course, you could always build your own Python application for reading them, but using code that someone else has created is a lot easier. The following list provides places where you can get code to read the MNIST dataset using Python:

>> https://cs.indstate.edu/~jkinne/cs475-f2011/code/mnistHandwriting.py

>> https://martin-thoma.com/classify-mnist-with-pybrain/

>> https://gist.github.com/akesling/5358964

The host page also contains an important listing of methods used to work with the training and test set. The list contains an impressive number of classifiers that should give you some ideas for your own experiments. The point is that this particular dataset is useful for all sorts of different tasks.

REMEMBER

You have worked with the digits toy dataset from Scikit-learn in a number of chapters in the book. To use this dataset, you import the digits database using from sklearn.datasets import load_digits. This particular dataset appears in Chapters 12, 15, 17, 19, and 20, so you gain a considerable amount of experience in working with a much smaller digits database when you work through the examples in those chapters.

Working with Pictures

The Canadian Institute for Advanced Research (CIFAR) datasets at `https://www.cs.toronto.edu/~kriz/cifar.html` provide you with graphics content to work with in various ways. The CIFAR-10 and CIFAR-100 datasets contain labeled subsets of a dataset with 80 million tiny images (you can read about how the dataset works with the original image dataset in the Learning Multiple Layers of Features from Tiny Images technical report at `https://www.cs.toronto.edu/~kriz/learning-features-2009-TR.pdf`). In the CIFAR-10 dataset, you find 60,000 32 x 32 color images in ten classes (for 6,000 images in each class). Here are the classes you find:

>> Airplane

>> Automobile

>> Bird

>> Cat

>> Deer

>> Dog

>> Frog

>> Horse

>> Ship

>> Truck

The CIFAR-100 dataset contains more classes. Instead of 10 classes, you get 100 classes containing 600 images each. The size of the dataset is the same, but the number of classes is larger. The classification system is hierarchical in this case. The 100 classes divide into 20 superclasses. For example, in the aquatic mammals superclass, you find the beaver, dolphin, otter, seal, and whale classes.

WARNING

Both CIFAR datasets come in Python, MATLAB, and binary versions. Make sure that you download the correct version and follow the instructions for using them on the download page. Yes, you could use the other versions with Python, but doing so would require a lot of extra programming, and because you already have access to a Python version, you wouldn't gain anything from the exercise.

This is an excellent challenge to take after you have worked with the digits dataset described in the previous section. Taking this challenge helps you to deal with colorful, complex images. If you worked through the examples in Chapter 14, you already have some experience working with images using the toy Olivetti Faces dataset.

Analyzing Amazon.com Reviews

If you want to work with a really large dataset, try the Amazon.com review dataset at https://snap.stanford.edu/data/web-Amazon.html. This dataset consists of reviews from Amazon.com taken over a period of 18 years, including ~35 million reviews up to March 2013. The reviews include product and user information, ratings, and a plain-text review. This is the dataset to tackle after you work through smaller datasets, such as MovieLens. It can help you understand how to work with user-generated data in a business context.

Unlike many of the datasets in this chapter, the Amazon.com dataset comes in a number of forms. Yes, you can download all.txt.gz to obtain the entire dataset (11GB of data), but you also have the option to download just portions of the dataset. For example, you can choose to download just the 184,887 reviews associated with baby products by obtaining Baby.txt.gz (a 42MB download).

TIP

Make sure to check out the bottom of the page. The site owner has thoughtfully provided you with the Python code required to interpret the data. Using this simple function makes working with the immense dataset a lot easier. Even if you choose to create a modified version of the function, you at least have a good starting point.

Interacting with a Huge Graph

Imagine trying to work through the connections between 3.5 billion web pages. You can do just that by downloading the immense dataset at https://www.bigdatanews.com/profiles/blogs/big-data-set-3-5-billion-web-pages-made-available-for-all-of-us. The biggest, richest, most complex dataset of all is the Internet itself. Start with a subsample offered by the Common Crawl 2012 web corpus (https://commoncrawl.org/) and learn how to extract and elaborate data from websites. The principle uses for this dataset are:

>> Search algorithms

>> Spam detection methods

>> Graph analysis algorithms

>> Web science research

Pay particular attention to the Contents section near the middle of the page. Clicking a link takes you to an entry at http://webdatacommons.org/hyperlinkgraph/ that explains the dataset in more detail. You need the additional information to perform most data science tasks. Near the bottom of the page are links for downloading various levels of the entire graph (fortunately, you don't have to download everything, which would be a 45GB download for the index file and a 331GB download for the arc file).

Don't let the idea of performing an analysis on such a large dataset scare you. If you worked through the examples in Chapter 7, you have worked with simple graph data. This dataset is a similar task but on a significantly larger scale. Yes, size does matter to some extent, but you already know some of the required techniques for getting the job done.

TIP

This particular site provides access to a number of other datasets. Links for these datasets are at the bottom of the page. For example, you can find "Great statistical analysis: forecasting meteorite hits" at https://www.analyticbridge.com/profiles/blogs/great-statistical-analysis-forecasting-meteorite-hits. In short, if analyzing the entire Internet doesn't appeal to you, try one of the other amazing (and huge) datasets.

Index

Numerics

About the Authors

Luca Massaron is a data scientist and a marketing research director who specializes in multivariate statistical analysis, machine learning, and customer insight, with more than a decade of experience in solving real-world problems and generating value for stakeholders by applying reasoning, statistics, data mining, and algorithms. From being a pioneer of web audience analysis in Italy to achieving the rank of top ten Kaggler on kaggle.com, he has always been passionate about everything regarding data and analysis and about demonstrating the potentiality of data-driven knowledge discovery to both experts and nonexperts. Favoring simplicity over unnecessary sophistication, he believes that a lot can be achieved in data science by understanding and practicing the essentials of it.

John Mueller is a freelance author and technical editor. He has writing in his blood, having produced 111 books and more than 600 articles to date. The topics range from networking to artificial intelligence and from database management to heads-down programming. Some of his current books include discussions of data science, machine learning, and algorithms. His technical editing skills have helped more than 70 authors refine the content of their manuscripts. John has provided technical editing services to various magazines, performed various kinds of consulting, and writes certification exams. Be sure to read John's blog at http://blog.johnmuellerbooks.com/. You can reach John on the Internet at John@JohnMuellerBooks.com. John also has a website at http://www.johnmuellerbooks.com/. Be sure to follow John on Amazon at https://www.amazon.com/John-Mueller/.

Luca's Dedication

I would like to dedicate this book to my parents, Renzo and Licia, who both love simple and well-explained ideas and who now, by reading the book we wrote, will understand more of my daily work in data science and how this new discipline is going to change the way we understand the world and operate in it.

John's Dedication

This book is dedicated to the truly creative people of the world — those who don't need to think outside the box because, for them, the box doesn't exist.

Luca's Acknowledgments

My greatest thanks to my family, Yukiko and Amelia, for their support and loving patience.

I also thank all my fellow Kagglers for their help and unstoppable exchanging of ideas and opinions. My thanks in particular to Alberto Boschetti, Giuliano Janson, Bastiaan Sjardin, and Zacharias Voulgaris.

John's Acknowledgments

Thanks to my wife, Rebecca. Even though she is gone now, her spirit is in every book I write, in every word that appears on the page. She believed in me when no one else would.

Russ Mullen deserves thanks for his technical edit of this book. He greatly added to the accuracy and depth of the material you see here. Russ worked exceptionally hard helping with the research for this book by locating hard-to-find URLs and also offering a lot of suggestions.

Matt Wagner, my agent, deserves credit for helping me get the contract in the first place and taking care of all the details that most authors don't really consider. I always appreciate his assistance. It's good to know that someone wants to help.

A number of people read all or part of this book to help me refine the approach, test scripts, and generally provide input that all readers wish they could have. These unpaid volunteers helped in ways too numerous to mention here. I especially appreciate the efforts of Eva Beattie, Glenn A. Russell, and Matteo Malosetti, who provided general input, read the entire book, and selflessly devoted themselves to this project.

Finally, I would like to thank Katie Mohr, Susan Christophersen, and the rest of the editorial and production staff.

Publisher's Acknowledgments

Associate Publisher: Katie Mohr

Project Manager and Copy Editor: Susan Christophersen

Technical Editor: Russ Mullen

Editorial Assistant: Matthew Lowe

Sr. Editorial Assistant: Cherie Case

Production Editor: Vasanth Koilraj

Cover Image: © oxygen/Getty Images

Leverage the power

Dummies is the global leader in the reference category and one of the most trusted and highly regarded brands in the world. No longer just focused on books, customers now have access to the dummies content they need in the format they want. Together we'll craft a solution that engages your customers, stands out from the competition, and helps you meet your goals.

Advertising & Sponsorships

Connect with an engaged audience on a powerful multimedia site, and position your message alongside expert how-to content. Dummies.com is a one-stop shop for free, online information and know-how curated by a team of experts.

- Targeted ads
- Video
- Email Marketing
- Microsites
- Sweepstakes sponsorship

20 MILLION PAGE VIEWS EVERY SINGLE MONTH

15 MILLION UNIQUE VISITORS PER MONTH

43% OF ALL VISITORS ACCESS THE SITE VIA THEIR MOBILE DEVICES

700,000 NEWSLETTER SUBSCRIPTIONS TO THE INBOXES OF

300,000 UNIQUE INDIVIDUALS EVERY WEEK